CONVOYS

CONVOYS

THE BRITISH STRUGGLE AGAINST NAPOLEONIC EUROPE AND AMERICA

ROGER KNIGHT

YALE UNIVERSITY PRESS
NEW HAVEN AND LONDON

Published with assistance from the Annie Burr Lewis Fund.

For information about this and other Yale University Press publications, please contact:
U.S. Office: sales.press@yale.edu   yalebooks.com
Europe Office: sales@yaleup.co.uk   yalebooks.co.uk

Set in Garamond Premier Pro by IDSUK (DataConnection) Ltd
Printed in Great Britain by TJ Books, Padstow, Cornwall

Library of Congress Control Number: 2022939282

ISBN 978-0-300-24697-1

A catalogue record for this book is available from the British Library.

10 9 8 7 6 5 4 3 2

Dedicated to the memory of Alan Pearsall (1925–2006) and to Captain Richard Woodman

CONTENTS

List of Illustrations   *ix*

Acknowledgements   *xii*

Note on Conventions   *xvii*

Maps   *xix*

Prologue   1

Introduction   6

1   Convoying Before 1803   11

2   The Admiralty and Trade Protection,   25
    1803–1815

3   Warships and Merchantmen   53

4   Coastal Waters and the Western Approaches,   81
    1803–1814

5   North Sea Convoys: Two Commanders,   103
    1804–1812

6   Escorting the Troops: Europe and the   134
    Overseas Garrisons, 1803–1816

7   The Mediterranean: Fruit, Sulphur and   162
    Soldiers, 1803–1814

8   The East and West Indies: Two Sources   181
    of National Wealth, 1803–1814

9   The Battle for the Baltic: Timber,   214
    Hemp and Wheat, 1807–1812

CONTENTS

10 The North Atlantic: War on Two Fronts, 244
    1812–1815
    Conclusion   273
    Epilogue: The Second World War   284

    Appendix: Losses of Small Warships   *293*
    by Station, 1803–1815
    Timeline 1803–1815   *319*
    Glossary   *329*
    Notes   *338*
    Bibliography   *356*
    Index   *375*

ILLUSTRATIONS

PLATES

1. The ship *Castor* and other vessels in a choppy sea, by Thomas Luny. 1802, oil. © National Maritime Museum, Greenwich, London (BHC3251).
2. The Cruizer-class HM Brig *Wolf*, by E.W. Cooke, from *Shipping and Craft*, 1829. Private collection.
3. Cherokee-class brig sloop, by John Ward. 1807, lithograph. © National Maritime Museum, Greenwich, London (PW5029).
4. Frigate and brig trying the rate of sailing, by Edward Bamfylde Eagles. c. 1805, watercolour. © National Maritime Museum, Greenwich, London (TO896).
5. Frigate with a convoy in strong gales, by Edward Bamfylde Eagles. c. 1805, watercolour. © National Maritime Museum, Greenwich, London (TO895).
6. A fleet of East Indiamen at sea, by Nicholas Pocock. 1803, oil. © National Maritime Museum, Greenwich, London (BHC1097).
7. 'Part of the Crew of the *Abergavenny* East Indiaman, delivered from their Perilous Situation', by Thomas Tegg. 1808, hand-coloured aquatint print. © National Maritime Museum, Greenwich, London (PU6369).
8. The West Indiaman *Ann* off Birkenhead, by Robert Salmon. c. 1810, oil. © National Maritime Museum, Greenwich, London (BHC3196).

ILLUSTRATIONS

9. The government transport *Harriet*, by Nicholas Cantimillari. n.d., watercolour. © National Maritime Museum, Greenwich, London (PY8448).

10. A British 74-gun ship, probably HMS *Superb*, convoying merchant ships through the Great Belt, by William Adolphus Knell. 1808, oil. © National Maritime Museum, Greenwich, London (BHC0578).

11. The capture of HMB *Tickler* on 4 June 1808. British School. 1808, oil. © National Maritime Museum, Greenwich, London (BHC0584).

12. The sinking of HMS *Arrow*, by Nicholas Pocock. 1805, drawing. © National Maritime Museum, Greenwich, London (TO894).

13. The HMS *Hermes* ramming and sinking the French privateer *La Mouche*. 1811, print. © National Maritime Museum, Greenwich, London (PW4787).

14. John Wilson Croker, by Samuel Cousins, published by and after Sir Thomas Lawrence. 1829, mezzotint. © National Portrait Gallery, London (NPG D34239).

15. Sir John Barrow, 1st Bt, attributed to John Jackson. c. 1810, oil. © National Portrait Gallery, London (NPG 998).

16. Portrait of Joseph Marryat, by an unknown artist. c. 1810, oil. © Horsham Museum & Art Gallery (1999.1801).

17. Sir John Gladstone, by Thomas Gladstones. c. 1830, oil. © National Portrait Gallery, London (NPG 5042).

18. Heligoland. n.d., lithograph. © National Maritime Museum, Greenwich, London (TO842).

19. Malta Harbour. c. 1809, aquatint. © National Maritime Museum, Greenwich, London (PAI1147).

20. Page of the *Oeconomy*'s signal book. © National Maritime Museum, Greenwich, London (HNL/101/9, T1015).

21. Memorial stone to the casualties of the *Queen* in Mylor churchyard, Cornwall. Imperial War Museum, London (WMR-69482), © Stuart Nicholson.

– x –

ILLUSTRATIONS

MAPS

1. Oceanic trade: convoy routes and rendezvous.   xix
2. Home waters: convoy routes and rendezvous.   xx
   Insets: Solent, Cork, Berehaven (southern Ireland),
   Long Hope (Orkney).
3. North Atlantic: war materials and bullion routes.   xxi
4. The Mediterranean.   xxii
5. The North Sea and approaches to the Baltic.   xxiii
   Insets: Gothenburg, Hano.
6. North Atlantic military expeditions and supply convoys.   xxiv

ACKNOWLEDGEMENTS

I have lived all my life alongside convoys. In the first years of the Second World War my father served in a large aircraft carrier which escorted convoys to the Arctic and later to Halifax, Nova Scotia. When I was two months old in June 1944, when my parents lived in Alverstoke at the top of Portsmouth harbour, nearby landing craft left for Normandy to be part of the greatest military convoy of all. I became aware of convoys again in the 1970s because of impromptu lectures on the Second World War given by the then Deputy Director of the National Maritime Museum at Greenwich, Lieutenant-Commander David (Willie) Waters. He had been in the Admiralty Historical Section in the late 1940s and had spent some years analysing and writing on the Battle of the Atlantic. He liked nothing better than to push aside the papers on his desk, leave the tiresome business of running a museum for a while and talk about the complexities of convoys. He was particularly fluent on the greater efficiency of the perimeter security of larger convoys and the slowness of the Admiralty to recognise the mathematics of this fact.

Convoys stayed in my mind, often a long way from archives and libraries. When sailing from a young age I grappled with the shoal waters of the Essex and Suffolk coasts. The strong tides and shallow waters of the Dutch coast and Scheldt estuary increased my respect, if that were possible, for Napoleonic seamen of any nationality. Many years of sailing in the Solent taught me that these friendly waters can never be taken for granted, full of curious tides and currents. This vast anchorage was the most important geographical advantage that Britain had over France in the days of the sailing navy. It can be entered and exited at the west and east entrances, with the wind virtually from any direction, and could absorb very large convoys, which gathered there before they sailed all over the world.

In the early 1980s I sailed in the fierce tides of the Brittany coast under the tutelage of Keith McDowall and Ian Morton-Wright, marvelling at first hand at the dangers experienced by those who had manned the warships that blockaded French ports. The Channel coast has its dangers, particularly the Portland Race, where in 1805 Captain John Wordsworth, brother of the poet, lost his life, with three hundred others, when the East Indiaman the *Earl of Abergavenny* went on the nearby Shambles, in near windless conditions. In the early 1990s, with my wife Jane, I had two long cruises in waters leading into the Baltic, as far north as Gothenburg, and learnt much from my fellow maritime curator, Boye Meyer-Friese. The sheer cliffs and bulk of southern Sweden contrasted with low-lying Denmark, and I remember the surprisingly swift currents of the Sound and the Belts and long days of windless weather that had been so dangerous to British convoys. Later, Charles Consolvo took us sailing in the Virgin Islands. Sailing in Turkey, Corsica and the Ionian islands helped me appreciate the great depths of Mediterranean waters and how scarce were safe anchorages.

What I learnt is as nothing to the knowledge of officers and seamen two hundred years ago. I was sailing in the summer, with modern navigational aids and sophisticated weather forecasting, supported by a reliable diesel engine. I was never more than a weekend sailor. They were all-year professional seamen, mostly young, strong, brave to the point of fatalism, and very tough, often impressed men or living a life during which the evasion of impressment was a continuous burden.

Of those ashore, for much-appreciated advice I would like to thank Daniel Baugh, Jonathan Fennell, John Hattendorf, Yolande Hodson, Paul Kennedy, Faye Kert, Andrew Lambert, Margarette Lincoln, Roger Morriss, Adrian Osler, Sarah Palmer, Nicholas Rodger, David Starkey,

Liza Verity, Tim Voelcker, Michael Wheeler and Martin Wilcox and, many years ago, Louis Cullen. The late Pat Crimmin gave great encouragement at the start of the project, as she had given me unstintingly since I was a young research student. I am particularly grateful to Grahame Aldous, Catherine Beck, Marianne Czisnik, Rory Muir, Bob Sutcliffe, Evan Wilson and Richard Woodman, who provided me with ideas, references and transcripts. The next generation of Napoleonic maritime scholars were most helpful: Sara Caputo, James Davey, Evan Wilson and Jeremiah Dancy.

One last long historical convoy connection. The only article on convoys in the Napoleonic war was published as long ago as 1959 in the *English Historical Review* by Tony Ryan, who taught at Liverpool University and who devoted his scholarly life to the navy and the Baltic in the early years of the nineteenth century. He examined my doctoral thesis fifty years ago. In recent years I supervised James Davey's thesis on the Baltic, though he needed little help, proved by the strength of his Napoleonic writing ever since. This has given the many years I have devoted to the history of the sailing navy a most satisfying symmetry.

I am indebted to Guy Chet and Adrian Leonard for their expertise on the history of marine insurance. Rear-Admiral James Goldrick, RAN (rtd) shared his experience of the human dynamics aboard small warships. Peter Cannon-Brookes kindly lent me the diaries of Thomas Bulley in his possession and allowed me to quote from them. From the other side of the Channel and North Sea I have benefitted from the French perspective of Silvia Marzagalli. Astle Wold, once of Edinburgh University, and now of the University of Oslo, provided me with an extensive translation of a Norwegian source, recounting how his country benefitted from a major British convoy disaster in 1810 from enemy action, off the Naze of Norway. Ida Jorgensen and Henrik Karlssen provided useful information about the Danish and Swedish coasts respectively.

Former colleagues at the National Maritime Museum have also helped: Pieter van der Merwe with pictures, and Gillian Hutchinson with navigational problems and with charts. The current staff, including Stuart Bligh, Gareth Ballis and Penny Allen, were always on hand to assist in the Caird Library. Anthony Simmonds helped me find books, as he has done for many years. The efficiency of the National Archives is such that on a good day one only communicates with machines, but the work that goes on behind the scenes I have constantly appreciated, both as a former archivist and as a reader of over fifty years. Further afield, I received help from Nathan Coyde and his staff at the Guernsey State Archives, Dawn Ridding at Gladstone's Library at Hawarden and Nikki Caxton at Horsham Museum. The Athenaeum Library has, as ever, surprised me with its useful sources, supplemented by the riches of the London Library, brought swiftly and cheerfully by Laura Doran.

Long book projects gather groups of behind-the-scenes publishing professionals, including my agents Peter Robinson and Jon Wood. My editor Heather McCallum has been refreshingly direct and decisive. Meetings during the pandemic have been few, but fast-moving. I must also thank Katie Urquhart, Charley Chapman, Felicity Maunder and Meg Pettit. Though not yet a professional, Eva Deal gave me early help with computerised maps.

Dan Baugh, Michael Duffy, Richard Harding, Gillian Hutchinson, Rory Muir, Bob Sutcliffe, Evan Wilson and Richard Woodman have devoted time and thought when reading drafts of my chapters. I am more than grateful to them for their time and knowledge. The two anonymous readers of the final script provided yet further reflection, ensuring that there had to be another final script. Of course, all the judgements here are mine, and thus all errors are down to me.

My wife Jane shared many of my adventures, providing me with historical navigational assistance in the same way as she did when we were sailing. She accompanied me to the archives, tirelessly transcribed documents and improved countless drafts, while the maritime knowledge that she has gained from cataloguing manuscripts as a volunteer over many years at the National Maritime Museum has been brought continually into play. My continued thanks to her for a long partnership.

ACKNOWLEDGEMENTS

I am dedicating this book to two men whose knowledge of convoys in the sailing navy was greater than mine. Alan Pearsall was never more at home than in the archives. When I came to the National Maritime Museum, he was the Museum's Historian and became my mentor and friend for forty years. He had studied early eighteenth-century British convoys. In common with many museum curators at the time, Alan published little, but what he wrote is eminently worth reading.

In sharp contrast, Captain Richard Woodman went early to sea and has had a distinguished career in the merchant service, ending it with the command of the *Patricia*, the flagship of Trinity House. During these years he has written an immense number of books on the sailing ships era, but also on twentieth-century convoys. Latterly, he was made an Elder Brother of Trinity House. Every word he has written has been informed by a profound knowledge of, and respect for, the sea.

I owe much to both of them.

Charlton, West Sussex

NOTE ON CONVENTIONS

This book contains the story of British convoys in the Napoleonic 'Wars' rather than 'War'. Between 1803 and 1815 Britain declared war on ten countries: France, Spain, Holland, the north German states, Prussia, Denmark/Norway, Sweden, Turkey and Russia, and after 1812, the United States. Merchant ships in British convoys and the warships that escorted them had to be constantly alert to changing circumstances.

Language and abbreviations have been selected both for clarity and, as far as possible, as contemporaries would have understood them. I have thus stemmed the tide of modern fashion by referring to ships as 'she' as well as the inanimate 'it'.

In this book warships and merchantmen are continually considered together. Every warship's name is preceded by 'HM' ('His Majesty') and followed by the number of guns she carried and the names of the commanding officers. These abbreviations came into everyday use as throughout these years the Admiralty issued more and more printed forms using the 'HMS' format, to save the time of hard-pressed pursers and clerks. I have followed further subtleties with the smaller warships. 'HMB' denotes a one- or two-masted brig, rather than a three-masted 'ship'. 'HMAS' stands for 'His Majesty's Armed Ship', one of the many merchant ships chartered by the government to act as warships, a distinction which regular naval officers were keen on using to distinguish between their own commissioned warships and those which were hired. Further details can be gleaned from Chapter 3 and the Glossary.

International variations of maritime place names have always caused confusion, and I have used the anglicised version. An exception is the anchorage outside Gothenburg which is here known as Vinga Sand, though it appears in British logs as Wingo or Wingoe Sound.

For inflated and comparative money values the reader is directed to websites and calculators using data from the Office for National Statistics.

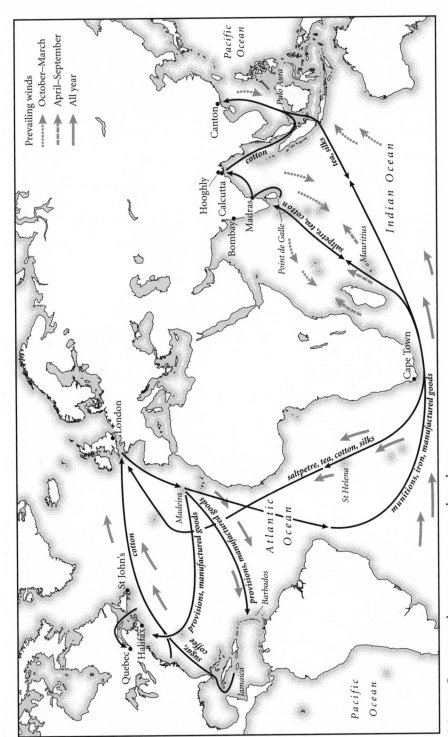

Map 1: Oceanic trade: convoy routes and rendezvous.

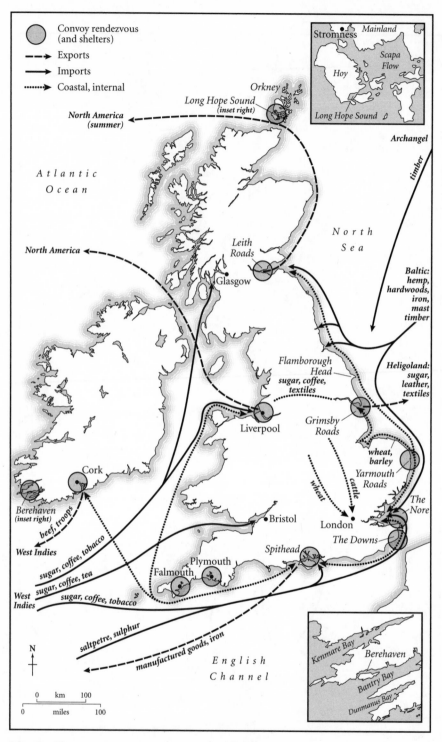

Legend:
- Convoy rendezvous (and shelters)
- ---▶ Exports
- ──▶ Imports
- ······▶ Coastal, internal

Orkney
Long Hope Sound (inset right)

North America (summer)

Stromness • *Mainland*
Scapa Flow
Hoy
Long Hope Sound

Archangel

timber

Atlantic Ocean

North America ◀

North Sea

Leith Roads
Glasgow

Baltic: hemp, hardwoods, iron, mast timber

Flamborough Head
sugar, coffee, textiles

Heligoland: sugar, leather, textiles

Liverpool

Grimsby Roads

wheat, barley
Yarmouth Roads

Cork

wheat

cattle

The Nore

Berehaven (inset right)

beef, troops

West Indies

sugar, coffee, tobacco

• Bristol

London

The Downs

sugar, coffee, tea

Spithead

West Indies

sugar, coffee, tobacco

Plymouth
Falmouth

saltpetre, sulphur

N

manufactured goods, iron

English Channel

Kenmare Bay
Berehaven
Bantry Bay
Dunmanus Bay

0   km   100
0   miles   100

Map 2: Home waters: convoy routes and rendezvous.
Insets: Solent, Cork, Berehaven (southern Ireland), Long Hope (Orkney).

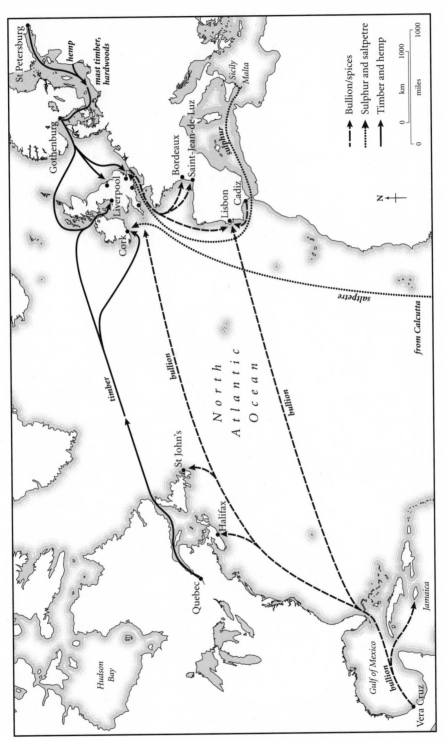

Map 3: North Atlantic: war materials and bullion routes.

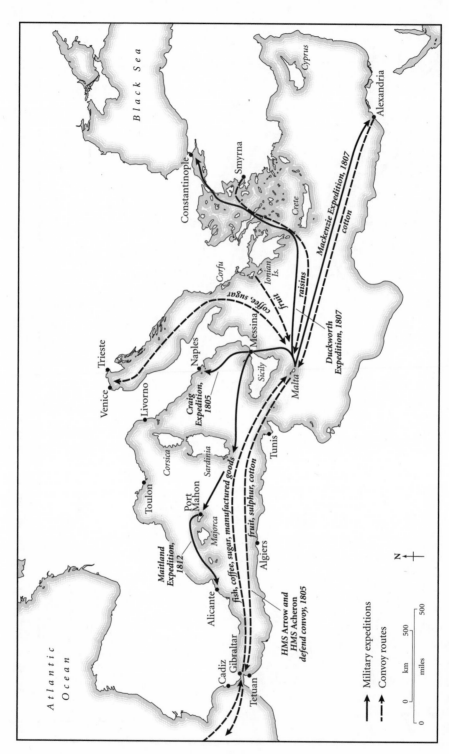

Map 4: The Mediterranean.

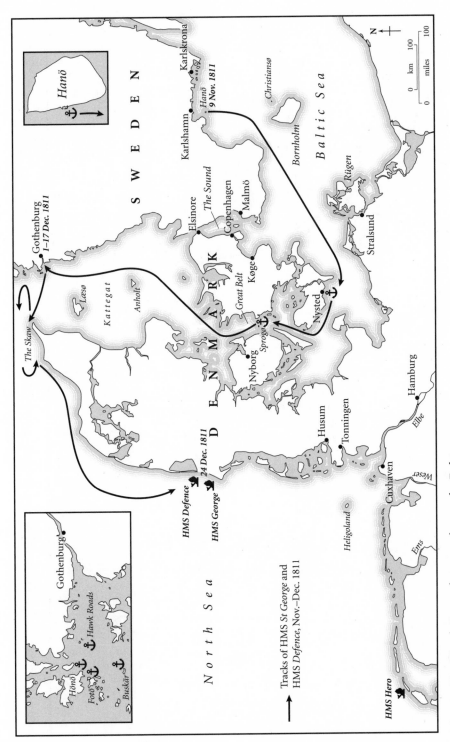

Map 5: The North Sea and approaches to the Baltic.
Insets: Gothenburg, Hano.

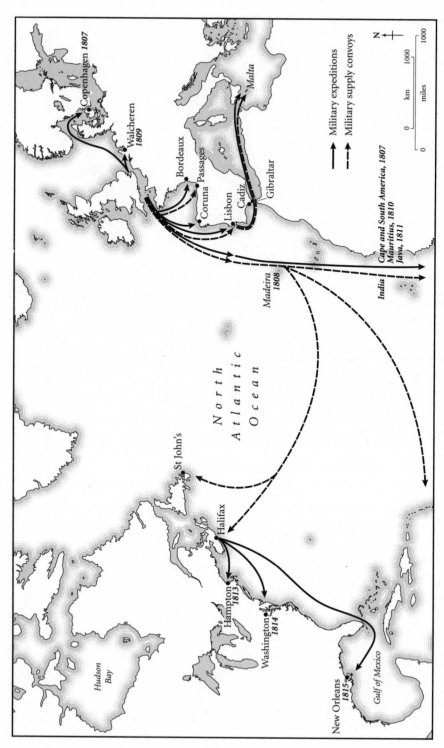

Map 6: North Atlantic military expeditions and supply convoys.

PROLOGUE

On 27 March 1804 a convoy of 67 merchant ships prepared to set out from Cork Harbour, bound for ports in the West Indies. The warship charged with escorting the convoy was the four-year-old 36-gun frigate HMS *Apollo*, which in her short life had taken or destroyed five privateers, and was now commanded by Captain John Dixon, rated by Lord St Vincent as one of the elite young captains.* With her 145-foot length, 943 tons and 260 crew, there could hardly have been a more powerful ship for the job in hand. She was assisted by a slightly smaller frigate, HMS *Carysfort* (32), Captain John Woolcombe.

The convoy weighed anchor in brisk, early spring weather: 'Strong Gales and squally', noted Augustus Dalby, the master of the *Carysfort*, in his log. For two days winds came from the north-east and the convoy made good progress on a WSW course, but on 30 March the wind changed to the north-west and then backed to westerly, compelling the convoy to steer to the south-east. The next day, 1 April, Dalby fixed their latitude as 40 degrees, 53' north and, by dead reckoning, longitude at 13 degrees 18' west. He calculated that the ship was well out into the Atlantic, 502 miles south-west of St Mary's on the Scilly Isles. The *Apollo* 'was now under her foresail, main and mizzen storm-sails; the wind blowing hard with a heavy sea'.[1]

At three a.m. on Monday 2 April, 'to the astonishment of everyone on board', HMS *Apollo* struck a shoal. She floated free but immediately

---

* Dixon appeared on a list of promising young captains which the admiral had drawn up (NMM, Nepean collection, NEP/7, Jervis to Evan Nepean, 4 Oct 1796).

grounded again heavily and repeatedly and started leaking. Captain Dixon and the officers, who had been off watch and were 'entirely naked, not having had time to slip on even a pair of trousers', did their best to maintain morale. The masts were cut away. All six of the ship's boats were swept away. Though she was newly built, the ship started breaking up as the incoming waves lifted and dropped her on the hard seabed. The waves continued to break over the hull, and the afterdeck sank below the surface. It was a miserable night for the crew. As the frigate drew over 13 feet, and was stranded on a gently shelving beach, the wreck was over 200 yards from the shore. Some of the men were swept off, others unsuccessfully tried to swim to land. 'About 30 persons had the good fortune to reach the shore.'*

The *Apollo* found herself on the Portuguese coast, 'on a long sandy beach reaching to Cape Mondego, three leagues to the southward', a hundred miles north of Lisbon. No fewer than twenty-seven West India merchant ships of the convoy followed her and were wrecked with her. Some merchant seamen gained the beach quickly, though the crews of some of these ships were completely lost. According to the *Naval Chronicle*, 'dead bodies were every day floating ashore, as pieces of wreck covered the beach upwards of ten miles'.

The 150 men still on the *Apollo*, however, remained in great danger. Those who did not attempt to reach the shore tried to hang on to pieces of wreckage, but some of these were dragged out to sea and perished. Captain Dixon was among them. The second night was even worse than the first, as one surviving officer recalled: 'The night drawing on, the wind increasing, frequent showers of rain, the sea washing over us, and looking every instant for the forecastle giving way, when we must all have perished together, afforded a spectacle truly deplorable, the bare recollection of which even now makes me shudder.' It was two days before the wind moderated sufficiently to

---

* Based on the uncritical account in the *Naval Chronicle*, which is at some variance with the *Carysfort*'s log (James, *Naval History*, III, pp. 261–4).

enable them to reach the beach safely. Sixty-one died from drowning, thirst or exhaustion.

The same day as HMS *Apollo* struck the shore, HMS *Carysfort*, sailing at the rear of the convoy, received reports of the groundings from the leeward merchant ships. Ships in the West India trade were larger than average. Most of those wrecked were over 200 tons burthen, nine were over 300 tons and one, the *Ark* from Bristol, was over 400. Over 7,000 tons of shipping were lost on the Portuguese coast on that night.[2]

The next day HMS *Carysfort* was still 'standing along the shore, offshore 6 or 7 leagues', or between eighteen to twenty-one miles out, when one of the merchantmen 'informed us that she saw the *Apollo* & 26 sail of convoy on shore yesterday dismasted & on their Beams'. Unsurprisingly, the master made no longitude entry in his log on that day, but as he sailed westwards to Funchal on Madeira on 4 April, borne now by light easterly winds, he corrected his log entry to 10 degrees 29' west, a crucial difference of three degrees of longitude to the previous entry, measuring 138 nautical miles at this latitude. Currents and the relatively slow speed of the convoy had pushed it to leeward far further than the *Apollo*'s captain and master had estimated. It had been a fatal miscalculation, demonstrating how fallible dead reckoning was even over a short ocean voyage.

Herein lay a curious British naval weakness. It had been known how to calculate longitude by the 'lunar distance method' since the mid-eighteenth century, requiring a sextant and a clear sky, but it involved a long and complicated calculation. John Harrison's chronometer had provided a practical improvement, whereby a position could be plotted in cloudy conditions when there was no sight of the moon. It was a copy of Harrison's chronometer that enabled Captain James Cook to complete his first round-the-world voyage in 1771. By 1788 the eleven naval and merchantmen in the First Fleet to Australia, equipped with chronometers, sailed separately across the southern ocean from the Cape of Good Hope, arriving at Botany Bay within two days of each other. The navy, however, neither required a young officer to know how to accomplish this calculation, nor provided a chronometer. By 1802, only 7 per cent of British warships had a chronometer on board and the navy only began to issue them in subsequent years, while ships in home waters did not receive them until the 1840s.[3] The rich East India Company was well ahead. By 1810 nearly every ship owned or hired by the Company had at least one chronometer.[4]

During these wars, dead reckoning had to be used. Convoys heading towards Newfoundland, for instance, would use the lead on the relatively shallow but well-charted Grand Banks to work out where they were. Those heading towards Europe would make their course along the latitude of a prominent high cape, preferably one with deep water in its proximity, such as Lisbon or Cape St Vincent.* Even the captain or master of a crack warship, such as HMS *Apollo*, lacked the capacity to plot his longitude. In 1812 a letter published in *The Naval Chronicle*, signed by 'A Captain in the Royal Navy', complained that 'Every man who has associated with naval officers for the last thirty years, must have heard their complaints of the want of good chronometers, which but few can afford to purchase, as they cost a hundred pounds each.'[5]

The more successful captains did purchase a chronometer. A contrast with HMS *Apollo* was provided exactly ten years later, in December 1814, by HMS *Leonidas* (38), commanded by Captain William King, which sailed with a convoy from Cork and hit south-westerly gales. King decided to turn back, 'having discovered by my timekeeper that we were drifted in three days sixty-eight miles of longitude to the eastward, and thereby drifting into the Bay of Biscay', and realised that his battered convoy was not going to weather Cape Finisterre.[6]

It was a mundane event, but it illustrates the difference between success and failure in this war, one of so many forgotten decisions which made up the complex organisation of worldwide British sailing convoys. The duration and size of some of them are still impressive today. In these

---

* It was around these high capes that privateers used to cruise in wartime, waiting for ships to make their landfall. More difficult was the approach to the French Atlantic coast, or English south-coast ports, from the west (Rodger, 'Weather', p. 194).

pages are scenes of majestic East Indiamen leaving Spithead for a six-month voyage to India or China, escorted as far as Madeira by a ship of the line; or a hundred or so homeward laden West Indiamen in the North Atlantic with brisk south-westerlies behind them, struggling to keep up with their escorting frigate. In the autumn off Gothenburg, several convoys of hundreds of small merchantmen, loaded with timber and hemp, would gather to sail from the Baltic to North Sea ports in England before the ice set in. The smallest convoy of all in these pages was a single valuable ship escorted by a naval sloop eastwards across the North Sea from the Humber to Heligoland, off the German coast. Her cargo, most likely of coffee and sugar, denied to Napoleonic Europe because of the British blockade, would then be smuggled to the mainland for great profit. At the same time smuggling undermined the Continental System designed by the Emperor to crush the British financial system.

INTRODUCTION

A convoy is a naval force, under the command of that person, whom government has appointed.

(Lord Mansfield, Hibbert v Pigon, 1782)[1]

Convoys were, and are, temporary gatherings of ships voyaging between friendly ports, keeping together to be protected by escorting warships. During the days of sail, the timing of convoys was governed by seasonal wind patterns and ocean currents, and in northern latitudes by winter ice. Sailings were also decided by harvest seasons and the quickest route to market.

Convoys have been overlooked as being merely routine, but in reality, life in a convoy of sailing ships was anything but dull, except in conditions of gentle, favourable winds and good visibility. Constant attention was needed to follow instructions, read signals, keep station and avoid collisions, particularly at night. Slower ships which fell behind had to be towed by faster ships, and those in trouble needed assistance; there was a constant anxiety that a storm might break up and disperse the convoy. Tension between the convoy commodore and the masters of the ships under his charge was often the rule. All this had to be surmounted whilst scanning the horizon for hostile privateers or warships.[2]

The convoy system was at the heart of British naval strategy, yet historians of the sailing navy have tended to regard convoying as incidental to the main business of winning the naval war. Victory was achieved by blockading enemy ports, or by battle. Thus the successful outcome of trade protection in the war against Napoleon has been presumed, a judgement shaped by the attitudes of many contemporary naval officers. They hardly mention their role in this everyday occupation.* Only a small minority of sea officers specialised in leading large convoys and were proud of it.

However they regarded it, officers and seamen in the Royal Navy spent most of their time convoying merchant ships, military transports and store ships, either in European waters or around the world. With a few exceptions, thousands of British merchant ships spent their time at sea under the protection of naval escorts, as required by convoy acts and insurance rules. The skill and perseverance of both naval and merchant officers and seamen brought the vast majority of the ships safely to their destination. In doing so, they demonstrated seamanship skills which in the twenty-first century have long been lost. We have hardly retained the knowledge even to appreciate what was achieved.

Much has been written in recent years about seamen in the sailing navy, but little attention has been paid to the skill levels of able seamen, ordinary seamen and landsmen, and the proportion of skills in warships at any one time. Since the time of John Masefield in the early part of the last century, the focus has been on the plight and condition of the seamen, with historians trying to reconcile the contradiction of the unfree, impressed seamen manning the warships which maintained English liberty against French aggression. Recent studies have examined and frequently disagreed over the extent of impressment, on the nature of naval discipline, and its relevance to mutiny and revolution, though this has more relevance in the politically unstable time of the Revolutionary War. The consistency of the data from muster books has attracted computer and database studies of manning and impressment and has led to new and significant judgements.[3] The meaning of nationality at this time when seamen from many countries moved from ship to ship has also been examined, of real relevance when

---

* This can be gauged by the entries in the biographical dictionaries of John Marshall (1835) and William O'Byrne (1849), which rely on the accounts of the officers themselves.

the issue was one of the causes of the declaration of war by the United States in 1812.[4] However, the demands of the sea and seamanship skills have somehow been overshadowed.

The difficulty of manning British warships was the navy's gravest weakness throughout the war and the situation was made worse by the condition of some of the warships (see Chapter 3). At the beginning of hostilities, in late 1803, the twenty-six-year-old HMS *York* (64) was ordered to sea to blockade the Texel. She had been built as the East Indiaman *Royal Admiral* in 1777, had completed four voyages to India and China for her original owner, then had a period as a 'dismantled' ship, before being sold, then contracted by the government to take 350 convicts to Sydney, and sailing on to China. A final voyage to Bengal for a cargo of rice was completed before she had been sold to the Navy Board in 1796 and renamed HMS *York*.[5] On the resumption of war, she was commissioned by Captain Henry Mitford, and set out across the North Sea in the second half of December 1803. She was never seen again.

On 6 March 1804 the *Hull Packet* newspaper carried a small notice that a large mast had been washed up on the beach near Peterhead in 'North Britain', while the lid of a box had also been found with the name of 'Henry Mitford' on it. A week later a notice appeared in the *Sun* that the wedge of carriage gun with 'York' carved on it had also been found. Just before the ship sailed, the captain had sent in her muster book to the Navy Board, with the last entry for 9 December 1803. The crew had consisted of 122 commissioned and warrant officers and able seamen; 112 ordinary seamen and 112 landsmen; 25 marines and 21 boys, in all 392 officers and seamen.[6] This single foundering cost only 50 fewer lives than the total number of 449 British officers and seamen killed at the Battle of Trafalgar, to be fought 21 months later.[7] Experienced officers, naval and merchant, commissioned and warrant officers, and able seamen, would win this long war of attrition, if there were enough of them. A dozen years of sea warfare had yet to play out, and shortages of skilled manpower towards the end of the war would be critical.

Warship casualties when convoying, blockading or cruising for privateers were to be heavy. Between May 1803 until the end of hostilities in 1815, during hostilities with Napoleonic France and her allies, and America from 1812, 409 British warships were lost. This was an annual average of ten warships a year more than those lost in the previous war against Revolutionary France between 1793 and 1802. Of these casualties, 250 warships were wrecked or foundered.[8] The great proportion of them were directly caused by the necessity of winter convoying and blockading. Even ships of the line were not immune; from the thirteen lost in all, eight were wrecked and two foundered.

Escorting ships out of the Baltic too late in the season was the most dangerous. One of these great ships went on shore in late 1810, and the same happened to three more in 1811. Two thousand, two hundred officers and seamen drowned. The last of these occurred on Christmas Eve 1811, when the 98-gun, 2,000-ton HMS *St George*, with a draught of 21 feet, and 850 men on board, was stranded on the shallow, sandy coast of Jutland. She had been dismasted, damaged and delayed in leaving the Baltic. On the shore helpless Danish onlookers saw five hundred men gathered on the quarter deck swept into the sea by one monster wave, although some still survived on the poop deck and some in the rigging. The next morning there was no sign of life aboard the wreck.[9] The long conflict at sea between Britain, European powers and America was to be dominated by winter weather.

The convoys were governed by a complex organisation, with tight rules. At its centre was a small team of Admiralty clerks, managed by the First and Second Secretaries of the Board of Admiralty, who sent orders for convoys to be organised by the admirals commanding in home waters or on distant stations (see Chapter 2). As with any great operation, dependent on communications which could go no faster than a horse or a ship, mistakes occurred. The number of warships acting as escorts was often insufficient. On one occasion in 1810, for instance, Danish gunboats in light winds captured an entire convoy of forty-seven merchant ships off the Naze of Norway (see Chapter 9).* In November 1812 a convoy of three ships set out to deliver munitions to Russia, sailing first to the Baltic, but it was sent back to England, then was ordered to the Black Sea, which it could not penetrate, finally managing to deliver them to the Baltic eighteen months later (see also Chapter 9).[10] This drawn-out warfare was only to be measured in sometimes imperceptible percentage gains and losses. The ultimate aim was to maintain British political and business confidence and the strength of the economy. If convoys had failed, and British trade faltered, so would the British economy. In such circumstances, France would have won this worldwide war.

The Napoleonic Wars were different from every conflict which had gone before, on sea and on land. All the industrial, manpower and technological resources of all the contestants were brought to bear to fight this desperate conflict. The successful protection of trade, particularly in the last seven years of the war during Napoleon's Continental Blockade, enabled Britain to maintain financial confidence. At the same time the army had to be transported to the Continent and beyond, and to be supplied with stores and reinforcements thereafter (see Chapter 6). British convoys and the networks they established laid the foundation of victory in 1815, and in doing so they established the country's naval and mercantile power at sea for a hundred years.

---

* The only other instance in this war was in 1805, when Villeneuve's fleet captured a complete convoy in the West Indies, which was extremely rare, even in well-known disasters. For instance, many merchantmen escaped the capture of the Smyrna convoy in 1693, and eleven escaped when PQ17 scattered in 1942 (see Chapter 1 and Epilogue).

ONE

CONVOYING BEFORE 1803

The Russiamen [the convoy homeward bound from Russia] are all run up the River before I could get here; and they will not take any notice of signals; which is very hard to be a convoy to have our signals not taken notice of. I fired several guns at them, which they did not mind, they outsailing me, this ship being so foul.

Captain John Lowen, *Ruby*, to Secretary of the Admiralty, 18 February 1708/9[1]

The principles and practicalities of convoying had been long established by the start of the Napoleonic Wars. Many lessons had been learnt in the previous 150 years. On the outbreak of war, a well-worn defensive strategy of blockade and trade protection was implemented, and convoys were also used to transport British troops overseas.[2] What was new after 1803 was the increased scale of the conflict, which, as will be seen, accelerated dramatically in its last years up to 1815.

Convoys were used far back in antiquity, but the system can here be conveniently traced back to the English Civil War, when the Parliamentary navy convoyed London trade, protecting it from royalist privateers.[3] The navy under Oliver Cromwell used patrolling warships in the Channel to combat Flemish privateers, although at first English warships, long at sea, were often unable to catch privateers, their bottoms well-tallowed, thus fast-sailing. The situation improved once a squadron was positioned off Dunkirk and Ostend.[4] As trade grew through the seventeenth century, so too did the need to expand its protection. One of the most difficult long-term problems appeared early in the relation-ship between the masters of merchant ships and naval captains, with the latter assuming that they would be rewarded for their escorting tasks. Direct payment was prohibited early by the navy.*

By 1674, after the Third Dutch War, the organisation of convoys developed, particularly in the Mediterranean, when trade with the Levant was threatened by Barbary corsairs. Regional squadrons began to be deployed with convoys. Early convoy discipline was established, with the principle that escorting warships should stay with the merchant ships and not pursue corsairs for prizes. As a result, trade flourished.[5] Convoys assumed greater importance in the war of William III between 1689 and 1702, when the French crown could not afford to maintain the royal fleet so adopted the war against trade. This was the period when French privateering admirals borrowed state warships and English and Dutch losses were considerable in these years.[6] French naval ships and seamen did in fact take part in the *guerre de course*.[7] Indeed, during hostilities over the next 120 years, the major, concentrated losses to British trade were caused by squadrons of French or Spanish warships rather than by privateers.

The most spectacular loss in the whole of the seventeenth century occurred in 1693. By any standards, the convoy from Spithead to Smyrna was enormous, consisting of four hundred merchant ships, escorted by twenty ships of the line under Admiral Sir George Rooke. Mediterranean convoys were particularly vulnerable to French or Spanish interception in wartime, as the convoy's southerly course ran parallel to nearly a thousand miles of hostile coastline.[8] On 30 May the convoy sailed south, accompanied part of the way by the Grand Fleet, but the joint commanders-in-chief had not received intelligence that the French Brest and Toulon fleets were at sea and that they had

* After the Third Dutch War, fines and imprisonment were meted out to those naval captains who had traded, although the practice of exacting a fee for the carriage of gold, silver and jewels in a warship still survived and did so into the nineteenth century (Davies, *Gentlemen and Tarpaulins*, pp. 179–80; Gough, 'Specie Conveyance', pp. 419–20).

combined. After the main body of English warships had turned back, the convoy continued onwards with its English and Dutch escorts, commanded by Rooke. On 17 June 1693, in the Bay of Lagos, east of Cape St Vincent, the great convoy met a very large French force which attacked it. The Dutch, in particular, fought a defensive action with great skill and three-quarters of the merchantmen escaped.[9] But ninety-two were sunk or captured: the losses were said to have equalled those of the Great Fire of London of 1666. Many merchants left the Royal Exchange, an eye witness recorded, 'with the faces of men under the sentence of death'.[10] The French prizes sold for the equivalent of the French naval budget for the previous year.[11]

In England this disaster caused immediate political friction in a very divided Parliament. The King was forced to appoint a new commander-in-chief, Admiral Edward Russell. The government attempted to come to the financial aid of the many merchant-insurers who had suffered losses, but the bill was thrown out by the Lords.[12] The discontent amongst the merchants, represented in Parliament, resulted in the Commons attaching to the 1694 Land Tax Bill a clause allocating forty-three warships to 'cruisers and convoys' only, effectively creating a second navy. This was the beginning of a long period of tension between the Admiralty and the merchant community in London.[13]

Financial exhaustion of both France and England subsequently led to the peace of Ryswick in 1697. However, the nature of warfare was changing from the set battles of the previous Dutch wars. Warships now spent long and monotonous periods at sea convoying trade. It was at this time, for instance, that convoys to and from Archangel expanded. Every year between 1702 and 1712 some fifty to seventy ships were convoyed north and back home.[14]

On the resumption of war with France in 1702, there were not enough skilled seamen to man both the navy and the mercantile marine and a general embargo on trade was declared immediately, prohibiting any merchant ship, already cleared outward, from sailing until she had turned over a quarter of her complement of seamen to the navy. For ships not yet cleared, half the crew had to be handed over.[15] Unsurprisingly, this led to further bad blood. Convoy delays and many complaints arose from naval captains about merchantmen failing to keep station or to keep a lookout, ignoring signals, leaving a convoy when they pleased, followed by complaints about another long-term problem: the different speeds and sailing capabilities of merchant ships, which made it difficult to keep them together.

Influence exercised by the merchants through Parliament forced the navy to impose very severe discipline on naval captains who were made a scapegoat for failures when protecting trade. In 1704 the *Coventry* (48), Captain Henry Lawrence, was captured when escorting an outward Newfoundland convoy, as well as several of the merchantmen. The verdict of the court martial on Lawrence was that he forfeited his pay and was sentenced to seven years' imprisonment. Later that year, Captain William Crosse of the *Elizabeth* (70) disobeyed orders to collect a convoy from the river Shannon, because of sickness on board. Instead, he turned back for Plymouth and his ship was captured by the French. At his court martial he was found guilty of 'notorious mismanagement'. His punishment was just short of that of Admiral Byng fifty years later. Crosse was dismissed from the service, lost all pay due to him and was imprisoned for life. Penalties of this extraordinary severity concentrated the minds of naval officers. 'Taken all in all, it did the service good', is the stern judgement of a modern commentator. Longer periods at sea and with the need 'to interpret precise orders ... would produce better discipline and understanding the nature of sea war. Above all, they became better seamen'.[16]

In London, though, continuing ill-feeling between the naval service and the merchant community led to a Parliamentary inquiry. In the autumn of 1707 an act was passed: 'for the better securing the Trade of this Kingdom by Cruisers and Convoys'.[17] As in 1694, forty-three vessels (out of two hundred) were allocated to trade protection, nine to cruising on the north-east coast, and three to the north-west. In order to preserve the experience necessary for operations in shallow coastal waters, seamen in the forty-three ships were forbidden to serve in ships other than in the cruising service.[18] These tussles for control in London were reflected in convoy indiscipline at sea, with the customary complaints from the naval captains that merchantmen would not obey signals and would leave the convoy when it suited them. In 1731 the situation was improved by the first publication of detailed instructions for convoys, 'established by His Majesty in Council', in the *Regulations and Instructions relating to His Majesty's Service at Sea.*[19] Both sides now had a book of basic rules.

Poor relations between the merchant community and the navy continued during the War of 1739–48. Losses were heavy in 1741/2, when over three hundred merchant ships were lost, resulting in heavy criticism of and pressure on the Admiralty, although a further Convoys and Cruisers Act was rejected by the House of Lords. This political controversy prompted the Admiralty to provide greater security and more resources to cruising for trade protection and convoys until the end of the war in 1748.[20]

The situation changed during the Seven Years War, fought between 1756 and 1763.* By the spring of 1758, Britain had achieved naval superiority, at the same time as significantly improving the organisation of the navy.[21] In 1759 she mounted a genuine blockade of Brest by stationing the Western Squadron off Ushant, and maintained an inshore squadron to keep watch. Here were a swarm of British warships and privateers positioned to intercept French ships returning to their home ports, particularly those of Brest, Rochefort and L'Orient. Further, their navy was rarely confident of knowing the position of the British fleet, which cut down the risk of heavily armed French raiding squadrons, enabling the British to employ smaller warships to protect convoys. The priority of privateers was the capture of merchant ships, and they

---

* In 1760 the total displacement of the British navy was 375,000 tons, that of France 156,000 tons and Spain 137,000 tons (Glete, *Navies and Nations*, I, p. 270). British warship losses by enemy action, shipwreck or foundering amounted to 73, of which 39 (53 per cent) were sloops or smaller (Hepper, *Warship Losses*, p. 212).

generally avoided warships.[22] The French neglected their trade protection, which had a disastrous effect on their trade and on the wealth of their port cities, and ultimately on the viability of the wartime finances of the French state.[23]

However, the British blockade was never complete, for gales blew the waiting warships off station, particularly when blowing from the land, allowing the French to slip away when the British were absent. This enabled French possessions to be supplied in India, the West Indies or North America, but the Western Squadron exerted enough control to wrest the worldwide strategic initiative from the French. The possibility of the breakout of French warships meant that the convoying of British trade was still essential.[24] Ever since the Smyrna convoy, escorting very large convoys, usually the outgoing East and West Indies fleets, south through the Soundings, put the British commander-in-chief in a quandary. He had to weigh up the consequences of leaving the Channel unguarded against ensuring the safety of the convoy. At times of threatened invasion, as for instance at Quiberon Bay in 1759, this became a critical strategic decision. Nevertheless, Britain exploited this advantage in the Western Approaches by making overseas conquests.[25]

The establishment of the Western Squadron changed the balance of naval power, which in turn brought about a new spirit of cooperation in London between the Admiralty and the merchant communities. Profits and politics forced them together, agreeing, for instance, the most efficient timings of convoy sailings.[26] Routines gradually became established, encouraged by lower wartime insurance rates for convoyed ships, with underwriters returning part of the premium to the merchants if their ships remained in convoy. In the 1739–48 war, for instance, 6 to 8 guineas per cent had been the average premium from London to Leghorn, compared to 1½ per cent premium in the peaceful 1730s. In the Seven Years War wine shipments from Madeira to London averaged 6 per cent without convoy, compared to 3 per cent if convoyed for the whole of the voyage. If there were added dangers, such as a hostile fleet known to be in the offing, rates would rise steeply.[27] Marine insurance remained a problem for homecoming trade. The outward voyage from Britain was usually fully covered, but many merchant ships sailed back to Britain uninsured, or only partly insured. Ships sailing for the East India Company were insured by the Company.* The first homeward convoy of 1757 from the West Indies, numbering 170 ships and valued at two million pounds, was almost all uninsured.[28]

The relationship between a well-insured (or even over-insured) merchant ship and a convoy under attack could be complex, and there were a steady number of complaints throughout the century about masters allowing the enemy to take their ship to claim insurance. The French experienced the same trouble, accusing their masters of selling some of the cargo on the voyage, and then claiming insurance on a complete cargo.†

Britain's naval strength at sea weakened during the American Revolutionary War, in part, at least, because of budget economies made in the early 1770s by the government of Lord North. The navy found itself short of small warships after hostilities with the colonists broke out in 1775, a weakness exposed even before the French entered the war in 1778 and the Spanish in 1779. American privateers were not only demonstrating considerable aggression in the North Atlantic, but soon became a danger to trade in home waters, as they were maintained and provisioned in French ports. Ships of the line were dispersed far and wide on trade protection duties, leaving question marks over the effective defence of the main Channel Fleet.‡ In 1777, Lord Sandwich, the

---

* From 1660 to 1834 the Company ran 1,577 ships, which made 4,563 voyages. Their ships were privately owned and chartered to the Company (Bowen, 'Shipping Losses', p. 324).

† In 1746 an officer in Admiral Conflans's squadron complained to the French Minister for the Marine: 'The captains of the ships in question did everything that was necessary to get taken, and succeeded in it; we have no doubt they had consumed part of their cargoes in the various ports where we were forced to stay, and being insured, were delighted to have an occasion to be captured' (D'Aubenton to Maurepas, 7 Nov 1746, quoted in Pares, *War and Trade*, p. 305).

‡ In 1775 Royal Naval tonnage displacement was 337,000 tons, the French 199,000 tons and Spain 198,000 tons (Glete, *Navies and Nations*, I, p. 271). 240 British warships were lost through enemy action, shipwreck or foundering, 165 (68 per cent of the whole) of which were sloops and smaller (Hepper, *Warship Losses*, p. 212).

First Lord of the Admiralty, complained to Lord Howe, 'The sea is now overspread with privateers on every part and the demands for convoys and cruisers so great that we know not how to supply them.'[29] The strategic situation worsened. In 1780 the Dutch declared war against Britain, and the Baltic states united in the hostile Armed Neutrality. The strategy of the successful Western Squadron, poised off the French coast, established in the previous war, was abandoned.

Convoys to supply the British army in North America were critical, but there were delays. Army transports were chartered by the Treasury and had to compete with the Navy and Victualling Boards, a system which was to be changed in 1794 by the creation of the Transport Board, which hired transports for all government departments.[30] Merchant ships assembling at Cork often had to wait for months for a warship to appear to escort them, and American privateers, operating in British waters, were only too effective.

This war witnessed the convoy disaster in 1780 that caused the greatest financial damage in the whole of the eighteenth century. The Admiralty took a risk in sending a large troop and supplies convoy, escorted by ships of the line, to relieve Gibraltar, besieged for several years by the Spaniards. Almost simultaneously, in August, sixty-three large merchant ships, bound for the East and West Indies, also sailed south from the Channel, loaded with not only trade goods, but also the 90th Regiment bound for Jamaica. The convoy had a strong escort, commanded by Captain John Moutray of HMS *Ramillies* (74), the new HMS *Inflexible* (64), an old 36-gun frigate, three 32-gun frigates, the HMS *Southampton*, HMS *Thetis* and HMS *Alarm*, supported by an old 74-gun ship converted into a store ship, HMS *Buffalo*.

One of the routines which the navy had evolved was for outward-bound West Indies convoys to call into Madeira to take on wine for the consumption and health of the crews before voyaging on to the Caribbean. Moutray's Admiralty instructions ordered him to Madeira, 'taking in there, without a moment's loss of time, such wine as may be necessary for the companies of the ships under your command'.[31] As the convoy sailed south, it met with Admiral Francis Geary, commanding the Channel Fleet of twenty-one ships of the line, looking for Spanish squadrons, known to be at sea. The Channel Fleet accompanied Moutray and his convoy south for a few hours, but Geary had been cruising for two months, his ships were short of provisions, their crews were suffering from scurvy and he himself was ill. On 2 August Geary turned north for home.

Seven days later, north-east of Madeira, Moutray's convoy met the hostile Spanish fleet, under Admiral Don Luis de Cordoba, who now commanded thirty-two ships of the line.[32] The British warships fled ignominiously. At one point, Moutray's ship, the *Ramillies*, had seven Spanish ships of the line chasing her.* Fifty-five merchant ships were captured, five of them East Indiamen. 1,350 seamen and 1,250 soldiers were taken prisoner, including the 90th regiment and its equipment.[33] A contemporary estimate was that four-fifths of the costs of £1,500,000 would fall on Lloyd's, the rest on the East India Company.[34] According to the official historian of Lloyd's, 'it shook Lloyd's to its foundations. Many underwriters failed, and thirty years later, at the height of the Napoleonic Wars, the month of August 1780 was still remembered as the blackest in the history of Lloyd's.'[35] The heaviest single blow had fallen on British trade since the disaster of the Smyrna convoy, eighty-seven years before, in a strikingly similar fashion, just beyond the extended cruising range of the Channel Fleet.

The next year, 1781, saw another enormous loss. The underlying cause was again a lack of capital ships in the Channel, which were engaged in another effort to relieve Gibraltar. Eighteen of a convoy of thirty-two ships sent home from the rich Dutch Caribbean island of St Eustatius were seized in February of that year by a force under

---

* John Moutray never commanded a ship again, ending his career as the dockyard commissioner at English Harbour in Antigua after the American war. Problems with his anomalous seniority caused difficulties with the ambitious young Captain Horatio Nelson, though personally there was no conflict, possibly because of Moutray's wife, with whom both Nelson and Cuthbert Collingwood had been infatuated. Moutray was clearly no firebrand (Knight, *Pursuit of Victory*, pp. 88–9).

Admiral Sir George Rodney. The convoy was attacked near the Scillies by a squadron of French ships of the line under Admiral de La Motte-Picquet. It was weakly escorted by a 74-gun ship, a French prize frigate and two captured Dutch frigates crewed by British seamen. In common with most warships sent home from the West Indies after some years' service there, they were not in good condition. The converging of rival convoys with powerful escorting squadrons, often with no knowledge of each other's whereabouts, led to major fleet actions, as occurred in 1781 at the Dogger Bank in the North Sea when powerful British and Dutch escorts happened upon each other.

Still the American privateers harassed trade in British waters. On 1 June 1782 Parliament took steps to hinder them extending their range of operations by outlawing the ransoming of merchant ships at sea. According to generally understood international law, if a privateer captured a merchant ship it was within its rights to do three things: take it to a friendly port to have it condemned by a prize court; remove the crew and destroy the vessel; or release the prize after removing armaments, valuables and any provisions or water required by the captor.[36] This last right was made illegal in British law by 'The Act to Prohibit Ransoming Act of 1782'.* Both the French and Americans contested this law until 1815 and, as we shall see, both naval and merchant seamen fell foul of it, to their considerable discomfiture.

It was, of course, a war that did not end happily for Britain, yet the loss of the American colonies in 1783 was followed by a decade of peace during which overseas trade to and from Britain dramatically increased, including that with the newly formed United States. By September 1792, just over 16,000 merchant ships were registered with the Board of Trade. The number of ships entering and clearing British ports increased and by 1792 they numbered 13,033 and 13,891 respectively. Between 1793 and 1801 the annual wartime average figures were 10,442 entering and 10,814 clearing.[37] Thus the task of trade protection in the French

* 22 Geo. III c.25.

Revolutionary War increased dramatically and the merchant community and the Admiralty agreed regulations for convoys contained in a Parliamentary Act passed in June 1793.*

The first two years of the Revolutionary War were marked by emotionally violent statements in the British Parliament and in the French National Convention. In 1793 the British planned to starve France by extending the 'contraband of war' to foodstuffs, although consequent tensions with Scandinavian countries led to abandonment of this plan.[38] In reply, in May 1794, the Convention passed a decree for all British prisoners of war to be executed.[39] In the same year the French sent a large convoy loaded with wheat from the United States to stave off hunger in Revolutionary Paris and the escorting French fleet met Lord Howe and the Channel Fleet off the French coast. The French warships lured Lord Howe deep into the Atlantic, away from the convoy, before being caught by Howe on the 'Glorious' First of June.

The greatest danger to British trade at the beginning of the French Revolutionary War was posed by powerful French raiding squadrons. In October 1795 a convoy of over sixty merchant ships homeward bound from the Levant, escorted by HMS *Fortitude* (74) and two other 74s, was attacked off Cape St Vincent by a squadron of six French ships of the line, commanded by Contre-amiral Richery. The British lost HMS *Censeur* (74), a French prize recently taken, which according to the captain of the *Fortitude*, was 'not half manned and had but little powder'.[40] The major loss, however, was the thirty-three merchant ships taken into Cadiz. Richery followed this by a raid on Newfoundland with seven French ships of the line, where he destroyed fishing vessels

---

* The other act passed early that year was the Traitorous Correspondence Act (33 Geo. III c.27), which prohibited the insurance of naval and military stores in any shipment to a French port, or of any cargo belonging to any person living in French dominions; but it allowed the insurance of non-military items, even to a French port (Wright & Fayle, *Lloyd's*, pp. 178–9; Avery, 'Naval Protection', p. 232). As we shall see, the private sector acted with remarkable independence from the state during the Napoleonic Wars, with considerable contact between British and French merchants, bankers and insurers.

and buildings and equipment ashore and threatened St John's. The British press fulminated over the French admiral's 'predatory incursions on the coast of Newfoundland . . . heroically committing acts for which a common plunderer would long since have been gibbetted'.[41] The potential damage that could have been achieved by French naval squadrons against British trade was never realised. Invasion attempts on Ireland in 1796–8, or the grand expedition to Egypt in 1798 took up French resources.

Enemy privateers made less of an impact in the first years of the war in north-west Europe, being less effective than they had been eighty years before during the Nine Years War and the War of Spanish Succession, for by the end of the century the Royal Navy had become relatively more powerful than it had been against the French in the earlier wars. In the 1790s, French privateering voyages were not necessarily profitable and posed a considerable financial risk for the ship's backers. Life for French privateer crews was dangerous and hard.* This was the time when French privateering was at its weakest, for it only reached a peak of activity in 1797–8, partly as a consequence of the naval mutinies at Spithead and the Nore, which encouraged the French to think that the Royal Navy's command of the seas had weakened.[42] This increased activity, particularly in the Channel and the North Sea, can be partially gauged by the number of French seamen captured in privateers and held as prisoners of war in British prisons and hulks. From 11,500 in 1796, this had more than doubled by 1799 to 25,000, after which these numbers dropped as a result of prisoner exchanges through cartels with the French.[43]

This increased aggression by privateers led to the Convoy Act of 1798, which made sailing in a convoy compulsory, at the same time as imposing a tax upon the merchantmen for protection. In its first year of operation, the convoy tax brought into the Treasury just under

---

* In a sample of 132 convoys between 1793 and 1797, 4 were attacked; out of 5,827 ships escorted, 398 straggled from their convoys and 35 were lost (Rodger, *Command of the Ocean*, p. 559; Avery, 'Naval Protection', pp. 242–50).

£1.3 million.[44] Some exemptions from sailing in convoy were allowed, including coastal shipping and those bound for Irish ports, Hudson's Bay Company ships and the well-armed East Indiamen. However, the latter usually sailed in convoy, escorted by a 74-gun warship, in the danger area to and from St Helena through the Western Approaches and the Channel.[45]

The Admiralty managed to contain merchant ship losses in the French Revolutionary War.* Estimates of British merchant ship losses vary, and calculations involve a number of assumptions merely to establish the overall size of the British merchant fleet. In 1799, for instance, the Registrar-General of Shipping recorded a total of 17,879, of which 13,518 were registered in England and Scotland.[46] This figure would be affected by losses from enemy action or 'marine causes', by the number of prizes recaptured, and by how many ships were operational or seaworthy at any one time. The Secretary of Lloyd's estimated that some 2 per cent were lost over the whole period, 1793–1815.[†]

Through the century, the Royal Navy and the commercial world had gradually established legal frameworks and routines to solve their differences. Relations between the Admiralty and the merchant communities in London and the various port cities on the question of trade protection in the Great Wars were constructive, although, not unnaturally, local grumbling arose over delays and mishaps. Lloyd's had grown powerful enough to bring pressure on clients as well as the government, and underwriters were clear that convoys made financial sense. In this,

* In 1800 British warships displaced 546,000 tons, the French 204,000 tons and the Spanish 227,000 tons (Glete, *Navies and Nations*, II, p. 376). British warships lost by enemy action, shipwreck or foundering in the French Revolutionary War amounted to 226, of which sloops and smaller totalled 153 (68 per cent of the whole) (Hepper, *Warship Losses*, p. 213).
† These are complex calculations with constantly moving variables. According to Mahan, *French Revolutionary War*, whose analysis of British losses extends to several pages, Lloyd's listed British losses by capture, 1793–1800, as 3,639 (less those recaptured) and those by losses from 'sea risk' at 2,967, a total of 6,606. To counterbalance the losses, in 1801, 2,779 had been brought under the British flag as prizes. Some of these figures were to rise sharply after 1803, with estimates of losses of as much as 5 to 6 per cent in the deep-sea trades (Mahan, *French Revolutionary War*, II, p. 226; Rodger, *Command of the Ocean*, p. 561; Sutcliffe, *Expeditionary Warfare*, pp.75–6).

they were supported by legal judgements defining liabilities which created conditions for reliable insurance. The Committee of Lloyd's was now accepted as the contact point for the Admiralty and they worked together.

Most convoy routes were sailed throughout the year. The likelihood of hostile winter weather did not much affect schedules and routes, though it sharply increased insurance premiums paid by shipowners reflecting greater risk. Overall, winter weather and hurricanes were responsible for the loss of far more ships, cargoes and lives than were sustained from enemy action.

Many of the trade protection tasks had remained the same for many years, including the dependence of Britain upon imported war materials. Shortages of seamen with the accompanying burden of impressment had long been experienced. Inadequate numbers of suitable naval escorts were a familiar problem. Incipient friction between lightly manned merchant ships, driven by profit, and naval commanders, raised on hierarchy and instant obedience, was an old problem, although, as we shall see, there were many variations in naval/civilian relations. Ahead lay twelve years of warfare. Steadily increasing in size and frequency, British convoys stretched further across the world than during any previous conflict, with an intensity never previously witnessed.* If the last six years of the French Revolutionary War are compared to the last six years of the Napoleonic Wars, it can be seen that at least three times the number of convoys escorted nearly three times the number of merchant ships than in the previous conflict. This could hardly have been foreseen in May 1803, when war broke out again.

---

* In the last six years of the French Revolutionary War (1796–1801), 508 convoys escorted 21,500 ships, an annual average of 85 convoys protecting an average of about 3,500 ships. Between 1809 and 1814, 1,674 convoys protected 57,448 ships, at an annual average of 279 convoys protecting 8,206 ships (Knight, 'Achievement and Cost', p. 126, figures compared between the appendices in Avery, 'Naval Protection', pp. 346–405; TNA, ADM 7/64).

TWO

THE ADMIRALTY AND TRADE PROTECTION, 1803–1815

The cargo intended to be laden consists of colonial produce, British Manufacturers etc more especially East India goods which must be paid for in Cash before they can be taken out of the Warehouses. A ready return is the Life & Soul of this Trade, which cannot be accomplished while vessels are tied down to Convoy.

> William Price, Commercial Chambers, to John Barrow,
> Second Secretary to the Board of Admiralty, requesting
> a licence to sail without convoy for the *Sybella*,
> 31 October 1811[1]

Nothing shall interfere with that most important object the protection of the convoys.

> John Wilson Croker, Secretary to the Board of Admiralty,
> to Admiral Sir John Borlase Warren, commander-in-chief,
> North American Station, 6 January 1813[2]

If there is a long theme to this history of convoys, it was the struggle between two very different instincts. The navy measured success by the number of enemy warships or privateers destroyed or captured, but this was of tangential importance to shipowners, merchants, brokers and insurers. Their primary concern was the safe arrival of their merchantmen. Fusing these separate motivations was one of the central problems for the Board of Admiralty. The others were to maintain a high level of trade protection at the same time as keeping that trade flowing; to ensure that imported raw materials were sufficient for domestic industrial expansion to take place, enabled by the continual flow of worldwide imports, exports and re-exports.[3] Britain's army, navy and ordnance also had to be transported with the maximum level of speed and efficiency, and support for their operations, maintained year by year in distant places. The population of Britain had to be fed with imported wheat in years of dearth. If these vital objectives were achieved, then it would follow that the financial confidence of the merchant community, in particular the City of London, would continue, providing the essential loan capital to add to tax income, so that the government could keep the war going.

For the twelve years of war, 1803 to 1815, threats to trade were extraordinarily complex and they changed continually, as did the seagoing trade patterns of neutral nations. Between those two dates, at different times and in different combinations, Britain was at war with France, Spain, Holland, the north German states, Prussia, Denmark, Norway, Sweden and Russia, and, after 1812, the United States of America.

A more complex and continual problem, however, faced the Admiralty throughout these war years. The shortage of seamen had been a long-term problem. At the height of William III's war in 1696, the number of seamen borne peaked at 47,000 men. The greatest number of seamen borne in the war against Napoleon reached 147,000 in 1813.[4] A parallel demand for merchant seamen increased their numbers from 54,000 in 1738 to over 91,000 in 1791.[5] Both the commanders of warships and merchant ships pursued skilled seamen, with the masters of merchant ships having the advantage of being able to offer greater wages and more freedom. Impressing seamen from merchant ships would bedevil relations between the navy and the ships they were trying to protect. The problem became worse as the number of available skilled seamen declined steadily throughout the war, so much so that the government changed the Prize Act in June 1808, redistributing proceeds away from senior commissioned officers and directing them towards the petty officers, the skilled seamen who were in such short supply.[6] It did not reverse the trend. The national manpower shortage in the last five years of this war came close to affecting its outcome.

Britain did, nevertheless, have some critical advantages. It enjoyed a clear lead over France in four key areas: financial expertise and available capital, industrial output, shipbuilding and shipping capacity and naval and mercantile seamanship.[7] It also possessed or controlled sheltered anchorages large enough for substantial convoys to gather. In home waters, the Solent and Cork Harbour were the most important, complemented to the north by Long Hope Sound in the Orkneys. As the war developed, the tacit agreement of the Swedish government led to the Baltic trade being able to depend upon Hano in south-east Sweden and the sheltered waters outside Gothenburg. Secondary anchorages, unsafe in easterly or south-easterly gales, were the 'Roads' outside Leith, the Humber, Great Yarmouth, the Nore in the Thames Estuary and the Downs off Deal. Vulnerability to easterly winds also affected Torbay, Plymouth Sound and Falmouth, while Berehaven in the west of Ireland was generally only used in emergencies. On the other side of the Atlantic, safety and numbers could be had in Halifax, Nova Scotia and St John's Newfoundland and further south, Jamaica in the West Indies.* All that the British lacked now was a deep harbour for gathering trade in the central Mediterranean. The retention of Malta in British hands in 1803 was to prove to be vital, and was the immediate reason for the resumption of war in 1803.

Neutral shipping played a big part in trade from the start of this war, with false flags and papers. In Bordeaux in 1803, for instance, a hundred French vessels registered under a foreign flag and half of them went to America. French cargoes were transported by neutral ships, which then 'broke' their voyage in a neutral port. In early 1805,

---

* The sheltered anchorages of Lisbon and Cadiz changed hands during the war. Spain had the advantage of Ferrol, but the French had the problem of west-facing entrances at Brest, Rochefort and L'Orient, difficult to use in contrary winds.

for instance, an American brig imported a cargo of brandy from Bordeaux to Newburyport, Massachusetts, which was then re-exported to Copenhagen.[8]

In May 1806 this changed when Britain imposed the Orders-in-Council announcing the blockade of North European ports.* These orders declared that all ports under French occupation were blockaded, and that any ships entering or leaving them were lawful prize, which kept the High Court of Admiralty busy in its task of deciding which prizes were condemned and which were not. This move was answered by Napoleon's Berlin Decrees in November, which began his Continental System. These opposing blockades effectively eliminated neutral shipping. Increasingly, licensed neutral or even enemy ships carried cargo, and subterfuge inevitably prevailed as most merchant ships now carried two sets of papers. The British now welcomed merchant ships of any flag into their convoys, provided the ship accompanied the convoy for the whole journey to a friendly port.

The Convoy Act of 1803, which built on that of 1798, set the framework by which the Admiralty regulated the convoy system. It declared that all ships engaged in foreign trade had to sail in convoy, in theory enforced by the power to punish ships' masters for 'running' from a convoy. From the time of the issue of printed and signed instructions by the convoy commodore to each master, the merchant ships were under his orders, and the insurance of ship and cargo was invalid if a merchant ship broke convoy and was then captured. Thus, merchant ship masters were usually instructed by shipowners to keep in convoy.

An exception to this Act was the coastal trade around Britain, undertaken by numerous small vessels, often on short, local voyages, and impossible to organise into convoys. As the Board of Admiralty reiterated to Lloyd's in 1809, with some irritation, 'The convoy Act does not compel any vessel to take convoy between any two Ports of the United

---

* The use of the Privy Council enabled commercially sensitive decision-making to be undertaken in secret, although usually by cabinet ministers. For the development of the use of the Council on naval matters, see Rodger, *Command of the Ocean*, pp. 96, 181.

Kingdom, and ships may freely sail without convoy from Port to Port, within the United Kingdom without taking out a License from the Admiralty ... the sailing of Ships without convoys from Port to Port is equally applicable to the Irish Trade.'[9] Small cruising warships patrolled off vulnerable points, such as headlands, although convoys were provided if requested by merchants, and government transports on coastal routes were protected as a matter of course.

When the risk from enemy warships and privateers was lessened, the Admiralty issued licences to enable well-armed merchant ships to sail independently. Pressure for such licences came from several sections of the merchant community, but particularly from those with perishable goods, such as fruit, cargoes which could not tolerate delay. The herring or pilchard trade to the Mediterranean, though salted and barrelled, needed to be expedited. Sometimes the Admiralty would grant them for a general area, for a limited time, or for a particular route. When British sea control was dominant, and the Board assessed the risk of capture by the enemy was small, many merchant ships were able to sail independently under licence.[10] This happened, for instance, in the Atlantic between 1809 and 1812, when French privateering activity was very low, and in Northern European waters after Napoleon's power had collapsed after 1812, though licences stopped abruptly once the Americans declared war. In the second half of 1814, for instance, because of the declining risk on some stations, the Admiralty issued 1,128 licences.[11]

This could lead to difficulties between the Admiralty and Lloyd's, as the latter always wanted convoys to be enforced. A strongly worded Admiralty statement of March 1809, in reply to a protest by Lloyd's, stated that licences to sail independently were not issued to a ship, 'unless she is manned and armed in such a manner as to give a reasonable assurance that she cannot be captured by an enemy's Privateer'. Another factor in such a decision was 'if she is in Ballast or has not a cargo of much value on board, but in general vessels having valuable cargoes on board are not permitted to sail without convoy', and the Admiralty claimed 'that the discretion exercised in granting Licences has been beneficial to the Public as there is strong reason to presume from the very small comparative number of Licensed vessels that have been captured by the enemy'.[12]

Both Britain and France were still dominated by mercantilist principles and, in the words of the historians of Lloyd's, 'aimed at the regulation rather than the prohibition of trade (and) were well content to see the enemy drained of gold by the purchase of such commodities as did not contribute directly to his fighting strength'.[13] One way of keeping trade flowing was to allow licensed trading with the enemy, while France also had a similar system. The Privy Council was the body that issued licences to permit trade with the enemy. This had happened before the imposition of the economic blockades after 1807. In early 1804, for instance, the Board of Admiralty instructed Lord Keith to use his control of the North Sea ports of Hamburg, Tonningen or Husum to let specie imports through to England. The blockade 'should be so far relaxed as to give permission for the exportation of bullion to this country ... and when the sum on board any one ship shall amount to £100,000 to proceed with it to Harwich and there to deliver it to such persons as shall be appointed to receive it on the part of those to whom it should be consigned'.[14]

At times, the amount of direct trade with the enemy was substantial. Poor harvests in Britain resulted in the import of grain from France and Holland, to be paid for in silver, an opportunity, as Napoleon saw it, to divest Britain of its bullion reserves. In the autumn of 1809, the Privy Council issued licences for ships registered in any country except France to import grain, meal or flour into England from ports of France or Holland. In May and June 1810 over 123 licences were issued for 585 ships to bring grain to an English port, which could return to France with colonial, East India and prize goods and British manufactures. When the grain shortage in Britain ended, these licences ceased.*

---

* Galpin, *Grain Supply*, p. 115. Chapter VI, 'Licenced Trade', pp. 83–122, lays out the complexities of the system. Galpin quotes thirteen Parliamentary Acts between 1793 and 1810 that contain clauses relating to licences and forty-three Privy Council Regulations issued. There were eighteen different types of licence.

For much of these wars, a convoy commodore could be forgiven for wondering from exactly which state he was protecting his merchantmen, and his knowledge of the state of diplomatic relations between the states of Europe would need to be constantly up to date. Further, if he captured an enemy warship or privateer, he had to calculate which ones might be worth taking to port as a potential prize. Which might result in costing him a great deal of money if it was not successfully condemned in the High Court of Admiralty? It was not easy to know then, or even from the evidence today, about the state of relations at a date when a capture might have taken place. Nor is it easy to generalise about the criteria used by prize courts in condemning prizes as there was a wide variation on the judgements of vice-admiralty courts in several countries. It was so complex and changing that a leading scholar today doubts whether clear-cut concepts of 'neutrality' and 'neutral shipping' were or are adequate definitions.*

Already-complex legalities were made doubly so by fraudulent licences, which could be purchased in every major seaport in the world. As a precaution, merchant masters carried alternative licences, although they had to ensure that they produced the correct licence whenever apprehended on the high seas. Much trickery was employed, on every side.[15] Merchant ships could be boarded by naval officers in enemy uniform to trick the captured master into giving him a set of incriminating papers.† American merchant ships, for instance, carried British cargoes to Russia in 1807, when Britain and Russia were at war.[16] Warships and privateers often saw a way through the necessity of using vice-admiralty courts at all by attempting to ransom a captured vessel, rather than take possession of it, made illegal in British law in 1782 and specifically forbidden in all the Prize Acts.[17]

---

* In 2016 Silvia Marzagalli called for a redefinition: 'neutrality should be conceived within an evolving system of relations in a given region, rather than as a clear-cut, objective legal determination of the status of neutral shipping and the maritime trading rights of a given flag' (Marzagalli, 'Neutrality issues in the Mediterranean', p. 131).
† See the example of the *Eliza Swan*, Chapter 10.

In addition to the licences granted by the Privy Council, there were those issued by the Admiralty. The first category was 'letters of marque', well developed by the mid-eighteenth century, which were documents bestowing the legal right on a non-naval ship to capture and profit from the taking of enemy ships, allowing them to bring their capture to port to be 'condemned' as lawful prize. British privateers did not flourish as they had done in previous wars because overall there was insufficient seaborne enemy trade to make it worth their while. There was a flurry of activity in the first few months of the Napoleonic Wars, and there were good years after 1808 for a period against Danish merchantmen and against American shipping after 1812.*

Between 1803 and 1815 letters of marque were issued to 1,810 vessels. Only 175 of these were private men of war, and the rest were well-armed cargo-carrying merchant ships which might find an opportunity to capture an enemy merchant ship. Private men of war were divided into 'deep-water', larger and intended for the Western Approaches and beyond, or the smaller 'Channel' private men of war, operating much closer to home. Compared to that of the American Revolutionary War, for instance, this was a very low level of activity. Nevertheless, what privateers there were attracted valuable and experienced seamen, which would have been more than useful for manning warships and merchantmen.[†]

The Board of Admiralty and its officials were generally closer to the powerful interests in Parliament than they were to the naval officers to

---

* Statistical research into the number of prizes at this time has not been completed, but preliminary findings suggest that, as the wars went on, the value of prizes went down but the numbers went up (Aldous, 'Prize Money', p. 17; Benjamin, 'Golden Harvest', pp. 6–7).
† 599 privateers came from London, 401 from Liverpool and 229 from east-coast ports, with the rest spread through many different ports. In July 1803, Letters of Marque declarations reveal that 91 'Channel' private men of war were crewed by 2,708 seamen, and 10 'deep-water' private men of war by 565, all these seamen denied to naval and merchant ships (Starkey, *British Privateering Enterprise*, Appendix 8; 'British Privateering Enterprise', pp. 130, 132, 137–8).

whom they gave orders. At the heart of Admiralty business was its relationship with the various strands of the mercantile community, primarily in the City of London. Very often these elements were made up of competing interests who did not necessarily see eye to eye, as, for instance, shipowners with the merchants or planters whose cargoes they were transporting. Rivalries existed between East and West India merchants, while merchants and shipowners combined when there was controversy over marine insurance.

The powerful influence of the City of London in convoy business arose from its representation in Parliament. Of a total of 2,143 MPs between 1790 and 1820, 180 members were merchants who traded overseas.[18] Two-thirds of them were based in London, although those from Bristol and Liverpool were increasingly represented. West India merchants numbered 35 MPs while 25 traded to the East Indies. However, the 'interest' of both these groups were swollen by 'nabobs' from India or planters from the West Indies. The East India Company was a powerful lobby, while in addition a number of members had been 'free' merchants in India. When Indian affairs were debated, there was no lack of expertise. The West Indies lobby, too, was influential. About 75 MPs in this period owned or were heirs to sugar fortunes.[19] However, both these groups were beginning to lose their power. Sugar prices declined steadily during the war, lessening West Indian influence, while merchants in Liverpool and elsewhere were actively working to divest the East India Company of its monopoly, led by John Gladstone, a wealthy Scots merchant, based in Liverpool. They were successful in 1813.

Lloyd's too had its critics, for pressure from merchants and shipowners, as well as their insurance rivals, brought about a Select Commission on Marine Insurance in 1811. The defence of the monopoly held by Lloyd's was led by Joseph Marryat MP, Chairman of the Committee of Lloyd's, which brought him to prominence. The interests of Lloyd's and the Admiralty, both of whom had a primary target of minimising risk and shipping losses, were closest. Both strove to assert the importance of convoy discipline. Complaints about the delays to convoys or recommendations for different arrangements from the Committee of Lloyd's were swiftly attended to by the Admiralty Board, as can be gauged today in the archives by the close annotations made by the Secretaries to incoming letters from Lloyd's.[20] What was never solved was impressment from merchant ships, leaving them dangerously short-handed. Lloyd's regularly made representations to the Admiralty, but the shortage of seamen which led to such high levels of impressment proved to be an insoluble question.[21]

The Admiralty Board and the Committee of Lloyd's were usually in agreement, though differences could flare up if losses of merchant ships mounted. And the Admiralty needed the cooperation of the underwriters at Lloyd's. In the previous war they had proved to the Admiralty that the war risks for 'runners', those merchant ships which left convoys, were between a third and half more than those which remained in convoy, and they adjusted their premiums to conditions accordingly.[22] The underwriters at Lloyd's, in the words of a study of convoys in the French Revolutionary War, 'helped to shape and to enforce maritime policy by their differential premiums'.*

Lloyd's also provided rewards to motivate naval officers by setting up the Patriotic Fund, which awarded elaborately decorated swords to naval officers, usually to the rank of post-captain and above, who had distinguished themselves in the protection of trade.[23] Eighty-two of these swords were awarded between 1803 and 1809, and charitable giving to seamen increased.[24] Direct lobbying played a part. One example of influencing a naval officer occurred in 1801 when the Levant Company invited Nelson to lunch. As a result of this contact with the 'Turkey merchants', as he called them, he knew exactly what to do in setting up the Smyrna convoys when he arrived in the Mediterranean as commander-in-chief in 1803. He wrote to the consul in Smyrna in

---

* One authority, drawing a parallel with the Second World War, suggests that Lloyd's was so close as to fulfil an operational research function for the Admiralty (Waters, 'Notes on the Convoy System', p. v).

October 1803, 'in everything in which I can be useful to the Levant Company I shall be truly happy to shew it'.[25] Vice-Admiral Collingwood, who succeeded Nelson as commander-in-chief, was less sanguine, recounting privately in January 1806 that he had been to Carthegena where a Spanish squadron lay. These ships did not need to go to sea as,

> their trade is so covered by the neutral flag, that it requires no other protection. The property of the enemy is thus secured, while we are buffeting the seas without ceasing, and with difficulty protect our own. What is the worst part of it is, that these invaders of our rights are, for the most part, ensured by English underwriters. It is a most nefarious practice, which has put me out of conceit with mercantile patriotism. They may give me fine vases and high praises, but they must shew the same regard for their Country which I feel, before they can gain my esteem.[26]

In spite of their differences over licences to sail without convoy, the question of enforcing convoy discipline most exercised the Admiralty and Lloyd's throughout the war. Masters of merchant ships found the naval regulations and the stream of orders by signal from the commodore irksome. In certain trades they would often 'run' from a convoy, often during the night, to reach port first when the price they could obtain for their cargo was high. 'Running' ships were a problem and always the most vulnerable to capture by the enemy.

It was extremely difficult to bring a successful prosecution against a master for infringing naval instructions, for witnesses were unlikely to be cooperative. Nor did the law help. The 1803 Convoy Act was ineffective because it did not cover the disobedience of signals and it was never used successfully to enforce discipline.[27] A case was brought in 1804 against Captain Barge of the *Annabella*, but the High Court of Admiralty found that there was no case to answer. In 1806 Lloyd's began sending copies of complaints about masters to owners, who were to dismiss them.[28] In 1807 Captain Sir William Bolton, commanding

HMS *Fisgard* (38), sent a party aboard the *Arethusa* merchant ship, master William Chivers. A thorough search found eight seamen who had deserted from warships, including the *Fisgard*, when at Cork. Chivers then sailed away from the convoy, when, as Bolton reported to the lawyers: 'I was compelled to make sail after him and bring him down with a shot.' When a second boarding naval party reached the deck of the *Arethusa*, tempers erupted. Chivers held a pistol to the chest of the naval lieutenant and, as Bolton reported, 'not satisfied with this outrageous violence, the Man endeavours to alarm the whole convoy by making signals of distress, and proceeds in the most wanton manner to hack and cut in pieces his own rigging'. The next day, Chivers produced an Admiralty licence, described by Bolton as 'appearing to me a sufficient justification for my suffering him to depart'. Bolton was not cast in the Nelson mould. A more flagrant breach of several laws could hardly be found, but the witnesses were dispersed. The case did not come to court until 1810, when it was thrown out for lack of evidence.[29]

Throughout the war, Sir William Scott, Judge of the High Court of Admiralty for thirty years from 1798 to 1828, was defining prize law with a long series of judgements with which naval officers had to be constantly familiar. Examples of his judgements included: which ships should be issued with letters of marque, or the definition of a neutral ship, or when a port was legally blockaded, or what should happen to prizes seized during embargoes before the declaration of war, or how prizes of great value, especially specie, should be awarded.[30] Throughout the war Scott upheld the power of the state and of British rights, particularly in the right of search of neutral vessels. He was, in the words of one recent commentator, aware that 'this was no ordinary war, but a fight for the civilisation of Europe'.[31]

Perhaps one of the most intricate judgements concerned the capture of the *Wight*, a British ship being convoyed down the ten-mile channel between the islands of Ithaca and Cephalonia in the Ionian islands by HMS *Thisbe* (28). In windless conditions, a privateer 'rowed out from the land by means of sweeps' and captured the *Wight*, though the warship's boats recaptured her within an hour, with the loss of one man. The captain of the *Thisbe* demanded salvage for the recapture, even though it was argued by the lawyers representing the merchant ship owners that it was neglect by the *Thisbe*, the convoying ship, that the *Wight* was captured in the first place. Scott, nevertheless, ruled that the ship had been properly captured, and found for the captain of the *Thisbe*.[32]

Britain had started the naval war against France in May 1803 at a profound disadvantage, due to the policies of the First Lord of the Admiralty, Admiral Lord St Vincent, who was consumed with a Whiggish passion for violent change and extreme economy, which reduced investment in the navy. He came to office in February 1801 and left with the fall of Henry Addington's administration in May 1804 and was followed by two First Lords, Melville and Barham, with trenchant personalities operating within weak governments. However, by a series of radical moves they rapidly restored the navy so that a sufficient fleet could fight the Battle of Trafalgar.* It was very unfortunate for the strategic direction of the navy that he was forced to resign. He was followed by the old but experienced Lord Barham, until the death of William Pitt in 1806, after which Lord Grenville's 'Ministry of All the Talents' lasted only fourteen months. Grenville appointed two inexperienced First Lords, Lord Howick (who became Lord Grey) and Thomas Grenville. The Tory governments which followed appointed Lord Mulgrave from 1807 to 1810, who left the office bowed down by the responsibility and took another less demanding Cabinet post; the

---

* Inheriting the repair backlog from Lord St Vincent, Melville forced a very reluctant Navy Board to repair ships by the quicker method of 'doubling', favoured by the East India Company. After Melville had left office, John Barrow wrote to him appreciatively that 'the battle of Trafalgar would not have taken place if the new mode of repairing ships had not been adopted ... instead of 34 sail of the Line, the Mediterranean Fleet would not possibly have exceeded 24 ...' (Knight, 'The Fleets at Trafalgar', pp. 70–74; *Britain Against Napoleon*, pp. 223–4).

decent but unassertive Charles Philip Yorke followed for two years until 1812, when the Baltic convoy disaster of late 1811 was a factor in his resignation. The second Lord Melville, who had a complicated relationship with his dominant father, became First Lord after Melville senior died in 1811.[33] All these first lords had to face the problems of running the navy with declining numbers of seamen.[34]

The Admiralty functioned under the First Lord who presided over six commissioners, three naval officers and three civilians, usually politicians, meeting in the Admiralty Office in Whitehall. The Office was a small department, with only fifty-four secretaries and clerks in 1805, which increased to sixty-five by 1815, as business increased with the increasing scale of the war. All the service and civilian commissioners were MPs, thus able to speak for the navy in the House of Commons. The Board was supported by a Secretary, of whom four served during these years.*

Convoy business was dealt with by only a small number of these officials because of the need for secrecy and speed. A draft of Admiralty working methods was drawn up by the veteran administrator, Lord Barham, when he was First Lord for nine months in 1805 and 1806. Responsibility for convoys at Board level was taken by the 'First Professional Lord' (or the senior naval officer) who undertook 'military correspondence, including with Port Admirals' (the commanders-in-chief of Portsmouth, Plymouth, the Nore, the Downs and eventually Yarmouth), much of whose business was the management of convoys. The Second Secretary dealt with reports on convoys from the port admirals and other officers, appeals against impressment and other general business: he had to write letters 'of a peculiarly secret & confidential nature'.

---

* Sir Evan Nepean until 1804, then William Marsden until 1807, William Wellesley Pole until 1809, when John Wilson Croker was appointed. All these officials were MPs, except Marsden. Board meetings were attended by the Secretary and the Second Secretary. The latter official was John Barrow, in post from 1804, with a short period when he was replaced by Benjamin Tucker, serving for a remarkable 45 years.

A step down the hierarchy was 3rd Confidential Clerk, Mitchell Hollinworth, a senior clerk from 1800 to 1807, mentioned in Lord Barham's notes as responsible for 'Orders and Secret Orders and Instructions to Admirals, Captains and others'.* Office rules for maintaining confidentially were strict. 'All papers sent out from the Board to be in locked cases; no Head Clerks are to suffer any person to come into their Office but who has business to transact; the Messenger to be under the direction of the Secretary and such a number kept in waiting as to be ready to set out at a moment's notice.'[35]

Operation of the shutter telegraph on the roof of the Admiralty, in sight of three lines of visual shutter towers, was one of the most important responsibilities of the Second Secretary. Two lines were operational from the beginning of the war, between the Admiralty and Deal (for ships anchored in the Downs), with a branch up to Sheerness (for the Nore), while a second line went in a south-westerly direction to Portsmouth. In 1806 an extension to Plymouth was completed and by 1808 a northerly line of towers to Yarmouth was operational.[36] The system was complicated. A message to Plymouth, for instance, in code, would have to go through twenty-two towers.[37] The efficiency of each of fifty-seven towers around southern England was dependent upon the discipline and efforts of a naval lieutenant and a small team of signallers. A fixed telescope was trained on the next station and so much concentration was required that signallers were organised into watches of only five minutes. Good visibility was, of course, critical: winter fogs and long winter nights brought communications to a stop. Nevertheless, on a fine day, a message could reach the Admiralty from Portsmouth in fifteen minutes and the system transformed the speed of Admiralty business. Naturally, convoy arrangements were a frequent subject for messages.[38]

---

* This had not changed since 1786 when the Third Established Clerk was responsible for correspondence with 'the Commanding Officers of the Ports and of the different squadrons, in which business he is assisted by three of the Extra Clerks' (*Commission on Fees, Third Report*, 17 Aug 1786).

The 'private signals' of the navy to all warships, merchant ships and coastal signal stations were also circulated by the Second Secretary. These were the means by which an enemy could be identified; if the ship under observation did not reply by hoisting the correct signal, it was presumed hostile.[39] The management of the line of signal stations established along the coast on headlands was the responsibility of the port admirals, communicating along the coast, watching initially for any signs of invasion, but after 1806 in the main for enemy privateers. In late 1807, for instance, John Barrow ordered the signal station lieutenants ('copied' to port admirals) to extend their brief to watch for smugglers, who 'unship their cargoes into smaller vessels in which they are smuggled on shore . . . such practice might be prevented if the Officers at the several signal stations were enabled by signal to apprise HM Revenue Cruizers wherever the same was observed by them.' He then added 'signal 104' to the list of private signals to signify 'smugglers'.[40]

The speed of the shutter telegraph messages from the Admiralty challenged the authority of the commanders-in-chief in home waters, and particularly the Channel and North Sea fleet. Commanded by Lord Keith since the beginning of the war, it consisted of over a hundred warships, mostly small, with which to defend the Kent, Sussex and Essex coasts. As the invasion threat began to lessen, and Napoleon's army marched away to central Europe from the Channel ports in the late summer of 1805, Keith's priority turned from invasion defence to commerce protection. His span of control was too wide. Admiralty orders sent by telegraph began to contradict his own. Keith, who was notably prickly, wrote to the Board of Admiralty in March 1804:

> since there are no ships or vessels under my command which are not expressly attached to particular duties of high importance . . . I cannot venture to incur the high responsibility of weakening them without their Lordship's positive commands . . . they will signify to me what station ships or vessels are to be withdrawn each time when a convoy is required . . .[41]

Trying to gain the high ground on what he regarded as an unreasonable demand from the Board, Keith undermined his own position by suggesting that their lordships should decide priorities within his command. It was therefore no surprise that when Keith relinquished his North Sea command on 18 May 1807, it was broken up into smaller stations, based at Leith, Yarmouth, Sheerness, the Downs and the blockading squadron off the Texel, each with its own commander-in-chief.[42]

The Admiralty Board might have thought that this would solve the problem of who was in command, but confusion still arose. In late November 1807, for instance, Vice-Admiral Thomas Macnamara Russell, on his flagship HMS *Majestic* (74) in the Yarmouth Roads, wrote angrily to Rear-Admiral John Wells, at Sheerness, on the diversion of yet another gun brig under his command, an order given by Wells, his junior. Russell's rage spilled out into official correspondence to an unusual degree. The order to Wells, he wrote, 'without having observed the common and most necessary etiquette of announcing to me by what authority or through what necessity you had diverted them from the execution of my orders. As you, Sir, so repeatedly disregarded my Orders, I can have no hope of redress but by communication of this expostulation to my Lords Commissioners of the Admiralty.' The Board's reaction could only have brought dismay to Russell. His letter was annotated by a minute stating that Wells was acting under Admiralty orders, 'which should have been communicated to the Vice-Admiral from the Admiralty'.[43] The problem of exactly who had operational command of convoys in coastal waters needed a solution, and was not reached until John Wilson Croker was appointed Secretary of the Admiralty Board on 12 October 1809.

Changes in the management of convoys, and of much else, came almost exactly halfway through the war, when this Irish lawyer and politician, aged only twenty-eight, came to the Admiralty. He had made his first reputation when he deputised for Arthur Wellesley, the future Duke of Wellington, at that time Chief Secretary for Ireland. He had become an MP in 1807 and had spoken very effectively in defence of

Portland's government. As a result, he was appointed Secretary by Spencer Perceval, the Prime Minister, who needed to call upon vigorous eloquence in the House of Commons to defend his government.* Croker was unknown and Perceval's decision to appoint him was risky, yet he proved to be energetic, fast-thinking, forceful and driven, always at his desk, with an extremely retentive memory. He made an immediate impact, a contrast with the two previous Secretaries, the amenable and scholarly William Marsden (1804–7), who was not an MP, or the efficient but colourless William Wellesley-Pole (1807–9).

It was a time of radical change in Whitehall in general. Many old bureaucrats were retired and given one of the newly created pensions.[44] Perceval's political position was so weak that he had to take risks to survive, also appointing Peel and Palmerston, both very young, to senior positions. At the same time the bureaucracy was being strengthened. Several Parliamentary commissions had reported and recommended wide-ranging reforms in systems and working practices in the civil service which were being implemented. Reforms in the administration of prize money and in the distribution of seamen's pay were undertaken by George Rose, Treasurer of the Navy.[45] The government operated with more transparency. In 1811, for instance, MPs were given up-to-date printed details of naval expenditure for the first time.

An early initiative by Croker was to confront a senior figure and long-term friend of George III, George Villiers, Paymaster of Marines, who had embezzled naval money for years. Croker refused to sign routine documents presented to him, without evidence of expenditure. Villiers tried every means to force Croker to comply, whereupon the new Secretary threatened to resign and the matter was referred to Spencer Perceval, who then informed an astonished King of the matter.

---

* Croker's appointment caused bewilderment in the political world. The daughter of Lord Spencer, First Lord of the Admiralty in the 1790s, wrote to her brother Robert Spencer: 'I wish I expected better things from him than I do. However, he is not much known: perhaps this connection with the navy may strike out of him some unsuspected talents' (Wyndham, *Correspondence of Sarah Spencer*, p. 89, 12 Oct 1809).

Croker won the battle of wills. Villiers was disgraced, and had his house and estate confiscated.[46] The young Secretary had immediately taken the high moral ground. With his department working much more efficiently, formidable in debate, fully supported by the Second Secretary, John Barrow, John Wilson Croker's position was unassailable.*

Within months he was able to exert great influence in Admiralty business, increased by the appointment of political nondescripts and weak naval officers to the Board, which he dominated. Croker described himself as the 'servant of the Board', but one of those weak members, the jovial Admiral Sir Joseph Yorke, a man noted for his humour rather than his brains, commented 'that it was precisely the other way round'.[47] Croker was described by Charles Greville, the diarist, as 'too over-bearing to be agreeable', which accords with the Secretary's own view of himself: 'I never have and never will (I hope) do anything for the sake of popularity: he that steers by any other compass than his own sense of duty may be popular, but cannot be an honest, and I think not a useful public servant.'[48] Rear-Admiral Sir Thomas Byam Martin, then Comptroller of the Navy Board, and a dominant personality himself, was at a dinner party at which Croker was also a guest. He was infuriated by Croker's 'impudent volubility and tyranny of talk [which] is a great damper to society, and often disgusting'.[49] This would be a fair reflection of the opinion of many naval officers of the most influential naval administrator of his generation, whose appointment at the Admiralty was to last for twenty-one years.

Croker's power, however, was circumscribed. Over civilian employees he had absolute sway.[50] However, the appointment and promotion of naval officers lay in the hands of the First Lord and the naval members of the Board, and party-political influence prevailed. By 1809, when Croker was appointed, 60 per cent of warships (400) were small and

---

* Strong personal power was buttressed by Croker's remarkable friendship with John Barrow, the Second Secretary. Both were establishment outsiders with literary talents, in retirement they shared a home and Barrow's oldest son married Croker's adopted daughter (Knight, *Britain Against Napoleon*, p. 472).

commanded by the junior ranks of commander or lieutenant. With his hand so firmly gripping day-to-day, operational business, needing speedy decisions which only he or Barrow could make, he wielded great influence, especially as a good proportion of these naval officers had little in the way of patrons of their own.* His orders became peremptory, as if he was on a quarterdeck, and his authoritarian tone was reflected in his communications with very senior people. In 1813 Lord Bathurst, Secretary of State for War, had to write to Wellington in Spain to sooth his feelings: 'You must not read Croker's composition as you would those of any other official person. He has a talent for writing sharply & with great facility. When this is coupled together, it is a great misfortune in an Official person. His style is often what it should not be, when he addresses himself to Departments . . . but I have not taken any notice of it.'[51]

Yet there were certain areas into which he could not trespass, including general strategy, which Melville kept in his own hands in his dealings with the Cabinet. Croker received many applications for passages in warships from civilians, but approval was very much in the hands of individual captains. When a direct cousin, a young lady, needed to go to Lisbon, she had to take passage in a merchant ship, 'in a convoy protected by three King's ships, in none of which I could take the liberty of asking a passage for her'. Likewise, he failed to obtain a passage for Lord Byron to go to the Mediterranean in a warship, a disappointment, no doubt, because of Croker's literary ambitions.[52]

Croker's appointment to the Admiralty in October 1809 came at a difficult time. The expedition to Walcheren had sailed three months

---

* The total number of warships in commission at the beginning of 1803 was 442. By 1809 there were 684, totalling 431,651 tons, when just over 400, or 61 per cent, were sloops or gunboats or vessels, approximately 25 per cent by tonnage. By 1813, all warships in commission had decreased to 570, at 404,303 tons, of which there were 344 sloops, 60 per cent, or 23 per cent by tonnage (James, *Naval History*, appendices 11, 17 and 21). See also Chapter 7.

THE ADMIRALTY AND TRADE PROTECTION, 1803-1815

earlier and was beset with difficulties. Upheaval took hold in the marine insurance world, when merchants and shipowners attempted to supplant the underwriters and brokers at both Lloyd's and the other insurance bodies. Lloyd's was the biggest institution, for the Corporations, the Royal Exchange and London Assurance and the Globe Insurance only handled a small proportion of the total marine insurance.* All of these bodies had been set up as long-established monopolies by Act of Parliament. Merchants petitioned Parliament and opened a subscription list to raise capital to enable them to place risks directly and eliminate the brokers altogether. The most serious complaint from merchants and shipowners was the difficulty of obtaining insurance cover for winter sailings from underwriters, but there were also allegations of failure to settle claims and other misdemeanours.† In February 1810 the House voted for a Parliamentary Select Committee into Marine Insurance, but, a year later, Lloyd's and the Corporations, led by Joseph Marryat, the Chairman of Lloyd's, defended themselves vigorously in Parliament, winning the critical debate by one vote, thus retaining their positions as the centre of the marine insurance market.[53]

Croker and Barrow together addressed the need to tighten up the operation of convoys. A first conviction was secured in 1809 with Francis Wayth, master of the *Cynthia*, for misbehaviour on a convoy from Newfoundland to Portugal, who was fined £50 with costs.[54] However, two events in July 1810 caused the Board to impose a much stronger control over trade protection. A complete convoy was captured by Danish sloops off Norway because of a lack of adequate escorts (see Chapter 8). In the same month as this disaster, when Barrow was visiting

---

* There were also shipowners' clubs, mostly in the north of England, small mutual businesses with only a small amount of capital. They only insured 'good' ships, chiefly coasters and government transports. In the latter case, the government provided an indemnity, leaving the clubs to bear the risk of 'marine peril' (Wright & Fayle, *Lloyd's*, pp. 254–5).

† 'A Practice appears to prevail at the Coffee-house … During the months of August, September, October, November and December, a great number of the underwriters withdraw from Lloyd's Coffee House. The merchants ascribe this to a dislike of winter risks' (*Select Committee on Marine Insurance*, Main Report, p. 1).

Ramsgate on Admiralty business, he saw two colliers taken by French privateers within sight of HMS *Cracker* (10), a gun brig, who made no attempt to defend her. According to Barrow, her captain was sleeping ashore.* None of the small warships at the Nore nor in the Downs made a move.[55] Barrow suspected that the complications and costs of securing prize money deterred any action by junior naval officers.†

There followed a period of intense Admiralty centralisation of decision-making, taking initiative away from commanders-in-chief. The escorting ship and departure of all convoys had to be approved by the Admiralty. Croker took over convoy organisation in the North Sea (see Chapter 6). He altered North Sea coastal signal stations.[56] Perhaps the most striking was the change in the relationship of the commanders-in-chief at Cork, the good-natured Vice-Admiral James Thornborough from August 1810 to November 1813, who was followed by the rather weak Vice-Admiral Herbert Sawyer, until the end of the war. It would not be unfair to say that Croker harassed these two officers by means of frequent letters, demanding detailed information, returns of merchant shipping at Cork and precise orders on convoying and cruising against the enemy.[57] The time lag between an order and a reply was approximately a fortnight, by express post from London to Holyhead, then by packet across the Irish Sea to Dublin, then by post-chaise to Cork. It took between five and eight days for a reply to reach the Admiralty, by the same route in reverse.‡ Even though Croker was trying to stretch the resources, he could do little with so few

---

* An examination of *Cracker*'s log for this period (TNA, ADM 51/2253) reveals a ceaseless round of sea time and maintenance, indicating that Barrow's criticism was unfair.

† The critical Richard Hall Gower agreed in 1811: 'If the tedious, expensive, and vexatious processes in law ... were differently managed, there would exist a stronger incentive to activity in our smaller ships of war. At present, the law expenses exceed the value of some captures' (Hall Gower, *Dangers Attendant on Convoys*, p. 8, fn.).

‡ A sample of letters sent from Cork to London between 1813 and 1815, comparing the date of writing with that of the Admiralty clerk's 'received' ink stamp, shows that it took between five and nine days for letters to arrive. Transmission was faster during the summer months, e.g. a letter of 15 February 1814 reached Whitehall on 24 February, while that of 10 July arrived on 15 July (TNA, ADM 1/629).

ships available, receiving frustrated letters from Admiral Thornborough, who had just received a request in June 1813 for more protection from the merchants of Glasgow: 'I have not sufficient ships in the squadron even to furnish the convoys required, much less to protect the home-ward bound trade and coast of this Kingdom from the American privateers.'[58]

Further tightening of control came with the declaration of war by the United States in June 1812.* Their very effective American warships and privateers threatened convoys in the western Atlantic, and the navy was overstretched. Licences to allow independent sailing of merchant ships were withheld. By this time convoy orders and schedules were printed in detail. Some survive today in Admiralty records. Those governing the vulnerable Atlantic 'cross trades' ('To and from Great Britain to the British North American Provinces and to and from thence to the British West India Islands') are heavily amended in ink, evidence of intense discussions. The anxiety of the overuse of printed documents and concern about keeping the information confidential is betrayed at the end of the document: 'Printed by Order of the Committee of Merchants, interested in the Trade and Fisheries of the British North American Colonies, *for the Information of the Trade only*; and the Committee are particularly anxious the same should not appear in any of the Newspapers.'[59]

As late as the autumn of 1814, Lloyd's were concerned that licences for independent sailing were still being issued. In the last few months of the war trade protection in home waters was being run ragged by American privateers, by now burning their captures, and an exhausted British navy, made ineffective by a lack of ships and seamen. Between May and September 1814, 172 ships were taken between the Canary

---

* By the autumn of 1812 Croker was demanding a daily detailed list of merchant ships lying at Cork, including their owners, masters, tonnage and cargo (TNA, ADM 1/624, 29 November 1812). The Admiralty Board also challenged a sacrosanct area of shipboard life when it examined ships' punishment records on the North American station which had become savage as morale plummeted. See Chapter 9 (Malcolmson, *Order and Disorder*, p. 199).

Islands and Great Britain, often those that had 'run' from convoys. Lloyd's pressed the Admiralty for 'a rigid adherence to the convoy system'.[60] When the delegation from the Committee of Lloyd's visited the Admiralty, led by the redoubtable Joseph Marryat, it was clearly a tense meeting.* The Admiralty had managed to obtain some convictions and a handful of masters went to prison for breaking convoy. John Newland, master of the *Coquette*, spent a month in the Marshalsea and three others joined him in 1814 and 1815.[61] These convictions were not brought under the Convoy Act in the High Court of Admiralty, but under the Act for the Encouragement of Seamen in the Common Law Courts.

The steady profits on marine insurance through the years of war have led to the assumption that convoys were effortlessly successful. Wartime insurance was, of course, more expensive, but trading opportunities were more lucrative and a remarkable number of ventures were not insured, or only partially so. At this point London had displaced Amsterdam as the most active insurance market with sufficient spare capital to back insurance on this scale. Insuring ships and cargoes for return voyages to Britain, say, from the West Indies, were thus problematic, with letters being sent ahead to agents in London to place the insurance with underwriters. It was quite possible that the insured ship might reach Britain before the message, it which case the owner might 'save the premium'.[62] An alternative method was to insure well ahead as, for example, Michael Henley did with the London Assurance House for the *Oeconomy* in April 1811, from St Domingo to London with a cargo of mahogany and fustic. The insurance did not cover 'capture,

* Later, released from the pressures of a world war, the relationship between the Admiralty and Lloyd's, and in particular between Croker and Marryat, deteriorated sharply in 1822 on the question of convoys for protection against Cuban piracy. Even allowing for the robust political debating standards of the day, this could only be described as a public, blazing row fought out in Parliament. The radical *Morning Chronicle* called Croker 'a reptile', 'a needy, shameless, quibbling trickster' and a 'briefless Irish lawyer, who tumbled into Parliament by accident'. Marryat eventually withdrew his motion (McCarthy, *Privateering, Piracy and British Policy*, pp. 140–41, 151–2).

seizure or molestation by the Government or inhabitants of Hayti' and the return voyage had to begin by 1 August of that year.*

The *Oeconomy*'s voyage was simple, but insurance questions could be complex, particularly those cases which involved licences to trade with the enemy, and these cases necessitated Lloyd's and the Admiralty working very closely together. For example, in July 1813 the *Charlotta* from London to Le Havre, armed with a licence to trade with the enemy, was captured, as John Bennet reported urgently to Croker,

> with a very valuable Cargo, and with these Licenses on board was captured on the 13th Instant and carried into Portsmouth by the *San Juan Baptista* privateer under Spanish Colours, but suspected to be owned by subjects of Great Britain. As such a practice would destroy the confidence hitherto reposed in these Licenses, greatly to the prejudice of the Trade ... and as Insurances to a large amount have been effected at Lloyd's.[63]

The prize had been detained by the Port Admiral at Portsmouth. The three elements of naval administration combined: Lloyd's provided information; the navy deployed physical force; the High Court of Admiralty applied the law.

In spite of these complexities, trade steadily increased in wartime. British control of the oceans cut France out of long-distance trade, enabled it to annex French territories and took over most of the commerce between Europe and the rest of the world. Metals and other manufactures continued to be exported. Crucially, merchants, through covert means, managed to re-export much of the produce which Britain had seized by conquest. For instance, twice the amount of sugar and

---

* The *Oeconomy* was insured for £3,000 and her cargo for £2,000, although the full value of the freight was estimated to be £3,500. At £6/6/0 per cent, the premium would have been £315. The manifest lists 707 logs of mahogany, 1,040 pieces of fustic, 1,262 of Nicaraguan wood, as well as those on the master's personal account (NMM, HNL/101/8: 9 & 10, 19 April, 10 July 1811).

three times the amount of coffee was re-exported to Europe between 1804–6 and 1814–16.[64] During the last six years of the war, between 1808 and 1814, there were three times as many convoys and protected merchant ship voyages (over fifty-seven thousand) than there had been in the last six years of the French Revolutionary War.[65] This was made possible by the wealth of naval and mercantile seamanship experience, and in spite of heavy losses, particularly of those skilled seamen. Much of the success in the last three years of the war can be attributed to French weakness following Napoleon's defeat in Russia in late 1812, but it was also achieved through convoying many neutral ships to Britain's advantage, better and faster merchant ships, an improvement in crew sickness rates through the virtual elimination of scurvy, enabling the country to overcome narrowly the shortage of skilled manpower which was the main threat to a British victory in the final years of the war.[66]

Croker's political guile, his ability to handle a tricky conundrum of obligations, and his control over Admiralty business are well illustrated by a three-way correspondence on convoying to India, which occurred in early 1814. It was between Croker's friend George Canning, by this time MP for Liverpool, and John Gladstone, a merchant who was Canning's chief supporter and financial backer in Liverpool and a passionate supporter of the move to break the East India Company's monopoly, which had just been achieved in 1813.[67] A convoy departing to the East Indies was thus a sensitive issue at this time. American depredations on British convoys had been heavy during the previous eighteen months, for which the government had been much castigated in Parliament. However, ships of the line from the Baltic and the Mediterranean had now become available for convoy duties because of the collapse of Napoleon's power in Europe. Losses to the Americans had to be avoided at all costs. The maintenance of convoy discipline was now all important.

John Gladstone, close to government and Lord Melville, the First Lord, tried to push his luck. He was hastening the preparation of his ship the *Kingsmill*, an armed merchant ship of over 500 tons, which was to make the first non-Company ship voyage to India from Liverpool, and he requested a licence to sail without convoy. This was refused by Croker, whom Gladstone suspected was taking such decisions, rather than the Board. Canning tried to explain this away to Gladstone, that 'the Secretary has a sort of right to expect that his opinion shall be final'. Gladstone believed that Croker was keeping correspondence away from the Board, though Canning denied this: 'It is impossible that the Secretary should have withheld any memorial from the knowledge of Lord M or of the Board – private letters he may, on the grounds that the decision of the Board was already taken.' The 74-gun HMS *Achille* left with convoy of forty ships for the East Indies on 11 May before the *Kingsmill* was ready to sail.[68]

As a final plea for a licence, Canning wrote a persuasive letter to Croker on 16 May. The ship was 'quite ready to put to sea this week. She is a venture of £40,000, and the delay of waiting for a convoy would be highly detrimental to the owner. That she was not ready for the last convoy which sailed is to be attributed to the novelty of the undertaking. The singularity of the case seems to preclude any danger of its being considered as a precedent for licences for merchant ships of smaller force.' Croker refused, writing to Canning the next day:

> The Rule is to act with perfect impartiality . . . if she is permitted to sail without, on what pretence can we refute the like indulgence to every other Merchant who may demand it? I am sure you will feel at once that in this case we have no option, & I hope you will believe me that it is with great regret that the Board feel themselves unable to comply with a request of yours.

But Croker held all the cards and he did not hesitate to play them. When he saw Canning the next day in the House of Commons, he told him 'that though he did not like to announce the fact in a letter, probably to be communicated to others ... a Convoy would <u>very speedily</u> be appointed under which the *Kingsmill* might sail to her destination.'[69] He made it sound as though special dispensation was being made. In fact, he knew that there would have to be another convoy because of further demand from shipowners and merchants. On 9 June 1814 HMS *Cumberland* (74) left England for India with a convoy of twenty-three ships, together with the *Kingsmill*, which returned to England fifteen months later having completed a profitable voyage. The Board of Admiralty, and in particular its Secretary, had to act as the focal point between political, commercial and naval interests, and deft handling of their differing requirements was essential for the success of trade protection.

THREE

WARSHIPS AND MERCHANTMEN

I deem it unnecessary to comment much upon the treatment I received at the hands of the captain of this seventy-four-gun ship, who being clothed with a little brief authority, rendered it necessary for us, poor merchant captains, to admit at this time to almost every kind of indignity, without any possible means of redress.

Samuel Coggeshall, master of the schooner *Eliza*, having been apprehended, interrogated and delayed for two days, Carlsham, Baltic, 7 November 1810[1]

The Causes of the Separation of so many of the Convoy may rightly & Chiefly [be due] to the Wind and the Weather, but must also be ascribed in great measure to the Inattention of the Merchantmen themselves . . . Fearful of getting to leeward, they are always averse to bear up however necessary for Others, whom they selfishly never consider . . . they try to weather each other & thus are found in the morning greatly separated from the Protecting Force.

Captain Philip Carteret, HMS *Pomone*, Tagus, to the Secretary of the Admiralty, 23 April 1813[2]

The number of warships available at the sudden renewal of war in May 1803 was disastrously inadequate. The First Lord of the Admiralty from 1801, Lord St Vincent, was convinced that wholesale venality existed throughout the navy, particularly in the dockyards and among contractors who built warships and supplied timber. Contracts were cancelled and state employees were fired. The result was a complete breakdown in relations between the Admiralty Board and the Navy Board. Labour relations within the navy's industrial establishments were badly damaged.[3] Convoys required ship sloops and brig sloops, of which there were 137 in commission at the end of the Revolutionary War in 1802, which St Vincent cut to 55 by 1803. From a worse than standing start, because of the poisonous relations between contractors and the Admiralty under St Vincent, it took 3 years before the number of 137 sloops was exceeded.[4]

St Vincent limped along for a year until the Addington government fell and William Pitt appointed Henry Dundas, now Lord Melville, as First Lord, who energetically reversed policies and revitalised the administration.* He also commissioned a swift confidential report on the sufficiency of shipbuilding timber following the loss of HMS *Apollo* and the twenty-seven merchantmen in her convoy, recounted in the Prologue. The report listed 438 ships (and their individual tonnages) lost by shipwreck, foundering or capture, from September 1803, a few months after the renewal of war, over the winter to May 1804, in all not far short of 2 losses a day. Winter weather had accounted for 294 merchant ships, and 144 had been captured by enemy warships and privateers while 12 warships had been lost to storms and 2 small ones had been taken by enemy privateers. Of these totals, 47 loaded timber ships went down in or sailing from the Baltic during October, November and December 1803, before the ice had set in. Between December 1803 and April 1804 over a hundred merchant ships were wrecked or foundered in the North Sea and the Bay of Biscay. In tonnage

---

* During his tenure, Melville put forward radical ideas of manning the navy based on a quota scheme on shipowners in proportion to their tonnage, a scheme that had been tried in Queen Anne's war (see Chapter 1). Ships were to be embargoed until they had provided the seamen, after which all the seamen on their own ships would receive protections. It came to nothing when Melville was impeached. It might have worked and no one else came up with a way to avoid impressment (Rodger, *Command of the Ocean*, p. 497).

terms, this represented 90,000 tons, which if extrapolated to a year, would mean an annual loss of well over 100,000 tons. In spite of the size of the British merchant fleet and the capacity of its shipbuilding industry, these figures were dangerously high.* They also emphasise the need for and importance of the Baltic timber and hemp convoys, which for most of the war were by far the most numerous of all.

In May 1803 the priority was to get ships to sea and as a stop-gap solution the Navy Board turned to chartering or purchasing merchant ships for converting to warships. The search was undertaken by Transport Board surveyors who were travelling around the ports in the country looking for prospective transports (merchantmen of over 200 tons suitable for transporting stores and troops). These ships, known as 'Hired Armed Ships' ('HMAS') or 'Hired Armed Brig' ('HMAB'), operated in an identical fashion as a warship, commanded by a commissioned lieutenant or commander, and subject to the Naval Discipline Act and the Articles of War. The chartered ships were contracted only for use in 'home waters', the waters around the British Isles, the Channel, North Sea and Irish Sea. Ninety-two were hired in 1803 and more than a hundred in 1804. The numbers of hired ships declined slowly as they were replaced with captured prizes, although in 1807 there were still 71 under contract, with a total measurement of nearly 9,000 tons.[5] Others were purchased. Between 1803 and 1815, 66 colliers and other types of merchant ships were taken into the navy, as well as 157 French, Spanish, Danish, Dutch or American prizes.

Some of the purchased ships were not much faster or more seaworthy than those they escorted. St Vincent, writing in 1803, noted, 'the ships purchased from the East India Company, so much complained of . . . as by the accounts we have received of them they are most applicable to

---

* NMM, MRK/015/11/47, 'Oak Timber', 12 July 1804. These two memoranda are in the papers of Rear-Admiral John Markham, a commissioner in the Whig administrations, and therefore a political opponent of Melville. The recommendations of the report included regulation of merchant ship building and the limitation of merchant ship size to 440–460 tons and 800 tons for East Indiamen, politically impossible to implement, reflecting the anxiety of officials.

Convoy Service.'[6] Most of the complaints arose from smaller warships. It was something of a lottery to be appointed to a fast and seaworthy ship and had little to do with an officer's talent or potential. When Thomas Grenville was appointed First Lord in 1806, Commander Henry Morris let him know his dissatisfaction with the ship to which he was appointed in June 1804: 'the *Espiegle* is without exception, not only the worst sloop in His Majesty's service, but the worst of the Merchant Ships purchased into the Naval Service in 1804.'[7] It illustrates how difficult it is to generalise about the speed and efficiency of sailing warships in this or any war.[8]

Frigates were traditionally the class of warship which led convoys, and for the West Indies trade, this continued to be the case. But as the Napoleonic Wars progressed, this created a real problem as the size of frigates was to increase substantially through the wars. Those newly built were designed with longer proportions as the Admiralty searched for more powerful ships and higher speeds.[9] In almost any wind, they were too fast for merchant ships. A merchant seaman, Samuel Jefferson, was returning from Quebec in 1808, with a cargo of oak timber and barrel staves, in a convoy escorted by HMS *Amelia* (44), a large French prize 150 feet in length. The convoy experienced the usual strong westerly winds, and the frigate 'would run ahead and out of sight of the fleet in twelve hours under bare poles with her yards "braced by", although the fleet was carrying all sail'.[10] In such conditions, with confused seas, it could be dangerous even for a frigate to sail 'under bare poles', for without enough speed the ship could broach, with the waves overtaking her, and she might then find herself parallel to the waves and in danger of capsizing.

Even the enormous 2,258-ton HMS *Canopus* (84), Captain Francis Austen, was discomfited in April 1806 on the voyage home to England from Jamaica after the battle of San Domingo, when she was 'scudding under a reef'd Foresail in a very violent gale of wind', when 'the tiller was carried away and the ship broached to'. We know that the ship was thrown violently on her side, because Austen's papers and accounts were with his clerk several decks below, and the papers became, as he reported to the Admiralty, 'so defaced and mutilated, by the water (of which there was then a considerable quantity on the Lower Gun-deck) as to be perfectly illegible'. As a result, Austen could not submit his accounts to the Navy Board and he could receive no pay. It was two years before the matter was resolved.*

Warships of all sizes were assigned to convoy duty, even ships of the line, usually when they were sailing to or returning from a foreign station and it was important that they did not sail too fast for the convoy. Many factors affected a ship's speed, including the obvious ones, such as whether or not the ship had recently been refitted, if the bottom of the ship was foul, or, alternatively, had been newly copper-sheathed. How the vessel floated, whether she was down by the head or the stern, was affected by the stowage of ballast or of cargo. Merchant ships sailing light with ballast only were slower and unresponsive to the helm. In 1809, Admiral Collingwood at Malta sent an order to Vice-Admiral Purvis at Gibraltar that all ships in ballast sailing in a winter convoy to Lisbon should have their own 'distinct convoy'.[11] The trim of warships could be even more finely calculated. In 1810 HMB *Helicon* (10) was not sailing well, but she was restowed and her speed was restored, as were the prospects for prize money. An observer noted that morale improved and that 'the men were more cheerful, desertions became more rare, look-outs were better kept.'[12] Poor stowage could affect much larger ships, as with the newly built 1,200-ton HMS *Liffey* (38), bringing a convoy back from Quebec at the end of the war. Her captain, John Hancock, complained to John Barrow, Second Secretary at the

---

* Austen ordered his clerk to make fresh copies, but there was so much material that this took a long time. It took three memorials to the Admiralty, requesting 'that the Rules of the Service ... may be dispensed with' before he received the pay due to him in January 1808 (Southam, *Jane Austen and the Navy*, p. 319).

Admiralty, that she laboured and that her main deck was constantly full of water. 'I am of opinion [*sic*] the uneasiness of the ship, and her deep and heavy rolling, arises from two causes, one, the Ballast not being sufficiently winged up in the Midships, the other, the very great lengths of the lower masts, and Top masts.'[13]

Sailing to windward, when the direction of the wind was from forward of the beam, determined whether a ship sailed well, although ultimately speed was governed by waterline length.* In May 1814 a west-going convoy to Newfoundland, led by HMS *Bellerophon* (74), was taking Vice-Admiral Sir Richard Goodwin Keats out to his station as commander-in-chief. Keats was a well-known stickler for detail and tested the ship of the line against two of his much smaller escorts in the mid-Atlantic. In a fresh south-westerly breeze, beating against the wind, a newly won American prize, HMS *Pike* schooner (14), a sixth of the tonnage of the flagship, raced the old battleship, but the latter sailed faster by a calculated one mile an hour. Two days later, but this time with a following wind, the two ships again raced, joined by the newly completed HMS *Medina* (20) of 460 tons, a quarter the size of the flagship. The speed of all three ships was 'found to be nearly equal'. The next day Keats had a different but familiar problem, 'with a stiff gale from the south-east … the *Bellerophon* running under her poles to keep company with the Convoy'.[14]

Thus it was that brig sloops, ship sloops, gun brigs and bomb vessels came to do most convoy escorting, but for the first two years of the war the priority was the rapid expansion of the fleet of shallow-drafted warships to defend the Channel coast and the creeks and estuaries of

---

* The innate skill of a windward helmsman was another factor, for it was felt that some seamen were born with it, and it was not to be learned. One captain was reputed to put the doctor or the cook on the helm of his ship if speed to windward was critical (Willis, 'Windward Performance', pp. 33–4).

Essex against French invasion barges. The roles of small warships were interchangeable and they were constantly multi-tasking. A sloop or brig might be on convoy or blockading a hostile port, cruising to assist an incoming convoy into a British port, or seeking out enemy privateers, or all three, in the space of a month, at least in home waters where most convoying took place.

For almost the entire war, shipyards all over Britain, from Cornwall to Scotland, and even Bermuda, built small warships.* The Admiralty ordered the Navy Board to contract for ship sloops, brig sloops, gun brigs, cutters and luggers of 300 tons or less. Between 1803 and 1813, 174 extra brig sloops were built and 87 smaller gun brigs.[15] The commander-in-chief, North Sea and Channel, Lord Keith, was pleased with his new, small vessels, and their shallow draft, writing to Rear-Admiral John Markham at the Admiralty Board in May 1804, 'I rejoice the gun-brigs are in a fair way, they are extremely useful among the sands.'[16] Two years later, he had changed his opinion, writing to Markham, 'I hope you are not building any more of the small sloop brigs, they do not answer, all complain they are wet, do not sail, and draw 12 feet, the large brigs are excellent . . .'[17]

These large brig sloops played a vital role throughout the war, and the most important design was the Cruizer class, a prototype designed by the Surveyor of the Navy Sir William Rule, launched in December 1797.† They were very fast and seaworthy. No less than 106 of these 2-masted, 300-ton, 18-gun brig sloops were built, steadily ordered through the war by successive Admiralty Boards. Their 24-pound carronades provided a blistering fire at short range and were extremely

---

* This was the first time that all shipyards were allowed to bid for Navy Board shipbuilding contracts. Between 1803 and 1815, 518 new warships of all classes were built, measuring 323,000 tons, trebling the tonnage that had been built during the French Revolutionary War (Knight, *Britain Against Napoleon*, pp. 357–9).
† For comparison, 36- and 32-gun frigates were also built continuously. Those in sea service, commissioned or in ordinary, totalled 69 (68,565 tons) in 1803 and peaked in 1814 at 139 (141,212 tons) (Winfield, *British Warships*, p. 142, using James, *Naval History*, appendix abstracts).

effective against privateers.* Other classes of smaller 16-, 14- and 10-gun brig sloops were also ordered and built, most notably the Cherokee class of 230 tons, designed in 1807 and the only class to mount 18-pound carronades on their broadside. Driven by the need for smaller ships, Lord Mulgrave's Admiralty Board ordered thirty of them.[18] Their manoeuvrability, for they were fast in going about and wearing, made them especially suitable for escorting convoys, but unfairly they came to be nicknamed 'coffin brigs'.[19]

In this, they contrasted with the less numerous, three-masted ship sloops which tended to retain their long guns, and were used as small frigates on distant stations. However, in a battle between a brig sloop and a ship sloop, the three-masted vessel always had an advantage because the two-masted vessels were vulnerable aloft to hostile fire. If the main mast of a brig sloop came down, it was difficult to make headway or steerage way.[20] An anonymous naval officer, 'Commander', writing after the war was enthusiastic, though he acknowledged that they were not easy to sail: '... if we put an officer who has always been accustomed to a line of battleship into one of them, and he proves head-strong and self-sufficient, ten to one he upsets her, but in the hands of a good brig sailor, they are as safe as any other vessel.' This author went on to warn against trying to put three masts into them rather than two, for 'the sailing qualities of the brig turned into a ship is ruined, because the most powerful sail in her, which is the fore and aft mainsail, is taken away'.[21]

Most small warships were suitable for more sheltered home waters rather than ocean crossings, but nevertheless they were sent out to convoy ships across the Atlantic and further. The small gun brigs and gun vessels of 10 guns were constantly assigned to tasks beyond their

* The Cruizer-class HMS *Raven* lasted only three months after she had been commissioned. In January 1805 she went ashore near Cadiz and was lost. Her captain, Commander William Layman, had already wrecked another ship in 1804 and was never employed again. He committed suicide in 1826 (Knight, *Pursuit of Victory*, pp. 649–50).

design capabilities. At the beginning of the war, some of them were basically oared vessels, but their design developed to one-masted vessels of about 50 foot and 40 tons, though the most well-known of these ships, the *Archer* class, were 80 foot long. They were deployed on the Spanish coast, on the Walcheren expedition and most notably in seeing Baltic convoys through the Sound and the Great Belt in the hostilities against the Danes. They took heavy casualties.

The design of some of these small vessels was also controversial. The Comptroller of the Navy Board, Sir Thomas Boulden Thompson, complained to Rear-Admiral Markham in 1806: 'Does it not appear singular that the people of Bermuda so long conversant in building small vessels shall have so much overmaster these schooners? They were built at Bermuda by old established builders, and according to their own plan, not from any draughts sent from here.'[22] And a persistent critic of the Navy, Richard Hall Gower, from the East India Company, railed against the design of small warships, arguing that windward ability in a ship was all-important: 'Cruisers, of necessity, must be Weatherly. It would almost appear from the present system of over-masting vessels for the sake of spreading canvas and giving spread before the wind ... but that no vessel of the ordinary construction ... is equal to the performance of a passage upon a wind in the open sea ... vessels need to be weatherly ... a circumstance that can never be attained by the present gigantic system of masting.'[23]

The faults of these brig sloops are best illustrated by HMS *Childers*, built in 1778 and ordered to run into the Rade de Brest in early 1793, where it was fired upon by the French batteries, providing the excuse for William Pitt to declare war on Revolutionary France. Measuring 200 tons, with 14 guns and a crew of 80, she was very fast, and lightly built, but was unstable in heavy weather, with a reputation for having to jettison her guns to maintain stability in a storm. The commander-in-chief of Newfoundland in 1807, Admiral Sir Erasmus Gower, writing to the Admiralty Board, was none too pleased to hear that she had been assigned to his station:

I believe she has now got rid of her guns three times, and is by no means calculated for the Newfoundland Station for she is so slite [*sic*] that if she even strikes against the loose Sea, I should have much Anxiety for her safety. She sails remarkably fast, and does extremely [well] in the Channel after privateers, particularly as she would have so many safe Anchorages to run for if the Captain found it dangerous staying at sea, or she would be admirably adapted between Cape Finisterre and Lisbon, where the small privateers are very troublesome.[24]

In early 1808, Commander William Henry Dillon, desperate for a ship after losing seniority because of a long period as a prisoner-of-war, accepted command of her. He agreed his appointment to the *Childers* with Admiral Gambier, a member of the Admiralty Board, and came down the stairs:

As I passed through the hall of the Admiralty, several officers of my acquaintance accosted me in the following terms: 'Is it true that you have accepted the command of the *Childers*?' 'Yes', I replied. 'Then go and insure your life without loss of time. She has returned to port having thrown her guns overboard to prevent her sinking. You will never come back again!' 'Very satisfactory news', I observed. 'However, I shall try what I can do with her.'[25]

The ship was ordered to Leith, where the commander-in-chief there, Rear-Admiral James Vashon, as Dillon described, 'gave strong symptoms of displeasure at having such a vessel under his Flag'. After a survey, and much work on the ship, further humiliation came in the shape of the refusal of the Leith merchants to be convoyed by the *Childers*: 'they protested against placing their property under the care of such an inefficient vessel of war, and they remonstrated.' Dillon was teased unmercifully by his fellow officers, but against the odds, he brought the ship up to a new pitch of efficiency, and impressed his seniors and the Admiralty by his success in a sharp fight with a much larger Danish war brig, for which he was promoted to post-captain and received a £250 reward from the Committee of Lloyd's.[26] Remarkably, HMS *Childers* survived until 1811, when she was broken up.

As we shall see, Dillon was rewarded with bigger and better ships. He improved the sailing performance of the *Childers* by many physical alterations, but above all he improved the discipline, morale and sailing efficiency of the crew, so much so that when he left the ship on promotion they petitioned to be transferred with him, though that was not possible. The importance of a strong character and competence in commanding these small vessels was paramount. Away from port for long periods, there was little space on board to avoid conflicting personalities. On large warships, by contrast, hierarchy, rules and procedures, as well as competent subordinate officers, could make life easier for a commanding officer. Aboard large warships there was spare manpower for much of the time. In 1805 one experienced hand on board HMS *Revenge* (74) compared his workload to that on board an Indiaman, and found the life relatively easy. He wrote home: 'We have very little work to do and plenty of men to assist when any work is to be done . . . Some days we have but little to do but on others nobody could believe that is unused to the sea what a hurry we are all [in] . . . when we have done our duty we may go to the fire to sleep, to read, write or anything.'[27]

If a small warship was a happy ship, then all was well. One young seaman, appointed to a schooner, wrote later that 'the crew of small vessels, like other small communities [are] much better known to each other and much more knit together than the crews of large vessels.'[28] On board a small warship life was extremely busy. When at sea in smooth conditions and at anchor, all were engaged in the constant maintenance of hull, rigging and sails. A senior army officer took passage for the Peninsula in September 1812 aboard the brig sloop HMS *Vautour* (16), and was deeply impressed with 'the constant activity during the voyage, not a moment's idleness; the sails were mended; the masts were repaired; the deck was caulked, and made watertight for the winter; the winter rigging was made ready; the sides of the ship painted. All this, besides the routine duty of the ship, was done whenever there was smooth water'.[29]

The Admiralty tried to alleviate pressure on seamen in small warships by enabling transfers to large ships. In 1812 two able seamen successfully applied for a transfer from the gun brig HMB *Growler* (12) to HMS *Bulwark* (74), anchored in the Basque Roads. Having served on the gun brig for eight years, they were taking advantage of an Admiralty Regulation 'which directs that seamen having passed a long servitude in small vessels may if it meets their inclination, and the Service will admit, be removed into large ships or vessels of a superior description'. To replace them, two seamen from the ship of the line were moved into the gun brig.[30]

But when not well organised or wisely commanded, things could go badly wrong on small warships, indicated by a collapse in morale. In October 1808, off Martinique, HMS *Carnation* (18), a brig sloop, fell in with a smaller French brig, *Palinure* (16). The captain was killed, the lieutenants and the master were also casualties, and the rigging destroyed. The sergeant of marines and several of the crew fled below, and the *Carnation* surrendered with ten killed and thirty wounded. At a later courts martial, thirty-two members of the crew were found guilty of cowardice and ordered to be transported to Botany Bay, though eventually this was not carried out. The sergeant of marines was condemned to death and hanged.[31]

Stress was part of life at sea and could be particularly so in small, unhappy warships. Long periods at sea in northern latitudes could take their toll. In 1812, James Whitworth, once a coxswain but demoted to landsman, was on board HMS *Portia* (14) on North Sea convoy and blockade duty, commanded by a very young captain who clearly thought that tough discipline was the way up the promotion ladder.* Based at

---

* Joseph Symes only entered the navy in 1801, and became a lieutenant in 1806, but he happened to be the nephew of Rear-Admiral William Domett, an Admiralty commissioner at the time. Symes was made a post-captain on 21 March 1812. His next promotion was to retired rear-admiral on 31 October 1846. Symes was followed by Commander Henry Thompson, who commanded in the same style.

Great Yarmouth, where it was impossible to get ashore for long periods to reprovision in onshore winds, Whitworth wrote a long series of depressed letters to his wife. Flogged and in irons, with a leg injury, ill with jaundice, in May he promised her 'I shall take the first chance that offers to make my escape from this floating Hell' and tried to desert. By September, Whitworth was utterly depressed: 'I am but a peice [sic] of useless lumber, a burden to myself and a Plauge [sic] to other people' . . . 'We expect a Court of Enquiry . . . with respect to our usuage [sic], and likewise hope we shall have our exchange of Captains.'[32] No exchange of captains took place, but instead, Whitworth was transferred to another ship.

It became a more complex matter when insanity bordered on high-level disciplinary infringements. In the same year, the mild and inoffensive Lieutenant Richard Gamage was second-in-command of the brig sloop HMS *Griffon* (16) with a complement of 100, stationed in the Channel. In the absence of his commanding officer, and goaded by the aggressive disobedience of the sergeant of marines, and quite out of character, Gamage lost his temper and ran the sergeant through with his sword and killed him. There was immense sympathy for Gamage, and every avenue of appeal was explored. He showed no signs of derangement and met his death with dignity. The address from the commander-in-chief, Admiral Sir William Young, was unusual: 'this kind, humane and compassionate man, commits the dreadful crime of murder. Let his example strike deep into the minds of all who witness his unhappy end . . . one moment of intemperate anger may destroy the hopes of a well spent, honourable life.' Gamage was hanged from the yardarm of the flagship on 23 November 1812.[33]

Very different circumstances governed a serious incident, only a month later, on the other side of the Atlantic, at the town of Sydney, north of Halifax, Nova Scotia. Commander John Evans, captain of the brig sloop HMS *Recruit* (18), became deranged when ashore. He challenged the town officials to a duel and his orders nearly led to a shooting battle between his marines and soldiers of the local garrison. Calm was not restored for three days, when Evans was arrested and kept in gaol for several months. He was taken back to England, confined in the navy's mental prison at Hoxton in London, where he died in 1816.[34] These matters were more easily dealt with on larger ships, where there was a good deal of tolerance for mental instability.[35]

The First Lord and his Board were faced with the problem of having far more sea officers than commissioned ships in which to employ them, although this was an old problem. By 1803, the over abundance of naval officers was even more marked.* A recent study has found that 'sixty-three per cent of all commissioned officers never served on active duty as anything other than a lieutenant'.[36]

Patronage was the basis of the Board of Admiralty's power and influence, much of which was tinged with political obligation. No one was more conscious of this than Thomas Grenville, First Lord for six months towards the end of 1806. He kept the leverage of patronage in his own hands and made a point of appointing as many half-pay officers to ships as he could, taking little account of experience. Their lack of experience may well have contributed to the fact that more small warships were sunk or captured during his tenure than at any other point during the war.†

The importance of patronage and influence did not end with appointment to a ship. Ships varied infinitely in performance, as we have seen, while the opportunities to earn prize money varied wildly from station to station. For the lucky few, a rich prize taken would dwarf the monthly wages of the crew. A great deal of money was made by the

---

* In January 1788, there were 57 flag officers, 424 captains, 181 commanders and 1,350 lieutenants; in January 1803, 132 flag officers, 666 captains, 410 commanders and 2,462 lieutenants (HL, STG 147 (35), 'Account of total number of officers').
† Twenty-eight small warships were lost in the winter of 1806–7. The details of Grenville's appointments, in the hand of his private secretary, are in his papers in the Huntington Library (Stowe Grenville Collection, ST/103; see also Appendix).

navy in this war, as usual widely but unevenly distributed; ships on the home stations were taking about a million pounds a year between 1803 and 1810. But a slow ship on the wrong station was not going to make anyone rich.* As one officer complained, writing in the *Naval Chronicle* in 1808: 'One ship, calculated for any variety of service, is kept constantly taking coastal convoys; while another of the same class and properties has a series of advantageous cruises.'[37]

It was the job of a naval officer, very often of junior rank and commanding a small warship, in his role as the convoy commodore, to keep his convoy together. Sailing in convoy was regulated by previously issued orders, activated by flag signals from the convoy commodore, or at night by the burning of blue lights and in fog by the firing of guns at regular intervals. The size of a convoy could vary from a single merchant ship to as many as three hundred, though these last were rare. The merchantmen were always of different lengths and tonnage and thus of very variable sailing performance. Their relatively small crews could not manage the constant sail-trimming required for precise station keeping. Very often warships would have to tow slower merchant vessels, or those which could not make a course to windward and drifted off course to leeward. To keep a convoy together, both naval and merchant officers and seamen used fine seamanship skills that today have long been forgotten and lost.

A warship was crewed by far more seamen than a merchant ship of equivalent tonnage, given the need to manhandle the guns. The numerous Cruizer-class brig sloops, of 18 guns and 300 tons, were manned by 121 men. Numbers declined sharply in the smaller 14-gun and 12-gun warships where the complements were 70 and 50 respectively, and a 10-gun sloop had no more than thirty-five crew members.[38] The smaller the crew and the ship, the harder it was to work, and at the beginning of the war the majority of the seamen would be rated 'able',

---

* A modern commentator summarised the situation by the Napoleonic Wars: 'it was inevitable that most officers were disappointed most of the time' (Rodger, *Command of the Ocean*, p. 522).

though this high standard was diluted as the shortage of skilled seamen mounted.

There was also much difference in the sizes of merchant ships that required convoying. In the North Sea and the Baltic trades, ships could be less than 100 tons. East Indiamen were the most lavishly manned, in principle carrying about a dozen men for every hundred tons. The largest measured 1,400 tons, though they could be as small as 750 tons. The latter had a complement of a hundred, which included six mates, five midshipmen, surgeon and purser, a boatswain, gunner, carpenter, caulker, cooper, cook, sailmaker, armourer, butcher, baker, poulterer and six quartermasters, and their various mates and servants. Approximately fifty would be seamen.[39]

The same ratio of seamen to tonnage could be found on one type of merchant ship, which was not much in evidence in wartime convoys. Slave ships, principally in these years from Liverpool, were large, fast, well-armed and well-manned, and they avoided convoys for at least the first two legs of their inhuman triangular journey to and from the African coast. One of the last to sail before the abolition of the trade in 1807 was the *Mary*, 500 tons, with 24 9-pounders and 4 carronades on the quarterdeck. She set out from Liverpool in 1805, as related by the captain: 'We were manned by between sixty and seventy men, thirty-six of whom were qualified to take the wheel, being an uncommon proportion of able seamen, at a time when it was difficult to procure a good crew.'[40]

The ratio of crew to ship size of a merchant ship varied from trade to trade, but averaged perhaps overall one seaman for every 15-ton measurement. This level of manning was kept as low as possible as the fixed costs of crew wages and provisions to feed them directly affected the profitability of a voyage, but for overseas voyages an extra mate would be hired. The *Norfolk*, 385 tons, owned by Michael Henley and Sons, on charter to the government in 1808 for a transatlantic voyage, was crewed by the master, three mates, two carpenters, a cook and a steward, with nineteen seamen, a total of twenty-seven, a man for every

14 tons. This was considerably more than the *Oeconomy*, 344 tons, with a cargo of mahogany from San Domingo to London, with a crew of only sixteen men in all, a man for every 21 tons.[41]

The meeting of two cultures, one a tight military structure, the other loosely organised and market-driven, inevitably led to friction. The navy's uniformed, hierarchical ways, laced with social snobbery, were little in sympathy with masters who were intent on reaching port first to get the best price for their cargo.* The traditional view is that naval officers disliked the tedium of convoy duty and the consequence was disdain, even contempt, for the masters of the merchant ships in their charge. They in turn chafed at the constant signals flown by the warship, and the consequent requirement for the watch to keep a sharp lookout and tacking and wearing to order. Station keeping by unwieldy cargo ships was difficult and the resultant lax convoy discipline by merchant ships was a constant irritant for convoy commodores. Disdain for convoy duty on the part of the navy was accentuated by the limited opportunities it offered for pursuing enemy ships for prize money.

Strict rules applied over not abandoning a convoy to pursue a prize. Captain Samuel Hood, for instance, when commodore in the West Indies in 1804, reminded his officers in a standing order that they would lose their prizes and be court martialled if they abandoned their convoys.[42] Yet convoys attracted enemy privateers and there were prizes to be had by the escorts, as well as the opportunity to impress senior officers. Yet prize money could still be found by ships blockading a port. Although few or no enemy or neutral merchant ships would be at sea, any incoming merchant ships could be apprehended when approaching port after a long voyage. The lack of French merchant ships at sea was

---

* To this extent, masters were in competition with each other, except for East Indiamen, all of which were chartered by the Company.

obviously a limiting factor, but after 1807 Danish, and after 1812 American, merchant ships were plentiful, enabling British naval officers and the crews of small warships to benefit from prize money, some of whom gathered rich rewards. Besides, considerable opportunities existed for commanders of naval vessels escorting convoys to earn freight money by delivering silver or gold, and not only for the lucrative routes for specie from Mexico to Europe.

While friction in running convoys often occurred, relationships were very complex and infinitely varied. The greatest social clash arose between naval officers and commanders of East Indiamen. In the West Indies trade, where large ships carried extremely valuable cargoes of sugar, coffee and cotton, some higher-ranking officers commanding powerful frigates, anxious to get home, took little care of their charges. Complaints about convoy commodores who sailed ahead and lost their convoys were more than occasional.

In the Baltic trade, by contrast, where less senior and less well-connected naval commodores escorted smaller merchant ships carrying bulk cargoes, there was a greater degree of cooperation. Warships and merchantmen faced hostile weather and ice together, often meeting again in subsequent convoys. They had more in common with each other than did those engaged in the more valuable trades.* In general, naval and merchant commanders, and more particularly the ship-owners, knew that it was essential to keep the convoy together. Besides, warships often came to the aid of merchant ships in trouble. After the decimation of the Baltic convoy in the ferocious gale of November 1811, Vice-Admiral William Otway, commander-in-chief at Leith, reported to the Admiralty the arrival of HMS *Alexandria* (36), which had towed a large, dismasted ship deeply laden with timber and flax

---

* Witness the easy familiarity in the calm waters of the Great Belt at the entrance to the Baltic, from Midshipman John Boteler of the *Dictator*: 'On fine days, the mids would ask for a boat and row among the different ships to see what they could pick up, generally asking if they had anything to sell, but it mostly ended by our being offered a bottle of schnapps, a chicken, a dried goose (split and smoked), a tongue, ham, sausage etc and one large ship gave us a whole bolt of duck cloth' (Bonner-Smith, *Boteler Recollections*, p. 22).

seed into Lerwick in the Shetlands, 'probably of the late Gothenburg convoy . . . other wrecks are drifting about in the North Sea'.[43]

This situation could be reversed. Merchantmen also assisted warships when in trouble, in particular when the deeper-drafted men of war were aground and the shallower merchant ships could reach them. When HMS *Brazen* (18), a ship sloop of 400 tons, with a draft of nearly 12 feet, found itself on a reef in the West Indies at Cape Francois, the master of the *Catharine of London* sent his boats to lighten ship, and was on board the whole night, and 'handsomely offered his Ship to receive the Guns and Stores, without any remuneration'. The Admiralty awarded the master a piece of plate worth £25. Seven awards were made in the first half of 1810, mainly in the North Sea. A Dutch schuyt was awarded £100 for assisting HMS *Nymphen* (42) when on the Haak sands in January.[44]

Occasionally, the merchant service surprised the navy. A long description appeared in the *Naval Chronicle* of the successful defence of the *Economy* transport, on passage home from Gibraltar in January 1811, from attack by a French privateer. On board as a passenger was an invalided naval lieutenant, Lieutenant Gill, who wrote to the Transport Board that the transport 'was not only defended in a most gallant and determined manner by the master and his little crew, but Mr Alexander Gordon shewed, in his arrangement for receiving the enemy, such coolness and presence of mind that I have never seen surpassed by any officer I have ever known in the British Navy'.[45]

But other pressures divided them, chiefly the commercial imperatives that governed the merchant masters' lives. They sought as much flexibility as possible, while the navy wanted certainty and order. Sometimes a perishable cargo might be damaged if the convoy was delayed, which might cause the master to break convoy to get his cargo to market.[46] Very often masters were only told the destination of their cargo at the last minute, for successful merchants depended upon up-to-date market intelligence, and the price of a commodity varied continuously from port to port. A merchantman taking a cargo of Baltic wheat back to England, for instance, would await his orders at Elsinore.[47] Then there were the complexities of marine insurance. The navy was on the lookout for scams, suspecting sometimes that masters deliberately tried to get themselves captured by the enemy to earn the government indemnity.[48] If necessary, masters were going to cut corners with insurance regulations, particularly if they could secure a low premium by being convoyed, but breaking away from the convoy at the earliest possible moment, if they could get away with it.

The navy had few sanctions at sea, though if a merchant ship master was inattentive, or obstinate, a commodore might fire a shot across the bows of the offender. If the naval officer was feeling particularly irascible, he might fire a shot at the merchant ship's hull. Disputes, particularly over breaking convoy, were much more likely to be resolved ashore by protests to Lloyd's, and to the Admiralty.

However, the greatest barrier to good relations between naval and merchant officers and seamen was caused by the impressment of seamen into the navy from merchant ships. This long-running and steadily increasing problem was the result of the acute shortage of skilled seamen in Britain as a whole.* For instance, in April 1807, Captain James Carthew, HMS *Crescent* (36) in the North Sea, was asked to account for being short of 40 seamen from a complement of 270. In the previous year, he reported, nine were dead (two overboard) and others were in a hospital ship, eleven had run, the rest had been discharged or promoted or had transferred to the marines.[49] Those ships with full complements saw a sharp lessening of crew skills.† The high attrition rate occasioned by shipwreck or by those taken prisoner increased the problem as the

* Some groups of seamen were protected by Parliamentary statute: masters and chief mates of merchantmen over fifty tons; seamen over fifty-five and under eighteen; landsmen in their first two years at sea; apprentices in their first three years. On shore, bargemen, lightermen, fishermen and coastal traders were protected unless there was an emergency, or 'hot press' (Brunsman, *Evil Necessity*, pp. 8, 65).
† E.g., extracts from the muster book for November 1810 of the storeship, HMS *Spy* (14) show 31 out of a complement of 36 to be able seamen, but 2 years later there were only 16 able seamen, vacancies having been filled by landsmen and invalids (TNA, ADM 1/625).

war continued.* By 1814, eighteen ships on the Irish station were short of a hundred seamen.[50]

These shortages drove naval officers to take able seamen from merchant ships, even on occasion in mid-ocean. If a merchant ship in a convoy was boarded by seamen from a naval launch, ship masters would fly their ensign upside down – the traditional signal for a ship in distress.[51] Since a master was responsible for manning his ship, there were likely to have been heartfelt protests. Occasional violence could erupt, but it was more likely to be a game of cat and mouse with a press gang searching the ship. Jacob Nagle was the gunner on the *Brilliant*, a merchant 'letter of marque' of 14 guns, and 60 crew, from Greenock on a voyage for logwood. Press gangs were searching the ship regularly, most notably when she arrived at Kingston harbour, Jamaica: 'No sooner than we came to anchor, but the flagship's boats were on board.' Nagle had a press protection which he had received from previous naval service, but the press gang search found the second mate. Nevertheless, sixteen seamen were hidden whom the press gang did not find.[52]

While some naval officers used their sanction of taking able seamen from merchant ships as punishment for disobeying signals, some instances of impressment arose from desperation. The lives of naval officers and their crew, required to sail complex ships in all weathers, were dependent on the seaman's skill and muscle power, and naval captains were constantly trying to increase their crews.[53] Their predicament grew worse as the war intensified. It was the one factor that created anxiety in merchant ships, afloat and ashore, and resulted in sheer inefficiency. In 1806 the Lord Provost of Glasgow complained to the Admiralty that crews of merchant ships coming into Glasgow went into hiding fifteen

---

* No recent estimates of seamen casualties in this war have been made. Michael Lewis' 1960 calculations do not make it clear whether small warships were included in his figures, while his choice of the year 1810 for detailed analysis does not appear to be statistically sound. The industrial growth which was achieved while the army and navy were so short of men in the last years of the war is still unexplained (see Appendix; Lewis, *Social History*, pp. 419–21; Wilson, *British Naval Officers*, pp. 54–5; Rodger, *Command of the Ocean*, p. 499).

miles below Greenock, leaving their ships to drift about the river at the mercy of wind and tide.[54]

One merchant seaman, Samuel Jefferson, resisted and evaded the press gang for the whole war. He joined a merchant ship at Hull as an apprentice in 1804, aged fourteen. Talented and hard-working, he was made a master at an early age. He wrote bitterly many years later of the 'cruel system of impressment dragging every English sailor into the Navy. In this glorious land of liberty they were taken by force from their homes to fight for the poor wages of thirty shillings a month, when foreign sailors in merchant ships were receiving five pounds for the same service.'[55]

Jefferson managed to outwit the press gangs, afloat and ashore. In 1807, returning from the Baltic, the captain of a naval schooner came on board his ship, mustered the crew and took (Jefferson used the word 'kidnapped') the biggest apprentice, who was the master's nephew. The next year, off Dungeness, Jefferson was hidden by the master, when boarded by another naval officer, 'in a place where we were almost suffocated, but H.M. service was so much detested on account of the tyranny then exercised, that a sailor would almost as soon suffer death as go into it'. When his ship was moored by Cherry Garden pier in the Thames in 1809, Jefferson had to stay on board for ten weeks, the only safe place from the press gang, at a particularly sad time for him, because his father had died and he wanted to visit his mother in Yorkshire. In 1810, when his ship was in the West India dock, he had gone to stay with a wealthy uncle in Knightsbridge, at a time when no press warrants had been authorised. While away from his ship, they were reinstated, so that he returned, in disguise, grandly riding a horse, because his uncle owned 'two fine chargers ... but, mounted as I was, I should have been bad to catch ... for I was well prepared for a race'. He was finally caught in 1811, though immediately released, when he was chief mate, as his ship was in the West India dock, where

the chief mates of ships were protected during the time that the homeward cargo was in the ship ... One day when I was crossing Tower

Hill, opposite the Mint, the vagabond pressgang seized me and dragged
me along through Rag Fair to their rendezvous in Rosemary Lane ...
the vagabonds detained me about two hours, although they knew they
could not keep me. They wanted me to drink and treat them, but soon
found they were on the wrong track.[56]

By a mixture of luck, caution and planning, Jefferson evaded service in
the navy for the duration of the war.

It was not unknown for the reverse to happen, when merchant
seamen, unhappy aboard their ship, turned themselves over to warships.
At Elsinore in 1805, for instance, two seamen belonging to the *Anatolia*
brig were entered into HMAS *Prince William*, under Captain Andrew
Mott. The log runs: 'Wm. Smith treated [them] ill, applied for assistance, Capt. Mott sent for them & they entered.'[57] On board the *Ellice*
at Malta in 1809, a quarrel between the chief mate and a seaman resulted
in them both being taken aboard separate warships, and the master had
to pay them their wages due at short notice.[58] At Jamaica in 1811, the
master of the *Edward* lost several crew during the loading of a cargo of
sugar. While the ship was waiting at Negril Bay for the convoy to collect,
as Landsman Hay reported, two more of them 'hailed a war boat when
passing and voluntarily went on board a man of war! Our Captain was
greatly irritated and rated the coxswain of the boat very sharply for
coming alongside to remove his men. "You may save your cheek music,
my brave fellow" said the coxswain, "if your whole crew have a mind to
step into the boat, I will take every man and Mothers son of them and
never once say by your leave".'[59]

At sea, however, it was different. If anything unified naval and merchant
seamen, it was hostile weather. When lives and ships were endangered,
the level of cooperation was very high. With their numerous crews,
warships were able to man ships' boats with great facility and lives

were saved. Surgeons carried by warships, for instance, attended to sickness and casualties on convoyed merchant ships. Naval carpenters and crew regularly went aboard merchant vessels to assist in their repair. Merchant ships which had lost a mast were towed by a warship for days, and convoy commodores regularly ordered the faster merchant ships to tow the slower ones in order to keep the ships together.

Relationships depended, too, on the skill and experience of the convoy commodore. In September 1805, Andrew Carr, master of the 328-ton *Norfolk*, sailing to Danzig for timber, told his owner, Michael Henley of Wapping, that the efforts of his escort to get the convoy out of the Thames Estuary in easterly winds were admirable: 'Our commodore is really indefatigable and seems to have the welfare of the convoy much in view.' Three years later, Carr, this time master of the 172-ton *Fame*, wrote highly critically from the Humber on 17 September 1808, of the captain of the old HMS *Vesuvius* bomb vessel, because of an impractical signal made for the convoy to bear up in very light winds, beyond the capability of most of the merchant ships: 'Our Commodore seems totally ignorant as to a convoy consequently I'm much afraid [we] shall meet with much detention between here and Gothenbro.'[60] But the *Fame* reached Stockholm by the end of November, loaded its cargo of pitch and tar, left under the protection of *Vesuvius*, breaking the ice of the Stockholm river, and arrived back in Portsmouth on 3 January 1809. His opinion of his convoy commodore can only have changed.

Stress was also caused by weather conditions. Limited visibility caused by morning or seasonal mists, or winter fog, was always a hazard. It was almost impossible even to count the number of ships in a large convoy accurately from a ship heaving and rolling in a mid-ocean swell. One convoy commodore reported in 1813 that he had sent half a dozen officers and seamen to the masthead to count his convoy and that they had all arrived at a different answer.[61] At night, any unexplained circumstance could cause fear, as recorded by a passenger on board a homeward convoy of fifteen ships from Newfoundland in

December 1812: 'much alarmed at a strange sail appearing close on our quarter carrying a light ... the passengers were preparing themselves to go on board an enemy cruiser, but our fears soon subsided when we found that we shortly lost sight of her ... she must have been a vessel outward bound'.[62]

Recognising ships at a distance was never easy and warships and merchantmen could be easily confused. At the end of the war, American privateers demonstrated particular ingenuity, adapting fast merchant schooners and using their speed to great advantage. Even professional naval officers had to guess the nature of strange vessels seen at long distance. It was the French rear-admiral Durand de Linois who made the most spectacular convoy recognition error, early in the war. He planned to ambush the large homeward China fleet in February 1804 off Pulo Aor, a small island north-east of the eastern entrance to (what is now called) the Singapore Strait. His squadron consisted of an 80-gun ship, 2 heavy frigates and a 22-gun corvette. The British ships, under the command of Commodore Nathaniel Dance, consisted of sixteen large East Indiamen and eleven 'country' ships. None of the East Indiamen were carrying guns on the lower decks, having stowed them in the hold to make room for goods, mainly for reasons of private trade. At best the only guns were 18-pound carronades, which were no match for the powerful French ships.[63]

Linois thought that the convoy of Indiamen was escorted by warships, but no British naval vessel was involved. He knew that large British warships were around and he wrongly believed that the Indiamen were frigates. His doubts were fed by a previous incident of mistaken identity two months earlier when a French 12-gun privateer had chased two British 74-gun ships, thinking that they were Indiamen. The privateer had 'the mortifying experience' of catching them. Dance aggressively formed his convoy into a line of battle and advanced towards the French. There was half an hour's firing and Linois withdrew. He was, and still is today, much criticised for timidity.[64] The chance for the French to strike a very heavy blow at the East India

Company, and to damage the credit of British trade in general, was missed, and such an opportunity never again arose in this war. Dance and his captains were much praised and rewarded by Lloyd's and the City when they arrived home in London. But the historian who has studied this aspect of the Napoleonic Wars in most detail puts the case fairly: 'The French admiral, in short, had a difficult problem. He had to do more than distinguish merchantmen and ships of war. There were merchantmen trying to look like Indiamen. There were Indiamen trying to look like men of war. There were Indiamen armed as men-of-war. There were men of war trying to look like Indiamen. And, to complete the circle, there were men-of-war, trying to look like ordinary merchantmen.'[65]

For the last three years of the war, the British navy was unable to get enough warships to sea, as was the case between 1803 and 1806, the result of Lord St Vincent's savage peacetime economies. Rather than a shortage of warships, however, the shortfall of skilled seamen was now the overriding problem, which had bedevilled naval administration since the seventeenth century. As a result, trade protection suffered badly, with the greatest damage suffered in home waters. The Admiralty Board, preoccupied with day-to-day business, failed to look ahead and made a series of muddled policy decisions.

The problem had been foreseen in May 1810, towards the end of his life, by Henry Dundas, the first Lord Melville. He had enforced real change when he was briefly First Lord of the Admiralty in Pitt's administration, by force of character and intellect. Towards the end of his life, and long out of power, Melville forced a debate in the House of Lords, arguing that too many ships of the line were in commission, facing severely depleted enemy fleets. Resources should be more usefully directed elsewhere. 'The naval establishment of this country is now upon a scale considerably exceeding that in wisdom, in sound policy and of every principle of economy, than it ought to be.' He calculated that the navy could afford to lose 40,000 tons.* Those in power, however, were not listening, even though by the summer of 1811 the government had firm intelligence that Napoleon's economic and manpower resources were running dry and that a French invasion attempt was now becoming impossible. Keeping so many British battleships in commission was untenable, with their crews of six hundred and upwards.[66] Yet, on 6 January 1812, in the last days of Charles Philip Yorke's tenure as First Lord, the Admiralty Board, still in the grip of traditional thinking, ordered 4 great battleships, measuring in total over 10,000 tons. In 1813 and 1814, work was still proceeding at Plymouth dockyard on two 100-gun battleships, *Britannia* and *St Vincent*. In the last years of the war at least seven were on order, although they were not completed until the peace.

The attempts of the Admiralty Board to rectify the shortfalls of small warship numbers were too little and too late. Following the first summer of war against the United States, on 18 November 1812 and again on 18 January 1813, it ordered the Navy Board to contract for a total of 25 three-masted 'sloops'. These were the new 'Conway' and 'Cyrus' classes, both of 20 guns and 460 tons, an implicit admission that casualties of smaller sloops of 300 tons and below were too high. These ships came to be known as 6th rates, enabling them to be commanded by a post-captain, and were crewed by between 150 and 135 men.[67] In all, 3,600 seamen would be required to get all of them to sea, but those seamen were just not available.[68] Only four of these new ships were commissioned immediately after launching, at the end of 1813. A dozen were put straight into ordinary to be laid up. The rest were delayed, one by as much as eighteen months, at a time when small warships were

* The specific issue was turning large warships into troopships, but Melville convincingly analysed the number of ships of the line that could be decommissioned. His estimate of all enemy ships of the line was seventy-one. Although long out of government, he was still an influential figure, but died in May 1811 (Sutcliffe, *Expeditionary Warfare*, pp. 156–7; Knight, *Britain Against Napoleon*, pp. 436–7).

desperately needed. For the purposes of protecting trade, the measure turned out to be almost useless.*

The war with the United States intensified the seaman shortage, with many deserting, while ships and men were concentrated on the American seaboard to blockade the enemy. Further pressure on seamen numbers came from merchantmen in Europe, where freight rates and wages were high with the expansion of trade. To make matters worse, Napoleon's abdication in April 1814 encouraged shipowners and masters into believing that the wars were coming to an end. Convoy discipline declined. American privateers had rich pickings in home waters preying on running ships in 1813 and 1814.[69] This was when the protection of trade in the waters around Britain was at its weakest.

---

* During 1814 it was a losing battle to get ships to sea. By the end of the year, ships of the line in commission had fallen from 99 to 47. 22- and 20-gun ships had recently increased from 23 to 34, but sloops and gun brigs had fallen from 263 to 196, a loss of 67 (James, *Naval History*, VI, appendices 22 & 23).

FOUR

COASTAL WATERS AND THE WESTERN APPROACHES, 1803–1814

The season is now fast approaching for the privateers from St Malos's pushing out to intercept our homeward bound trade on the outer edge of the Soundings and off Cape Clear; and if frigates employed for the protection of the trade in those parts are not kept within proper limits, you must expect to hear of great injury being done to our commerce, particularly to that of Liverpool, Bristol and the ports of Ireland; short days and long nights being very favourable to the enterprise of the Malouins.

Admiral Lord St Vincent, commander-in-chief, Channel
to Thomas Grenville, First Lord of the Admiralty,
30 October 1806[1]

The entrance to the Channel was the bottleneck through which all convoys had to pass on passage to and from the Atlantic or distant stations. The vulnerability of square-rigged ships when sailing against strong winds in this area had always been Britain's disadvantage in the wars against France, whose vessels were able, for instance, to reach the West Indies more quickly from more southerly French ports. The area of the 'Soundings', as it was often known, was largely of deep water, with cliffs and headlands that could be seen from afar on clear days to aid navigation. But it was dominated by tides, very strong at springs, while visibility could be reduced by thick winter fogs or spring and autumn mists, and heavy swells and breaking seas could be devastating in winter storms.[2] For the first years of the war, at least, nowhere in the world did

British shipping suffer more casualties from winter weather than in coastal waters and the Western Approaches. With an unlucky combination of adverse wind and tide, these could be very demanding waters, and the long winter nights brought more casualties and difficulties for convoys.

On 2 January 1804, the powerful HMS *Courageux* (74), 180 foot in length and measured at 1,772 tons, with a crew complement of 590, led a convoy of 133 ships from Spithead headed for Jamaica and the Leeward Islands. She was captained by Captain Albemarle Bertie and was also transporting Rear-Admiral James Richard Dacres out to his command in Jamaica. The sloop HMS *Ranger* (16) accompanied the ship of the line. The convoy was immediately hit by westerly gales which continued relentlessly. A month later, *Courageux* gave up the struggle, and limped into Plymouth on 3 February, accompanied by only forty merchant ships. She was leaking and had sprung her foremast; moreover, she had jettisoned her upper deck guns as she was 'in so much danger'. Dacres transferred his flag elsewhere. *Courageux* was in dock for a long refit, which included having her poop cut away and, according to the newspaper report, was 'not so crank when she first went to the West Indies'.[3] All this occurred at the same time as the disappearance of HMS *York* (64), presumed to have foundered, and the wrecking of HMS *Apollo* and her convoy on the Portuguese coast was soon to follow.

Nine warships were lost to winter weather in the Channel in 1805, but worse was to come.* The storm of 13–18 February 1807 saw sixteen warships perish in five days, half of them having been purchased, hired or converted from a French prize. Unhappily, Thomas Grenville's Admiralty Board had just sent some small warships to blockade French ports to underpin the proclamation of the British Orders-in-Council of 7 January 1807. The ships were on station as political tokens. The only small warships available were unsuitable: four gunboats, a bomb vessel and a fireship, the last two so slow and unweatherly that they would be

---

* Of thirty-nine small warship casualties in the Western Approaches, 1803–14, twenty-seven foundered or were wrecked, almost all of them in winter (see Appendix).

completely unable to sail to windward to claw their way off a lee shore. They either foundered or were wrecked ashore near Dieppe, Etaples and north Brittany. Over 180 seamen were drowned, over 70 taken prisoner. Further south, it was difficult to blockade the mouth of the Garonne as it was a dangerous lee shore in south-westerly winds. As a consequence, French trade was able to get in and out of Bordeaux, Bayonne and Nantes, for blockading warships were always thinly deployed. During 1807, for instance, 197 American ships entered Bordeaux.[4] During these years, Nantes was the main privateering port, though smaller ships from Bayonne were relatively successful as well.[5]

Progress down the Channel against the prevailing winds caused considerable damage to large and small merchant ships. More than a handful of large East Indiamen, equipped and crewed for a voyage of ten thousand miles, never made it past Land's End. In January 1809, HCS *Admiral Gardner* and HCS *Britannia*, outwards from London, both went aground on the Goodwin Sands. Though the loss of life was light, financial losses were estimated at £200,000.[6] Just how brutal winter gales could be in the Channel and Western Approaches was demonstrated again in late 1810 by the *Elizabeth*, a country ship of 650 tons, bound for Madras and Bengal, setting out in late October from the Thames to join the first convoy of 1811 at Spithead. The ship was taking 347 lascar seamen back to India, who were frequent passengers in outgoing ships, having manned homecoming East Indiamen, after their original crews had been depleted by desertion, naval impressment or disease. Some of them acted as the *Elizabeth*'s crew.* Northerly winds prevented her from calling at Spithead and she missed her convoy. Off the Isles of Scilly she sprang a leak and went onto Cork, and waited for

---

* Though efficient seamen, contemporary opinion did not rate lascars highly when it came to manning guns when an Indiaman was under attack, and they suffered from a high mortality rate from cold temperatures (Bulley, *Country Ships*, chapter 13). When the HCS *Brunswick* was taken in February 1805, Thomas Addison commented that the ship was 'very weakly manned ... not having twenty effective European seamen on board. Our guns were consequently wholly manned with Chinamen, excepting one European to each' (Parkinson, *Trade*, pp. 213–16; Laughton, 'Addison', p. 356).

the weather to moderate. On 17 December she again set out to try to reach the convoy, but south-westerly gales drove her back over 400 miles up the Channel. She anchored off the South Foreland on 27 December. Here her cables parted. The ship now drifted across the Channel where she grounded near Calais, lost her rudder and was finally wrecked on the beach north of Dunkirk. Only twenty-two of her crew and passengers survived.[7]

Rarely today do we have an insight into life aboard a merchant ship in such circumstances, but the letters of Thomas Longstaff, master of the *Ellice*, chartered as a government transport, to her owner, William Mellish, the principal meat contractor to the Victualling Board, show how difficult it could be to get out of the Channel. On 20 March 1812, the *Ellice* left for the Mediterranean in a convoy of thirty-three ships from Portsmouth. They were escorted by HMS *Pelorus*, Commander Joshua Ricketts Rowley, a new Cruiser-class brig sloop, which was a small warship for the size and distance of the convoy. It was over two weeks before the convoy managed to leave England. Firstly, it could not weather the Isles of Scilly, so it went back to Torbay. 'We have had a decent trial in a Seaway, I think [I] never saw a Sea more Severe than on the 21st,' Longstaff reported. 'The Ship tho' deep is like a Seagull when the sea does not break, but one Sea broke on board us on the 21st from which she made a fixed stand until she could recover, but what will you think of the *Serapis* (44) Storeship, having at the same time all her Starboard Bulwark swept away by a Sea?' (Though old, HMS *Serapis* was 886 tons, the *Ellice* was something over 300.) On the evening of 26 March, the convoy again put to sea. The *Ellice* missed stays off Penlee Point, at midnight, so Longstaff again ran back to Plymouth, as did the rest of the convoy. One ship had been driven onto the rocks, two had lost their bowsprits. On 29 March Longstaff again wrote from Plymouth, by this time from the inner harbour, the Cattewater, repairing the damage, especially to his warps. He wrote to London: 'These Equinoxial gales are truly oppressive,' but concluded optimistically, 'This weather must be at an end.'[8]

The wind went finally round to the east, and the convoy left on 5 April, the *Ellice* making a fast passage of sixteen days to Gibraltar, exactly the same amount of time that the convoy had been delayed by high winds on the south-west coast of England. However, the same prolonged spell of high pressure set up alarms in Lloyd's about incoming trade. John Bennet reported to Croker on 17 April at the Admiralty that two merchant ships had arrived at Cork on 10 and 11 April short of water and provisions: 'In consequence of the prevalence of Easterly winds ... a great number of ships from the West Indies ... and other quarters must from the known period of their sailing be beating about at the entrance of the Channel and it is presumed many of them in want of Provisions and Water ...'* Croker's large, urgent scrawl minuted the letter: 'Sir Robert Calder [commander-in-chief, Plymouth] to make exertion to push out any cruizers which may be within reach with supplies of water & provisions for the merchant men who may be beating about the chops of the Channel. Acqu[ain]t Lloyd's.'[9] That message would have been transmitted down the line of the shutter telegraphs to Plymouth. Searching for overdue convoys was a regular task for small warships commanded by the commander-in-chief, Irish Station at Cork, the main western rendezvous for west and south-going convoys. Vice-Admiral Edward Thornborough, a good-natured and experienced seaman, in post from 1810 to 1813, took most of the strain in this demanding task, with only a handful of small warships. As well as Atlantic convoys to worry about, and the defence of Ireland, his warships had to convoy merchant ships from Liverpool and further north, guard against smuggling, as well as dealing with extra tasks heaped onto him by detailed orders from the demanding Croker.[†]

---

* Bennet listed sixteen overdue ships from Demerara and Surinam, Berbice, Honduras and Jamaica, as well as the packet from Antigua (TNA, ADM 1/3993, 17 April 1812).
† For instance, in August 1813 Croker ordered Thornborough to send three warships, which he named, to guard the western Scottish fishing fleet near Cape Wrath. Thornborough did so, but wrote back, 'but their Lordships must be well aware that by doing so the North West coast of this Kingdom to the Clyde and round to Belfast is entirely left defenceless, and I have no means to protect the same' (TNA, ADM 1/625, Thornborough to Croker, 14 August 1813; see also Wilson, 'Defence of Ireland', p. 571).

The infrequent calms or very light winds in the Channel created different problems, giving the well-manned privateers the advantage over heavily laden merchant ships. In one tragic case, in February 1805, light winds and a strong ebb tide led to the destruction of the outward bound 1,200-ton HCS *Earl of Abergavenny*, Captain John Wordsworth, the poet's brother. She had four hundred passengers aboard, as well as a valuable cargo and 250,000 ounces of silver to pay for cotton in Bengal, which she was then going to transport to Canton. The convoy of East Indiamen left the Motherbank in the Solent on 1 February, but separated from the escort HMS *Weymouth* almost immediately, and suffered three days of south-westerly gales, before the wind fell light. It was decided to anchor in the Roads off Weymouth, but, with a pilot aboard, on 5 February the ship ran aground on the Shambles immediately to the east of the Portland Race. Wordsworth thought she could be got off, and did not immediately fire distress guns, but the ship started leaking immediately and the pumps were ineffective. By this time, the wind had got up and the boats from the shore could not approach the ship. Wordsworth lost his life, as did three hundred others, though a hundred who clung to the rigging were saved the next morning. The silver was salvaged from the wreck a year later.[10]

The Channel was also dangerous in northerly and easterly gales, for the anchorage in the Downs was extremely vulnerable when the wind swung from the south-west to the north, transforming a sheltered anchorage into an open roadstead. The height of the waves could build up quickly, causing a rough and uneven strain on anchor warps, even if the anchors held.* On the day after the February gale in 1807, Admiral Russell reported to the Admiralty that all the warships were safe except for HMS *Snipe*, 'gone to pieces, people saved ... but the Havoc among the Merchant ships is a Melancholy Sight'.[11] Of 150 ships at anchor, not

---

* In a south-westerly wind, on the other hand, the Downs was a very sheltered anchorage, as Admiral William Young described during a respite from the blockade of the Scheldt in 1812: 'The sea here is so trifling when compared with what we are accustomed to off the Scheldt, that if we had not heard the howling of the wind, we should not have suspected that we were riding in a storm' (Marsden, *Brief Memoir*, p. 143, Young to Marsden, 26 October 1812).

more than 30 remained, and most of them had lost masts and rigging. Thirteen vessels were on shore between Deal and St Margaret's Bay. Most of them had been proceeding down the Channel to join outward-bound convoys, some in ballast, but others with valuable merchant goods on board. The brig *Regard*, *The Times* reported, 'laden with King's slops [clothing], bound for Portsmouth, is also lost'. The day after the gale, at Dover, 'the shore was lined with people a-wrecking. The beach for several miles between Dover and Deal is covered with pieces of ship timber, soldier's belts, cartouche boxes, hats, shoes, empty casks and remnants of wearing apparel.'[12]

Those small warships that survived these storms were more than likely to be badly damaged. The escorts were much smaller and lighter than their merchant charges, and suffered badly in any collision, as the commander of HMS *Sparkler* gun brig reported in the Downs in November 1807. She had just brought a convoy from Harwich to anchor, when the wind again swung to the NNE. A transport drove on board her, which 'stove the whole of her Stern Frame in, carried away the larboard catthead knees, the bowsprit sprung, fore and main channels carried away, jolly boat carried away, the Bow Much damaged, main boom gone, and other material damages which I am afraid will cause the Brig to be ordered to a Dockyard before the defects can again be made good'.[13]

Only Cork Harbour and the Solent were safe anchorages in all winds, but the narrow western entrance of the latter, particularly when the direction of the wind was blowing against that of the tide, could be very dangerous in certain conditions. The master of HMS *Pomone* (44), returning in late 1811 from a very successful three years in the Mediterranean, with the capture of six French privateers, and another burnt to avoid capture, felt confident enough to take the ship through the Needles channel at night, intending to anchor in the Yarmouth Roads. On 14 October, within two miles of the anchorage, the ship hit a rock just by the Needles and sank slowly. Her crew and £55,000 worth of specie were saved, as was a passenger, the diplomat Sir Hartford

Jones, British minister in Persia, and the Arabian horses he had brought back with him. Some of the crew broke open the spirits on board. The court martial exonerated the captain and reprimanded the master. Overconfidence neither was nor is wise in these waters.

At any time of the year, the coastal trade in the waters around the British Isles contained an immense number of merchant ships, most of them of no great size, upon which the working of the British economy depended. The need to keep these routes open throughout the year meant that they were vulnerable to French privateers, who not only were able to take advantage of the long hours of darkness, but who also set sail on the tail of winter gales at a time when warships were not on station, having sought shelter behind headlands, and when convoys had been scattered by the storm. In the Western Approaches, dispersal could happen after a convoy sailed, with strong south or south-westerly gales. But the great advantage to the privateers, which were more interested in avoiding warships because of their superior firepower and crew size, was that merchant ships engaged in the coastal trade were not obliged to join a convoy by the 1803 Convoy Act.

It was impossible to organise such numerous and seasonal traffic. Coastal trade carried bulk cargoes from one British port to another, throughout the year, vital in view of costly and generally unsuitable land transport.* It also often involved cargoes of perishable agricultural produce, which had to sail without delay. Many small merchant ships

---

* Canal building was just beginning to take traffic away from the vulnerable coastal trade, and the construction of the Wey and Arun Canal, to join the Thames to Portsmouth harbour, was intended to cut out the necessity of coastal traffic. It was begun, though was not fully operational, before the end of the war. More ambitious plans were outlined in a prospectus in 1824 for a 'Grand Ship Canal from London to Arundel Bay', justified by the claim that 110 vessels were shipwrecked annually between the Isle of Wight and the Forelands, and that the value of shipping captured in the Napoleonic Wars was at least £3 million. All these investment plans were brought to an end by the introduction of steam power (Vine, *London's Lost Route*, pp. 31–67, 98–9; Knight, *Britain Against Napoleon*, pp. 165–8).

operated on much shorter routes supplying local markets with cattle, beer, flour, groceries and other everyday necessities, though beer did not travel well and tended to be brewed as near the point of consumption as possible. Some supplied London with coal and grain from east-coast ports in very large quantities, and the same could be said for butter, flour, oats and casked provisions from Ireland. For instance, the *Salome* of Barmouth, from Newry to London in March 1814, which was wrecked on the Atherfield Rocks on the south-west coast of the Isle of Wight, was 'laden with 600 tierces and barrels of pork, 200 firkins of butter and 90 hales of bacon'.[14] Newspaper reports on shipping casualties in home waters mention cargoes of oats, herrings, planks, tar, iron, dye wood, bale goods, coal and 112 tons of potatoes from Jersey, all heading to London.[15] From the capital came cargoes of manufactured or foreign goods, such as ironware, cotton and wool clothing, down the Thames Estuary, then either up the North Sea or down the Channel.

Travelling by sea rather than by road was the cheaper option for passengers as well, and large, specialised craft known as 'Leith smacks' moved large numbers of people up and down the east coast between London and Scotland. Fast and immensely powerful to windward, with long bowsprits and a huge mainsail, they kept out of trouble because privateers would not trouble to chase them as no cargo was carried. Seamen needing to travel would hitch a lift on an available merchant ship and make themselves useful, as did Samuel Jefferson in March 1807 in Bridlington in Yorkshire, under orders to join his ship in London, when he made a passage south along the North Sea coast in the brig *Venus*, demonstrating how fast it could be done with a fair wind:

When we left the harbour we had no provisions cooked, and the mate was on the sick list, but no sooner had we cleared the harbour than a hard gale sprung up at north east, with a heavy sea, and almost constant snow showers. The vessel being very deep laden with wheat, she shipped such quantities of water on deck that we stood up to our middle at the pumps, with nothing to eat, as no cooking could be done: the wind being fair we gained the Nore in two days, got some beef in the coppers, and were so hungry that we eat it half boiled.[16]

Government transports, however, were always escorted by naval vessels, such as those contracted by the Navy Board to distribute materials including timber, iron or coal to dockyards or shipyards, or provisions from the London market to waiting fleets or foreign-going convoys. Those transports working for the Board of Ordnance took a constant stream of substantial cargoes of gunpowder from the mills around London to depots or floating magazines at Chatham, Portsmouth, Plymouth or Yarmouth, as well as shipping the return of unexpended powder to the mills for drying and dusting before re-use.* An example of coastal trade cargoes of great value were the guns and shot cast by the Carron company in Scotland, which had to make their way down the east coast to Woolwich Arsenal for their proof tests, which had to be passed before the Ordnance would accept them.[17] The commander-in-chief at Plymouth, Admiral Sir John Colpoys, complained to a member of the Admiralty Board about the removal of a cutter permanently stationed at Falmouth to ensure the safety of regular tin convoys eastwards, the only means by which this precious and heavy commodity could leave Cornwall: 'I hope some substitute will be appointed, as ... we may expect Lurking Privateers hovering about the coast in Long winter nights...everybody knows the Clammer [sic] it occasions. Therefore, I mention all this to prevent the Board falling under the lash of Coffee House Politicians.'[18]

The exigencies of war, soon called for some coastal convoys in the Western Approaches. As the winter of 1804–5 approached, the implementation of a regular weekly convoy from Portsmouth to Cork was ordered following several storm-dispersed West Indies convoys. Sending more ships to Cork, John Bennet, the Secretary of the Committee of

---

* A significant amount of gunpowder was at sea any one time. A 74-gun ship ordered for foreign service was issued with 330 ninety-pound barrels of gunpowder, and 295 barrels if on Home Service, as well as the requisite amount of round, case and grape shot (Cole, *Arming the Navy*, p. 81; Saunders, 'Upnor Castle', pp. 170–74).

Lloyd's, argued in his letter to the Board of Admiralty, 'would prevent such a large fleet rendezvous at Spithead as is generally the case at the approaching Season, and probably be the means of avoiding similar Disasters to those which occurred to the First Fleet from Portsmouth ... under convoy of HMS *Courageux* ... only a single instance of the many which occurred last year'. The letter was minuted: 'Direct Admiral Montagu [commander-in-chief, Portsmouth] to give the Protection requested.'[19] Another change came about in November 1807 after pressure from Lloyd's, which persuaded the Admiralty to stop using Falmouth as a regular gathering point for convoys. Not only did convoys from Portsmouth have to lose valuable windward miles by turning north, but John Bennet outlined recent mishaps, one convoy having to sail to 'the newly conquered Dutch Colonies ... without any protection whatever', while the mid-April Jamaica convoy, stopping at Falmouth, missed 'a noble wind' and took two months to reach Jamaica, 'leaving the ships little better than four weeks to discharge their outward Cargoes and load for the July convoy'.[20] This came into force after it had been agreed with the Committee of West India merchants.

The 280-mile stretch of water between the Lizard and the North Foreland saw an elaborate battle of wits between French privateers and British seamen, in tricky tidal and wind conditions. The distance to the hunting grounds for privateers from Dunkirk or Dieppe in the east of the Channel was considerably shorter.[21] From Dieppe to Dungeness it is only 58 miles, while the North Foreland is only 90 miles away, visible on a clear day from mid-Channel.* These high chalk cliffs had a line of coastal signal stations that signalled to each other, thence

---

* The distance from St Malo to the Lizard is 145 nautical miles, to Portland Bill 113, to the Needles 127 and to Beachy Head 178. From Dieppe to the Needles is only 115 miles. Portsmouth to Falmouth is 160 miles, and Portsmouth to the Downs 119 miles. Measured in nautical miles, with the course at safe distances off each headland (Coote, *Shell Channel Pilot*, I, pp. 20–21; II, p. 10).

to the commanders-in-chief at Plymouth, Portsmouth and the Downs, to warn them of privateers and to direct warships to cut them off.[22] They were also the navigational mark for ships taking a northerly course to the southern North Sea. This part of the coast, north of the Thames Estuary and the Nore anchorage, is low, with extensive sandbanks parallel to the shore, making local knowledge essential, but the privateers' captains, in peacetime often fishermen from the northern French ports, knew these waters well. The complexity and shallowness of the waters and the weight of traffic hindered the arrangement of convoys and the local commander-in-chief positioned patrolling cruisers to protect shipping, but from the start of the Napoleonic Wars, fishing vessels, colliers and merchantmen were taken regularly by privateers.[23] French activity and success rates were notably lower as were profits than in the Revolutionary War, which peaked in 1797–8, when their privateers were emboldened by the mutinies in the British fleet at the Nore and at Yarmouth.[24]

Most of the crews of the French privateers were merchant seamen, unable because of the war to ply their trade. They brought seamanship and local navigational expertise to their ventures, in many cases more so than British officers, who were likely to have less experience of the complicated tides and fickle weather in these waters. Privateers in the eastern Channel were small ships, sometimes as little as 20 tons, mostly lugger rigged, without square sails, so that they were able to sail close to the wind. They were heavily manned to aid capture and so that enough crew could be spared to sail prizes to the home port. They used headlands for cover, ambushing the rear ships of a convoy and stragglers, particularly when dispersed going to windward, often sailing with the convoy for a time, making a capture and then steering to their home port at night.[25] Lack of stowage space for the provisions required for a large crew meant that these small ships were unable to stay at sea for a long time. Their forays were raids rather than cruises.

Nevertheless, even a small government convoy could lose a ship to the privateers on the 110-mile passage from Portsmouth to the

Downs. In late January 1808 HMS *Chichester*, a 700-ton armed store-ship, was escorting two transports contracted to the Navy Board, sailing in convoy with 'light colliers'. The *Findon* and the *Sussex Oak*, loaded with wood, set off from Spithead in a strong westerly, heavily reefed. The much larger storeship sailed ahead, and by the time the two transports had sailed clear of the moored ships around Spithead, the *Chichester* was halfway to St Helens. According to the master and owner of the *Findon*, the next time he saw her was in Dover and he presumed the *Sussex Oak* had been captured. His letter of complaint reached the Admiralty Board: 'I never saw such conduct from a convoy and I think it proper that the Navy and Admiralty Boards should be made acquainted with his Conduct for it is Hazardous to sail under such Convoys as we frequently do to be left to the Mercy of the Privateers.'[26]

This convoy mishap was due to impatience, but another hazard was navigational error of judgement. Just how difficult winter navigation on an unlit coast could be was demonstrated by an eastbound coastal convoy of twenty-seven ships from Plymouth to the Downs on 5 December 1809, escorted by HMAS *Harlequin* (18), commanded by Lieutenant Philip Anstruther. The wind was fair for two days and from the southerly point of Bolt Point in South Devon, the course to Beachy Head, 158-miles distant, was almost entirely out of sight of land. At its furthest point, the convoy would be 30 miles from land. Once past Beachy Head, ships would head on a more northerly course to follow the coast. At five o'clock in the morning of 7 December, 'when most were in their hammocks', thinking that the convoy had passed Beachy Head, the course was altered. But the tidal calculations were wrong. It was very dark. *Harlequin* struck the beach at Seaford. 'Little did we think at the time we were so near the shore,' according to one officer, 'all of us thought we had struck on a rock; and we immediately fired our guns and burnt blue lights till all were expended; yet the convoy continued to follow us and six of them struck; the rest hauled their wind and got safely off; those on shore soon went to pieces.'[27] The local captain of Sea Fencibles wrote immediately to Croker at the Admiralty: 'although the surf was very high, we succeeded in saving the crew, excepting two, but with pain I have now to add that the greater part of the Crews of the Merchantmen are Drowned and the whole of the vessels totally lost.'[28] Forty seamen perished. Lieutenant Anstruther, a lieutenant of fifteen years seniority, survived the shipwreck: unsurprisingly, he was never promoted. It was a miscalculation that a French privateer would not have made.

Beachy Head marked the dividing line between privateers from St Malo and those of the more northerly French ports. The Malouins headed towards the high points on the English south coast such as Portland Bill or Beachy Head, across the tidal flows of the Channel, or took a more westerly course out to the Soundings or Western Approaches. French privateers taken by British warships off Cape Clear, the most southerly point on the south-western coast of Ireland, were very much larger than those in the east of the Channel, in areas where greater seaworthiness counted. Some were as large as 350 tons, although the average was between 130 and 180 tons. These ships were capable of carrying stores and provisions for a long cruise, well-manned, although their armament was comparatively weak if they came up against a British warship. HMS *Seagull*, Captain Henry Burke, a 300-ton brig sloop, had escorted a convoy to Cork in August 1803, and received intelligence that a privateer was off Cape Clear. He found an East Indiaman, HCS *Lord Nelson*, by now flying French colours, as she had already been captured by a powerful French privateer, *Bellone*, 34 guns and 260 crew, and was manned by a prize crew. The *Seagull* now attacked the much larger East Indiaman, while the privateer made her escape. The action lasted through the night, during which the British sloop received severe hull and rigging damage, two were killed and several wounded, before she stood off.[29] She was about to renew the action, at which point a squadron of four British ships of the line arrived on the scene, commanded by Admiral Pellew, which retook the much-battered East Indiaman, which had suffered from two successive actions against different enemies. Trade protection in the Western Approaches was on an altogether different scale than in the eastern Channel.

Just how vulnerable a British merchant ship could be in the Western Approaches can be illustrated by the *Norfolk*, 385 tons, hired as a government transport, under the convoy of HMS *Gluckstadt*, originally a Danish prize of 18 guns. She was on passage from Plymouth to Vigo in January 1809 during the rush to evacuate troops after the retreat to Corunna, and was, presumably for this reason, without a cargo. She was captured by *La Valeur*, a French privateer of 16 guns, crewed by 150 men, and, as the master of the transport, William Coates, reported to the owner, Michael Henley:

> They were going to burn the ship after proposing to Ransom the Ship which I would not agree to, the first sum was £2000, then £1500. I offered £700 but they would not hear of that they came to £1000 and would not go for any less. I consulted within my own Mind and thought that I better pay than let the ship be destroyed as I thought the service we were going upon was so urgent that government would not hesitate about paying the Ransom . . .

The ransom was agreed, the document signed, and the mate, James Tate, agreed to go with the French as hostage for the payment of the money. By the time Coates wrote the letter, the ship was back in Falmouth, where it was weather-bound for some weeks.[30]

Neither Coates nor Tate knew that ransoming had been made illegal twenty-five years earlier by Act of Parliament. Henley was adamant that no ransom should be paid. By May 1809, Tate was pleading for payment, otherwise he would be moved from St Malo, 'or I will be sent to prison in the country', and asked that Henley told his father in Wapping of his predicament. Remarkably, the owners of the French privateer were represented in London by Baring Brothers, who a year later pressed Henley for the money. 'We shall be glad to be favoured with your determination in this business as soon as possible.' Joseph Henley replied the next day: 'The payment of the ransom was unlawful according to the existing laws of England, consequently we cannot have anything to say to it.' The result was that Tate spent five years as a prisoner of war. He sent increasingly desperate letters to Henley, who ignored them. 'The most deplorable situation that I am reduced to ... the state I have so long endured as a sacrifice for your property; which is three years since the capture of the *Norfolk*'. He did not reach London until November 1814, and received some compensation from the government.[31] Whether Tate received any from Henley is unknown, but it seems unlikely.

Losses in the Channel were the subject of complaint from Lloyd's to the Admiralty in March 1809, a time of low political and military confidence, just after the evacuation of the British army from Corunna. In a robust reply the Admiralty provided loss statistics for the previous six winter months between 1 September 1808 and 1 March 1809. Seventy-two merchant ships had been lost, which included '43 from Foreign Ports to the United Kingdom, several of which are running ships', but 24 of them had been recaptured, a net loss of 48 ships. In the same period, the Admiralty pointed out, 1,519 convoyed ships left ports in Great Britain and Ireland, 1,221 received homeward bound instructions, and 972 sailed without convoy with an Admiralty licence, a total of 3,762, 'without including the coasting and Irish trade, which it is well known to a very great proportion of the general commerce of the Country'. During the same period, 33 enemy warships and privateers had been captured.* Losses of 1.3 per cent justified the Admiralty's confidence, which it did not fail to convey to the Committee of Lloyd's.

---

* Lloyd's challenged the Admiralty's winter statistics for the Channel with its own 'List of ships taken and Retaken November to March'. 1805–6: 104 captured, 22 retaken; 1806–7: 79:24; 1807–8: 82:25; 1808–9: 80:25. Total for four winters: 345 captured, 93 retaken, thus 252 taken by the enemy into port (TNA, ADM 1/3993, 17 March 1809).

Considering the very great extent and magnitude of the British Trade, and the extreme difficulty of guarding against the activity and enterprise of all the numerous privateers belonging to the enemy upon the coasts of the Channel where the run from shore to shore is so short, it will be found a ground of satisfaction that the Commerce of the Country could have been so well protected, than of complaint that the captures alluded to have been made by the enemy.[32]

Nevertheless, there followed a difficult period in 1810 and 1811. Napoleon tightened up the Continental Blockade and inflicted damage on British trade, especially in Northern Europe.[33] This was the period when Croker and Barrow at the Admiralty were attempting to reform the convoy system in home waters, while a Parliamentary enquiry into marine insurance shook confidence in London (see Chapter 2).[34] The *Hull Packet* reported in January 1811 that 'the risk in the Channel is now considered so great that it is with the utmost difficulty any insurance can be effected as the merchants and others concerned in shipping cannot afford to pay premiums adequate to the indemnity of the underwriters.[35] Two days later the *General Evening Post* thundered: 'The depredations daily committed upon our Commerce by the Enemy's Privateers in the Channel, imperiously demand the Attention of the Admiralty Board ... Is it not a disgrace to a country which prides itself upon its Naval superiority, that insurances cannot be effected upon vessels bound up Channel, but at the most exorbitant premiums?'[36]

French privateers went on the offensive.* One captured by HMS *Nymphen* (42), Captain John Hancock, in March 1811, had six

---

* It was never easy for a French privateer to make enough money to cover the cost of the crew, provisions and fitting out the ship, and there were instances where a privateer could take several prizes during a cruise, yet still make a loss. There was a decline in privateering between 1804–5, when French merchantmen could trade with the United States with more chance of profit than attacking British commerce (Crowhurst, *French War on Trade*, pp. 51, 203).

Americans aboard, their purpose to act as a prize crew to aid the disguise of a prize on its journey to the home port.[37] Sometimes French corsairs operated in small groups. In June 1811, between Dover and Folkestone, four privateers brazenly attacked a timber ship that had just completed a rough crossing of the Atlantic and appeared to be damaged. A crowd of spectators watched the action from the cliff tops above Folkestone. The *Cumberland* had a crew of 26, and the number of the combined crews of the four privateers was estimated at 270. The master of the *Cumberland* skilfully hid his crew below decks, armed with long boarding pikes, who surprised the boarding party. Those Frenchmen who were not immediately killed jumped overboard. Three subsequent attempts at boarding failed. The incident was celebrated with the publication of a print, and the crew were given three-year impressment protections by the Admiralty.[38]

French warships combining as raiding squadrons remained a danger. In February 1812 two French 44-gun warships, the *Arianne* and the *Andromache*, together with the *Marmalouck* (16), left Nantes for a cruise. They shook off their immediate pursuers and were at large in the Western Approaches for over three months, in which time, as the list drawn up by Lloyd's for the Admiralty itemised, 'captured and destroyed' twenty-nine British and American merchant ships. HMS *Northumberland* (74), Captain Henry Hotham, was ordered to lie in wait for them off L'Orient. Finding them on 22 May, he attacked the French ships as they returned to port, driving them on shore, even though they were under the protection of shore batteries. Under fire, two of the French ships exploded. When the *Northumberland* returned to Plymouth, she was cheered up the harbour; nevertheless, the merchant losses were considerable.[39] By contrast, in April 1813, HMB *Teazer* (10) was cruising to protect the trade in very light winds between Cape Clear and the Scillies, when she was chased by a French frigate, potentially much faster. *Teazer*'s commanding officer, Lieutenant John Julian, ordered all the guns to be heaved overboard, except the stern chaser. For forty-six hours, with the 'great exertion' of the crew on the sweeps, he kept ahead of the large French ship. The name of the gun brig was at least appropriate.[40]

At the beginning of 1814, one of the last wartime tasks to be undertaken by convoys and small warships was to deliver gold and silver coin to pay Wellington's troops, now fighting their way into France from the southern border near Bayonne, which the British army was still besieging. Without specie for soldiers to pay for food and luxuries, and to keep them from looting, Wellington was reluctant to move forward. In addition, the armies of Russia and Austria were moving rapidly towards Paris and it would not do to miss the denouement of a twelve-year war. On 8 January, Wellington was at St Jean de Luz, near the French border, writing to Earl Bathurst, the Secretary of State for War, and described the situation as 'incontestable that this army, and all its departments, and the Portuguese and Spanish army, are paralysed at this moment for want of money'. British forces were 'in debt in all parts of Spain, and are becoming so in France'.[41]

On 22 January at Portsmouth, HMS *Desiree* (36), Captain Arthur Farquhar, a former French warship taken as a prize of 1,000 tons, received 60 boxes of specie, worth £400,000. She departed the next day, escorted by HMS *Zealous* (74), which was on her way to North America. Five days later they hit heavy weather. *Desiree*'s log recorded that the crew hoisted 'Runners and Tackles up to secure the mast'. The following day the two ships lost contact with each other. By 29 January, *Desiree* 'shipped a great quantity of Water, battened down the hatches', and fought her way through 'Hard Gales', which blew to 2 February. She arrived at Passages in northern Spain on the 3rd, and sent the money ashore on 5 February. The same day Farquhar recorded in the log that a rum cask of 64 gallons was opened, a reward for an exhausted crew.[42] But the next morning, in trying to get out of the narrow harbour, she went aground. Wellington moved his army forward on 12 February.

More specie was, however, needed. At this time, the north of Europe was being scoured for French gold and silver coin by Nathan Mayer Rothschild and his agents, under a contract made with the British government on 11 January 1814. The specie was to be delivered to Wellington by 11 March, for which Rothschild would receive 2 per cent of all money provided, at his risk.[43] This brought about the chance involvement of HMB *Earnest* (10), 185 tons, with a complement of only fifty men, commanded by a forty-year-old lieutenant, Richard Templar.

At the beginning of January 1814, *Earnest* was at Harwich, under orders for a humdrum job: the delivery to Helvoetsluis, at the mouth of the River Rhine, of the luggage of the new Ambassador to the Netherlands, the Earl of Clancarty. Squalls and a 'strong frost' marked the crossing of the North Sea, and the gun brig had difficulty in making Helvoetsluis Haven as ice floes were coming down the river. Templar had to anchor off the Haven as, according to the log, 'the Ice came down so thick and heavy', and only on 18 January could he get into harbour with the help of men heaving on lines from the shore. He delivered the luggage and prepared to return to England, but, beset by frost and snow, was unable to leave the Haven. On 30 January the ship was battered and damaged by a storm when moored at the pier, lost its gig and the two men in it and had to hire Dutch shipwrights to repair extensive damage. Misfortune upon misfortune, on 14 February Templar discovered that *Earnest* was 'neaped' – the ship could not move and had to wait for the next spring tides to arrive.[44]

Two days later, Mayer Davidson, Nathan Meyer Rothschild's principal clerk, arrived at Helvoetsluis. With him were twenty-nine casks of specie and nowhere to store them and no British soldiers to guard them. HMS *Comus* (22), the warship under orders to take the specie to the south of France, was nowhere to be seen. Davidson complained bitterly in a letter to Rothschild that there was no 'Store house, no seals, no weights, & no lodging to be got for money'. Templar agreed to take the specie aboard the *Earnest*, together with further consignments that arrived as they were loading, amounting to fifty-four chests of French silver and seven chests of gold Napoleon d'Or and Louis d'Or, worth £101,850.[45]

HMB *Earnest* still could not get away because of the weather, but eventually sailed on 19 February in a small convoy, reaching the Downs in two days, where the ship received coals and bread from the depot ship moored there. A small gun brig, with a king's ransom on board, was at considerable risk from American privateers. On 24 February Templar joined a convoy of thirty ships heading to Passages in northern Spain, which had just left the Solent, escorted by HMS *Seahorse* (38).[46] Templar went aboard her to seek permission from her captain to join the convoy, which then was hit hard by south-westerly gales, with sleet and snow, after which the winds fell light and variable: 'the winds round the compass' was recorded in the log on 26 February. But then a north-easterly gale struck the convoy, during which Rothschild's treasure was at its greatest peril. *Earnest*'s log runs: 'the ship laying on her beam and waterlogged. For her preservation and the crew cut away the lee anchor and the guns', but she recovered when relieved of the weight of the guns. During the night the decks were swept clear of all casks and all loose gear. Finally, the convoy reached Passages and on 8 March Templar was able to deliver sixty-one chests ashore.

It was not until five weeks later, on 15 April, five days after the hard-fought battle of Toulouse and a day after the abdication of Napoleon, that HMS *Comus* arrived at Passages with £235,283. She had taken her time. When she finally reached Helvoetsluis, she wasted a day on an inspection from the Duke of Clarence, just promoted to Admiral of the Fleet and engaged in ceremonial duties taking Louis XVIII back to France. Later she was four days anchored in Plymouth Sound, taking on water, the mark of a captain not in a hurry.[47] Bayonne surrendered on 27 April. It was not until 18 May that the bomb vessel HMS *Thais* arrived in the River Garonne near Bordeaux with £215,202 on board.[48] Only the gun brig had delivered within the contract date.

By May 1814, the government owed Rothschild a million pounds. The Prime Minister, Lord Liverpool, remarked later to Castlereagh, 'I do not know what we should have done without him last year.'[49] In 1816, John Charles Herries, the government official who had worked very closely with Rothschild, wrote a summary report on the specie contract for the Prime Minister: 'operations were undertaken ... through the agency of Mr Rothschild ... which proved highly efficacious ... the Chest in the South of France was furnished with French Gold from Holland by shipments at Helvoetsluis so rapidly and completely that the Commissary-General was abundantly supplied for all his wants.' Herries carefully covered his back and Rothschild's reputation by advancing the specie delivery date of each of the warships by three weeks.[50] Nathan Rothschild had taken risks, and was richly rewarded for it, though he probably never knew how close he had been to losing £100,000 in the *Earnest*.

FIVE

NORTH SEA CONVOYS
Two Commanders, 1804–1812

*We became bewildered in the middle of the North Sea and the
captain determined to anchor, which we did in twenty-eight fathoms
of water. We veered to three cables on end and rode very pleasantly,
but pitching tremendously at times bowsprit under, and the water
coming over the forecastle poured into the main deck. We remained
at anchor three days and were visited by two fishermen, who gave us
our bearings. We weighed very easily and we found our way to the
Swin and Sheerness.*

    Midshipman John Harvey Boteler, HMS *Dictator* (64), 1811[1]

HMS *Dictator* was returning from a successful summer in the Baltic,
when her experienced captain lost his bearings. The ship's draught of 18
feet obliged him to be cautious. The North Sea is fiercely tidal, shallow
and largely featureless. High land to aid navigation is scarce, with the
Dutch and German coasts especially low-lying. Flamborough Head
immediately north of the Humber, and Heligoland, the island off what
is now the German coast, are the most prominent features.

    These are difficult waters. The summer convoys were easier, with
long hours of daylight, usually escorting a smaller number of merchant
ships. Voyages to the north German ports from the east coast of England
averaged between three and five days. But it was the winter convoys
that took their toll on ships and men. These convoys were generally
much bigger because of the end-of-season Baltic trade, returning to
Britain before the ice set in and it was dark for much of the day in such

northerly latitudes. While this gave convoys protection from privateers, storms and fog made it difficult to keep the ships together. The value of having specialist convoy officers operating constantly over familiar routes became apparent.*

The reality of the lives of naval and merchant officers and seamen who maintained the blockade and escorted the convoys in the harsh conditions of northerly latitudes is the subject of this chapter. Commander John Hancock of HMS *Cruizer* (16) specialised in blockading the French and Dutch coasts and hunting down privateers. Commander Peter Rye of HMAS *Providence* (14) patiently convoyed merchant ships to and from the Humber to German, Danish and Swedish ports. But it is a mistake to categorise blockading and convoying as two separate strategic functions, for ships constantly did both, sometimes simultaneously. Hancock was impetuous, aggressive and hard on his men. Rye was in a different situation because he commanded a merchant ship contracted to government, with a volunteer crew who were paid merchant wages. He was careful, commanding by personality rather than by punishment. He was also to cultivate his own brand of independence from admirals and the Admiralty.

Before the beginning of the war the careers of both officers had followed similar paths, having been born within a year of each other in 1765 and 1766 and entering the navy within a month of each other in 1778. Neither had a patron and both were held back by lack of employment during the peace after 1783, and thus were relatively old when they became lieutenants. When Rye was twenty-six he was included in the large naval promotion in 1791, which followed the Nootka Sound crisis. Hancock was ignored, as he later described it, 'through want of interest', and nearly left the navy, 'to retire for ever from a profession which he had embraced with ardour, and never ceased to adore'.[2] The French Revolutionary War, however, improved their

---

* Similarly, the captains and crew of the fast and weatherly North Sea packets kept out of trouble, sailing on the same routes throughout the year from Harwich and Yarmouth to the Continent (Knight, *Britain Against Napoleon*, pp. 293–9).

prospects. Hancock was made lieutenant in 1794. Both junior officers were in the thick of the action and in early 1801 both achieved the rank of commander, and were appointed to brig sloops before the Peace of Amiens. At this point their fortunes diverged. Peter Rye's sloop was paid off, Hancock retained his command through the peace.

John Hancock thrived in the first years of the war, commanding the five-year-old HMS *Cruizer*, as part of the blockade off French and Dutch ports to prevent invasion. Late in the summer of 1803, *Cruizer* cut out and captured a French national schooner and a brig near Cap Gris-Nez and early in 1804 burnt another at Sluys. But it was not only privateers and warships that were her prey. The ship also captured French and neutral merchant prizes, which were still at sea during the early years of the war. By the time Hancock left the *Cruizer* in early 1806 she had taken at least ten prizes, earning Admiral Keith over £450 for his 'flag eighth'. The ship's total prize money would thus have been over £3,600 in under three years.[3]

In the meantime, Peter Rye was stuck on shore on half pay, approaching his fortieth birthday. He had the misfortune to be the nephew of an MP, Joseph Jekyll, who had criticised the Addington government, which had not endeared him to the First Lord, Lord St Vincent.[4] Jekyll told Rye that he had written to the First Lord on his behalf in February 1802, with no result.* On 25 March 1804 Rye wrote an exasperated letter to William Marsden, the Secretary of the Admiralty. It was more than usually direct and forceful and shows the lengths to which unemployed officers had to go to attract the attention of the Board:

Please to remind their Lordships of my early and numerous offers of Service by letters, also three Personal Applications which detained me in Town from my Residence in Northamptonshire, at a considerable

---

* In the same letter Jekyll congratulated his nephew on breaking off an engagement, as it was 'an act of great imprudence to marry in these expensive times on half pay unless the wife brings money with her' (NRO, Rye/X/7244/069, 19 February 1802).

Expense, to no Purpose, as I never had the Honor of seeing their Lordships since my last Application. I have been four months at Sheerness in hopes of being serviceable or employed, my five and twenty years of Service entitle me to hope for a ship or the Sea Fencibles. [Annotated, dated 29 March] Their Lordships cannot employ him at present.[5]

Rye's luck in his search for a ship turned soon afterwards. He was appointed to a brig sloop HMAS *Providence*, an ex-collier of 291 tons, to be armed with fourteen carronades. Although it may not have seemed to have been a propitious appointment, he was to stay with this ship for over eight years. *Providence* was at North Shields, which Rye reached on 16 May 1804, by which time the owner, William Clarke Jnr, had already raised a civilian crew of forty-three men and three boys. This included a master (who would effectively be the owner's representative), a surgeon, a boatswain and a carpenter, but the ship had no marines, nor a purser nor a captain's clerk. *Providence* was of similar tonnage to a *Cruizer*-class sloop, but the crew was only a third of the latter's size, generating less firepower from their carronades. However, the consumption of less water and provisions gave the *Providence* a much greater cruising range. According to a regular Admiralty return, when fully stored she carried three months' provisions, cooking fuel and candles for twelve weeks and nine tons of water, with consumption at three-quarters of a ton a week.[6] Rye was loyal to the ship which he commanded for so long, later describing her to the Admiralty as a 'well-found and good sea boat'.[7]

The day after his arrival, Rye mustered the crew and commissioned the ship, taking care to write to inform William Marsden, Secretary of the Admiralty, that he had done so.[8] The ship took on four guns so that he would not be defenceless on the voyage south and by 22 May he had sailed from the Tyne. Six days later the *Providence* anchored at the Nore and drew stores from Sheerness dockyard. On 3 June yard artificers were fitting chocks and carriages for fourteen carronades, which were sent on board from the ordnance yard at Queenborough. That was the last time that HMAS *Providence* went near a royal dockyard until 1812: stationed at the Humber for eight years, she was maintained in Grimsby docks and on occasion her copper sheathing was repaired on the mudflats of the Humber when the tide was low.

The *Providence* set sail two days later, just two months after Rye's appointment. The first task recorded in the log: 'scaled the guns and loaded them with shot'.[9] The ship's muster books reveal an experienced and mature crew, with an average age of over twenty-five and more than half of them married. Most were able seamen; only five of them were rated as ordinary seamen.[10] All except one were from the north-east, and only half a dozen were not from North Shields or Sunderland, giving the crew a strong regional bond, unlike commissioned warships, which had to take mixed pressed men and volunteers as crew, randomly and unwillingly assembled. The crew was more highly paid and the ethic on board was very different from the harsher discipline of the regular navy.* Rye allowed them freedom ashore and plenty of leave. Remarkably, in over eight years, no record of any disciplinary proceedings appears in the logbooks of the *Providence*.

One experienced rear-admiral, James Vashon, commander-in-chief, Leith, wrote to a member of the Admiralty Board in 1807, warning against impressing the crews of hired armed ships, which technically a regularly commissioned warship could do, for the owner would have found and signed on the crew and paid them. In Vashon's opinion, hired armed ships 'are well calculated for the convoy service and cause less trouble than I generally experience in Men of War Brigs and Gun Brigs, which are constantly having their people Desert'.[11]

Providing the crew was only a small part of the shipowner's contractual tasks. He had to procure and supply provisions to feed the crew and to equip the ship to the specified standard laid out in the contract. For

---

* They were forerunners of the armed merchant cruisers run by the Admiralty during the First and Second World Wars. Twentieth-century merchant seamen were required to sign a form known as 'T124', which rendered them liable to naval discipline.

this the owner was paid every two months, at a price per ton per month, usually about fifteen shillings, as well as £5-10-0 per month for each of the crew. As a result, though his expenses were high, Clarke made a great deal of money. At the start of the war, he was preparing five large copper-sheathed colliers for chartering by the navy. Three of them, the *Providence*, *Charles* and the *Prince William*, were of similar size, about 300 tons, with 14 guns, though the first was a two-masted brig sloop, and the other two were ship-rigged with three masts. The three ships were to be based on the Humber, sailing with each other until 1812.*

Hired armed ships could be rapidly mobilised but were expensive and the Admiralty sought to replace them by prizes and by warships recently built under contract by merchant yards.† The hiring of the ship required constant accounting, to be undertaken by the commander, who had no assistance from a purser or captain's clerk. Every two months the commander had to provide the Navy Board with a crew muster, a state and condition report, as well as a certificate so that the owner could receive his Navy Board payment. If there was a man short for any reason, an abatement was made on the bill paid to the owner. Any repairs and refits, or charges for docking, were also charged to the owners, which would be deducted from the regular payments made by the Navy Board to the owner. The provisions account also had to be drawn up and balanced. The commander was only too aware that if there were mistakes, he would be held liable for the shortfall.

Financially secure, Peter Rye immediately married a much younger woman. In July 1804 he took his first convoy to Elsinore. While the waters off the Thames Estuary and East Anglia were much contested in 1804, full

---

* HMAS *Prince William* was commanded by Lieutenant Andrew Mott from 1804 to 1812, convoying to the Baltic or Heligoland, and in some years with as many as seven crossings (there and back) of the North Sea. The longest command was that of Lieutenant John Watson of the gun brig HMS *Aggressor*, 177 tons with a 50-man crew, who served on these routes from 1803 to 1814, usually with small convoys, but on one occasion with 65 ships to the Baltic (TNA, ADM 7/64).
† When the *Providence* was finally discharged in 1812, the total of the imprest paid to Clarke was £44,986, and other North Sea brig sloops, HMAS *Prince William*, £50,177, and HMAS *Charles*, £58,226, all owned by William Clarke of North Shields (TNA, ADM 49/99, Imprests relating to hired ships, 1804–18).

of action and hostile privateers, the northern North Sea was comparatively peaceful, so much so that Rye took his newly married wife Eleanora (whom he called Elinor) with him in the *Providence* on a voyage to Elsinore. Unsurprisingly, nothing appears in the official records.* After his gentle introduction to the North Sea, he got down to the year-round routine of escorting convoys. He was based at Grimsby, where the convoys gathered in the Roads outside the port. Only Leith in Scotland and Long Hope Sound in the Orkneys were more northerly convoy assembly points.

John Hancock's life at this time was very different. In November 1804 *Cruizer* performed her most famous exploit when she chased the large privateer lugger the *Contre-Amiral Magon*, with a crew of sixty-seven. She was commanded by an infamous Dunkirk captain, Jean Blanckman, who had already captured forty British merchant ships since the beginning of the war. She was sighted off the coast of Flanders and in a freshening wind she fled north, parallel to the shore. The wild pursuit continued through the night. *Cruizer* lost most of her studding sails, her main top gallant mast and fore-topsail yards and the privateer lost her topmast. In the hold of the privateer were twenty masters and seamen of English vessels, prisoners already captured, who had to endure the tension of this wild nine-hour pursuit of ninety miles, knowing that they would be in a French prison if the privateer escaped. They also knew that no British warship would be likely to catch her, although one prisoner remarked, as reported in the *Naval Chronicle*: 'I have little hopes, indeed, unless it should fortunately be the *Cruizer*, for she sails like the devil.' It was a deserved reputation. When she towed her prize to the Yarmouth Roads, two thousand people lined the jetty and beach of Yarmouth to

---

* The next year he wrote to her from Elsinore when she was at home in Grimsby recalling their visit: 'Today I went on shore and wandered alone through every walk in the Royal Gardens, and yet not alone . . . for the different points of the view we admired over again, the same seat we sat upon . . .' (NRO, Rye/X/7244/084, p. 7, 1 June 1805).

see her and the famous Jean Blanckman as a prisoner.[12] A year later, Hancock took another large French privateer, the 14-gun *La Vengeur.*

In 1805 and 1806 Hancock was the senior officer of the blockading squadron off Flushing and Ostend, as he reported in his journal, 'in sight of Ostend for week after week'.* When the weather was calm, he took the opportunity to complete the unending task of maintaining the ship. In February 1805, anchored off Blankenburg, the log reads: 'Employed painting ship and tarring the rigging.'[13] Hancock had plenty of seamen. In early 1804 the *Cruizer* had 114 crew on board, with 34 of them able seamen, just short of her complement of 121. By early 1805 the able seamen had increased to forty-two, with twenty young ordinary seamen and only eighteen landsmen.[14] These were the days of plentiful seamen, a situation that did not last.

In the first three months of 1805 Hancock in the *Cruizer* captured four prizes, impressed men from them and escorted his captures back to Harwich or Yarmouth. Most of his prizes were incoming ships to his blockaded port, but in June that year he demonstrated remarkable aggression. Off Ostend his squadron chased a galliot and forced it to run up onto the beach, and as his log recounts, 'sent a boat to her which was forced to return by the artillery on the beach. Came to in 7 fathoms, sent all the boats armed to the Galliot. Boats returned with the Galliot.' The next day he mustered the ships company. 'Performed Divine Service', appeared in the log for the first time, as well he might, given the success of such a risky venture.[15] But Hancock was far from satisfied. In later years he recalled in disgust that, 'he never received the value of a teaspoon from Lloyd's, or any other commercial association: thanks he certainly received in abundance, but always at the expence [only] of postage.'

Hancock, however, continued his aggressive activities. In January 1806 he disguised the *Cruizer* as an American merchant ship and

---

* Hancock's journals were informal and scrappy, according to Lord Keith, to whom he submitted them, 'not being kept in the form prescribed by the Lords Commissioners of the Admiralty . . . cannot be forwarded to the Board'. Keith ordered Hancock to 'pay due attention', retained them and one, at least, is still in Lord Keith's collection (NMM, KEI/30; KEI/L/108, 2 February 1806. Keith to Hancock).

decoyed cutters and luggers out of Flushing which were smuggling goods to England. He seized a thousand tubs of Geneva gin, 26,000 gallons of spirits, tobacco and other contraband, sailing back with his convoy of prizes in triumph. However, a surprise awaited him on shore. He later wrote that 'he had been included in the grand Trafalgar promotion, which took place only seven days before he made this valuable and important capture, and of which he was at that time ignorant'.[16]

As a post-captain, Hancock could not continue in command of such a small ship as a brig sloop and he was immediately superseded and had to leave the *Cruizer*. In vain did he write to the Admiralty for further employment, stressing his five years of experience of navigating the Dutch coast and his expertise in detecting prize cargoes in neutral ships. Three years elapsed before he had a permanent command again, during which the Admiralty found him a variety of temporary jobs. Such were the vicissitudes of a naval officer without interest. But he was not finished with the North Sea.[17]

The maintenance of British sea control of the North Sea was vital. To the south, any invasion attempt on the Essex and East Anglian coasts had to be kept at bay by a blockade of French and Dutch ports. Similarly, British coastal trade needed protection from Dunkirk privateers. To the north, it was essential that the huge quantities of Baltic timber, hemp and pitch to maintain shipbuilding production, as well as wheat, reached British ports in several thousand ship voyages a year. In addition, two to three hundred merchant ships made the difficult voyage north into the Arctic Circle to Archangel every summer, most of them laden with coffee and sugar, bringing back cargoes of iron, timber, hemp, cordage, tallow and corn.[18]

Convoys from the Nore and the Humber to German ports ensured a flow to the Continent of many re-exported tropical products, including coffee, sugar, tobacco, indigo and raisins and British manufactured exports. Most of the merchantmen escorted by Rye in *Providence* were loaded at Hull with goods which had come from the Manchester area across the Pennines and down the Aire and Calder navigations. It was a period of rapid expansion of canals and river navigation and of long squabbles between the Manchester merchants and the canal companies over the provision of enough canal boats and compensation for damage caused to goods in transit.[19] The route over the Pennines and thence by river to Hull, according to the Manchester Commercial Society, was 'the key through which our manufactures can alone find a passage for the markets of Germany, Switzerland and the borders of Italy'. For the owner of a cargo the risk of goods being too late for the Italian fairs, for instance, might outweigh the regulations for the ship to keep with the convoy, and a master of a merchant ship might well be following the owner's orders to break convoy if delays were excessive.[20] It was of incidental importance to merchants that these smuggled goods were undermining the Napoleonic economy after the imposition of the Continental System, but, in spite of the Emperor's efforts to prevent these goods from landing, they were shipped and landed in large quantities.

The Humber was well placed for trade for northern Germany, being on the same latitude as Emden at the mouth of the Weser, the southern-most German river, giving the east–west route a considerable sailing advantage in the prevailing south-west/north-east winds. Exports from Hull were already well established, including metal and metal goods, particularly lead, chemicals, textiles and imports of naval stores and corn.[21] Emden had 'an inconsiderable trade' in agricultural products up to 1803, but in 1804 the number of ships arriving there suddenly increased to over 1,200 and to almost 1,600 during 1805. The Berlin Decrees of November 1806 and the occupation of Hamburg pushed the trade north again and the ports of Tonningen and Husum became very busy with 'neutral' goods.[22] Hull grew at the expense of London in trade to Northern Europe, as ports in Holland and Germany fell into French hands.

For the first years, *Providence*'s convoys sailed mainly to Tonningen, some way up the river Eider in southern Denmark, and not an easy river to enter, described by one senior captain as, 'very shoal & on the Bar at high water there is not above 3 fathoms'.[23] Cuxhaven at the mouth of the Elbe was also an occasional destination. Another was the island of Heligoland, with its high cliffs, west of the Elbe, although still three hundred miles from the English coast.[24] Immediately upon the declaration of war with Denmark in September 1807 the island was captured, without bloodshed, by a force under Rear-Admiral Thomas MacNamara Russell. He enthused over his capture, writing to the Board of Admiralty, that, 'with a small expense this island may be made a little Gibraltar, and a safe haven for small craft, even in the winter'.[25]

Heligoland was to be an extraordinarily valuable acquisition. The island was easy to find for the gently shelving soundings provided a trustworthy guide for making the island, essential in the thick weather so prevalent in the Heligoland Bight. In February 1811 a lighthouse was built there by Trinity House, with the aid of a Treasury grant, giving a fixed white light visible for sixteen miles in clear weather.[26] The holding in the anchorage was firm, though with a rocky bottom which took its toll on anchor cables. In September 1809 the owners of the *Ocean* brig complained to the Transport Board that the ship had been held at Heligoland since May and the new cable on the ship was now nearly worn out: 'while our vessel continues in that Perilous situation we shall not be able to get a Farthing Insurance effected upon her'. They enclosed the report of the master, who hoped for 'a prospect of going from this horrid place ... I have been under the necessity of cutting twenty fathoms of my small bower cable. I spliced it twice and it again stranded in two places, being so long in continual motion.'[27]

There was also the problem of the Heligoland pilots. George Coggeshall's experience with one of them in 1809 led him to call them 'a vile set of extortioners, who would scarcely save a drowning man without pay; in a word, they are a notorious set of unprincipled rascals'. He had to threaten the pilot who was guiding his ship into the River

Eider with a loaded pistol.[28] The pilots were also responsible for the safe anchorage of ships between Heligoland and Sandy Island, but who had by local custom an alarming conflict of interest: if any ship was wrecked ashore, then salvage rights went to the islanders as a whole.

The sad story of the *Atlas* merchant brig was recounted in a deposition under oath by her master, Peter Fisher. The ship had been convoyed from the Nore in early October 1808, but when anchored was caught by a SSW gale, lost a cable, then drove athwart the hawse of another ship. The pilot refused to take the ship to sea, in spite of being repeatedly requested to do so. 'Therefore the pilot ran us on shore for the preservation of our lives, which as he said was all that he had in his power ... but so little did the pilot appear to apprehend danger after the vessel was on shore that he laid him down & slept, so soon as he had informed the commander that the ship & Cargo was now prize to the island.' Thomas Brown, the Harbour Master appointed by the navy, sent a boat to rescue the crew, but it was followed by boats full of islanders:

> the Heligolanders immediately demanded possession of Ship & Cargo under pleas that all vessels going on shore belonged to the Island ... The conduct of the Heligolanders became most outrageous resembling that of Pirates than men wishing to claim salvage, they entering the cabin by force, broke the padlock on the same ... and swore that unless their demand was complied with, the Commander and the crew with that of Mr Brown's boat would be thrown overboard.

The cargo was eventually taken onshore by naval employees, but only after considerable violence. The ship was a total loss.*

In spite of these considerable local difficulties, trade with the island increased exponentially. By the spring of 1808 'an extraordinary network of Anglo-German merchants' began to use Heligoland for large-scale

* A copy of this deposition found its way to the desk of Lord Castlereagh, Secretary of State for War (TNA, CO 118/1, 3 November 1808, John Bennet, Secretary of the Committee of Lloyd's, to Castlereagh, enclosure of 10 October 1808).

smuggling. By the summer some two hundred merchants, mostly from London, Hamburg, Edinburgh, Bremen, Liverpool, Frankfurt and Manchester had settled on Heligoland, many of them making use of warehouses prefabricated in Manchester.[29] Vast quantities of coffee, raw and refined sugar, raisins and pepper came as cargo from the Nore and the Humber and were then smuggled from the island in fishing and other small boats to the German states. Manufactured goods, hardware, tin plate and cotton twist followed, as well as a great variety of such goods as salt, logwood and coal.[30]

For a short time, the value of the goods which passed through Heligoland was phenomenal. The value of the goods between 1809 and 1811 amounted to £86 million pounds.* The Chamber of Commerce explained to the Committee of Lloyd's that Heligoland was 'the only medium through which the North of Germany and the countries upon the Rhine can receive their supplies'.[31] Fortunes were made, but it was very risky, and much depended upon the effectiveness of the naval cover provided by convoy or patrolling warships. Underwriters would not insure cargoes sent to the island as smuggling was illegal. One who ignored the warnings of his more cautious business associates not to go there was Nathan Meyer Rothschild, based at this time in Manchester. He established an agent there and made a great deal of money.[32] But by 1810 the island began to lose its edge and by 1812 the downturn came, when the price of coffee and sugar on the Continent began to drop sharply. Other merchants lost their fortunes.[33]

The British capture of the island immediately increased demands for convoys. An army garrison was established on the island and had to be supplied.[34] Arms and ammunition were also shipped there to encourage covert operations against the Napoleonic regime in German states. These were unsuccessful and the island began to be used more and more

---

* The Chamber of Commerce charged 0.25 per cent for the levies for local costs, thus the total value of goods came to £86.3 million, which as Jan Rüger points out, exceeded the smuggling through Malta and was a little more than Britain's annual public budget for 1811 (Rüger, *Heligoland*, p. 25).

for the withdrawal of troops from the Continent.[35] It was trade, however, which accounted for the greatest amount of shipping movements. The number of ships convoyed between 1808 and 1813 totalled 946. Two-thirds of this figure arrived in 1809 and 1810, after which the numbers fell away sharply. The larger convoys came from the Nore, the largest in September 1809 consisting of forty-seven ships. In the main, however, trade operated in very small convoys, sometimes as little as one merchantman protected by a single warship. All three of the sloops based on the Humber completed these single-ship crossings.[36] On the *Providence*'s first crossing with a single ship, she towed it eastwards for two days and when they neared Heligoland, she cast off the merchant ship and returned directly to Grimsby.[37]

Rye's time in the *Providence* is an unusual story because he was stationed in an independent, even isolated, position over a long period. The admiral to whom he reported was stationed at Great Yarmouth, a hundred miles to the south of Grimsby. Rye gradually assumed more responsibility, providing his own local motivation and leadership, since the means of enforcing the navy's traditional intense discipline through hierarchy, instant obedience, marines at attention and the threat of flogging, were far distant and did not apply.

Yet nowhere in his log over nine years is there mention of any punishments of his crew of over forty, in the confines of a ship of about 90 foot in length, which would allow little space for each man to sleep, let alone live and eat in comfort.* There could be little physical distance between the commanding officer and his crew and it is clear that the trust between them was very strong. For instance, on 11 January 1807, with *Providence* in dock in Grimsby, he mustered the crew, and then marched

---

* The logs of other hired warships are likewise free of disciplinary entries, in contrast with the regular naval sloops of this size. See Chapter 2.

the men to church. In November 1809, when anchored in the Grimsby Roads, he 'sent most of the ship's company on shore to attend the funeral of one of our men that was unfortunately drowned in Grimsby Dock'. Less than a month later he sent them again to the funeral of a crew member who had died of a 'putrid sore throat and a malignant fever'.[38] Perhaps the most conclusive evidence for this trust is a list in Rye's papers of subscribers to the 'Collection for poor William Westcott's Widow'. Every member of the crew gave something, Rye leading with three guineas, the officers with a guinea. The total came to £23-3-0, a remarkable sum for so small a crew. The list is neatly drawn up in Rye's strong and decisive handwriting; one can read into the document considerable satisfaction on his part.[39]

The loyalty shown by the crew to Rye and the *Providence* is remarkable. In the nine years of his commission only two men deserted, both in 1810, one of them just two days after Rye had mustered the crew when the ship was in Grimsby dock, and paid eight months' wages.[40] When the ship was decommissioned in September 1812, fourteen of the original crew were still on board, by which time the first and second mates had worked their way up from young able seamen of nineteen when they joined in 1804. There had been death through accident and sickness, and crew members retiring as 'unserviceable', but the retention rate was exceptional.[41]

To wield a strict disciplinary regime was anyway impractical, because for some weeks of each winter *Providence* was hauled into the wet dock in Grimsby. Though there was sometimes a lull in winter activity, during which essential maintenance had to be done, the ship sailed for almost all the year. As the crew was required to work on the ship at the town quay or in the dock, it was impossible to confine the seamen as would be necessary in most warships. *Providence* required constant maintenance in harbour and at sea and work on the ship was unceasing for his crew. Besides, by using commercial docks and some labour, the owner was charged against his contract for all repairs that were not completed by the crew, but it was Rye who had to keep these complex accounts. With reports on the condition of the ship, they were transmitted to the Admiralty regularly and adjusted by the accountants in the Navy Office.[42] The relationship between owner and government could be difficult. In 1808 William Clarke protested furiously at an accusation that there had been irregularities over the provisioning accounts aboard *Providence*.* In 1809 Rye himself had to remonstrate with the Deputy Comptroller of the Navy Board, Captain Sir Francis Hartwell, 'I am in 1807 brought in debt to Government £214 (a sum that will nearly ruin me) . . . it is my firm belief that Government will be gainers by me were they to balance the account, for had I proper persons in the capacity of Clerk and Steward the balance would have been in my favour.'[43]

Rye also had to solve maintenance problems continually. Winter conditions in particular resulted in constant wear of the ship, as Rye reported to Marsden in December 1806: 'The *Providence* having strained very much in very severe weather both in going to and returning from the Baltic'.[44] Many examples of heavy weather are recorded in Rye's log. Off Flamborough Head in the autumn of 1807, for instance: 'Strong gales with long heavy Squalls, a high cross sea and constant small rain. The Ship labouring much and shipping a great deal of water ... starboard topsail sheet broke and the main topsail went to Rags. Set close reefed main staysail and bent another storm sail.'[45]

When the ship was at Elsinore in the summer of 1806, he enlisted help: 'delivered instructions to three masters of merchantmen two carpenters belonging to them assisting ours in caulking the decks'. Within the month he had a problem with the main mast, bringing the cross trees down to repair them. Sometimes he heeled the ship for copper sheathing repairs below the water line, and new copper sheets were supplied from Hull and transported by the ship's launch to

---

* Clarke wrote to Vice-Admiral Douglas, who forwarded the letter to Wellesley Pole at the Admiralty. The letter concluded: 'I most seriously wish I had the opportunity of confronting the author of so vile a calumny; I have however the satisfaction of knowing that in all my engagements with Government – they have always been fulfilled with that strictness which will I trust render it ever unnecessary to have recourse to the meanness complained of in their Lordship's letter' (TNA, ADM 1/1427, 4 November 1808, enclosure, 28 October 1808).

Grimsby. In November 1807, after a rough crossing, Rye entered in the log: 'hauled up the spare Sails to air, found the Rats had got into the sail room'.[46] Repairs to the hull were even more of a problem. In July 1810 the crew managed to repair the hull within the space of a tide. Rye ran *Providence* on the flats of the Humber, as the log ran: 'set sail and run the ship on the Flats for the purposes of stopping a leak we had discovered . . . nailed new Copper on the bottom where wanting, and got clear for hauling off the shore with the flowing tide'.[47] The crew would have had to work fast before the rising tide re-floated the ship.

The same problem arose every winter when the ship was in the dock at Grimsby, for the projected lock gates had not been built by this time and it was therefore a 'wet' dock rather than a 'dry' dock.[48] Every winter the ship was docked, but it would seem that a temporary dry dock was made in the mud at the end of 1811, but, as ever, there were problems, as the log had it, for the ship was 'wholly prepared for going into the dry Dock, but retarded owing to the unavoidable circumstances of the Dock not being completed, it being under repair'. Yet again Rye had a problem with insufficient height of a spring tide: 'this morning's Tide been so much taken off as not to leave a sufficiency of water to take us out of the Dock'. 'Neaped in dock', Rye noted, and the ship was stuck without enough water to float her until the next spring tides a fortnight later. On 19 December the ship 'prepared to leave Dock . . . but was prevented by the Tide not flowing high enough'. Finally, on 20 December the ship was hauled out.[49] Not many commanding officers of the time had to deal with maintenance problems of this complexity.

Aside from convoy duty, the *Providence* had an aggressive role, cruising to police the middle part of the North Sea to ensure that it was clear of enemy privateers, and also to intercept the enemy's trade. Throughout the years 1804 to 1812, Rye's log reveals his ship was constantly chasing, challenging and boarding ships to examine their papers, particularly the licences of neutral shipping, as well as searching British ports for smugglers attempting to bring in gin, brandy or French luxury goods. As a result, he made some successful prize captures, the first in April 1805 when, two days out from Grimsby with a convoy to Tonningen, *Providence* chased a strange sail and was eventually joined by HMS *Thames* (32), which was escorting the Leith convoy, and HMS *Scorpion* (16), a Cruizer-class brig sloop. The 'chase' hoisted Dutch colours and, being completely outgunned, fired a gun to leeward and struck. The prize was *L'Honneur*, a 12-gun Dutch schooner bound for Curacao, carrying despatches and a thousand stands of arms. She was taken back to Yarmouth by the *Scorpion*, with whom Rye and his crew would have had to share the prize money, but the incident demonstrated the effectiveness and depth of the British blockade and the totality of its control of the North Sea.

Other very necessary but unglamorous tasks had to be undertaken. In 1804, for instance, Rye transported thirty-seven casks of bar silver from the British consul at Elsinore to the agent of Daniel Bayley in London, a task for which he would have received freight money.[50] Busy with convoying, it took Rye two months before he reached the Nore with the silver, as he informed the Admiralty, which immediately ordered him to embark twenty-five seamen to a ship at Yarmouth, a frequent task for convoy escorts in the North Sea.[51] Another task was the transmission of intelligence from German ports to the Admiralty of the rapidly changing military situation in Northern Europe, in addition to bringing home letters.[52] More burdensome was ferrying troops, and transferring seamen or prisoners of war, a task which increased as seamen and soldiers became more and more scarce. The quickest way to transport a large body of men several hundred miles was by sea and warships were immediately available.*

Rye was especially solicitous of the merchant ships he was escorting. He was off Heligoland at the end of his first year in command, in December 1804, in thick fog that turned to 'Strong gales with snow', as the log recorded. At daybreak he discovered that the *Triton*, one of his

---

* For instance, the *Hull Packet* reported in early 1807 that HMAS *Hebe* was sailing from the Humber to Sheerness with over a hundred carpenters and shipwrights to prepare for the Copenhagen expedition of later that year (*Hull Packet*, 20 January 1807).

convoy, had lost her bowsprit and foremast. *Providence* 'bore down to her assistance, sent an officer and 6 Hands to help them, also a Jib'. During the night the *Triton* managed to lose *Providence*'s boat, so Rye sent another to take his men off, then took the *Triton* in tow. Two days later they anchored in the Grimsby Roads.[53] Assistance of this kind was not forgotten, nor was it the only instance, and Captain Rye came to be much admired and respected by shipowners and merchants in Hull and Grimsby.[54]

Only once did Rye sustain serious damage during his long commission. In late February 1806 *Providence* had just escorted a convoy across to the Elbe, and was at anchor in the Cuxhaven Roads in a heavy gale, when a Swedish merchant ship dragged her anchor and was driven by the wind across *Providence*'s anchor cable. It was an extremely dangerous situation which could have led to the foundering of both ships. Rye cut his cable and ran up river, tried to get into Gluckstadt harbour on the north bank, but its entrance had been blocked by the wreckage of five whaling ships sunk in the gale, with, as Rye learnt later, the loss of nineteen lives. The ship was driven further up the river, and ran up on a bank, but the pilot 'unfortunately run us at the top of high water upon the small island of Pogen ... which was totally overflown, a circumstance which never happens, but in extraordinary heavy gales of wind from the NW or NNW ... the returning tide rose not so high by four feet.'[55] Rye had been 'neaped' on the top of a very high spring tide. A more potentially embarrassing situation could hardly have been selected in all Europe, for in early 1806 the border between Denmark and Hanover was a diplomatic hotspot. Prussia was negotiating a treaty with France to enable it to occupy Hanover, and since late 1805 the British had been preparing an expedition to the Elbe to prevent a takeover by Prussia.[56]

The *Providence* was stranded for five weeks. Rye and the crew worked ceaselessly to get themselves out of their predicament. The crew lightened the ship, as Rye reported to William Marsden at the Admiralty: 'We have a clean, swept hold, the Stores and Provisions are lodged in

His Danish Majesty's Storehouses at Gluckstadt.' With the help of a hundred Danish labourers, a 473-foot-long channel was dug in six days, 30-foot wide and 8-foot deep. A constant worry was whether or not he would be arrested. Rye wrote to the local Danish commander in nearby Gluckstadt, 'I cannot suppose in my helpless situation the French or the Prussians will consider the sand or Island of Pogen as Danish territory, their Banner is not displayed thereon, or a King's vessel bearing her flag riding there off.'[57]

Rye kept the crew busy by digging under the ship to enable the keel and rudder to be repaired, and caulking, which was completed by the next spring tides on 6 April. Even then, it was difficult, for the channel started to fill with sand as the water rose, but the *Providence* came off on 6 April, 'late in the evening after the most fatiguing exertions of officers and ships Company as the sand they worked upon after a certain Depth was forced up again and renewed their Labour', as Rye described it to Marsden. When the ship at last made its way downriver to Cuxhaven, Rye found that a British embargo on Prussian ships had come into force. A more senior captain of a British warship lying there ordered him out of the Elbe immediately so that the ship would not be detained. Had he been captured, Rye and his crew would likely have been prisoners of war for the eight years until the end of the war. Rye returned to convoy duty by escorting four ships back to Grimsby, 'but a heavy gale attended with continual thick snow storms obliged me to lay off till daylight', before he could come to anchor in the Grimsby Roads.[58] In his report to the Admiralty, Rye concluded: 'Please to inform their Lordships also that every Officer and man exerted themselves to the utmost', which earned him a congratulatory letter from their lordships.[59] It was not an ideal way to get noticed, but the incident demonstrated Rye's ingenuity and enterprise.*

---

* The British consul at Hamburg sent a bill for £1,155/3/3d to the Navy Board for the hire of labourers and other expenses while the ship was stranded; this amount was paid by the Navy Board and then deducted from the *Providence*'s owner's two-monthly hire payment (TNA, ADM 49/99, Imprest volume, 'Providence').

Rye's escorting duties were proving as difficult as ever, best illustrated by a convoy in late 1806 to Elsinore. He issued instructions to twenty-three masters at Grimsby on 13 September but by the next day had 'lost sight of all the convoy from the thickness of the fog'. Severe weather was to follow. Two days later the *Supply* brig 'made the signal of distress, sent the 1st Master and six hands on board to assist her at the Pumps, she having 5 foot of water in the hold'. Two days later the *Robert and Mary* flew a signal of distress, 'being leaky', though not wanting immediate assistance. Rye ordered her master to keep near the *Providence*. On the sixth day out the *Mary* also flew the signal of distress, 'having carried away her Foretopmast close to the Cap, and the Head of her Main Top Mast'. The convoy reached Elsinore on 21 September, eight days out. The *Mary* limped in three days later, and Rye sent six men on board to assist her. The *Providence* herself had carried away her crosstrees at the main mast, which needed immediate repair. This was nothing like his idyllic visit to Elsinore in the summer two years before when he took his wife Elinor.

The return convoy of twelve vessels, too, was full of incident, for it was blown back to Elsinore by contrary winds. On 30 September a Russian squadron with five ships of the line passed through the convoy. On the same day he met and boarded the *Iphigenia*, 'brought the master and his papers on board, and finding that she was under false colours detained for legal adjudication, and sent the First Master and two men aboard', and she joined Rye's convoy. This was the 700-ton prize that Rye recalled many years later.[60] More convoys in heavy weather followed that year. In late October he sailed with eighteen vessels, three days out, 'convoy much scattered'. On a return passage from Elsinore on 7 November, with thirty-six ships, he notes in his log, 'Heavy gales with snow squalls and a High Sea', which forced him on 12 November to run for Lyngor, a Norwegian port, which he made with the aid of a pilot, where it blew so hard that the crew 'carried out hawsers on the starboard bow and quarter to rings in the rocks for steadying the vessel'.

Relations with merchantmen were not always good. Rye referred in one letter in 1804 to 'the wilful inattention to convoy instructions without any Intention of obeying them but merely to recover the Premium on Insurance', and recommended changing the system so that the convoy commodore should furnish masters with a certificate at the end of the voyage that they had obeyed signals, before the ship could claim the lower premium.[61] He wrote to Marsden at the Admiralty, enclosing his convoy lists, and a list 'of those Masters of Merchantmen who behaved particularly Ill, and showed a total disregard to convoy Instructions, which Instructions were rendered still more plain by the Flags and Pendants being coloured'.[62]

In 1806 Rye avoided promotion to a larger ship by the unusual means of a doctor's note. On 21 October 1806 the Admiralty appointed him to HMS *Vulture* (16), fully 100 tons larger than the *Providence*, and with a crew of a hundred.[63] The *Vulture* had been built in Shields, but purchased by the navy rather than hired, and thus commissioned, enabling it to go further afield than the hired armed ships, which were confined by contract to 'home waters'. Instead of accepting gladly, Rye replied by enclosing a letter from Thomas Bell, a Grimsby surgeon, who certified that he had attended Rye in the summer, and his opinion was that 'any foreign voyage would be extremely dangerous and prejudicial to Captain Rye's future Health it being by no means reinstated'.[64] His health does not seem to have been good, and he certainly suffered from rheumatism later in life. Two years later, in April 1808, he even applied unsuccessfully to the Admiralty for a vacant captain's shore-based position running the local Sea Fencibles, the local volunteer defence force.[65]

Rye did not leave the Humber.* Instead, the focus of the war changed. Lord Keith's command was broken up on 19 May 1807 into independent squadrons, under rear-admirals based at Leith, Yarmouth, Sheerness, the Downs and off the Texel.[66] Not long after, in June 1807, Rye sailed *Providence* down to Great Yarmouth, to talk with the new

* By this time, Rye had put his roots down in Grimsby and he and his wife had six children there. Elinor was born on 17 August 1805, Peter 18 March 1807, George 3 December 1808 (but died three days later), Henrietta in 1809, Mary Anne 1812 and Maria in 1813 (NRO, Rye/X/ 7245/28).

commander-in-chief, Rear-Admiral Billy Douglas, whose command stretched from Harwich in the south to Newcastle in the north.[67] Rye was given the responsibility for coordinating the two other Grimsby-based hired brig sloop convoy-escorts, HMAS *Prince William* and HMAS *Charles*, both of 14 guns and the same tonnage as *Providence*, escorting convoys to and from north German ports, Heligoland, Gothenburg and Elsinore. They each averaged at least half a dozen return crossings a year and were commanded by junior officers of immense convoy experience.*

Rye was given further responsibilities. He was to issue convoy instructions to all ships leaving Hull, and those passing through the Grimsby Roads, such as those from London to Archangel.[68] However, because he was still commanding a hired ship, promotion from commander to post-captain was refused, in spite of his wide-ranging responsibilities. He had no clerk and the many surviving drafts in his strong, legible hand testify to many hours of writing. Informally, therefore, Rye was Senior Naval Officer, Humber. He had to reconcile the number of escorts available, of which there were never enough, with the demands of Hull merchants, some of whom wanted convoys delayed to await cargoes, while others wanted them to sail immediately. On 8 October 1807, for instance, four shipowners complained about delays to a convoy to the Baltic,

> detaining those Ships at a great expense in the Humber that were ready to join the *Charles* on the 8th ... We hope you will be pleased to take into consideration the great hardship we are under in having to wait at this advance season of the year, for the loading Ships that are expected to winter, and that you will be pleased to give directions for the *Charles* to proceed with those Ships that are ready on Saturday morning agreeable to the time fixt.

Yet the next day four different merchants wrote asking for the convoy to be delayed:

* Lieutenant Andrew Mott commanded HMAS *Prince William*, 1804 to 1812; Lieutenant Robert Hexter commanded HMAS *Charles* from 1807 to 1811.

From the very great quantity of manufactured goods known to be coming from Manchester, and their unexpected late arrival it will be almost impossible to get the ships down in time to join the Baltic convoy if it sails on the morning of the 10th. We therefore beg leave to solicit the favour of your allowing it to wait for the ships which will go from hence tomorrow at high water. On account of the Great Bustle which prevails in the harbour for all the ships to leave these Roads until that time and on this account we hope you will not consider our request improper or unreasonable.[69]

Rye had to solve these problems armed only with a junior naval rank. A large amount of the 'Great Bustle' in Hull was due to the vast amount of goods shipped to Heligoland.

It was no coincidence that the busy period between 1807 and 1810, dominated by the convoys to Heligoland, were good years for Peter Rye. He supervised the sailing of convoys from the Humber, recording each sailing in his log which paint a picture of constant movement in and out of the Humber, and also the arrival of warships with prizes. He took ships to Gambier's fleet in 1807 for the attack on Copenhagen, 'where he found 400 or 500 sails'. Through the summer of 1808 he was continuously at sea, chasing and checking every ship in sight, taking a Dutch prize in June. In September, in light winds, *Providence* beat off an attack on a convoy from Gothenburg by five Danish gun vessels. Admiral Douglas wrote that he 'highly approve(d) of your conduct and exertions on the occasion'.[70] Rye was similarly busy in 1809, managing in early July to include a two-day visit to Shields, the home port of most of his crew. This was unlikely to have been authorised, but the popularity of the visit can hardly be doubted. In October he escorted a convoy to Karlskrona, making his only passage through the Belt and into the Baltic.

In March 1810, before the Baltic convoys had re-started, *Providence* sailed down to Lynn looking for privateers or smugglers. In May Douglas allowed Rye to cruise after privateers 'within the limits of your command

and you will use the utmost vigilance to intercept any of the enemy's cruizers or vessels captured by them, but making the convoy service an object of primary importance and your absence from the Humber is never to exceed the period of seven days'. On 31 August 1810 Douglas hauled down his flag at Yarmouth, 'expressing my entire approbation of the manner in which you, Captain Mott and Lieutenant Mitchell have conducted yourselves and the convoy service at the Humber'.[71]

In contrast to Peter Rye, John Hancock had a lean time between 1807 and 1810. Without a ship, he went aboard HMS *Resolution* (74) as a volunteer on the expedition to Copenhagen, the captain, as he wrote to the Admiralty Board, 'having assented to receiving me if it meets their Lordship's approbation'. The letter is annotated: 'No objection'. When he reached Copenhagen, he found that new regulations prevented a half-pay officer from serving on a ship. He accompanied the army during the siege.[72] A succession of temporary commands followed. The first half of 1808 saw him as acting captain of the new 44-gun HMS *Lavinia*, Captain Lord William Stuart having leave of absence. He served off Rochefort, then escorted a convoy down to the Mediterranean, returning in September, though with some damage: 'Tiller broke and Rudder damaged by the Ship taking the Ground'. Hancock reported that Stuart was resuming the command on 19 October 1808, and his report to the Admiralty Secretary, William Wellesley Pole, was accompanied by his usual supplication to their lordships, emphasising his 'readiness to serve whenever they think proper'.[73] His next temporary command was the 80-gun Danish prize, HMS *Christian VII*, 2,132 tons, with a crew of 670, which he had to give up to Captain Sir Joseph Yorke on 27 April 1809, again with his usual request 'to make an offer of my Services wherever they may think proper'. A year later the well-connected Yorke was on the Board of Admiralty, and Hancock was asked for his opinion on the *Christian*

VII's sailing qualities. He gave a glowing report, 'The finest Man of War I ever was on board of ... never once missed stays', and once when 'working into Cawsand Bay with Sir John Duckworth's squadron, blowing very hard ... she came round like a top to the admiration of the whole fleet'.[74] Hancock's seamanship was clearly well-respected and the design of the *Christian VII* was copied when HMS *Cambridge* was launched in 1815.[75]

Professional reputation, however, was not yet enough to obtain the full command of an appropriate ship. In the second half of 1810, Hancock refused another acting captaincy, that of HMS *Monarch* (74) and also the regular command of HMS *Fisgard*, a 38-gun French prize, which had been captured in 1797 and had seen very hard service and, as it proved, was only two years from her final decommissioning. Finally, he was appointed to another Danish prize, the relatively new HMS *Nymphen* (36), though she mounted 42 guns. He took up the commission, as he wrote to the Admiralty Secretary, 'without loss of time'.[76] A year later, he was married.

Hancock's final period of service in the North Sea in HMS *Nymphen*, over 900 tons and with a crew of over 250, was a success. He served under Admiral Pellew during the admiral's ten-month North Sea command, during which *Nymphen* took a 14-gun French privateer. After Pellew moved on, Hancock served under Admiral Sir William Young, who commanded the blockade of the Scheldt. By February 1812 Hancock was commanding the blockading squadron off the Texel. In July of that year he was sent up to Shetland to protect the Greenland whaling ships, mostly from Hull.* In the early years of

* In the spring of 1808, the British briefly captured Torshavn on the island of Stromso in the Faroes, disarmed the garrison and spiked the guns in the fortifications defending the harbour. Lieutenant Thomas Baugh of HMS *Clio* (a Cruizer-class brig sloop) justified his actions because the harbour would have been 'a rendezvous for the enemy's men of war and privateers to have annoyed our Greenland trade homeward bound in the autumn and a protection to their vessels coming north about'. As this capture was not within his orders, Baugh wrote anxiously to the c-in-c, Leith, 'I trust my conduct will not meet your disapprobation as my motive for attacking Torshavn castle was merely to weaken the enemy's force and give greater security to the British trade' (Hattendorf et al., *British Naval Documents*, pp. 428–9, Baugh to Vashon, 21 May 1808).

the war, the main threat in these latitudes had been French privateers working out of Norwegian ports.[77] Very soon it was to be the Americans.

Nymphen's long and uneventful assignment had its own logistical problems. Hancock had to secure twelve bullocks when moored in Bressa Sound off Lerwick. Though she chased some suspicious sails, there were no prizes and a low expectation of reward brought discipline problems, including theft and drunkenness. On one day, five seamen received 182 lashes, followed the next day by 24 for another seamen for insolence.* The following day *Nymphen* supplied HMS *Cracker*, a gun brig, which was accompanying them, with a month's provisions.

In May 1813 Hancock took a convoy of sixty-one ships from Gothenburg to Yarmouth, when he most likely would have received his orders from Captain Peter Rye, by this time stationed at Gothenburg. His log is full of entries which show his disgust and frustration at the disorderliness of his merchantmen.[78] By mid-August, he was back on station off West Cappel, off the Dutch coast, responsible to Admiral Sir William Young. In November 1813 the admiral feared for the *Nymphen's* safety when her ship's boats were found drifting at sea. Young's description of his relief when he heard from Hancock goes beyond the normal formalities. 'I cannot describe the delight which your letter of 22nd afforded me, for I much feared that I would never see your handwriting again. I do most heartily congratulate you on your escape from danger.'[79]

The next year Hancock came to command a large new pitch-pine frigate, HMS *Liffey* (50), built rapidly to face the Americans, but all he was ordered to do was to take a convoy to Quebec in late August 1814, experiencing the usual violent autumn weather, and returning with another one. The ship was laid up in the summer of 1815, and John

---

* This episode of harsh discipline apparently had a lasting effect, for during the winter of 1812/13, 'no corporal punishment was inflicted aboard the *Nymphen*'. Admiral Young commented: 'considering the great number of foreigners among her crew (at least one fourth part of the whole) does great credit to the system of discipline Captain Hancock must have established...' (Marshall, *Naval Biography*, p. 28).

Hancock came ashore. He was never able to repeat the stylish achievements of his time in HMS *Cruizer* in the first years of the war.

Rye's period of independent command was soon to end. His anomalous
position in coordinating Humber convoys required direct correspondence with the Admiralty Secretary, saving time in sending information
to London, rather than through Vice-Admiral Douglas in Yarmouth, a
hundred miles to the south. This arrangement had worked well enough
while William Marsden and William Wellesley-Pole were Admiralty
Secretaries, but once the abrasive centraliser, John Wilson Croker, had
been appointed Admiralty Secretary in 1809, it was only a matter of
time before Rye's way of life was to change. Henceforth, Board approval
was needed for the sailing of all convoys and which ships were appointed
to escort in the Downs, Harwich, Yarmouth, the Humber and Cork.[80]
Rye's modest, informal command over the Humber was dismantled.
The merchants of Hull reacted by sending Croker a letter to be delivered personally by the MP for Hull, John Staniforth. The letter was, as
described by the merchant who drafted it, as

> signed by a majority of the most eminent merchants & ship owners of
> this place, in recommendation of the services you have afforded them,
> during your long residence on this unproductive station, and earnestly
> recommending you to their Lordships for promotion – being the spon-
> taneous wishes of the parties to whom you were personally unknown,
> but who duly appreciated your services in protecting the trade of
> Hull.[81]

This plea for promotion to post-captain was not well timed. At the end
of the year HMAS *Providence* and HMAS *Prince William* were ordered
to Cork on convoy duty, leaving on 13 January 1811 for Yarmouth for
orders.[82] There Rye was to hand over his responsibilities for the Humber,

a chastening experience, described by the Port Admiral, Rear-Admiral Lord Gardner, in his report to Croker: 'Captain Rye left at the Admiral's Office a Pacquet of Orders relating to the Duties performed by him while Senior Officer in the River Humber.'[83] No formal handover took place.

The ships made their way to Cork with a convoy, from which they escorted another one back to the Downs, via Portsmouth and thence back to Cork again. Transports then had to be escorted to Liverpool, reached in early April. By 4 May, a month later, the two ships were back in the Grimsby Roads. Rye was still acting senior officer in the Humber and indeed, soon received an order from Admiral Gardner (Douglas's successor) in Yarmouth to appoint a convoy for a ship to Spithead.[84] A Baltic convoy had to leave, but Andrew Mott of the *Prince William* was stricken by gout, 'confined to his Bed on shore in a Dangerous illness'. Rye therefore gave command of the convoy to a non-commissioned officer, Thomas Campbell, who had been master of the *Prince William* for seven years. He returned safely with six vessels on 29 June.[85]

Without a commissioned officer in command, the convoy was not by definition legal, which had insurance implications. Croker turned on Rye ferociously, annotating Rye's letter: 'Call upon him to account for his not having gone with the convoy himself in the *Providence*.' Rye in reply enclosed a copy of a letter from Vice-Admiral Robert Murray, the new commander-in-chief at Yarmouth, who had ordered him to remain at Grimsby. This excuse, Croker penned in reply, was not valid. 'Acquaint him that the Admiral's letter by no means authorises his having sent the convoy under the command of the master.' Rye had to apologise, which he did in a very short, tight-lipped letter to Croker. Two weeks later Rye's regular request to Croker for £10 for stationery expenses was refused, a petty response. Croker's letters to Admiral Murray now took a hectoring tone, asking why he did not 'order the *Providence* to take convoy and not to suffer her to continue an Useless Vessel?' Murray's answer was that a letter from John Barrow ordered him to ensure that a sloop was always on station to guard the Humber and that was what the *Providence* was doing.[86] By 13 July, Rye had left Hull with a convoy of eleven vessels to Gothenburg, where he was detained to oversee convoys, under the orders of the commander-in-chief, Baltic. During 1811, *Providence* sailed 5,000 miles.[87]

The winter followed a similar pattern to the previous year, with maintenance to be overseen in Grimsby dock. Then *Providence* set out on convoy duty again on 1 January 1812, escorting ships to Cork, then accompanying troop transports before arriving back again on the east coast. At the end of April she spent a week at Sheerness receiving stores, her first dockyard visit since 1804. She took a large convoy north, then sailed in June to Gothenburg and finally, on 29 July, escorted 138 ships, accompanied by three brigs, including the *Prince William*, back to the Nore. On 30 July *Providence* chased a privateer from the convoy. Ten days late Rye ordered a licensed Norwegian ship to join the convoy and gave a final tow to a slow galliot. The convoy reached the Little Nore on 14 August 1812. Rye then finally received his commission as a post-captain, dated 12 August. He made his last log entry in HMAS *Providence* at Sheerness: 'hauled down his pendant and put the Brig out of Commission' on 21 September 1812.[88] He had crossed the North Sea in her, there and back, thirty-four times, and had sailed 40,000 miles.

For the next year, from May 1813 to January 1814, Rye spent time as a post-captain in HMAS *Ceylon* anchored in Vinga Sand outside Gothenburg, coordinating convoys up through the Belt to the Baltic and back over the North Sea. He issued instructions, conveyed despatches, provided medical aid and supervised victualling arrangements. He was responsible to the commander-in-chief, Baltic, and did this well, receiving rare praise.* His final posting was to HMS *Porpoise* (16), a guardship at Harwich, an ignominious appointment for a man who had overseen the defence and trade protection of a critical part of

---

* Rye received the information from Commissioner Hartwell of the Navy Office that Admiral Hope was ' ... perfectly satisfied ... with your management of the business entrusted to your care' (NRO, Rye/X/7243/408, 25 October 1813; also Journal of HMAS *Ceylon*, Rye/X/7242/07, 8 April 1813–14, January 1814).

the North Sea. In September he retired, wracked with rheumatism.* For most of the war he had maintained his independence, but in the end the hierarchical ways of the navy, and the bureaucracy controlled by John Wilson Croker, beat him down.

Captains Rye and Hancock, both exemplary seamen, served for very long periods at sea, in the most difficult of waters, winter and summer. Peace in 1815 finished their seagoing careers when they were at the height of their powers and experience. Their failure to achieve further active promotions demonstrates the problems faced by those who lacked a powerful patron. Both had tricky decisions to make, including resisting Admiralty appointments to ships that by their condition or size would hamper their careers. With their different roles and temperaments, the two officers were major contributors to the maintenance of Britain's control of the North Sea. That dominance was achieved and maintained by junior officers who commanded brig sloops of no more than 300 tons.

---

* 'I was attacked by so severe a Rheumatism as to render me a complete cripple . . . it is only within these few days I have been sufficiently recovered to move without assistance from room to room . . .' (NRO, Rye/X/7244/095, draft, Rye to unnamed Admiralty official, 12 September 1814).

SIX

ESCORTING THE TROOPS
Europe and the Overseas Garrisons, 1803–1816

The Salisbury transport was lost on the Long Sand, on Tuesday night last, when 241 soldiers and part of the crew were drowned. The Captain is saved and is arrived at Deal. Thus, in a moment, more lives have been lost to their country than it cost to obtain possession of the Danish capital and arsenal.

Kentish Gazette, 20 November 1807[1]

Through the week all is bustle, every hand is employed, the same cheerfulness prevails, no cursing or swearing or rope's end is employed. The word of command or Boatswain's pipes is sufficient to set this mighty living machine in motion. Two evenings a week is devoted to amusement, then the Boatswain's mates, with their pipes summons 'All hands to play'. In a moment the scene is truly animating . . . Thus my time is passed in the midst of health, pleasure and contentment.

Private William Wheeler, 51st Regiment of Foot, on passage to Spain aboard HMS *Revenge* (74), February 1811[2]

Convoys had to protect the transports carrying the army to overseas operations and permanent garrisons. Once the troops were landed ashore, they had to be resupplied with stores, provisions and reinforcements, year in, year out. Britain had met with no military success in repeated expeditions against Continental Europe during the French

Revolutionary War, though much experience had been gained. Bitter memories remained over the convoy casualties wrecked in the Channel during the Abercromby-Christian expedition to the West Indies in 1795–6.[3] These misfortunes had to be set against the broad strategic success of overseas expeditions, when 135,000 British troops had been transported to five theatres of war, an effort which culminated in the dramatic success of the Egyptian expedition of 1801.[4]

After the Peace of Amiens, the French were even more militarily dominant on the European mainland. The British had control of the sea, enforced by blockade, and continuing superiority at sea made it possible to lessen the numbers of ships stationed outside Brest and Rochefort. British squadrons in the Baltic and Mediterranean increased correspondingly.[5] However, offensive operations on the French coast were limited to raids or rocket attacks and operations were restricted to the south at Naples (1805) and to the north in Heligoland and Copenhagen (1807), until the government tried using massive force to land troops on the Continent at Walcheren in 1809. This proved to be decisively unsuccessful.*

As the war continued, expeditions and supply convoys made longer and longer passages to more distant destinations. Safely escorted shipping gave Britain a great advantage over Napoleonic France. For instance, when the Emperor ordered thousands of veteran French soldiers in the Peninsula to move north across Europe to the Russian border during 1811 and 1812, as a preliminary to the invasion, they had no choice but to march overland for months, needing to be expensively fed on the way. It took a year for Napoleon to assemble his army on the Russian border.

By contrast, the British used convoys all the time for routine troop movements around the British Isles, as well as transporting them to

---

* Though there was a complicated confrontation in April 1809 in the exposed Aix Roads outside the River Charente, on which Rochefort is situated. Four French ships of the line were burnt, but an opportunity was missed to do further damage to what remained of the French Atlantic fleet (Rodger, *Command of the Ocean*, pp. 555–6; Davey, *In Nelson's Wake*, pp. 283–6).

foreign stations. Because of social and political unrest in Ireland, a heavy military presence was required there. Troop transports were constantly criss-crossing the Irish sea, which also had to be protected. Movements were constant, all year round, between Dublin and Liverpool, or from English south-coast ports to Cork and back. Convoys enabled the army to reach and maintain a presence overseas. Britain sent troop convoys north to Germany and the Baltic, and far south to Lisbon and Cadiz in order to achieve an unopposed landing. Overseas, they went regularly to India, the Cape, the West Indies and Canada, and occasionally to South America, Egypt and also in the Indian Ocean to the islands of Reunion and Mauritius, and in the last years of the war to North America.

A substantial and steadily increasing number of soldiers served abroad. By 1808 the figure was over 100,000 and this figure peaked at 180,991 in 1813.[6] Troops required for overseas garrisons varied with the ebb and flow of the conflict. By 1814 they were set at 73,500 officers and men.* The greater number of troops were transported and convoyed in the amphibious expeditions, examined later in this chapter. It is difficult to say exactly how many British and allied soldiers were transported near and far in convoys during the war against Napoleon, or later against America, allowances having to be made for replacements for repatriation of the wounded. If return journeys back to Britain are discounted, it is probably true to say that between 1803 and 1815 a quarter of a million soldiers were taken out, in large amphibious expeditions and routine supply convoys. This was, in other words, approximately double the number transported in the French Revolutionary War, though over a longer period.

Escorted transports full of troops, guns, horses, provisions and stores, therefore, could and often did travel long distances. The threat to

* The 1814 the total consisted of East Indies (India) 25,000, Leeward Islands 10,500, Canada and Nova Scotia 8,000, Jamaica 5,000, Gibraltar 5,000, Malta and Ionia 5,000, the Cape 4,000, Mauritius 3,000, Ceylon 3,000, Bahamas and Bermuda 1,000, Africa 800, for relief purposes 5,000 (Burnham & McGuigan, *British Army*, p. 5, quoting Wellington, *Supplementary Despatches*, vol. 14).

these convoys came from hostile weather rather than enemy action, as privateers were primarily seeking merchant cargoes, and, in any case, a transport containing perhaps two hundred soldiers, each armed with a musket and bayonet, was not easy to overcome. American privateers late in the wars did take army store ships from these convoys, ransacking and then ransoming them.* The average troop transport was, however, not large: it was over 200 tons, but often not much more and chartered from the market in London through agents.[7] As we shall see, winter storms and accidents exacted a heavy cost when these transports were shipwrecked, foundered or sunk by collision, amongst which were the horse transports, which had their own problems.†

There were many complaints about the small size of the transports, and the great length of time taken to embark and load a large convoy was a real disadvantage. So often the assembly of these convoys was delayed so that they were unable to sail until the dangerous winter months. General Sir John Moore noted that the average battalion needed seven or eight transports and thought that warships of 1,000 tons should be converted to troopships, the extra stowage capacity enabling them to bring stores and equipment belonging to the troops being transported. Disembarkation could then be accomplished more efficiently. His other objection was the independence and insubordination of the civilian masters, not subject to military discipline. 'What can a convoy of 200 small brigs do, commanded by north-country skippers,

---

* George Coggeshall, master of an American letter of marque in March 1814, captured four transport brigs from an outbound convoy to San Sebastian, taking cargo out and then giving each master his freedom. After taking provisions and other useful stores, he and his crew also helped themselves to 'officers' and soldiers' clothing, cocked hats, epaulettes, small arms, instruments of music etc' (Coggeshall, *Thirty-six Voyages*, pp. 176–7; for another instance of the taking of a military transport, see Glover, *Corunna to Waterloo*, p. 117).
† Each horse was transported in a sling which kept it upright, but the resulting pressure on the horse's abdomen could cause digestive problems. (The reader need not be troubled by the remedy for this blockage.) More harrowing was seasickness for horses, for they are unable to be sick, and as a result could turn violent. The animal would have to be put down. A pistol ball could not be used for fear of injuring someone in the confined space and the horse would be killed with an axe, an essential implement in the equipment of the regimental farrier. The carcass would then be hoisted out of the hold and slung into the sea (Gray, *Veterinary Surgeon*, p. 39).

who will do nothing but what they like themselves?' he complained in 1808.[8] A similar opinion was voiced by a subaltern in the Guards on a Peninsula transport, converted from a collier: the master was 'a drunken Northumbrian, familiar only with the North Sea', and his ship, 'an ugly, slow and leaky drowning machine – always going to leeward like a haystack'.[9] As ever, warship escorts had to slow their progress by sailing under bare poles or heaving to at regular intervals.*

There was considerable debate amongst politicians in 1811 about the possibility of converting larger warships, with their lower guns removed, to act as troopships to replace the much smaller transports. With France no longer in the possession of overseas territory or bases, the elder Lord Melville pointed out in the House of Lords that far too many ships of the line were still in commission, and put forward the idea of converting thirty to forty larger warships held in reserve to troopships.[10] Though wholesale implementation of this idea was rejected, it was adopted on an ad hoc basis.† Which service was ultimately responsible for discipline on board was a thorny issue and had previously led to high-level tensions in the French Revolutionary War, not entirely dispersed.[11] Another army officer, Henry Bunbury, writing in later years remembered: 'It was a badly arranged service, and equally disagreeable to the officers of the army and navy, who were always quar-

---

* Even here there were exceptions, as recorded by Samuel Jefferson in 1805 aboard the 300-ton *Mary Ann*, when bringing Russian troops from St Petersburg to Swedish Pomerania. His ship carried thirty-two Russian cavalry horses and men, but the escorting warships were overcrowded. One three-decker had 1,500 troops on board, in addition to the crew. 'The men of war got on so badly in the Gulf of Finland that we ran away from them off Dagherot and made the best of our way for Rugen Island' (Jefferson, *Merchant Marine*, p. 11).

† Private Wheeler of the 51st Regiment was taken to Spain in the relatively new HMS *Revenge* (74 guns, 1,954 tons, commissioned 1805). According to one military memoir, on 1 January 1811 the entire 28th Regiment sailed for the Peninsula from Plymouth in this large warship. One thousand two hundred men were aboard, with more than a hundred women. The ship lost its convoy and had a narrow escape when a fragment of burning tobacco fell into the rum issue. Though the flames were quickly doused on the deck, they spread up the rigging, eventually to be extinguished with wet blankets. 'Never do I remember anything like that thrilled to the depths of my soul like that cry of fire, on the wild waste of the waters'(Clammer, 'Soldier's Wives', pp. 62–3, quoting G. O'Neil, *The Military Adventures of Charles O'Neil* (Worcester, MA, 1851), pp. 38–40).

relling.'[12] The lack of flexibility between the services on this matter was criticised in Parliament.* In any case, there could be friction on the transports between the senior army officer and the transport agent, usually over accommodation.[13]

Regimental orders were detailed on questions of cleanliness, exercise (the men were to use dumb-bells) and firearms drills, and officers were to defer to the master of the ship on the question of smoking. Spirits were to be mixed with three parts water.[14] The jealousies between the officers contrasted with mutual dependence and good relations between seamen and soldiers when aboard ship, a judgement informed by anecdotal evidence.[15] What happened in port, after drink had been taken, might be another matter.

At least, by chartering the smaller merchant transports for military use, their similar size enabled them to maintain approximately equal speeds with trade ships to enable a convoy to keep together, though this was difficult enough, as we have seen. The Admiralty could therefore mix military and trade ships in one convoy without difficulty. Most of the army supplies came in mixed convoys, with government transports sailing alongside merchant ships.

Just one example of many of these routine movements took place in the summer of 1807, when a battalion of the 29th Regiment of Foot was ordered home from Nova Scotia after five years' garrison duty at the various forts, islands and settlements there. With its headquarters in Halifax, it had clearly been a successful deployment, since its citizens presented a silver chalice to the regiment on its departure. The convoy was to be escorted by HMS *Mermaid* (22), which had spent three years in the West Indies and needed a refit at a home dockyard. On 18 May

---

* The Earl of Galloway commented: 'The troopships to be commanded by sea officers, navigated by seamen, to whom the naval articles of war would apply; but would any reasonable man contend that from thence there could arise any difficulty of holding, when necessary, regimental courts martial on board troopships? To imagine such difficulty were to suppose the officers, both naval and military, to have laid aside all regard and attention to the interests and duties of the service to which they belong' (*Cobbett's Parliamentary Debates*, 17, 1810, col. 89).

38 officers and staff and 744 rank and file boarded 5 transports, the *Amphitrite, Crisis, Dominica, Sceptre* and *Zephyr*. The *Mermaid* took an army captain, lieutenant, 3 sergeants, a drummer and 65 privates to perform the duties of marines, as well as 30 French and Spanish prisoners of war. It was a quiet crossing. Day after day, the log merely records, 'Convoy in Company', with the occasional entry for reefing topsails. *Mermaid* chased two strange sails, one an American brig, the other *Princess Amelia*, a Jamaica packet, which did not stop until *Mermaid* fired a gun at her. Fog caused some excitement near the Isle of Wight, as it often does, and at least one of the transports had to wear suddenly off St Catherine's Point to avoid the shore, but on 20 July the convoy was standing in for St Helens. On 5 August *Mermaid* was anchored at the Nore, where she was decommissioned, with her crew turned over to HMS *Marlborough*.[16] As with many midsummer convoys, it was uneventful.

The routine of these regular convoys was interrupted by large amphibious operations, dictated by the strategic situation. Such expeditions were on an altogether grander scale. If all went well, they would leave British shores in the late spring, but delays could easily occur as they were the most complex organisational task attempted by the eighteenth-century British state. Coordination at Cabinet level was required between the Treasury, Admiralty, Navy Board, Transport Board, Victualling Board, Commander-in-Chief of the Army (the Horse Guards), War Office and Board of Ordnance.[17] The accumulation of sufficient stores and provisions for shipment was a significant task. Further transports had to be chartered. The purchase of the necessary extra provisions alone required a lead time of six months.[18] Smaller preparatory convoys, often from Ireland or Scotland, were sometimes needed to bring battalions of infantry or cavalry to ports of departure and all units had to march considerable distances to do so. They would gather at seaport towns so that embarkation could take place at the Downs, Spithead, Weymouth, Plymouth Sound or Falmouth. For the north of Europe, Harwich, Grimsby or Hull for the Humber or even

Leith was used.* One of the immediate problems was accommodation for the troops at the ports of embarkation, which led to the use of the Parkhurst Barracks on the Isle of Wight as a general army depot to which smaller units would be sent before being embarked on transports at Cowes. One soldier estimated in 1808 that two thousand soldiers were billeted there and he called it 'a complete hotbed of demoralization', with 'not more than from half a dozen to one hundred belonging to any one regiment'. He had to witness continual punishments during his brief stay. 'Drunkenness, disobedience of orders, absence from tattoo, roll-call, breaking out of barracks at night, petty pilfering etc were the usual crimes that called the <u>cat</u> into play.'[19]

A total of thirty convoyed combined or amphibious expeditions took place between 1803 and 1815, of which fifteen were of major, strategic importance.† Eight of the latter were broadly successful, or not opposed by the enemy, furthering British war aims, of which the 1807 expedition to Copenhagen, and the concurrent taking of Heligoland, must be accounted the most successful. The continuous landings of the army in Ostend and its nearby beaches in May and June 1815 before Waterloo constituted the most confused and hastily arranged.

Those expeditions that have been most analysed were those which were successful in landing the army, but which subsequently met with military failure. These include several convoys resulting in landings in Montevideo and Buenos Aires in 1806 and 1807, General Mackenzie's

* Hull and Grimsby were used to embark troops for Copenhagen in 1807. The 7th and 8th Regiment of Foot had come from Ireland and had marched from Liverpool via York across to Hull. An unusually positive comment on early nineteenth-century soldiery appeared in the *Hull Packet*, 28 July and 4 August 1807, which reported that twenty-eight ships had arrived at Grimsby to embark the King's German Legion, who had 'obtained the respect of the inhabitants of this place to a particular degree, by the exemplary order and propriety of their conduct'.
† Davey, *In Nelson's Wake*, chapter 8; Marcus, *Age of Nelson*, p. 401. Wareham, *Star Captains*, has a comprehensive list of the thirty expeditions, pp. 153–5, together with participating frigates, useful to demonstrate how these ships were used, thus making them unavailable for convoying.

landing in Egypt in 1807, and the landing of the army led by General Sir David Baird at Corunna in late 1808 and its subsequent evacuation in January 1809. The huge Walcheren expedition managed to get to sea in late July 1809, but had been delayed by contrary winds.[20] Although Flushing was bombarded and taken, the main objective of reaching Antwerp and destroying the shipbuilding yard there was never considered achievable once the expedition had reached the Scheldt. The army was then destroyed by Walcheren fever, with nearly four thousand deaths and over eleven thousand sick.[21] These misjudged episodes left much evidence for historians in the papers of subsequent Boards of Enquiry.*

By contrast, two 'conjunct' operations were so unsuccessful that they have been largely ignored, because on these occasions the army never fired a shot in anger and slunk home. Sir John Moore's expedition of ten thousand troops, which arrived in Gothenburg in May 1808 to bolster the Swedish state, had the makings of a farce, faced as he was by the unstable Swedish King who, it turned out, did not want any help. The troops did not land and Moore was fortunate not to have been made prisoner by the King.[22]

More than a year earlier, the government's decision to send 26,000 troops to defend Hanover in late 1805, which was dependent on Prussian good will, floundered when the latter hesitated on hearing of Napoleon's successes at Ulm and Austerlitz. Eventually, on 10 December 1805, HMS *Leopard* (50), with two gun brigs, set off with 120 transports with Lord Cathcart's force of 26,000 from the Downs. It immediately hit a severe north-easterly gale, with hail and snow. Many ships, including the escorts, returned to the Downs, but on 14 December the *Jenny* and the *Ariadne* transports went on shore near Calais, with over four hundred soldiers made prisoner. Among those aboard the *Jenny* were six young children, one of which was born the night before the

---

* Details of further successful examples of amphibious operations can be gained from the Timeline appendix. They include the occupation of Madeira (1807), Guadeloupe (1810), Reunion (1810), Mauritius (1810) and Java (1811).

grounding. According to the *Moniteur*, they were well treated before being marched off to prison.[23] But others did not escape with their lives. The *Maria*, with 270 troops on board, went on the Haak sands in a snowstorm. Some clung to the rigging: only twenty survived. The *Isabella* was wrecked in the Texel, with just half of the three hundred soldiers saved. The *Aurora* went down with three hundred, including the commanding officer and entire staff of the Cameronians. Those ships which returned to the Downs and Harwich set out again on 22 December, but another gale hit them. By this time there was ice on the river Weser. The *Helder*, a large converted Dutch prize with six hundred soldiers on board, went ashore at the Helder: in spite of strenuous attempts to save her by the boats of the escort HMS *Regulus*, all were taken prisoner when they reached the shore.[24] Sailing in midwinter, most of the expedition had not even reached the Continent, yet a thousand soldiers had drowned and over four hundred had been taken prisoner.*

The success of the Copenhagen operation, which started on 7 September 1807, was blighted by heavy loss of life on the homeward passage. The convoy left on its homeward voyage on 3 October, at the signal gun fired by one of the escorts, HMS *Inflexible* (64), known to be a bad sailer. Four days later, according to the Captain's log, fifty-three ships were in company and by 25 October off the Scaw, having joined another convoy, which by now totalled 189 ships. Two days later, the *Inflexible* 'ran foul' of a very large transport, the *Augustus Caesar*, with five hundred troops aboard.† Ten minutes after the collision the transport's main mast came down, five minutes later it was followed by the mizzen. It was nearly an hour before the ships got clear of each other.[25]

---

* This weather took a terrible toll on the cavalry horses. Some were landed from a transport at Chatham after spending three weeks at sea. When their slings were removed, 'they lay down at once and were only got up with difficulty' (*Times*, 22 January 1806; Grocott, *Shipwrecks*, p. 210).

† The log of the *Inflexible* uses the phrase 'ran foul'. *Lloyd's List* called the *Augustus Caesar* a 'very fine' transport, indicating that she was new, which would account for the fact that she did not break up on the Dutch coast, allowing the troops to escape with their lives, if not with their freedom (TNA, ADM 51/1686; *Lloyd's List*, 16 November 1807).

The boats of the warship took off 130 of the troops, but the *Augustus Caesar* drifted helplessly towards the Dutch coast, with only her foremast standing. All those left aboard survived to be taken prisoner.[26]

Worse was to follow. When the transports reached the Yarmouth Roads, they were not allowed into the congested waters of the River Yare in the port and were ordered down Channel to Portsmouth. On 19 November on their way south they were hit by a gale. The *Salisbury* was lost with 241 men, the *Eagle* packet with 180 of the King's German Legion 7th Line Battalion. The *Endeavour* transport struck on the Goodwin Sands: twenty-four men and twenty-three horses of the 3rd Light Dragoons of the King's German Legion perished. A further two horse transports were sunk, one of them run down in the Dover Roads. In all, nearly five hundred soldiers of the King's German Legion lost their lives.[27] The same storm caused two big losses from a small convoy in the Irish Sea, both the *Rochdale* and the *Prince of Wales* packet taking troops from Dublin to Liverpool. Not long after leaving they hit the gale. They tried to turn back but ran ashore on the south side of Dublin Bay. The soldiers were volunteers for the Queen's Own German Regiment and from the Cork and Mayo Regiments: 267 in all died from both ships. From the *Prince of Wales*, the master, crew and two ladies were saved, but 150 soldiers who were below were drowned.* According to one report, 'On the following day, the 20th, the shore presented a frightful scene. From Dunleary to Blackrock, it was almost literally covered with the dead bodies of men, women and children.'[28]

A happier outcome from the stormy weather of the winter of late 1807 concerned the transport *Antiope*, which was carrying part of the 90th Regiment of Foot from Portsmouth to Cork, leaving on 20 December. On Christmas Day, with the Irish shore in sight, the wind

---

* The severity of the storm of 19 November 1807 cannot be in doubt. The *Hampshire Telegraph*, 30 November 1807, reported: 'Nine miles from Holyhead, the mail coach, on the 19th, stuck fast in the snow, nor could any help extricate it until the next day, when thirteen men and many cart horses were employed. The wind was so strong, that the horses would not face it nor could the men keep their feet.'

rose, went round to the west, accompanied by thick fog. With the pumps clogged, the soldiers baling, the ship ran before the wind towards the Welsh coast. All on board were five days without a change of clothing and starving, 'the ship was left to the mercy of the waves, sailors and soldiers fell on their knees to prayers for deliverance from their dreadful situation.' The ship drifted into St Bride's Bay on the Pembrokeshire coast, ringed with high cliffs, but in spite of a small number of casualties, most managed to get ashore. The next day 243 men of the 90th Regiment marched into Haverford West. The report concluded: 'In the midst of this shocking scene, a soldier's wife was delivered of a fine boy and both are likely to do well.'[29]

The Transport Board's charter party drove a hard bargain and shipowners had to provide a great deal of equipment; amongst the specifications were at least six carriage guns, with twenty rounds for each gun; coppers and furnaces; platters; spoons; candles and lanterns for the use of the troops. Pumps and buckets were to be provided for water for the horses. To ensure that the vessel was adequately manned, a scale was used which determined that for every 100 tons burthen, the ship had to carry five men and a boy.[30] Critically, the shipowner was responsible for keeping the ship in repair. If it was unable to perform its agreed service, the owner was fined, as in the case of the *Harry Morris*, owned by Michael Henley of Wapping, which was at Spithead in March 1811 when it missed its Lisbon convoy because two of its crew deserted just before sailing. The master hired two more men, the ship chased the convoy down the Solent to the Needles, but did not catch it. The Transport Board pronounced that the ship 'will be out of Pay until she proceeds with the next Convoy, and will be mulcted for short complement'. Henley duly 'noted protest', sworn before a notary, but the Board could see 'no reason to alter their decision in this case'. The ship arrived in Lisbon only five days after the original convoy.[31]

At the height of these expeditions, the transports never stopped. 1809 was one such year. Henley's ships furnish a number of examples: the *Hawke* took troops to the Baltic via Gothenburg, then to Rostock, Memel, Karlskrona; then back to Spithead and from there to Corunna; back to Plymouth, then Portsmouth, down to the Channel Islands, before ending in Portsmouth. In the same year, between January and September, another of Henley's ships, the *Lady Juliana*, sailed from London to Portsmouth.* She then sailed with troops and horses to Lisbon, back to Plymouth, then Portsmouth, Ramsgate, Flushing and Deptford.[32] Nor should one forget the stores that supported the army. In July 1809, for instance, the *Fame* was convoyed to Cadiz with a cargo of gunpowder, but returned early the next year with a mixed commercial cargo: wine, tobacco, tallow, wool, copper, bark, cochineal and balsam.[33]

As a result of this constant use, repairs on the transports were neglected. The owner had to make a judgement on the risk to a vessel: whether or not to lose income and repair it, or to continue with the government contract and hope for the best. The consequences of unseaworthy transports could be tragic. The *Alexander* was an old hospital ship on the long passage from Montevideo, returning with 110 wounded soldiers as well as some widows of officers who had been killed, after the ill-conceived expedition there of 1806/7. The ship left in a convoy led by HMS *Unicorn* (38) and HMS *Thetis* (38) on 9 August 1807. Being very leaky, the master of the *Alexander* had to shorten sail, and lost sight of the convoy, but reached the North Atlantic between 39th and 40th lat. North. The leak then became unstoppable, the ship was

---

* The *Lady Juliana*, 397 tons, was by this time over thirty years old, having been built in Whitby in 1778. Before Henley owned her, the ship had been to Botany Bay with the Second Fleet. Henley had purchased her in 1791 (for £650) and sold her in 1825 (for £3,200, allowing for wartime inflation), underlining the fact that the efficiency (and sale price) of a wooden ship depended not on age, but on the quality and regularity of refitting and repair, and of its day-to-day maintenance. In the thirty-four years that Henley owned her, the ship had been almost everywhere in the northern hemisphere, making money for her owner: Archangel, Riga, Honduras, Quebec, and had carried troops on several expeditions (Currie, *Henley's*, p. 33; NMM, HNL/77/37–73).

abandoned in calm weather, but suddenly foundered with women and most of the sick soldiers still aboard. The captain had abandoned ship and left in a small boat, but thirteen sailors, fifteen soldiers, a woman and child managed to get away in the long boat, taking with them 3 gallons of spirits, 1 pound of raisins and four biscuits. An American ship found the boat six days later, 'during which seven soldiers died, two of whom lay dead in the boat when they came alongside; they had cut one man up and had eaten of his flesh; some remained in the boat when they saw the ship; but on seeing her they threw it overboard.'[34]

The condition of another transport, the *William*, is described in detail by the retrospective journal of Private John Morris Jones of the 2nd Battalion of the 39th Foot, which set off from Falmouth to Malta on 20 February 1808. HMS *Antelope* (50) led a convoy of forty ships. 'Our little brig was a slow sailing, clumsy old craft, formerly a South Shields collier,' according to Jones, 'I should utterly fail, were I to attempt to describe the compound of vile smells ascending from between decks. The breaths and exhalations proceeding from so many human bodies crowded below, added to the smells of pitch, tar and bilge water, from the depths of the hold, baffles all description.'[35]

The brig was the slowest sailer in the convoy and at the approach of nightfall was urged to close up by the escort. The master shook out some reefs, against his better judgement, but the added strain of faster speed started a leak in the bows of the ship and the pumps were immediately manned. The ship filled quickly, the provisions were underwater and the wind got up. Unhelpfully, the convoy commodore in HMS *Antelope* (50) answered the transport's signal of distress by ordering the master to make his best way to Gibraltar. A long night followed. The pumps choked, then broke and were mended, using leather from people's shoes. By the morning of 24 February, the wind eased and at six a.m. the *Antelope* sent a carpenter aboard, who pronounced the situation hopeless. The order was given to abandon the *William*. The other troopships closed up and sent their boats, and everyone rapidly scrambled off the ship, with no chance to collect personal possessions. Twenty minutes later the *William* sank. The captain of the company, for whom Jones had unbridled contempt, 'lost not a single particle of his baggage – all had been carefully preserved, even to his two pointer dogs'.

Jones now found himself aboard a much better troopship, the *Richard*, but contrary winds delayed arrival at Gibraltar until the middle of March. Here he was put on another transport, 'a crazy, leaky old craft', the *Minerva*, in which he had travelled before. Again, he described bad conditions, 'the creaking of badly fitted bulkheads, the groaning of rickety timbers, the oozing of water through the deck of our berths – all conspired to make us devoutly wish for the termination of our voyage.' Jones eventually reached Syracuse in Sicily, where after making complaints he eventually secured a berth to Malta aboard the troopship HMS *Monarch*, an old 74 cut down to a troopship, arriving on 7 April. His journey had taken forty-six days in four ships.[36]

The deteriorating condition of hired transports was raised in September 1810 when Admiral Berkeley, commander-in-chief, Portugal, wrote to the First Lord of the Admiralty, Charles Philip Yorke from Lisbon, though in a private rather than an official letter: 'The Transports in this River are most of them in so dreadful a state from being copper'd over iron fastenings, and being patched up for the sake of Hire, that some of them are not actually fit to trust to sea with Troops, and have been condemned on Survey.'[37] Those transports which were copper-sheathed were paid a higher rate per month, but were not normally copper-bolted; the electrolytic action weakened the old iron bolts leading to leaks and worse.

The main military task for convoys in this war was supplying the Peninsular army from 1808, throughout summer and winter until 1814. Overall, 175 convoys were to leave British ports for Lisbon and the Mediterranean between 1808 and 1814, protecting 4,896 ships south. One hundred and twenty-five convoys returned to Britain containing

3,865 ships. Some of the largest convoyed over a hundred merchant ships, some a handful, but the average was between twenty-five and thirty-three ships per convoy.[38] The destinations of these south-going convoys were mixed three ways. Some went only to supply the army at Lisbon, Oporto or Cadiz, or later in the war the north coast of Spain at Santander or Passages. Others were mixtures of transports and merchant ships, sometimes destined for the Mediterranean, but some could be putting into Lisbon. Calculation of exactly how many convoys or ships went to support the Peninsular armies is therefore not possible.[39] Outgoing convoys faced the considerable difficulty of beating across the Bay of Biscay against the prevailing south-westerlies. They were heavily laden, bringing fresh troops, artillery, horses with their feed for the cavalry and for the wagon train, and provisions for the soldiers. By the end of the war, Wellington's increased army was consuming 40 tons of biscuit a day.[40]

Troop convoys began sailing to the Peninsula at the very end of 1807. Political trouble had been brewing for Napoleon in Spain during this year, watched closely by the British government, which ordered a small force of five thousand troops under Major-General Sir Brent Spencer to Lisbon. His sealed orders told him that if his force could not get ashore in Portugal, he was to proceed to Gibraltar. As with the case of the Hanover expedition, the convoy left from Spithead desperately late, on 20 December 1807. The convoy commodore was Captain Robert Corbet aboard HMS *Neriede* (36). Shortly after weighing anchor, the ships were becalmed. Against naval regulations, the army officers made visits between ships. Predictably, this was followed by a gale on Christmas Day and every ship in the convoy, except the *Neriede* and one other, gave up and ran back to Falmouth. They did not leave Falmouth for nearly two months, sailing on 23 February. Unsurprisingly, the convoy was far too late to make an entry into Lisbon as the French had already occupied the city. It sailed on and reached Gibraltar on 12 March 1808, at which Spencer's force, too small to make a difference, was largely ineffectual until it joined Wellesley's army in Portugal later in the year.[41] It was not an auspicious beginning.

The two 1808 midsummer troop convoys to the Peninsula, on the other hand, were brilliant successes. Wellesley's army of nine thousand landed in Montego Bay on 1 August. His already assembled force in Cork had been destined for an attack on the Spanish empire, but the orders to go to Portugal were issued hurriedly to take advantage of the Spanish uprising against the French occupation. Seventy-five transports cleared Cork Harbour on 12 July 1808. The landing was assisted by an advance guard of 320 marines from Admiral Cotton's fleet, which held the fort at Figueiras, commanding the bay.[42] It was a successful period for British convoys. In the same month, General Romana's army of nine thousand Spanish troops, previously allied to the French, was spirited away in thirty-six transports from Denmark to Santander in northern Spain. Organised by Rear-Admiral Sir Richard Goodwin Keats, it was an impressive display of naval and mercantile convoy discipline.[43]

The second expedition ordered in response to the Spanish uprising against Napoleon in May 1808 was to send 12,500 troops under General Sir David Baird, who sailed to Corunna in north-west Spain in September of that year with 200 infantry and horse transports. Baird arrived in mid-October, so that his army could join up with the army of Portugal, by now commanded by Sir John Moore.[44] The transports stayed there and at nearby Vigo.

It was as well they did. The British army retreated back to Corunna in confusion and were evacuated under fire between mid and late January 1809. Twenty-nine thousand troops were taken back to England with a following, but rising, wind by 227 infantry and cavalry transports, victuallers, forage and store ships, all of them crowded with sick and exhausted soldiers.[45] The last ships to leave were large warships. One of them, the first-rate *Ville de Paris*, took General Baird and his staff, 743 soldiers, 40 wives and 7 children; together with 600 crew, the ship carried 1,300 people in total back to England.[46] It was rather a four- or five-day straggle than a convoy, being hit by a gale as they reached the Channel. The *Dispatch* transport, with seventy

7th Light Hussars and thirty-four horses aboard, struck the rocks on the Cornish coast near the Manacles; the master was allegedly drunk in his berth. Only six survived. The *Smallbridge* struck the coast with two hundred King's German Legion on board; there were no survivors.* In spite of these losses, the British had been lucky. The official despatch of Rear-Admiral Michael de Courcy, who commanded a squadron at Corunna, pointed out, 'Had the Wind been otherwise than Southerly the whole of the shipping would probably have been lost.' This sentence was carefully omitted from the public printing of the despatch.[47]

Partly as a result of the setbacks and reversals of early 1809, Wellington was constantly short of seasoned, trained troops in the Peninsula. A frenzy of convoy activity in March and April brought soldiers from Britain so that by May he had 23,000 troops.[48] By September 1810 he had 40,000 and 6,000 horses.[49] His army slowly expanded, although sickness and casualties in action were a constant drain on his strength. In the year as a whole, 20,000 additional troops were sent out from Britain. Seventeen convoys escorted 429 ships to Portugal, but a further 21 brought 635 ships, listed as for both Lisbon and the Mediterranean.† In all, in May 1813, 259 transports were supporting the army in the Peninsula, in a number of roles, and a stream of drafts of soldiers supplemented battalions already serving in the Peninsula, though fewer soldiers were sent in 1813.[50] Wellington sent one untrained infantry battalion to Gibraltar, by convoy, to allow a more experienced one to take its place.[51] In 1813, the number of convoys and ships to the Peninsula more than doubled, surprising in view of the other demands on government transports in that year, particularly to

---

* By a terrible coincidence, two hours after the *Dispatch* struck the rocks, and only a mile away, HMS *Primrose*, an 18-gun sloop, escorting an outgoing convoy of thirty ships to Corunna, was also wrecked, and 120 seamen were lost (TNA, ADM 7/64; Grocott, *Shipwrecks*, p. 273).

† One convoy that left Cork for Lisbon in May 1812 was escorted by HM ships *Leonidas* and *Leopard* with the 1st Battalion of 5th Regiment of Foot, numbering 1,025. Also in the convoy was the *Archduke Charles* transport bound for Botany Bay, which left the convoy after it reached the latitude of Lisbon (TNA, ADM 1/624, Admiral Thornborough to Croker, 16 May 1812; Sutcliffe, 'Bordeaux to Ostend', p. 4).

North America after the outbreak of war. What is remarkable is the number and size of winter convoys: 14 convoys with a total of 525 ships were sent south in November and December.*

Transporting horses across the Bay of Biscay to Portugal posed particular difficulties and it was little wonder that Wellington continually complained about a lack of them.† In January and February 1810, for instance, Cornet John Luard of 4th Dragoons took forty-two horses in the *Perseverance* transport to Lisbon. They marched from Guildford to Plymouth in 'exceedingly cold weather'. Crossing Dartmoor was 'very disagreeable'. Unsurprisingly, given the time of year, they had a grim passage to Lisbon, leaving Plymouth on 24 January. While good progress was made for the first four days, sixteen days of gales followed, 'as severe as ever I saw them when in the navy'.‡ Near the mouth of the Tagus, the transport was becalmed and had to cut her anchor cable to escape drifting onto rocks. Two horses died during the passage.[52]

On return to Britain, the ships carried officers on leave, the sick and wounded and prisoners of war. All of the latter had to be heavily guarded. This was by no means an easy task. On board the transport *Frances* in October 1810, one Royal Marine officer, Richard Fernyhough, had only 15 marines to guard 270 French prisoners. Contrary hard gales, easterly and south-easterly, kept them at sea for a month. The ship lost touch with the convoy and for three nights was clawing its way off the rocks off the Scilly Isles. In this situation, he wrote a letter to his family in case he managed to find another homegoing ship:

---

* The Admiralty sent the following statistics of Peninsular and Mediterranean convoys and ships to Lloyd's: Peninsula only: 48 convoys, 1,395 ships. Lisbon and Mediterranean: 22 convoys, 1,218 ships. Total sent south in 1813: 70 convoys, 2,613 ships (TNA, ADM 7/64).
† Wellington wrote to Lord Bathurst, Secretary of State for War, 28 July 1812, after the battle of Salamanca: 'I likewise request your Lordship not to forget horses for the cavalry and artillery.' Two weeks later he wrote to Admiral Cotton, 'I am sadly apprehensive that our horses will fall off terribly before the campaign will be over.' In any case, Wellington's horses were ultimately dependent upon green forage, which did not appear in the countryside until the spring, a factor that regulated the speed of his advance northward, as he pointed out to the Prime Minister, Lord Liverpool, in a letter of 23 November 1812 (Gurwood, *Wellington Dispatches*, IX, pp. 318, 347, 564).
‡ Luard cannot have been in the navy for long as he was never commissioned.

I am obliged to keep a sharp look out, as we are daily nearing the French coast, having no particular desire to have my throat cut. I have generally for my bedfellows a brace of loaded pistols and my sword, and the men follow my example. The nights being very dark, I never permit more than a few upon deck at one time to breath the fresh air . . . If they do not make an attempt to carry the ship into a French port, I must confess I shall consider them a set of very inoffensive fellows.

The prisoners below suffered miserably during the gale. He also had to deal with insubordination from the guard and threatened to 'shoot the first man that flinched from his duty'. Then the ship managed to hail a warship, and Fernyhough explained his predicament. Rockets and blue lights were supplied for use if there was trouble. Finally, the wind went to the south-west and the transport was soon back in Spithead. Fernyhough rounded off his account by remarking, 'During one of the gales, we threw overboard several of the unfortunate Frenchmen, who had died during the passage from illness.'[53]

In spite of these mishaps, naval capacity to move troops and equipment gave British troops critical logistical advantage over France in the Peninsula. Seaborne support for the defence of Cadiz, which lasted from February 1810 until August 1812, kept the French army in Andalusia at bay. The greatest support was given to Wellington and his army. During the defence of the lines of Torres Vedras, north of Lisbon, not only did the navy protect his flank with gunboat and signalling, but transports were kept in the Tagus in case the army had to be evacuated. By March 1811 256 transports totalling 75,000 tons were at the ready. In one historian's judgement: 'The risks involved in the retreat through Portugal in 1810 could never have been accepted without this maritime insurance policy.'[54]

Once British, Portuguese and Spanish troops began to advance northwards, keeping close to the coast, convoys kept them supplied, using Passages and Santander during and after the siege of San Sebastian. The north coast of Spain is a notoriously difficult coast, with deep water and few harbours. Wellington's lack of appreciation of maritime constraints was marked. Historians have emphasised friction between the army and navy, but much was achieved by cooperation at local level. The irascible (younger) Lord Melville, by now First Lord of the Admiralty, wrote to the prickly Wellington in mid-1813: 'I will take your opinion in preference to any other person's as to the most effectual mode of beating a French army, but I have no confidence in your seamanship or nautical skill.' Wellington wrote back: 'All that is required from His Majesty's navy is to convoy the supplies for the army coming from England and elsewhere, and to convoy back the empty transports.'[55] Wiser heads in London replied to Wellington in more moderate tones.

One of the other dangers for transports in a convoy was collision. Poor visibility was usually the cause, particularly during long winter nights. Often these incidents were not of much consequence, with perhaps damage to rigging from entanglement, repaired by the crew.[56] But they could be much more serious, as in a sudden accident in February 1811 in the Channel. A 36-gun frigate, HMS *Franchise*, Captain John Allen, was taking a convoy of ninety-one ships from Plymouth to Lisbon and the Mediterranean. A French prize, she was unusually large for an escort for military transports, 143 foot long and 898 tons. The convoy left on 19 February, among which was the *John and Jane* transport, which was one of several taking the 11th Regiment of Foot to Cadiz. On board were 252 soldiers, wives, children and crew. After a gentle start down Channel with a south-easterly wind, off Falmouth it started to blow fresh from the southwest. Allen headed for shelter in Carrick Roads in Falmouth harbour, but by the time the convoy reached the entrance, it was too dark to enter.

Off the coast, at three a.m. on 21 February, the signal was given to tack by gunfire, at the same time as a squall hit the convoy, the crew of the *Franchise* reefing the sails. It was too late. The ship was travelling extremely fast, estimated at nine knots, a huge speed for an escort.

She hit the *John and Jane* amidships. One of the *Franchise*'s officers described the conditions as,

> uncommonly dark, squally and raining, in the act of wearing this ship ran on board a transport, and from the velocity with which we were going at the time the shock was so great that we very nearly cut her in two and she sank under our bows in less than five minutes . . . The darkness of the night, the howling of the wind, the cries of the poor fellows in the water, together with the view of several bodies lying on the wreck of the spars, presented a scene of indescribable horror.[57]

A few seamen, an ensign, three sergeants and nineteen soldiers from the transport managed to scramble aboard the *Franchise*. Two hundred and fifty-five officers and soldiers drowned, with fourteen women, seven children and six seamen. Captain Allen took the *Franchise* and the convoy into Falmouth, anchoring in Carrick Roads.[58] Further tragedy struck when a boat with the three surviving sergeants onboard capsized.

The major in command of the battalion tried, by writing to the Adjutant-General, to get an enquiry into the incident, maintaining that the accident was due to faulty orders regarding navigation lights and unclear signalling instructions. Despite a promise from the First Lord of the Admiralty, nothing transpired. One officer commented that had the *John and Jane* shown lights in answer to the signal made, 'there can be no doubt but the catastrophe would not have happened'. What he did not explain is why the warship was going so fast. Almost certainly, Allen's lack of convoy experience played a part. His subsequent naval career did not flourish.* The convoy did not set out again until mid-March, reaching Cadiz by 27 March. The still-shaken

---

* Allen was about 37 years old at the time of the collision and had been made a post-captain in 1802, but had not served afloat for eight years from the time of his promotion until 1810 when appointed to the *Franchise*. He appears never to have commanded a convoy before. His curious seagoing career ended soon after this and his last appointment was Agent for Prisoners of War in Newfoundland, 1813–15. He had a large pension for wounds, though he did not die, a rear-admiral, until 1853 (O'Byrne, *Naval Dictionary*).

battalion was inspected by a major-general in mid-May: he commented on their 'loose marchings and inaccurate formations'.[59]

Worse was to come. On 26 December 1813 HMS *Melpomone* took a convoy of nine transports from Lisbon, bound for Portsmouth. After a rough passage, the warship brought eight of them to anchor into a crowded Carrick Roads, south of Trefusis Point opposite Falmouth Town, on 7 January 1814. The transport which arrived late, the large, copper-sheathed *Queen*, 358 tons, with a crew of 21, was later said to have stopped at Passages on her way north. On board were some French prisoners of war, 325 invalided artillerymen and soldiers of the 30th Regiment of Foot, accompanied by 63 women and 58 children. The total number of passengers was 473; by any measure, the *Queen* was overloaded. By the time they anchored off Falmouth, there can have been no one on board who did not think that they were safe in England.

The succession of events was witnessed by John Bechervaise, master of a ship half a cable ahead of the *Queen*, who recorded that she came to anchor on 13 January. The wind went round to the south-east, which leaves the anchorage very exposed. It was clear from the sky that a gale was coming. The minute guns were firing out in the Roads to warn of the impending gale. The *Queen*, however, had only one anchor down, possibly because this stop in Falmouth was only temporary before setting out for Portsmouth. The other was ready to be let go with the cable ranged out on the deck. Berchevaise claimed that the *Queen* fired guns from eleven p.m. onwards, which would tend to confirm reports that the master, Joseph Carr, was ashore. A violent squall with snow came at five a.m. and the ship started to drift, 'but at the moment the men who had the watch called out, men, women and children rushed up the hatchway, and so completely filled the range, that to have let go the anchor must have crushed nearly all those in the range to death, and before they were removed, the ship was on the rocks'.[60] According to Berchevaise, the ship hit a rock 40 yards from the Trefusis Point shore. Within three-quarters of an hour the ship had broken up, was on her side and in two pieces.

It is hard not to conclude that her old iron bolts were rotten, worn away by the electrolytic action caused by more recently applied copper sheathing.* 369 people died. Only a handful of women survived. Only two of the crew were lost. In 1827 a publication alleged that the master and the crew had been ashore, 'and many were intoxicated'.[61] Mass graves were dug in local churchyards. Three memorials were erected. The best-preserved today is in the churchyard at nearby Mylor.

The early months of 1814 saw more troop movements as the war against Napoleon reached a crescendo. The Haak Sands off the Texel claimed more lives as troops were moved to Holland for the operation against Bergen-op-Zoom in early March 1814.[62] Militia units were sent to still-troublesome Ireland. So many stores were being brought back from Spain that transports were congested in the Thames. Strict convoy discipline had to be maintained because war against the United States was still continuing.

Twenty thousand Peninsular veterans were transferred to the North American theatre of war, sailing directly from French ports to Halifax and Quebec. By October 1814 there were over two hundred transports on the North American station and the number would rise until well into 1815.[63] Casualties continued. Three troopships sank in the St Lawrence. The survivors of the *Charlotte* transport managed to survive for thirty-seven days in June on the island of Anticosti in the Gulf before being picked up by a warship. In October the *Sovereign* transport, sailing at seven knots, struck a rock on the island of St Paul, between Cape Breton Island and Newfoundland. Out of 239 soldiers, women, children and crew, only 27 were saved. On 30 April 1815, a converted 36-gun frigate, the *Penelope*, was wrecked on the Gaspé Peninsula, in very cold weather; some of the soldiers mutinied, some succumbed to the cold, though the majority of the crew reached Quebec in other transports.[64]

* There is further reason to think that the *Queen* was not in good condition, as it was chartered on 27 February 1813 at a time when the Transport Board was having difficulty in obtaining transports. Shipping demand had been stimulated by Napoleon's Moscow defeat in 1812. Charter rates rose to the high level of 30 shillings per ton per month (Sutcliffe, *Expeditionary Warfare*, p. 228). I am grateful to Bob Sutcliffe for further details on the *Queen*.

But seemingly hopeless situations could be retrieved. In October 1814, under convoy of the HMS *Sultan* (74), the *Baring*, a sizeable transport of 700 tons, carrying eighteen officers and over three hundred men of the 40th Regiment, was ordered to Berehaven, the one sheltered anchorage in Bantry Bay in the south of Ireland. The ship went on the rocks and drifted across the Haven to Bear Island. 'By the advice of the Master, through the exertions of the officers, the men were in great measure kept below, until the water was ankle deep on their deck.'[65] By keeping the weight of the troops below, the decks were kept clear for the seamen. Though a few men were drowned by jumping overboard prematurely, over three hundred were saved. Military discipline saved the day.*

Occasionally, the daring American privateers were bested by troop transports. Off Jamaica on 1 November 1814, the *Saucy Jack* of Charleston, which had recently taken seven prizes, came across what appeared to be a large unescorted merchantman at night, which looked easy prey. This was the *Golden Fleece*, with 250 troops aboard, escorted by the bomb vessel HMS *Volcano*. When the crew of the privateer attempted to board, they were met by a wall of bullets and raked by a broadside from the bomb vessel, which killed eight men and wounded fifteen. Though the *Saucy Jack* was badly damaged, she managed to struggle back to Charleston.[66]

On 1 March 1815, Napoleon escaped from Elba, marking the start of the Hundred Days, but because of the slowness of communications the British government had considerably less time to get an army to Brussels.[67] A frantic period ensued. The transports were diverted at very short notice. The government stripped Ireland of troops, overcoming

---

* Troopship disasters continued after the battle. On 30 January 1816, six hundred troops returning from the Continent via Ramsgate and Deal died in three transports, the *Seahorse*, *Boadicea* and *Lord Melville* (Grocott, *Shipwrecks*, pp. 390–98).

the protests of the Irish government. In the two months from 25 March, Wellington's army had increased by over 21,000 men.[68] Though peace had been signed with the Americans at the end of December 1814, convoys were still operating in the Atlantic. A convoy of transports on passage to Bermuda with Peninsular veterans was intercepted in the Atlantic by a fast warship with orders to return to Deal, from where it proceeded to Gravesend where the troops transferred to smaller transports.[69] The need for convoys was not so acute, with sloops and frigates patrolling the Straits of Dover. Transports poured out of Harwich, Ramsgate and the Downs in great numbers towards Ostend. Between 8 and 23 April, for instance, 160 transports ferried 8 regiments of cavalry from Britain to Ostend, with the loss of only 1 artillery horse.[70] Offloading horses onto the beach called for great skill, not least because of the fierce tide that runs parallel to the shore, leading to at least one transport crashing into the jetty, before coming to rest on the beach with an ebb tide, enabling the horses to be hoisted overboard and swum ashore.* Several accounts mention the chaos on shore. One officer wrote, 'the bustle and noise were inconceivable. The Dragoons and our men (some nearly, others quite, naked) were dashing in and out of the water . . . Disconsolate-looking groups of women and children were to be seen here and there . . . roaming about in search of their husbands, or maybe a stray child, all clamouring, lamenting, and materially increasing the babel-like confusion.'[71] Great skill was displayed by the masters of these transports. By now they had had a great deal of experience in handling army horses.

Major Edwin Griffiths of the 15th Light Dragoons embarked at Cork for Ostend on 12 May 1815 on the transport *Mary*, part of a convoy of transports containing 18 officers, 425 men and 399 horses of the regiment. He feared that the passage would take a fortnight or three weeks and, as he wrote to his sister, 'I detest a transport, but more for

---

* An officer in the 16th Light Dragoons reported that the weather was so calm on 11–12 April that, for the sake of speed, 'horses were put loose in the hold, and it being fine weather, we did not lose any' (Cohen, 'Brothers in War', p. 59).

my poor horses who will suffer much from the confinement . . . I would give a month's pay to have gone through England.' He particularly feared the Isles of Scilly. Rough weather was experienced in the Irish Sea, but once round the Scillies three days later, the convoy made seven or eight knots up the Channel. Across Lyme Bay it made nine knots, then went close to the Isle of Wight, which he knew well. Griffiths wrote to his sister:

> Beachy Head was then in sight, distant 6 or 7 miles. Ere soon after-wards saw the lighthouse at Dungeness, & dined off Folkestone where we were fired at several times & brought to by the *Nightingale* gun brig, who sent for our Capt. On board . . . At sunset we were in sight of Dover & heard the drums of the garrison beating the retreat. We glided quietly through the straits, & at bed time were just under the South Foreland lighthouse. This was altogether a charming days sail: we passed numerous vessels, bought some fresh macarel [*sic*], & were never a moment without something to interest one.[72]

After a day's calm, by the evening the *Mary* was in Ostend, and the horses were landed on the beach nearby. The voyage from Cork had taken five days and four nights. When moving troops by sea in midsummer, progress could be very swift and there were rarely accidents; the French had nothing like it. It is not too fanciful to conclude that had Napoleon challenged the allies in the winter months, Waterloo could not have taken place.

In the long Peninsular War, it is estimated that between 50,000 to 60,000 died. More certain figures exist from late 1810 until May 1814: of 35,000 deaths, more than 11,000 were killed in action.[73] Sickness and disease accounted for 24,000.* For a British soldier in the Napoleonic

---

* This was proportionally less than casualties from disease in the French Revolutionary War. Total deaths of private soldiers and NCOs in the West Indies totalled 43,747, 1793–1801, and 6,000 died in North Holland in 1794–5. At Walcheren, 3,960 soldiers died, though the effects of fever on those left alive were long felt (Duffy, *Soldiers, Sugar and Seapower*, p. 375; Howard, *Walcheren*, p. 229; Burnham & McGuigan, *British Army*, pp. 212–13).

Wars, death in battle was a less likely fate than dying by sickness or disease. Army casualties when at sea, from drowning or hypothermia, can be set against these figures. Between 1803 and 1816, this was the fate of at least six and a half thousand British soldiers in transports. Of the transports that sank or were wrecked, twenty resulted in a hundred or more deaths. Sixteen of these were in the waters around the British Isles. In view of the estimate of a quarter of a million transported over the whole war, this was perhaps a small percentage, but losses on this scale were very significant in the context of the grave manpower short-ages in the last three years of the war. Virtually all of these fatalities were caused by winter weather. This was the cost of the strategic flexibility which the military convoy system gave Britain over Napoleonic France.

Some of these soldiers were accompanied by their wives and chil-dren, who also died, instilling, even at this distance in time, the memory of these troopship disasters with still-powerful feelings of poignancy and tragedy.

SEVEN

THE MEDITERRANEAN
Fruit, Sulphur and Soldiers, 1803–1814

Malta is the most gossiping, gormandising place I ever heard of. The merchants there, who two years since were very little men, from the extension of their trade, the exclusion of all other nations from participating in it, and the ample protection given to their specula-tions, are suddenly become exceedingly rich. I have heard that some of them have made a hundred thousand pounds, and several of them from ten to fifteen a year.
Vice-Admiral Lord Collingwood to J.E. Blackett,
18 February 1809[1]

Cuthbert Collingwood, commander-in-chief of the Mediterranean fleet after the Battle of Trafalgar until his death in March 1810, did not much care for merchants, nor would he count trade protection as his greatest priority. Britain never dominated the naval contest in this region of Europe as it did, for instance, in the Baltic. Immediately Collingwood reached the Mediterranean in early 1806, he received news of the Treaty of Pressburg, signed after Napoleon's brilliantly successful campaign against the Austrians, by which France took over Venice, Istria and Dalmatia. This completely changed the situation in the Mediterranean. War with Russia followed the Treaty of Tilsit in July 1807, with hostilities with Turkey soon after. Collingwood saw off these threats, which encompassed expeditions to the Dardanelles and Alexandria. In early 1808 he also had to counter the potentially dangerous incursions of the substantial French squadrons of the French admirals Allemand and Ganteaume, which met at Corfu, though their voyages, unsupported by good intelligence and sufficient stores and provisions, came to nothing. Peace was made with Turkey at the beginning of 1809 and by the end of that year the Russian Mediterranean Fleet ceased to exist, although war between Russia and Turkey continued in the Black Sea.[2]

For the British, from 1810, the action swung to the Western Mediterranean, dominated by fighting in Spain. Port cities in south and south-western Spain, primarily Cadiz, Seville, Tarragona and Barcelona, were successively under siege and counter-siege. Often the critical advantage of the allies over the French was the ability to move troops and supply them with stores and provisions from the sea, all achieved through convoys. The same could be said for military operations in Naples, Sicily, the Ionians and the Adriatic.

At the same time, the French were not swept from the seas. Their coastal convoys supported their army throughout the period, well-protected by a series of coastal fortifications containing 4,000 cannon, with a concentration of 110 guns around Toulon.[3] In 1811, for instance, small, fast French convoys moved between Toulon and Corfu without interruption.[4] For almost all of the war, a substantial French fleet at Toulon was building, ready for a breakout. Collingwood's successors, Admiral Sir Charles Cotton (1810–11) and Vice-Admiral Sir Edward Pellew (1811–14), were both on the defensive.[5] Their job, in the words of one historian, was 'to win by not losing'.[6]

Nor did the British eliminate French privateers, whose main bases moved between Corsica, Crete or Algiers, and far fewer were captured than in the previous war.[7] Yet Collingwood's disparaging comments on the prosperity of the merchants of Malta highlights the general effectiveness of British sea control and of its trade protection in the Mediterranean, and of his own success in bringing this about. The numbers of British merchant ships arriving in the Mediterranean rose during the war, with flourishing cross trades between regional ports, but the military and maritime struggle was never won until after

Wellington's advance north towards France from Spain and Napoleon's defeat in Russia in 1812.[8]

The trade patterns of British convoys in the Mediterranean were complex, and made more so by the military campaigns, but they all hinged on Malta, the struggle for control of which brought the peace of Amiens to an end and the resumption of the war in May 1803. The island had been in French hands since 1798 when Napoleon had taken it unresisted from the Knights of St John. Thereafter, the French garrison had been under continuous siege until British and Neapolitan forces had finally forced it to surrender on 5 September 1800. The harbour was put to immediate use as the assembly and supply point for General Abercromby's successful expedition to defeat the French army in Egypt in 1801. The return of the island to the Knights of St John was a clause in the Treaty of Amiens, but a further breakdown of trust between Britain and France had led the Addington government to repudiate the clause, which became the immediate cause of the renewal of war. When the British Ambassador left Paris, he took his leave of Napoleon, who affected disbelief at the outbreak of hostilities, 'the cause of which is so small since it is merely a miserable rock'.[9] Despite this dismissal of Malta's importance, it was one of the more significant of the British government's second thoughts; strategic control of the island was retained for 167 years, although its prosperity plummeted when Napoleon's Continental System unravelled by 1813, and merchants returned to Leghorn, Trieste, Messina and Palermo.[10]

Malta was a priceless asset for it was already a complete naval base with facilities built by the Knights of St John, though they were outmoded and badly needed modernisation.[11] The island offered a different strategic advantage from Gibraltar, a thousand miles to the west. Before the Spanish revolted against French rule in 1808, Gibraltar was crucial in enabling the French and Spanish fleets in Cadiz to be blockaded. To support the fleet, Gibraltar's victualling yard was essential.[12] But the anchorage there was dangerously exposed and the loss of anchored ships in winter storms was common, added to those captured by Spanish gunboats from Algeciras across the bay when calm conditions prevailed.* 'When it is calm weather,' the Secretary of the Lloyd's Committee complained to the Admiralty Secretary in 1805, 'it is almost impossible for any vessel in passing through the Gut to escape them.'[13]

Britain had not invested in the building of a safe harbour on the western side of the Rock because the facilities of Lisbon, the capital of its Portuguese ally to the north, and Port Mahon, Minorca, under British occupation for much of the eighteenth century, were nearby. After the Spanish changed sides in 1808, the situation was reversed. Between 1810 and 1811, Cadiz was occupied by British and Spanish forces. It was surrounded by the French army and merchant convoys were needed to withstand the siege. At this time, Port Mahon came into British naval use, and while it was used by the fleet, but it was not central enough for trade convoys.[14]

When the war resumed in 1803, therefore, the British had in Malta an immense, deep-water and easily defended harbour, sheltered from storms, well-supplied with fresh water, a natural centre for both British military and trade shipping. The dockyard at Malta became an important refitting centre and, to avoid dependence on the two thousand-mile voyage from Britain, the navy started to procure timber and hemp from the Adriatic and by 1808 a new ropery had been built.[15] Convoy escorts from Britain rarely went further than Malta. From there, ships and British goods were protected by escorts from the commander-in-chief's squadrons and redirected to Italian ports, the Adriatic, Venice or Trieste to evade Napoleon's Continental System, and to the eastern shores of the Mediterranean.

The Levant Company in London had a network of factories in the Eastern Mediterranean, the chief of which were in Constantinople and

* For example, during a storm at Gibraltar on 20 January 1805, twelve square-rigged vessels sank, including a transport, though three hundred soldiers from the 57th Regiment were saved. Nine days later another storm destroyed sixteen vessels (*London Gazette*, 18 March 1805). Concern over the losses to Spanish gunboats led to the court martial of Commander William Mansell, HMS *Sophie* (18), 4 September 1806, for the loss of a brig from his convoy to a Spanish gunboat when the breeze failed. Mansell proved that he had a tow rope ready and was acquitted (TNA, ADM 1/5375; also Mackesy, *Mediterranean*, p. 275).

Smyrna, but with lesser bases in Cyprus, Tripoli and Alexandria in North Africa, and they spread through islands in the Aegean, Chios, Tinos, Paros, with Zante in the Ionians and Athens, Patras and Salonica on mainland Greece.[16] No commander-in-chief needed reminding of the importance of protecting this trade, not least because of the influence of the Levant Company, strengthened by several of their number being MPs.[17] Nelson was fully aware of the influence of the 'Turkey merchants', but he realised that it was impossible to please everyone or even anyone. He complained in a long letter to Sir Alexander Ball, now the de facto governor of Malta: 'The late Admiralty thought I kept too many [ships] to the Westward of Sicily; the Smyrna folks complain of me, so do the Adriatic, so they do between Cape de Gatte and Gibraltar. But all I have are to the Eastward.'[18] By 1807 the privateers were using Tunis as a base and Admiral Collingwood, short of escorts, was concerned that the Mediterranean could become impassable. The 'runners' were his main problem, merchant ships whose masters would not accept the convoy delays and went ahead by themselves, only to be captured by a privateer.

Demand for grain was maintained at a high level by the need to feed concentrations of seamen and soldiers, who were continually fighting until 1814, in various combinations of nations against each other, whether Russian, French, Spanish, British or Turkish.[19] British control over sea routes and convoys enabled Malta to become the hub of every maritime network in the central and eastern Mediterranean, but the acquisition of the island came with a price tag, for it was far from self-sufficient. The garrison of about five thousand soldiers and the dockyard employees had to be fed, in addition to the population. The constant requirement to feed and supply Malta remained a heavy drain on the time of small escorting warships.[20] The Adriatic supplied spars and timber to the dockyard, the transports all requiring protection.[21] A continual stream of Victualling and Ordnance Board transports from London brought provisions and stores, but in order to feed Malta, grain was needed from local sources. Sicily supplied a great deal. The French tried to invade that island for the last time in 1810, by which time there were over 23,000 British troops stationed there, and a ship of the line was moored at both Messina and Syracuse as a defence against a possible French incursion.[22]

The Barbary States were also important suppliers of foodstuffs, as was Alexandria. A good deal of Collingwood's time was spent in keeping the North African states friendly, gaining supplies of wheat but also fresh meat in the form of live bullocks.[23] Great quantities came to Malta – cattle from Benghazi, olive oil from Tunis and dates from Tripoli. British sea control ensured that not only was the traditional scourge of North African corsairs diminished, but the established trade of Barbary merchant ships to French ports was diverted to Malta.[24]

Wheat, oats and barley came not only from North Africa but further afield, from North America and for a period from the Black Sea.* Merchant ships needed protection for voyages as far as the Russian port of Odessa in the Black Sea to obtain wheat for the island.[25] Demand for cereals was so high that in 1810 Admiral Cotton had trouble with the islanders of Majorca and Minorca, who resisted sending wheat to the British fleet because of their own shortages on the islands.[26] Food convoys also came with cargoes from further afield, such as salt fish from Newfoundland. One Leith ship brought a cargo of fish from Shetland to Barcelona.[27] The usual British exports to the Mediterranean can be found in extant customs books: tin, lead, ironware and cotton goods. Sugar and coffee were re-exported from Britain to be smuggled past the Continental Blockade through ports in the Adriatic.

Malta was the rendezvous for the homegoing trade, which would assemble in Valetta Harbour four times a year, 1 February, 1 May, 1 August and 20 October, to be convoyed close to the North African

---

* It is worth emphasising the international nature of merchant ship owning at this time. A list of ships boarded by HMS *Amazon* in the Mediterranean, 4 November to 22 December 1803, belonged to the following ports: Altona, Bergen, Flensburg, Hamburg, Gothenburg, Cadiz, Barcelona, Port Mahon, Ragusa, Majorca, Leghorn, Zante. Between 13 May and 7 June 1804, HMS *Arrow* boarded ships from Venice, Trieste, Chiozzo, Curzola, Ragusa and Denmark (Wellcome 3667, Nelson documents).

coast, as far away from French privateers as possible, past Gibraltar and back to England.[28] Many cargoes listed 'merchandise' or 'sundries', which could include brandy, wine, sugar, coffee and soap. Less frequent entries in the lists included 'barelli', a Mediterranean plant that when burnt produced soda ash, used in the manufacture of soap and glass. High-value goods included silk from Aleppo, and medicines from Asia Minor such as opium or scammony.[29]

The bulk cargoes to Britain included cotton from Alexandria, currants from Patras, wheat from Salonika, olive oil and wine from the Ionian Islands. Figs and raisins, all transported after the harvest, needing urgent dispatch before they rotted; one group of masters in ships at Gibraltar in April 1804 requested an urgent convoy as their cargoes consisted of 'green fruit and other perishable articles'.[30] Of the fruit, the most important for the war effort were lemons. Lemon juice, considered by 1795 by the navy as an essential part of the seaman's diet to resist scurvy enabled extended operations at sea, such as blockading enemy ports and long periods in the Baltic.* By the early years of the war against Napoleon, acquiring a sufficient quantity of lemon juice was the major problem for the Sick and Hurt Board in London, which was now seeking new supplies in the West Indies and Portugal.[31] Nelson, when commander-in-chief between 1803 and 1805, took his own steps to procure it for the fleet from Sicily in early 1804, sending his surgeon, Dr John Snipe, to Messina to arrange supplies to be sent from an English merchant there named Broadbent. Nelson was able to write in his diary in October 1804, 'Not a sick man in the fleet'.[32]

None of these commodities were as of high value as some from other trade routes, as, say, bullion, or as important to the British war effort as hemp or timber from the Baltic, but there was one unique mineral that was of very high strategic value. The sulphur ore ('brimstone') from the

---

* An estimate of 1796 calculated that annually 171,093 gallons of lemon juice were needed by the navy. The Sick and Hurt Board continued to supervise the pressing and bottling, to be transported in partitioned boxes of nine bottes each (Vale & Edwards, *Trotter*, p. 120). Scurvy was still a factor in naval warfare; see, for instance, the pernicious effects of scurvy on the Swedish navy in 1808 (Davey, *Transformation*, pp. 113–14).

1. A convoy getting under way, as the frigate escort, heaved to in the centre of the picture, gathers the ships, possibly off Portsmouth. The picture was commissioned by the owner of the *Castor*, the West Indiaman in the foreground.

2. HM Brig *Wolf*, a Cruizer-class brig, pictured by E.W. Cooke, heaved to and waiting for a pilot. She was built in 1814. Designed in 1797 by Sir William Rule, Surveyor of the Navy, over a hundred of this 300-ton class were built, making it the most numerous and effective convoy escort.

3. A Cherokee-class brig sloop drying its sails. The smallest of the brig sloops acquired an unfair reputation as 'coffin brigs', despite the fact they performed well and, with a crew of only 75, were economical to run. The class was revived from the 1830s and HMB *Nautilus*, which is portrayed here, dates from that time.

4. A frigate and a brig trying the rate of sailing. It was important to know the relative speeds of warships when escorting convoys; the greater waterline length of a frigate's hull could be expected to outrun a brig. However, the powerful fore and aft mainsail gave the brig an advantage when beating as it enabled it to point closer to the direction of the wind.

5. Frigate with a convoy in strong gales, painted in a naïve style by a young officer who was undoubtedly present. The picture does not exaggerate the impact of a storm at sea on a convoy, with the loss of control and the difficulty of seeing other ships.

6. Meticulously painted by Nicholas Pocock, this fleet of East Indiamen running back from China in 1802 demonstrates the ideal of a convoy: well-laden merchant ships, at speed, with the wind behind them. The convoy is led by HCS *Hindostan* (1248 tons), flying the signal 'to wear, sternmost and leewardmost first'.

7. HCS *Earl of Abergavenny* had set off from Spithead with 400 passengers in a convoy to the East Indies, and was battered by south-westerly gales in the Channel, after which the wind fell light. Off Weymouth she went onto the Shambles sandbank. The captain thought that the ship would rise with the tide, but she had been holed and the pumps could not cope, and in the night the wind got up again. Only 100 seamen and soldiers, who managed to cling to the rigging, were rescued the next morning.

8. The *Ann* West Indiaman off Birkenhead. Smaller than East Indiamen, ships in the Atlantic trade were nevertheless powerfully built and rigged.

9. The *Harriet* government transport, one of the hundreds of merchant ships chartered by the Transport Board. These ships were numbered for easy identification and '660' can be seen painted on her hull just under her anchor.

10. The confined waters of the Great Belt were very dangerous for British convoys, as can be seen by the packed merchant vessels escorted by an unidentified 74-gun ship, possibly HMS *Superb*, in the operation to ensure the escape of Spanish troops from Denmark to Spain in 1808. A captured Danish privateer is seen in the left foreground.

11. The capture of HMB *Tickler* on 4 June 1808 by Danish gunboats. Warships were vulnerable in light winds in the narrow waters of the Sound and Great Belt, where the advantage lay with boats powered by oars. *Tickler* surrendered after a four-hour engagement, her captain killed.

12. HMS *Arrow* (24) was sunk in the Mediterranean on 3–4 February 1805, but the convoy she was escorting escaped (described in chapter 7). She was outgunned and outnumbered by the French warships *L'Hortense* and *L'Incorruptible*. *Arrow* was experimental and lightly built, armed with carronades only, which can be seen in this drawing by Nicholas Pocock.

13. HMS *Hermes* sinking a French privateer in heavy weather off Beachy Head, 14 September 1811. At 500 tons and a hundred foot long, the British warship demonstrates how small privateers could be. Ramming an enemy was unusual, hence the incident was celebrated in this contemporary print.

14. John Wilson Croker, Secretary to the Board of Admiralty, 1809–1830, was appointed when only 28 years old. He was a driven man who by all accounts came to dominate the Board. A critical part of his role was the defence of the navy's performance in Parliament, as well as relations with the City of London and other commercial interests, particularly on the business of convoys.

15. John Barrow, Second Secretary to the Board of Admiralty, was in post 1804–1806 and between 1807 and 1845. Barrow was responsible for naval communications. His close alliance and friendship with Croker was of prime importance in running the Admiralty during the war.

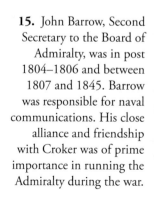

16. Joseph Marryat was a West India merchant and shipowner who became an MP in 1808 and Chairman of the Committee of Lloyds in 1811 until his death in 1824. He was a dominant personality and had a continuous and powerful influence on the administration of convoys, though he and Croker fell out in the 1820s when the pressures of war no longer existed.

17. Sir John Gladstone was an entrepreneur with many business interests, eventually settling in Liverpool. He became Chairman of the West Indian Association in 1809 and was prominent in the movement to end the East India Company monopoly. He later became an MP and invested heavily in sugar plantations in Jamaica.

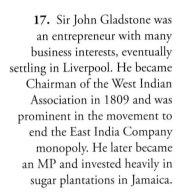

18. Heligoland was captured from the Danes in 1807 and immediately used by
merchants as a base from which to smuggle goods into Europe, evading Napoleon's
Continental System. For about four years, an immense quantity of merchandise was
stored there, to be smuggled in fishing boats to German ports thirty miles away.

19. Malta, with its great fortifications and sheltered harbour, gave the British an
important advantage in the Mediterranean after its capture in September 1800.
Homeward convoys gathered there, and it was used as a base by merchants from
which to smuggle goods into Europe, in a similar fashion to Heligoland in the north.

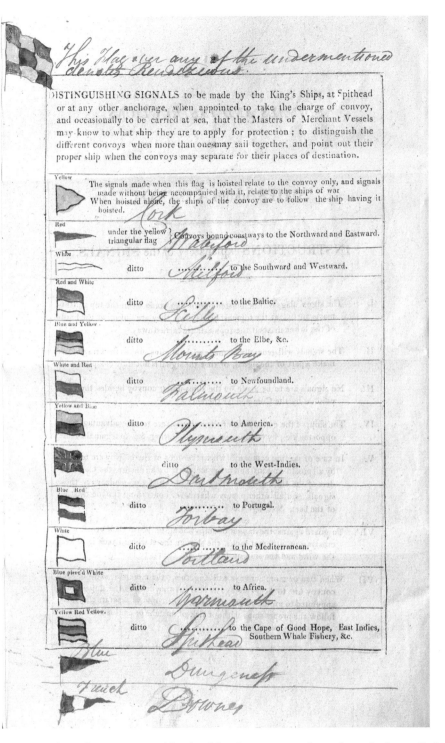

This Flag over any of the undermentioned denotes Rendezvous.

DISTINGUISHING SIGNALS to be made by the King's Ships, at Spithead or at any other anchorage, when appointed to take the charge of convoy, and occasionally to be carried at sea, that the Masters of Merchant Vessels may know to what ship they are to apply for protection ; to distinguish the different convoys when more than one may sail together, and point out their proper ship when the convoys may separate for their places of destination.

Yellow	The signals made when this flag is hoisted relate to the convoy only, and signals made without being accompanied with it, relate to the ships of war. When hoisted alone, the ships of the convoy are to follow the ship having it hoisted.	
Red	under the yellow triangular flag	*Cork* Convoys bound coastways to the Northward and Eastward.
White	ditto	*Waterford* .... to the Southward and Westward.
Red and White	ditto	*Milford* .... to the Baltic.
Blue and Yellow	ditto	*Scilly* .... to the Elbe, &c.
White and Red	ditto	*Mounts Bay* .... to Newfoundland.
Yellow and Blue	ditto	*Falmouth* .... to America.
	ditto	*Plymouth* .... to the West-Indies.
Blue Red	ditto	*Dartmouth* .... to Portugal.
White	ditto	*Torbay* .... to the Mediterranean.
Blue pierc'd White	ditto	*Portland* .... to Africa.
Yellow Red Yellow	ditto	*Yarmouth* .... to the Cape of Good Hope, East Indies, Southern Whale Fishery, &c.

Blue .... *Spithead*
Dungeness
French .... *Downes*

20. A page from the convoy signal book of the *Oeconomy* merchant ship, which travelled to and from the West Indies in 1811. Each merchant ship carried a signal book, by which a convoy commodore sought to control the course of the ships under his charge. This sheet is a key to destinations but has been overwritten with a set of Channel ports.

21. A memorial stone in Mylor churchyard, Cornwall, remembering the 369 casualties of the shipwrecked *Queen*. On 13 January 1814 she dragged her single anchor in a gale and struck a rock 40 yards from Trefusis Point in Falmouth harbour. She had nearly 500 passengers returning from the Peninsular War. She broke up very quickly. Caused by incompetence and even drunkenness, this was the most avoidable shipwreck of the war.

mines of Sicily was a critical element in the manufacture of gunpowder in Britain. Much less sulphur was used than the main ingredient, salt-petre, but nevertheless several thousand tons a year were transported to Britain. In 1802, for instance, the last year for which any Ordnance records survive, some 2,500 tons were imported by the Board.* On the resumption of war, stocks were being renewed. In September 1803 six ships with cargoes of sulphur for England were at Malta, their masters requesting a convoy home from the commander-in-chief.[33]

Fortunately, sulphur ore is odourless and was easy to transport, a contrast with the blue flame and acrid smoke with which it burns. It had to reach the state powder mills near London and at Ballincollig, near Cork in Ireland, which manufactured most of the gunpowder and distributed the raw materials to private contractors who made the rest. Less strategically sensitive sources for sulphur than Sicily were sought, for the mineral could be extracted from gypsum and pyrites, but the quality of Sicilian sulphur was paramount. After trials of gunpowder made from sulphur from Anglesey in 1799, Lieutenant-General William Congreve, Comptroller of the Royal Laboratory at Woolwich wrote to the Board of Ordnance: 'I am clearly of opinion that the Anglesea Brimstone should not be used at the Royal Powder Mills as long as it is possible to procure Brimstone from Mount Etna.'[34] In spite of the complications of supply, neither the army nor the navy, which used by far the greater amount, ever went short of gunpowder during the war.[†]

For Nelson, wedded to a forward, aggressive blockade of the French fleet in Toulon, Malta was operationally useless. It was six hundred miles downwind from where he wanted his fleet. In the twenty-three

---

* The mixing proportion of British gunpowder was saltpetre 75 per cent; charcoal 15 per cent; sulphur 10 per cent (West, *Gunpowder*, p. 7). When the British fleet withdrew from the Mediterranean between 1796 and mid-1798, imports of sulphur dropped to almost nothing, but in 1798, 1799 and 1800, 80,000 hundredweight came into Britain (Cole, *Arming the Navy*, pp. 70–71).
† There are sparse references to the transport of sulphur to England, though it seems likely that the ore was transported from Messina to Malta, before convoy to Britain (e.g. *Lloyd's List*, 7 January 1814).

months of his command, he spent only two days on the island, when he first arrived in mid-June 1803, paying his respects to Alexander Ball.[35] One of Nelson's first tasks was to organise the salvage of part of the Elgin Marbles, which had sunk in the *Mentor* before he had arrived in the Mediterranean.* In Nelson's absence afloat, complex naval administrative tasks at Malta were undertaken by the energetic Senior Naval Officer at Malta, Captain Graham Eden Hamond, with the guidance of Ball. His biggest task was to organise the military expedition of Lieutenant-General Sir James Craig to Naples, including the transport and convoying of six thousand troops, which left Malta on 3 November 1805, all of which required coordination with the Russians.[36]

Convoys were at greater risk in the eastern Mediterranean. A day before he reached Malta in 1803, Nelson sent orders for a heavy frigate, HMS *Anson* (44), with HMS *Arrow* (28) and HMS *Bittern* (18), to 'expedite our commerce to and from the Adriatic and the Levant, keeping the French Privateers from being insolent in the Morea, and about Cerigo and Zante'. From this point he never stopped issuing detailed orders, trying to find the most efficient way of covering convoys with insufficient small warships, under constant pressure from merchants to do more and often despairing of the shortage of escorts.[37] As Nelson sailed back to England in July 1805, he wrote to the Secretary of the Admiralty: 'The force which, always when I had it, I judged necessary to keep to the Eastward of Sicily was – and not less is wanted now – one Frigate 12 pounders, four sloops of war, the *Spider*, *Renard* and *Ventura* Schooners, and *Hirondelle* cutter, to which I often added *Anson* frigate and *Cameleon* and other sloops.'[38] In spite of the complexity of his command at a critical time in the war, Mediterranean convoys were never

---

* Nicolas, *Nelson Dispatches*, VI, p. 188. There can be little doubt that the removal of the Elgin Marbles had the approval of John Wilson Croker. After the war he wrote to the c-in-c Mediterranean: 'I apprehend that those kind of fragments are plenty as blackberries on the Tripoline Coasts, and they would be useful and ornamental in my drawing room' (Hamilton, 'Croker and Patronage', pp. 53–4, quoting Croker to Admiral Penrose, Croker papers, William L. Clements Library, 18 February 1818; Wheeler, *Athenaeum*, pp. 56, 337). Archaeologists have been diving on the wreck of the *Mentor* since 2011.

neglected. He wrote to another officer: 'I consider the protection of our Trade the most essential service that can be performed.'[39]

At the beginning of 1805, a uniquely fierce convoy action took place, off the Algerian coast, when two small British escorts were destroyed after fighting two much larger French warships, but their resistance enabled almost all the convoy under their protection to escape capture. The convoy of thirty-four ships, originally from Smyrna, had left Malta for England, loaded mainly with fruit, together with one transport, though with no troops on board. The two French ships they encountered were part of Villeneuve's fleet, which left Toulon on 17 January 1805, heading for the West Indies only to return after storm damage. The frigates had become detached during that storm and were making their way back to Toulon. In an age of carefully calibrated notions of honour, ships of equal armament might fight to a standstill, but it was understood that the smaller ship in an unequal contest would surrender after a token broadside, to avoid unnecessary bloodshed. However, the action that took place on 2 February 1805 was anything but equal.

Captain Richard Budd Vincent had been out in the Mediterranean since the beginning of the war in HMS *Arrow*, which was 128 feet long, 386 tons, complement of 121, long, narrow and lightly built, to an experimental design by Samuel Bentham. She had none of the orthodox long guns, being armed only with twenty-eight 32-pounder carronades, very effective at short range, but not at any distance. She was, according to a dockyard officer, unhappy with the radical design, 'built too slight'.[40] She was fast and Vincent was an assiduous and aggressive commander. In late 1803 he impressed eight seamen from two of the merchant ships he was escorting, but soon after he had put *Arrow* on a rock, news of which misfortune reached Nelson. Six months later he destroyed a French privateer at the island of Fano, in which three of his crew were killed and seven wounded.[41]

HMS *Acheron*, Captain Arthur Farquhar, the second escort, was a bomb vessel of the same tonnage, only 108 feet long and with a complement of only sixty-seven. 'Bombs' were frequently used for escorting convoys because their slow speed made them suitable to accompany heavily laden merchantmen. In addition to her two mortars for coastal bombardment (thus useless in this engagement) she had two huge 68-pound carronades and six 18-pounders.* Their French opponents were the new frigates, *L'Hortense* (40) and *L'Incorruptible* (38), armed with 18-pound long guns. Each had on board three hundred soldiers, as well as a crew of the same number.[42] Their tonnage would be three times as great; and they were very fast and the winds were very light.

Once Vincent had established that the two ships were hostile, he signalled to the convoy to scatter, the ships to make their way to Gibraltar, the next rendezvous, not far away. After much light-wind manoeuvring through the night, when 'everyone was at their quarters', and an exchange of shots, the two British ships put themselves between the convoy and the enemy. At daybreak the battle was joined for an hour and a half, at which point *Arrow* struck her colours. According to a letter from one of her officers, by now a prisoner in Cartagena, the *Arrow*

> was a complete wreck, floating like a log on the water for the last minutes of the action ... About three hours after they took possession of us, the Frenchmen found she was sinking fast, as we had upwards of thirty shot holes under water ... in spite of all the efforts made by the French and Englishmen, she sank about one o'clock in the afternoon, with three unfortunate wounded Englishmen on board, who could not possibly be taken out.

Arrow had thirteen men killed, two of whom were officers, and twenty-seven wounded. When *Acheron* saw *Arrow* strike, she set sail with one of the French frigates in pursuit, taking up more time for the

---

* The weight of the broadsides of the two British ships were 896 pounds and 244 pounds, while those of the French frigates were 720 pounds and 684 pounds, but the range of the guns was the critical factor, as was the *Arrow*'s light build.

convoy to escape. She had three killed and eight wounded. The officer reckoned, 'We think ourselves very fortunate in not having more officers killed', while the French 'own themselves they never thought of engaging them'.[43] Only three of the convoy of thirty-four were captured and burnt, the rest reaching Gibraltar. The master of the *Rambler*, one of the escorted merchant ships, thought, 'there was very little wind during the action, or [all] the merchantmen would have escaped'.[44] Rich praise for the defence appeared in the English press. Both commanders were promoted to post-captains, immediately after the conclusion of the courts martial on the loss of the two British warships. Farquhar was from Aberdeen, and received particular praise from the *Aberdeen Press and Journal*, 'in supporting so unequal a contest for four hours, for the sole purpose of giving the convoy time to escape, is beyond all praise'.[45]

The circumstances of this action were exceptional, with unexpected local French superiority and little chance of manoeuvre or escape in light winds. Early broadsides during the night would have told the French that they were dealing only with short-range carronades. Bentham's radical gun armament solely of carronades left the *Arrow* at a disastrous disadvantage, a problem that was to make other appearances in the war against the Americans from 1812. In spite of the narrowness of the margin of the weight of the broadsides, such determination on the part of the smaller ship was unequalled in this war in the defence of a convoy. The motives of a naval officer going into action were a complex mixture of honour, hopes of promotion and the possibility of prize money. Honour and the protection of commerce rarely went quite so far.*

Nelson's lament about never having enough frigates is well known. When he left the Mediterranean for the last time in January 1805,

---

* One similar defence, on 24 March 1804 by the experimental HMS *Wolverine* (13), enabled her Newfoundland convoy of eight merchantmen to escape. She was attacked by a much larger French privateer, after which the British ship rolled over and sank, once her crew had been made prisoner (Henderson, *Frigates, Sloops and Brigs*, pp. 291–3).

he had a dozen ships of the line, a dozen frigates and ten sloops.[46] During Collingwood's four years, as we have seen, the task of commander-in-chief, Mediterranean, expanded and grew more complex. Just before Lord Barham stepped down from being First Lord of the Admiralty in January 1806, he reckoned that Collingwood should have thirty sloops and smaller warships at his disposal.[47] Apart from watching the main French fleet in Toulon, and maintaining commerce protection, the commander-in-chief had to guard Sicily and watch the Dardanelles, after the Turks had joined the French. It proved to be impossible to reach Constantinople through the Dardanelles, while the attack on the Turkish Empire in Alexandria was a failure. In March 1807 a convoy of thirty-nine transports left Messina for Alexandria with five thousand troops on board, escorted by a 74-gun ship, a large frigate and a brig sloop. The city surrendered immediately, but the troops were defeated when they attacked Rosetta and the expedition withdrew ignominiously, achieving nothing.[48]

The convoy load increased in early 1809, when the Admiralty, taking all spare warships to evacuate troops from Corunna, had no escorts to spare for the Mediterranean, and ordered those protecting south-going convoys to return north when they reached Gibraltar. Ongoing convoys to Malta had to be covered by Collingwood's ships. Collingwood wrote to his deputy, Rear-Admiral John Child Purvis: 'The regulation that the convoys are not to come further than Gibraltar is exceedingly embarrassing, for as every power we make peace with claims from us protection, the duties of fleet increases as we make friends.'[49]

The number of seamen and soldiers in the Mediterranean grew steadily and substantially. By 1810 there were 33,000 seamen on station and the same number of soldiers, 23,000 of whom were in Sicily, 4,500 in Malta and 6,000 in Gibraltar.[50] Troops and crews needed despatches, medical support, stores and feeding, for much of the basic provisions were convoyed from Britain. It was a time of high freight rates. Under the umbrella of British trade convoys, regional neutral shipping thrived and the latter found a natural home in British convoys in the Mediterranean. Greek shipowners and merchants, especially from the Ionian islands, did well.[51]

Trade to and from Britain increased as well. In 1808 those arriving in Malta accounted for 8.4 per cent of total British exports, and for the next two years some six hundred ships in a dozen convoys came from England to the Mediterranean.* By 1812 the British exports to the Mediterranean had swollen to the significant total of 12.2 per cent of the whole, as the difficulties of trade with Northern Europe through the Baltic were considerable in that year and merchants found other ways of getting their goods into Europe.[52] By 1813 the number of British and neutral merchant ships and government transports sailing from England to Malta had doubled to over a thousand, sailing in twenty-two convoys.[53] Many of them were neutral carriers. Scandinavian-flagged ships dominated, but American vessels increased; by 1807 there were as many as five hundred in the Mediterranean.[54]

After the imposition of the Continental System by Napoleon in 1807, and the consequent Orders-in-Council from Britain, British shipping in the 'cross trades' rarely returned to Britain. An example of this was the *Ellice*, a hired government transport, fitted as a troop transport, which could take four hundred troops. She was owned by the major beef contractor in London for the Victualling Board, William Mellish. The ship's master, Thomas Longstaff, commanded the ship for eighteen years and for eleven of them, from 1806 to 1817, she was in the Mediterranean. She was big, fast and well-armed, with a crew of twenty-one, a good proportion of the seamen from the Mediterranean. Her busy schedule is chronicled in a surviving copy letter book between master and owner.

For the first six years the *Ellice* moved between Malta, Palermo and Messina, though she undertook many jobs, as Longstaff wrote to Mellish: 'we are too well known to the Men of War . . . and that when a

---

* Statistics from the Admiralty/Lloyd's List (TNA, ADM 7/64) are complicated by the number of ships on south-going convoys leaving them to go to Lisbon.

Ship of despatch is wanted the *Ellice* will (as usual) be singled out'. Though there is more than a hint of pride in this statement, his concern for Mellish is the cost for wear on the ropes and gear, for which the owner had to pay. The *Ellice* undertook many different tasks for the commander-in-chief, including trying to salvage a shipwreck that contained bullion, being ordered to Marsala to bring back a cargo of wine for the fleet, and transporting the army commander, Sir John Stuart and his deputy Lord Forbes, with their extensive followers and families, to Gibraltar. Longstaff let Mellish know that there would be less wear and tear in the winter months of 1808/9, writing from Messina, 'I have got into a snug corner of this harbour, and think of passing another month or two of the winter in it.'[55] As Mellish was paid by the Transport Board on a tonnage-per-month charter, this was quite acceptable, for it was always his aim to keep his ship in the Mediterranean.

Damage was however sustained the following October in a curious incident when jumpy troops in two ships in a convoy started shooting at each other, convinced that the other was an enemy privateer. On a very dark night off Cape Spartivento, the southerly point of Sardinia, and in spite of all efforts to stop the firing, Longstaff reported, 'Soldiers with Musquets in their hands, and in the dark, were not to be stopt from using them', in spite of 'a good light at the Masthead all the time'. On board the *Ellice*, one officer was killed and a soldier wounded, with similar fatalities aboard the other ship. Eighteen hundred shots were fired in all.[56]

Longstaff maintained the ship in profit, though 1811 was a bad year, with the rate of exchange for sterling weak, but it was generally a lucrative station for a merchant ship hired by government. During the winter of 1811–12 *Ellice* took six months out of service, running with the wind back from Malta to London in twenty-three days. On her return, she had a very difficult passage out of the Western Approaches.* For the next two years, the *Ellice* spent her time based in Minorca and

* See Chapter 3.

Alicante, supporting the army at the siege of Tarragona. By 1814 she was again back in the Ionians and Malta. The undoubted skill of Thomas Longstaff as master of the *Ellice* for those years in the Mediterranean is highlighted by the fact that immediately after he retired and was back in London, the ship was wrecked under another captain on the coast of North Spain in November 1817. She had 146 people on board and 13 were drowned.[57]

The level of military activity on land meant that the French naval and maritime shipping increased, especially in the Adriatic. It was a good time for prizes for British warships and the French lost much shipping.[58] The opportunities for small cruising warships in the northern Adriatic can be illustrated by cases of alleged ransoming of twenty-five enemy merchant ships by HMS *Unite* (38), commanded by Captain Patrick Campbell, between 1805 and 1809. Campbell was accused of ordering his surgeon, who spoke Italian, to 'compromise' with the merchants of Trieste to arrange for the release of captured ships, 'without adjudication or any legal investigation into the merits'. Campbell had also issued licences and had accepted presents from Trieste merchants. As the historian who uncovered this case commented, it was little more than a 'protection racket'. The case was sent by the Admiralty in 1812 to Admiral Pellew, when he was commander-in-chief, with an order to investigate, but little came of it and it seemed to do Campbell's career no harm.[59]

However, French privateers were a constant threat, based in Corsica and before the Spanish changed sides, from their east-coast ports.[60] At the end of 1808, after the arrival of the French Marshal Murat at Naples, Neapolitan vessels joined the enemy privateers and the losses continued.[61] At Collingwood's death in 1810, the ships of the line under his command had tripled to thirty, but the smaller warships had only doubled to twenty-two frigates and twenty-four sloops or smaller.[62] The numbers never reached the level Lord Barham had recommended.

If anything, the naval and military situation became marginally simpler in the Eastern Mediterranean after Collingwood, but intensified in the west, dominated by fighting in southern and south-eastern Spain, as did the activities of French privateers, which took a steady number of Spanish merchant ships between 1810 and 1812.[63] These campaigns were made complex by the intrigues of Spanish politicians and guerrillas and edgy relations between them and the British. The French army took Seville in January 1810 and went on to besiege Spanish and British forces in Cadiz for two closely fought years, during which the population of the city swelled to 100,000. With the French occupying the northern side of the harbour, the constant stream of provisions and reinforcements were supplied by convoys. An illustration of how many were involved is illustrated by a south-easterly gale on 27 March 1811, which wrecked fifty-three merchant ships and damaged hundreds of others.[64] The French finally lifted the siege in August 1812 and retreated north. There was heavy fighting around Valencia in 1811 and Tarragona fell to the French at the end of June 1811, although the British navy managed to evacuate two thousand Spaniards.[65] This intense naval activity took place at the same time as heightened activity in the Adriatic, with the successful frigate battle of Lissa against French forces on 13 March 1811. Venice continued to be blockaded, but with British goods and tropical products slipping through to Europe. Imports from this region to Britain held up, though with a slight dip in 1811, so that overall convoys continued and thrived through this period.[66]

One reason they did so was that the British midsummer convoys, when protected by a large warship, were unassailable. One example was when HMS *Leviathan* (74), commanded by the promoted Captain Patrick Campbell, after a two-year commission in the Mediterranean, and due for a refit, was ordered home with the trade. His orders were signed by the Rear-Admiral John Laugharn, on board *Trident* at Malta, 20 April 1813. Campbell was to escort 'such Merchant Vessels entitled to your protection and willing to accompany you, as may be bound hence to the Westward'. *Leviathan* was given extra tasks, and sent on a course to the north of the Mediterranean. She was to transport invalid officers and men and prisoners of war, and also call at Cagliari at the southern tip of Sardinia to embark 'the British Minister to the Court of Sardinia'. Campbell was also ordered to leave ships at Gibraltar 'in security', including the *Intrepid* and *Dolphin*, which were transporting corn to the allied armies in southern Spain. He was then to collect whatever ships were bound for Britain, set sail for the Downs, leaving ships 'at intermediate ports in the British Channel'.[67] She arrived in England with seventy-five vessels on 13 July 1813.[68]

As was the case on other stations around the world, one of the continual problems of the commander-in-chief was the deteriorating condition of warships, large and small. When Admiral Cotton reached his command off Toulon in early May 1810, he wrote to Croker of his concern at the condition of his warships. He also remarked pointedly that, 'An increase of small vessels is particularly desirable at this time, more effectually to prevent the coasting trade which the enemy must necessarily establish in this quarter for supplying their forces on the coast, and which appears to be carried on to no small extent in every direction occupied by the French Army'.[69] By 1813, with a new war against America in the North Atlantic to fight, the Admiralty withdrew four frigates from the Mediterranean, and similar numbers were transferred from the North Sea and the Baltic. To compensate, Pellew was given five more sloops, pushing the final total to thirty-five by July 1813.[70] By this time, the Austrian army and the British navy were steadily taking over French conquests. The net result of all this conflict was that Austria had Venice and all her territories, while Britain retained Malta.[71]

The Mediterranean presented escorts and convoys with unusual hazards. Plague was rife at various ports at different times, especially at Gibraltar. Long periods of quarantine were strictly enforced. During his extraordinary eighteen-month convoy journey from the Baltic to the Black Sea and back, Samuel Jefferson in the *Mary Ann* found himself in Malta in mid-1813, and was ordered to the Quarantine Mole:

The dead boats ... passed up the harbour where we lay, twice a day, about sunrise in the morning and again at sunset, laden with the dead bodies ... To get people to bury the dead they had to employ the slaves and convicts for this dreadful work at a dollar a day, together with their liberty if they survived, for although every precaution was taken to preserve these men by clothing them completely in an armour of oilskin from head to foot, many of their number died.[72]

Storms were perhaps not as severe or long lasting as elsewhere on the globe, though the fickleness of light winds was particularly trying for convoys. An exception to this was in the Western Mediterranean, which experiences the strong north-westerly mistral, that 'chilly and searching wind', as Admiral Smyth called it, which can last for days, and damaged even large warships.* Lightning could be a particular problem. Half of the ships of the line in Admiral Pellew's fleet, when watering off the mouth of the Rhone, were damaged by lightning. But this was as nothing compared to the ravages caused by hurricanes in the Atlantic and cyclones in the Indian Ocean, which we examine next.

---

* Smyth, *The Mediterranean*, pp. 211, 242–5; W.H. Smyth started his naval career in the Mediterranean in 1810, becoming famous for writing on the navy in later life, including his *Sailor's Word Book*, published posthumously in 1867.

EIGHT

THE EAST AND WEST INDIES
Two Sources of National Wealth, 1803–1814

In reviewing the disasters of the last convoy from Jamaica, find that 25 ships have miscarried out of 102 which left under convoy of HMS Magicienne . . . *besides very considerable damage to the ships and cargoes of the 77 which did reach Great Britain. It is calculated that from two to four out of 100 generally miscarry from one misfortune or other, the extra number of twenty odd in this instance is to be ascribed to leaving Jamaica so late in July . . .*

John Bennet, Secretary of the Committee of Lloyd's, to
William Marsden, Secretary of the Board of Admiralty,
31 December 1806[1]

In a few days . . . we fell in with a French 74 gun ship. She came down upon us, but the Lyon man of war standing out of the fleet for hur, she hall'd off and doged round us . . . but she followed us three days and nights, expecting it would come on to blow and scatter the fleet, but in the night we sailed in close order under the com[modore's] command. The fourth day she left us.

Jacob Nagle, seaman, *Neptune* East Indiaman, in a convoy from
Canton to the Cape of Good Hope, May 1807[2]

The largest and most valuable outward convoys to leave Britain during any year were the combined East and West India fleets. They would set out together down Channel, but headed their separate ways, usually parting at Madeira. On 28 January 1806 a very large convoy was making its way out of the eastern end of the Solent, at St Helens, its escort led by HMS *Canada* (74), commanded by Captain John Harvey. In the Channel, the convoy met up with a powerful British squadron of six ships of the line, commanded by Rear-Admiral Sir Richard Strachan in HMS *Caesar* (80). Off Start Point, following naval instructions, Harvey handed over the command of the convoy to the senior officer. By the time the convoy had been joined by those ships waiting in Falmouth, on 2 February *Canada*'s log recorded '246 sail in sight'.[3]

Three months earlier Strachan had commanded a squadron which had chased and captured four French ships of the line and the Admiralty had sent him out to repeat this distinguished performance, this time to hunt down a French squadron under Contre-amiral Willaumez, which had broken out from Brest.[4] Strachan was, however, temperamentally unsuited for trade protection, for he had a famous temper. William Richardson, the gunner of the *Caesar*, who witnessed the following scenes, said of the admiral, 'the sailors liked him for all that, as they knew he had a kind heart, and thought no more of it when his passion was over. They gave him the name of "Mad Dick", and said that when he swore he meant no harm, and when he prayed he meant no good.'

The convoy encountered good weather and a fair wind, but it became very dispersed. As there were known to be a good many French ships in the Western Approaches in that post-Trafalgar period, Strachan needed the convoy to close up. As Richardson related, 'we fired gun after gun with the signal up for them to close nearer, but without much effect, and we then began to fire shot near them'. When some of the cannon balls flew close past HMS *Montagu* (74), the captain, Robert Otway, sent away a lieutenant in a launch to protest to the admiral. As Richardson commented: 'The poor fellow could not have been sent on a worse errand: the Admiral got foul of him and drove him into his boat, and bawling after him, told him to tell his captain that if he did not keep his proper station, he would fire at him as soon as any other ship in the fleet.'

This was not an empty threat, because soon afterwards Strachan signalled to the convoy to heave to, to wait for a slow ship, the huge three-decker HMS *St George* (98), commanded by Captain Albemarle Bertie. But Bertie kept on sailing, according to Richardson,

> in order to have a start ahead when the squadron filled her sails again, and in doing so there could not be much harm as she was a bad sailer. But Mad Dick got into a passion, and ordered me to fire right into her. She fortunately hove to just at the moment I was going to fire, and I was ordered to stop; and glad I was of it, for perhaps some innocent man might have suffered by it.[5]

Had Richardson fired, it would surely have been a celebrated incident, an 80-gun ship firing into a 98-gun ship, not a recalcitrant merchantman, but one of his own squadron. Bertie's subsequent career demonstrated that he would have been quite prepared to bring matters to a court martial.* Strachan had by chance been placed in command of both a convoy and a squadron, for a short period, thus combining the twin necessities of war and trade. Patience, not impetuosity, was needed to command a convoy, of any size or purpose.

Combining, when possible, the outgoing East and West Indies convoys was an obvious saving of time and resources, although the escorted merchant ships were very different. By the end of the war, the larger East Indiamen were built to a standard 1,200 tons, three to four times larger than the average West Indiaman. East Indiamen were larger in tonnage, and comparatively well-manned and well-armed, but far fewer in number than the West Indiamen, while the distance to India and China

---

* Bertie was the illegitimate son of an aristocrat and had much to prove, as evidenced in a career littered with controversy (Rodger, *Command of the Ocean*, pp. 494–5).

was nearly three times that to the West Indies.* East Indies convoys had much smaller numbers.† In 1809, for instance, 5 convoys (59 ships in total) left Britain for the East, in contrast to the 28 convoys (1,462 ships in all) that went to the West Indies. In 1813 the same number of ships departed for the East Indies as four years earlier, but for the West Indies the numbers increased to 37 fleets, numbering a total of 1,702 merchant ships, with an average of around 50 per convoy, leaving in every month of the year.[6]

The combined convoys usually left Spithead or Cork, steering south against the prevailing south-westerlies to pick up north-easterly winds off Africa when south of Madeira, using them to steer across the Atlantic. At the beginning of the war, Lord St Vincent, with his customary precision, outlined the dates of outgoing convoys from Spithead to the Chairman of the Court of Directors of the East India Company: 20 December, 20 February and 20 April. Escorts would 'see their convoy safe through the S.E. Trades, into variable or westerly winds and then proceed on to St Helena'.[7]

This timetable was subject to every sort of variable, aside from the weather. The West Indies fleet set out from Portsmouth and called at Falmouth to pick up further ships and escort vessels, but this arrangement often led to convoys being missed, as in 1807 when those of 4 January, 3 March and 16 April were unprotected for at least part of their voyage. Heading for Falmouth also brought the ships near the coast, as the Secretary of the Committee of Lloyd's pointed out to the Secretary of the Admiralty: 'they sometimes get so near the coast they are pinched to weather the Scilly, whereas if they do not call at Falmouth they would probably keep a good offing with a sure wind which would

* The course made good distance. Britain to Calcutta is over 11,000 miles, and the duration of the voyage made by an Indiaman was generally estimated at six months. Portsmouth to St Helena is 4,330 miles. Portsmouth to Jamaica is just over 4,000 miles, with a voyage of anything between 10 and 14 weeks (Marshall, *British Empire*, p. 13).
† East Indiamen were labelled 'HCS', short for 'Honourable Company Ships', indicating that they were chartered by the East India Company. This differentiates them from 'Country' ships, usually owned in Bombay, which were allowed to trade between Asian ports, their principal trade being the export of raw cotton to China (Parkinson, *Trade*, pp. 337–8).

carry them clear'.[8] Lloyd's kept up the pressure on the Admiralty on West India convoys. Over three years later, in January 1810, Bennet was writing to John Wilson Croker that the outgoing convoys were too large, suggesting that a limit of seventy should be sent with two ships of war directly to Jamaica, without going to Barbados. Croker listened very carefully, and immediately sent for the chairman of the West India Committee.[9] The outgoing convoys from that point were smaller.[10]

Nature and economic conditions also linked the East and West Indies trades. World weather patterns, combined with the timing of harvests and markets, determined that some of these large convoys set out down the Channel and Western Approaches at the most dangerous time of the year. But the two trading routes, largely London based, had more similarities than differences. The tropical storm season, with monsoons or hurricanes, had to be avoided.

However, the strongest link between the two trades was the combined wealth that they brought to the British state, enabling the war against Napoleon to be prosecuted for twelve long years. The value of imports, for instance, on which duties were levied, rose from just over £50 million a year in 1804–6 to £65 million in 1815–16, almost entirely consisting of raw materials (54–6 per cent) and foodstuffs (42 per cent).* Tea came from the East and sugar, coffee and raw cotton from the West, together with the import and export of gold and silver. Almost a quarter of all exports were re-exports of these goods. This was possible because Britain, in the words of a distinguished economic historian, had 'gathered into its hands nearly all the commerce between Europe and the rest of the world'.[11]

The islands of the West Indies were completely dependent upon goods from Britain, neither having the capacity to manufacture nor to feed

---

* Duties levied on tea, for instance, which had been very low in the 1780s, had crept up again until they reached 96 per cent by 1806 (Davis, *British Overseas Trade*, p. 46).

the population, land being scarce and directed towards sugar or coffee production.[12] Cargoes included hats, haberdashery, furniture, saddlery, blankets, glass, linens, soap, candles, tools and copper boilers.[13] These cargoes were high value, and some manufactured items dense and heavy, very different from the lighter and bulkier raw materials brought back to Britain. Many of the outward convoys had ships which were in ballast, or only half loaded, making them clumsy sailers and difficult to escort.*

A typical mix of the manufactured and processed goods that left Britain on both the long-distance trades would come from all over Britain. Tin came from Cornwall, copper from North Wales. Ironmongery from the Black Country was exported through Bristol. Linen came from Belfast. Cotton goods from Manchester dominated. By 1807, 29 per cent of rapidly expanding cotton exports went to the West Indies, bolstered by trade with Spanish and Portuguese colonies, which increased dramatically after the Spanish came over to the British side in 1808. Early in that year it was thought that more Manchester goods had been sent to Rio in the course of a few weeks than had been taken there in the previous twenty years.[14] The Spanish, curiously, were wedded to cheap linen from Germany, rather than better quality linen from Ireland. One route for this was from the Continent to Leith, where the linen would travel along the Forth and Clyde canal, to be convoyed across the Atlantic from Glasgow.[15]

Provisions were continually shipped out. The best quality ('planter's') beef was transported to the West Indies, mostly from Cork, which had well-developed agricultural-based industries to supply naval and merchant ships. Casked foodstuffs were even sent on the long route to India, though most were procured locally by contractors.[16] In addition, several thousand seamen and soldiers serving on both stations needed

---

* Historians have long been critical of the East India Company's business inefficiency, stemming from its monopoly of trade, but a recent study has countered this view (Bowen, Business of Empire, pp. 246–52).

to be fed.* For instance, in November 1805 the Victualling Board ordered to the East Indies 160,000 8-pound pieces of beef, 200,000 of pork and 80,000 pounds of suet.[17] At a more prosaic level, each ship had to clear foodstuffs and provisions for the crew through Customs. The *Oeconomy*, 344 tons, owned by Michael Henley of Wapping, was outward bound in ballast to St Domingo in late 1811, to bring back mahogany and fustic. A crew of sixteen, victualled for three months, needed twenty casks of beef and pork, two tons of biscuit, three tons of flour and three of pease, and two tons of potatoes. Cheese, strong and small beer, spirits and wine were also included, as were coal for cooking, candles, salt and vinegar. For maintenance, spare canvas, leather for pumps, pitch and tar and twine were also listed on the Custom House document.[18]

Finally, small arms and munitions formed a significant part of cargoes. The Company's armies in India needed arming. One modern calculation is that between 1809 and 1829, 699,059 muskets, carbines, fusils and rifles were sent out to India.[19] Some of these weapons undoubtedly were destined for enemies of the British state, for in both India and the West Indies clandestine trading with the enemy was long established.

The most frequently repeated historical judgement is that naval captains of the time did not like convoy duty, but this was not always the case. An exception was Captain the Hon. Charles Paget, one of the most stylish frigate captains, who, though young, was already something of a legend for his daring rescue of the crew of a shipwrecked French warship when in command of the frigate HMS *Endymion*. In 1808 he

* The number of seamen in British warships in the East Indies averaged between eight and ten thousand, until the capture of Mauritius in 1810, when it decreased. The greatest number in the Caribbean was 17,259 in 1805, and did not slip below 14,000 until the last two years of the war (Knight & Wilcox, *Sustaining the Fleet*, p. 222). For army numbers, see Chapter 4.

was appointed to HMS *Revenge* (74), with a complement of 590 officers and seamen. Paget received his orders (he was 'very unexpectedly, tho' agreeably, surprised', as he explained in a letter to his brother) on 1 September to escort thirteen ships as far as Madeira, destined for the East Indies. Here they were to ship wine, and then he would take them further south to 'the Tropic' (of Cancer), when the convoy would continue and the *Revenge* would sail back to England.[20] 'I suppose if I had written the orders myself, they could not have been more to my satisfaction.'[21] He was pleased with his new ship, launched only three years earlier.

Paget sailed out of Portsmouth harbour on 5 September, with thirteen ships to escort. They had a fast passage south. Following winds pushed the *Revenge* on, 'reduced to scudding under bare poles, and having even then having many occasions to bring to allow the Ships to come up', often a dangerous point of sailing, even for large warships, but the *Revenge* was untroubled. By 18 September Paget was anchored in the Funchal Roads, Madeira, watering, provisioning and shipping Madeira wine, as were undoubtedly the rest of the convoy.* Since Madeira was fortified with spirits, it improved after months in the warm hold of a ship and thus graced the tables of West Indian planters and the British in India. Paget ordered a pipe for an army friend, shipped it aboard one of the Indiamen under his charge, to be taken to India and eventually brought back to England in about eighteen months, by which time it would be perfect for drinking.

The *Revenge* took the convoy as far as the Tropic of Cancer (latitude 23 degrees north), from which he had been ordered to return to

---

* Madeira was 'probably the most important shipping services node in the entire Atlantic commercial system' (Hancock, *Citizens of the World*, p. 142; see also McAleer, 'Atlantic Islands', pp. 98–105). A pipe of Madeira provided forty dozen bottles. In 1805, 6,250 pipes of Madeira were imported into India, providing 3,000,000 bottles, prompting Northcote Parkinson to wonder if this vast amount of wine was connected to the high mortality rates among young East India officials, 'considering the comparatively small number of people in a position to drink wine at all' (Parkinson, *Trade*, pp. 74–5). Madeira was also the only wine consumed in quantity in the West Indies, usually drunk with water and lime juice, a mixture known as sangaree (Horsfall, 'West Indian Trade', p. 183).

England. He then sprang a subtle surprise on the Indiamen. As he was about to depart, he hoisted the signal for mail home to be delivered to the ship. As he related to his brother, in a letter written later at sea:

> When their boats shoved off to come here, mine shoved off to visit there – *not* however with the same object, but to get a few men. I did it in the mildest and least annoying way, for I wrote a civil note to all the East India Captains to *allow* the officer from the *Revenge* to have their crews mustered in his presence in order that *one* or *two* men were desirous of volunteering for the *Revenge* . . . In *this* way I accordingly got 16 seamen, and might have got double the number, but that I would not take more than two from each of them.

Not many naval officers managed such gentlemanly impressment, nor was there any mention of the episode in the log, though it records that the *Revenge* 'hove to' on 10 October before leaving the convoy. Among Paget's catch were two musicians, bringing his ship's band up to twenty-two. On the return journey the *Revenge* called at St Michael's, one of the islands in the Azores, where he purchased a dozen bullocks, vegetables and 50 tons of water, which he got on board in twenty-four hours. By 18 November he was back in Cawsand Bay in Plymouth Sound.[22] It is difficult to imagine a more effective naval captain of the time than Charles Paget.[23]

But this was an example of the aristocracy at work, offering 'volunteers' a homeward-bound voyage in a crack ship. Impressment by the navy was fraught and violent wherever it took place, and these incidents highlighted the fractured lines of command between the military and civilian worlds. Just what power did a convoy commodore, of whatever rank, have over Company captains? The more flexible naval officers would use conviviality and the dinner table as a way of establishing a relationship, for the captains of East Indiamen dined well. Not so Rear-Admiral Troubridge, when escorting a convoy out to the East Indies. With none of Paget's social advantages, and well known for confrontation, this admiral's irritation with the lack of urgency from the East Indiamen soon led to anger. He immediately antagonised the company commanders by leading the convoy out of Spithead westward by the narrow Needles channel, rather than the wide east end, against Company orders. On the voyage he issued a thundering memorandum, as if from his quarterdeck, full of pejorative phrases: 'The great negligence of many of the convoy ... has been already a serious delay ... improper and inattentive manner ... pointed neglect to signal ... neglect ... unseamanlike management'.[24] It made little difference – the East Indiamen started deliberately disobeying him and by the end he lost contact with a number of ships.*

Senior naval attitudes had not changed four years later, when his successor, Rear-Admiral William O'Brien Drury, wrote to the Admiralty after an impressment row: 'The Captain of an Indiaman is but a mongrel kind of Gentleman, or officer – turbulent, insolent and over-bearing. Their conduct should be severely reprehended by the Court of Directors and the most rigid means adopted to punish them for their repeated outrages against His Majesty's Flag.'[25] Drury's jaundiced view of the Company led to his pressing the Admiralty, unrealistically and unsuccessfully, for naval base facilities with docks at Trincomalee to make the navy independent of the Company for ship maintenance.[26] Cooperation at working level was not easy when those at the top held such extreme opinions. One commander of an Indiamen commented in 1809:

> The young men in the Navy are too often impressed with such high
> notions of honour and consequence which attach to them from being

---

* Attitudes to speed and urgency were not shared, and Company ships were not as well-manned as warships, discouraging frequent manoeuvres and fast sail handling. Nor were East Indiamen fast: 'long, deep and narrow ships were all more or less crank' (Parkinson, 'East India Trade', p. 146). Benign tropical weather called for patience. See, for example, the slow progress of a convoy, fifty years earlier, up the Malabar Coast, sailing at different times in the night as the land cooled down, anchoring, then waiting for a different breeze. 'There was no alternative to falling into the leisurely rhythm of this timeless trade imposed by the wind system' (Sutton, *Maritime Service*, p. 59).

in His Majesty's Service that they are very apt to forget what is due to the Officers in the Company's Service, of equal respectability and possessing as nice a sense of honour as themselves, and imagine that they may just speak and act towards them as they think proper.[27]

It was not impossible, however, to find a middle way. Captain Francis Austen, brother of Jane, was one who did. In spite of his dismay at his appointment to the old HMS *St Albans* (64) in March 1807, and the convoying task that went with it, money could smooth the way. He had served in the East Indies early in his career and he knew the ways of his Company captains. In a sympathetic letter to the Company, after his first convoy, he recommended the appointment of Captain Hay of HCS *Retreat* to a better ship, citing 'his indefatigable attention ... in carrying a great press of sail day and night, which the wretched sailing of his ship, when not in tow, rendered necessary'. Austen certainly knew how to deal with the Company, negotiating convoy payments of 200 guineas in January 1808 for 'care and attention' in escorting a convoy of 13 vessels from St Helena to England, 400 guineas for further escorting and 500 guineas 'in anticipation' of his convoying out to China in April 1809.* On completion of this voyage, when he escorted thirteen ships back to England in 1810 from China via Madras and St Helena, he received £525. He also delivered to the Company's agent at Deal '93 Chests of Treasure said to contain 470,000 Dollars or Bullion to that amount'. After pressing the Company for more, Austen accepted £1,500 freight money.[28]

Although freight money was seemingly money easily earned by commanders of warships, matters could go awry. In March 1810 HMB *Cheerly* (10), under Lieutenant Thomas Foulerton, arrived at Spithead from the River Plate. He had been entrusted by a merchant called Hodgson in Buenos Aires with 21 casks of silver coin worth £15,000,

---

* These payments harked back to the seventeenth-century custom of paying captains for escorts. See the Introduction.

to be carried back to England, at 2½ per cent. When it came to handing over the casks in Portsmouth harbour, it was found that two were missing. They contained 5,865 dollars, worth £1,407, four times the value of Foulerton's freight money. Hodgson sued the naval officer. Judgement was not delivered until 1813, but the judges likened the responsibility of freight to that of a merchant ship's bill of lading and found that Foulerton was liable. He had to pay the merchant back the missing funds.[29]

The abolition of the slave trade in 1807 made little difference to British convoys, as the large, fast slave ships, generally from Liverpool, made their own way outwards and avoided convoying. It was much more likely that they would join a homegoing convoy when loaded with sugar and coffee for the third leg of the triangular route. There was a curious exception, in October 1807, after the slave trade had been made illegal in Parliament, but before the legislation came into force, when the last four legal slave ships were escorted across the Atlantic by a frigate.[30] In general, however, convoys operated separately from the slave trade, notwithstanding the support they provided in wartime to a slave-based economy.

Of more significance economically was the Spanish revolt against French domination in Madrid, which started on 2 May 1808. There had been trouble in the country beforehand, and in Britain the navy and the merchants were ready. West Indies convoys grew larger after 1808, swollen with ships from the new trade with South America. On 9 May a convoy of thirty ships left Spithead for Brazil escorted by HMS *President* (44), and ten days later another of twelve ships left Falmouth protected by HMS *Undaunted* (44). During 1808, in all, five convoys consisting of a total of eighty-five ships left for Rio de Janeiro and the Brazils, and although the rate decreased over the next few years, it remained steady at about half that number. By the summer of 1809, Vice-Admiral de Courcy, commander-in-chief, South American station, was asking for more warships for trade protection.[31]

For inward convoys, cargoes increased because of the demand for raw cotton caused by the explosive growth in demand for manufactured cotton goods, centred on Manchester. Cotton wool was grown in Brazil and the East and West Indies, but primarily in the southern United States, exported mostly through Amelia Island, in the north of present-day Florida, to which the Charleston merchants sent their shipments. Total import figures into Britain in 1809 reached a record 92.8 million pounds, but in 1810 that figure grew sharply to 136.6 million pounds, partly because merchants were building up stocks ahead of the threatened American Non-Intercourse Act.[32]

From the other side of the world, the increase in the volume of tea imported from Canton can only be described as spectacular. Every year the volume of tea imported into Britain increased steadily by 1½ to 2 per cent, with the effects of war and the need to convoy barely affecting the growth. In 1803 the quantity of tea sold came to 22 million pounds and peaked in 1813/14 at 30 million. In 1809 the Treasury increased the tax, but the volume sold quickly recovered.[33] Goods from Canton accounted for 67 per cent of all East India Company sale income earned in London between 1803 and 1808.[34] From there also came delicate, high-value goods such as raw silk, nankeens, pepper and spices.*

In general, however, the raw materials and foodstuffs that came back to Britain were bulky and the weight was difficult to distribute evenly through the ships. Known in India as 'gruff goods', these included sugar and indigo. The most difficult of all the cargoes was saltpetre from Bengal, crystals of potassium nitrate, which formed the greater part constituents

* The value of imported Company goods in 1809/10 was calculated for a Parliamentary enquiry. They totalled £5.9 million, of which £3.4 million was tea (57 per cent); Indian cotton goods 18 per cent; Chinese silk and nankeens 11 per cent; drugs and sugar 6 per cent; saltpetre 4 per cent; pepper and spices 3 per cent (Bowen, *Business of Empire*, p. 245, quoting Parliamentary Papers, *Fourth Report of the Select Committee on the affairs of the East India Company* (1812), p. 493).

of gunpowder, and was potentially explosive.* Demand increased because of the operations of Wellington's army in the Peninsula. In 1808 the Company contracted with the government to supply 6,000 tons a year. By 1812 that figure had doubled to 12,000 tons.[35]

From the West Indies came raw cotton, which was so light, even when it was compressed that, for one schooner at least, extra pig iron was needed along the keel to safeguard the ship's stability.[36] Sugar was loaded in thirteen hundredweight hogsheads and during the voyage across the Atlantic would lose 10 per cent of its weight. A cargo of sugar had a pungent smell that pervaded the entire ship and, according to one elegant passenger, her cabin was covered with a sort of leaden surface which came off on clothes. Coffee, on the other hand, would absorb the smell of other cargoes so that it would spoil if it was stowed near rum. In spite of lowering duties, coffee never became very popular in Britain and was, instead, re-exported to the Continent, often through Heligoland. It mostly went there via London, but an alternative route was through Glasgow, along the Forth to Clyde canal, to Leith and thence over the North Sea.[37]

Perhaps the most valuable item in terms of the war effort, however, was the bullion from the silver mines of Potosi in Mexico, which came via the port of Santa Cruz on the country's eastern coast, a thousand miles west of Jamaica. At the beginning of the war, there was much movement of capital around the Atlantic in the wake of the Louisiana Purchase. By this transaction Napoleon, who had just gained this vast tract of land from the Spaniards by the Treaty of Aranjuez in March 1801, sold it to the United States in April 1803. This exceedingly complex deal was arranged by a powerful Paris banker, Gabriel-Julien

* On 23 July 1794, the main Ordnance saltpetre warehouse at Radcliffe in East London blew up. According to *The Times*, some of the saltpetre was blown six miles away (Cole, *Arming the Navy*, p. 71).

Ouvrard, with Barings in London and Hope and Son in Amsterdam, enabling trading to take place with the Spanish Empire when Spain and Britain were still at war.[38]

This silver was transported either in fast and powerful British frigates or in Spanish merchant ships protected by British convoys.* Sometimes they were used to cloak secret operations. In 1804 HMS *Revolutionaire* (40), Captain Henry Hotham, a powerful French prize frigate, was given secret orders to collect £200,000 in Spanish or American dollars from the Bank of Norfolk in Virginia, which 'had become due to HM Government by the Government of the United States'. Hotham was to escort the East India convoy, to 'proceed with them as expeditiously as possible consistent with their security' as far south as latitude 15 degrees north, signal them to disperse on to their destination. He was then to proceed west and north to Norfolk.[39]

More remarkable was the extensive export of silver from Vera Cruz, arranged on commission from the British government by another firm of London merchants, Gordon and Murphy, who had high-level contacts in Madrid. Between 1801 and 1811 42 specie transactions took place at Vera Cruz, totalling 29,408,015 pesos or dollars, at the exchange rate of about 4 dollars to the pound, the equivalent of over £7 million. Over 18 million pesos were transported by British warships, and the rest by Spanish or neutral merchant ships.[40]

In late 1806 the newly-built HMS *Resistance* (38), Captain Charles Adam, was ordered to Vera Cruz. Since Spain and Britain were still at war, she was forced by the Spanish Viceroy to anchor fifteen miles away from the port. Without charts, the ship went aground. On 1 January 1807, her log records, she began to take treasure on board. A week later she had stowed 1,043 boxes, a total of over 3 million dollars, and sailed on 14 January for England. She had a remarkable passage. For six weeks,

---

* Protecting both British and Spanish trade could lead to confusion. Captain Fraser of the *Avon* (18) escorted specie to Philadelphia at the request of the Spaniards. Croker ordered the c-in-c, Jamaica, Vice-Admiral Bartholomew Rowley, to supersede Frazer for abandoning his station, but as the protection of Spanish trade was in Fraser's general orders, Admiral Rowley sensibly decided to ignore Croker's instructions (TNA, ADM 1/262, 20 January 1811).

the ship averaged over a hundred miles a day. On three consecutive days her distance run was over 190 miles, on another 204 miles (with 'double reefed topsails'), averaging over 8.5 knots, an exhilaratingly consistent speed for a warship of over 1,000 tons. After a voyage of over 5,000 miles in only forty-three days, she picked up a buoy at Spithead on 26 February. On 16 March Adam entered into his log, 'Came alongside 2 lighters for the Treasure. Employed loading ... Sent all the Treasure on Shore.'[41] This was just at the time when the government in London was becoming desperate for specie.[42] The *Resistance's* voyage from Santa Cruz, at least twice as fast as a convoy, can have done Adam's career no harm, a reasonable assumption since by 1835 Admiral Sir Charles Adam was First Naval Lord at the Admiralty Board.*

Much of this silver bullion went to London, sometimes via Cadiz, but it was destined for other purposes. Regular payments were taken, via Jamaica, to British troops in Guadeloupe and Martinique, for silver was needed when bills of exchange drawn on London were not acceptable. Halifax, the garrison and naval base in Nova Scotia, Canada, was particularly vulnerable because it was not self-sufficient and needed to be supplied constantly with silver merely to feed itself. Supplies of wheat were obtained from American farmers, even after hostilities had begun in 1812. Some cash came from England but between 1806 and 1815, 85 per cent of the money reaching Halifax dockyard was shipped from Jamaica.[43]

British, Spanish and Portuguese troops in Spain were the main recipients of Mexico's silver. Cash was essential for paying the troops and for purchasing local supplies. During 1809, for instance, seven Spanish ships departed from various ports in Spanish America to Cadiz; the *San Justo* in February left Vera Cruz and Havana with 6.7 million

---

* In 1841, the year that Adam retired, HMS *Resistance*, which had been in ordinary since the end of the war, was converted into a troop ship and was commissioned for another ten years. While it might be wide of the mark to ascribe sentiment to a tough Scot, it could be no coincidence that Adam was in post when the decision to prolong the ship's life was taken. He certainly remembered the voyage for his entry in O'Byrne's *Naval Dictionary* (1849).

dollars on board. None of this would have reached Cadiz safely without British trade protection. In spite of this stream of silver, by 1810 those defending Cadiz against Marshal Soult's encircling troops were desperate for money and credit. Two British 74s at Cadiz were sent directly to Vera Cruz, taking quicksilver, in order to pick up treasure, purchased with British government bills of exchange. HMS *Bulwark*, Captain Charles Fleeming, got safely into the harbour on 11 July 1810 and loaded thirty-two chests of dollars and small arms for the Spanish government, leaving on 2 October. The second ship, HMS *Implacable*, commanded by Captain George Cockburn, reached Vera Cruz on 23 November, but there was little coin. Instead, the crew loaded hundreds of bales of indigo and some cochineal, a valuable substitute for silver. In the four weeks that the ship was in port, Cockburn had to record the deaths of fifteen of his crew after an outbreak of scurvy on the outward journey.[44] By 25 February the ship was back and moored in Cadiz harbour. It took two days to unload the indigo and cochineal.* The British Treasury Agent there reported to the commander-in-chief, Jamaica: 'After the despatch of the *Implacable* it is not likely that any Dollars will remain to be forwarded'.[45]

Yet before supply dried up, the bullion flow was a critical factor in the Peninsular War. In the words of a Spanish historian: 'Without Mexican silver, neither the Regency nor the Cortes of Cadiz could have survived the powerful offensive of the Napoleonic army, particularly during the terrible years of 1809–11'.[46] Between October 1808 and February 1811 an average of almost one million dollars a month was sent from Vera Cruz to Cadiz and London, approximately half of all the silver mined at Potosi. The British navy kept the busy and thriving port of Cadiz open during the two years of the siege. British merchants came to dominate trade there. The City of London needed silver for the East India trade with China, for Spanish dollars were the currency of

---

* In 1810 the price of 'Spanish Caraccas' indigo rose from 4/8d per pound to 11/5d, while 'East India Superior' rose from 9/6d and peaked at 14/-. The price of cochineal rose from 32/- to 42/- a pound (Tooke, *High and Low Prices*).

the Far East too. These newly minted dollars thus played a vital role in the war against Napoleon.

The naval commands of the East and West Indies stations were the most problematic of all to manage. It is difficult to see how the Admiralty could have filled these commands without substantial contributions to senior naval incomes from the various merchant communities; fortunes were made by senior officers from freight money and from prizes. The lure of these potential riches therefore led senior officers to take up these commands and they were not always of the first calibre. They attracted those who were particularly keen, often through disadvantages of background, to increase their fortunes, and as a result some very weak appointments were made as commanders-in-chief on both stations.* They had to shrug off the potential dangers of tropical cyclones or hurricanes during the long sea voyage, or the risk of disease: one East Indies commander-in-chief drowned, two died suddenly in India, and another in the West Indies.† Long-term difficulties on station were well known and included a shortage of officers and an acute shortage of seamen, while a lack of maintenance facilities left warships that had been on station for any time in a dangerous condition.[47] Relations suffered between the navy and the West Indies merchants in Jamaica, as well as the East India Company in Bombay, Madras or Calcutta. An indication of the immaturity and ineptitude of Admiral Drury was the report in 1809 that he had challenged the Governor of Prince of Wales Island at Penang to a duel, in response to Company commanders refusing to drink to his health.[48] However, these problems were not quite as destructive as rivalries between warring senior naval officers, for

---

* The total of c-in-cs of the two stations for the duration of the war was ten. If Bertie at the Cape is added, at least half of these officers can be described as second-rate.
† Rear-Admiral Sir Thomas Troubridge, 19 December 1806; Rear-Admiral William O'Bryen Drury, 6 March 1811; Vice-Admiral Sir Samuel Hood, 24 December 1814; Admiral Bartholomew Rowley, 7 October 1811.

they were responsible for organising convoys between India and China, and homewards across the Indian and Atlantic Oceans to England.

The Admiralty had been fortunate in its appointment of Admiral Peter Rainier to the East Indies, who had held the command for twelve years from the beginning of the French Revolutionary War. He returned, a rich man, to England in 1805. For the rest of the war the situation was never less than fraught, and it was particularly bitter between 1806 and 1809, a period marked not only by internal rivalries but also by very high East Indiamen losses. Rainier was succeeded by Rear-Admiral Sir Edward Pellew, a brilliant leader and frigate captain, but ruthless in his pursuit of prize money and in promoting his two sons up the naval ladder. His command was bedevilled by the hasty and additional appointment on 23 August 1805 by Lord Melville of Rear-Admiral Sir Thomas Troubridge to the eastern half of the station, including the prize-rich Madras and Hoogli river. Pellew, incensed that half of his command was to be taken by a more junior officer, exploited a qualification in the Admiralty order which allowed him to declare that there was an emergency situation, and he refused to implement the order.

Troubridge had been over promoted for years due to the enthusiastic endorsement of his patron Lord St Vincent, who saw potential only in those whose characters were mirror-images of his own, and they both shared a vile temper. Troubridge had recently been a member of St Vincent's Admiralty Board, where he had made a fool of himself on more than one occasion.[49] In 1806, political opponents of Melville, by now in power, tried to find a compromise by making Troubridge commander-in-chief at the newly acquired Cape of Good Hope, news that Troubridge received in October 1806. His perceived humiliation at this outcome tipped him over the edge.*

---

* Pellew described Troubridge as 'A Weak Man, entirely commanded by his passion . . . every week dishonouring himself by striking some of his Midshipmen or any body else who comes in his way'. This evidence comes from Pellew in a letter to a personal friend of 10 January 1807. Although obviously hostile, this is strong evidence of a very tense time (Taylor, *Commander*, p. 200).

Troubridge was determined to leave Madras before Pellew was due back in the port. He therefore ordered his flagship, HMS *Blenheim* (90 guns, cut down to 74), now forty-five years old, to be made ready for sea. She had recently been aground and her pumps were needed just to keep her afloat while she was at anchor in the Madras Roads. It was towards the end of the favourable north-east monsoon season. Troubridge overruled the representations of her captain, who urged him not to put to sea, and he ignored the offer of Pellew to return in another warship. The *Blenheim* sailed for the Cape on 12 January 1807, accompanied by HMS *Java* (32) and the brig sloop HMS *Harrier* (18). The squadron hit a cyclone south-east of Madagascar on 1 February 1807. The last sight of the *Blenheim* from the *Harrier* was of the flagship settling low in the water, while *Java* had disappeared.[50] The combined complements of these lost ships were not far short of a thousand men. The affair divided the navy. St Vincent was never again to talk to Pellew, once one of his protégés.[51]

The West Indies station, too, was riven by passion amongst the senior navy. The quarrels at Jamaica, with money as the issue, led to the only court martial of an admiral in the Napoleonic Wars. Vice-Admiral Charles Stirling was commander-in-chief between 1811 and 1813. He had already spent part of his career there as the dockyard commissioner, and it was with one of his successors in this post, Isaac Wolley, that a dispute arose. Wolley was quarrelsome and had also fallen out with the previous commander-in-chief, Admiral Rowley, whilst Stirling lacked tact and was not popular in Jamaica.[52]

Wolley accused Stirling of claiming his flag-share of freight money on a warship that had escorted two British merchant ships to Havana, when no specie was actually carried. The court martial charge was 'For allowing HM Ships under his command to be hired as convoy to vessels going to the Spanish Main and/or taking money for the same'. Stirling's agent made the arrangements, and the question before the court martial, held on board a warship in Portsmouth harbour in June 1814, was how much Stirling knew about the matter. Wolley claimed that this practice was common, and he was probably right; Stirling's offence, if indeed it was such, involved a small amount of money compared to other payments. The verdict reflected the discomfort of the admirals and senior captains in reaching a decision: no court martial ever sat on the fence as much as this one. Stirling was 'To remain on the half pay list of Vice-Admirals of the Navy, and not to be included in any future promotion'. Stirling later managed to extract concessions from the Admiralty, though he never served again. Again, the affair split the navy for years.*

The wider divisive issue, however, which bedevilled both commands, was impressment, for the shortage of seamen on the East Indies station was acute. During 1805 Pellew started his command by issuing protections to the crews of East Indiamen, but when his warships were weakened by disease, he used his powers more freely. The Company's Committee of Shipping in London later established that in that year 818 seamen had been impressed from a total complement of 6,155 from outward-bound East Indiamen. In 1806 the figures were 694 out of 4,215. The navy took at least 10 per cent of the crews of East Indiamen for warships, but individual cases of impressment took far more. On one occasion Troubridge, when at Penang, took forty-one men from HCS *Perseverance*, out of a crew of not much more than a hundred.[53]

Apart from the lack of seamen, the difficulties caused by the profusion of money and the squabbling and obstinacy of fellow officers, a further problem for commanders-in-chief was the condition of warships that had to get back to England, taking a convoy with them. The dockyards at Port Royal, Jamaica, or English Harbour in Antigua had no docks for hull maintenance, while the Company dockyard at Bombay, the only dockyard outside England which had the capacity to dry dock a 74-gun ship, was many hundreds of miles from the main centres of activity on the east coast of India.[54] Just two years after the sinking of the *Blenheim* and the *Java*, Pellew returned to England in his flagship

---

* Ralfe's *Naval Biography of Great Britain*, published fourteen years later in 1828, devotes thirty-four pages to Stirling's trial and concludes that he 'was convicted upon the slightest evidence that, we believe, was ever offered to a court of justice' (vol. III, pp. 86, 98).

HMS *Culloden* at the end of his command, escorting a convoy, and he too ran into a severe cyclone.* But, unlike the *Blenheim*, the *Culloden* was in good condition, having had a two-year 'Large Repair' in Plymouth dockyard during the Peace of Amiens. She was relaunched at the beginning of 1803. It was also fortunate that *Culloden* had had her rigging overhauled in the harbour at Penang just before the voyage.[55] Nevertheless, the storm was nearly catastrophic. Pellew wrote afterwards to a friend: 'Had it continued six hours longer with the same violence, I believe she would have all our accounts in this life ... Had not the old *Culloden* been in good condition, she must have gone down.'[56] The ship never went to sea again after this voyage. She was laid up on her return and broken up in 1813.

The condition of warships in the West Indies, which might have been on station for as long as three years, were a potential hazard, with high humidity playing havoc with the rigging and teredo worm with hulls, in spite of the protection of copper sheathing. None of the naval bases in the West Indies could do more than caulk the upper works of a larger warship, or repair or replace spars, pumps or sails. Warships requiring docking had to return to England. Initiative was often needed to get home safely. In April 1809, Lieutenant William Ward of HMS *Bacchante* (20), when escorting a homeward convoy, discovered a leak of 'such magnitude as to compel my pushing for the first port'. He abandoned his convoy, but not before installing one of his passengers, Lieutenant Goodwin, on board one of the merchant ships, hoisting a convoy commodore's pennant. Goodwin had been the captain of a schooner that had been wrecked at Jamaica, and he escorted the rest of the convoy to the Downs. When the *Bacchante* finally anchored at Spithead there was 6 foot of water in her hold. Ward's report to the Admiralty was tinged with anxiety: 'I trust their Lordships from the defects of the ship will perceive the absolute necessity of my quitting

---

* Ironically, Troubridge had commanded *Culloden* from 1794 to 1800, years that saw two serious mutinies. The ship nearly took part in the battle of the Nile, but she went aground in Aboukir Bay on the approach to the battle.

the convoy and that they will not disapprove of my proceedings.'[57] *Bacchante* was an old French prize and was sold out of the navy three months later.

Considerable ingenuity also had to be employed in 1810 after HMS *Inconstant* (32) had sustained heavy damage to her keel on the rocks in Saldana Bay near the Cape. Not enough materials were on hand to repair her properly for the return convoy, but the Master Shipwright at the naval yard, 'being a clever man in his profession, patched her up so completely with sheet lead, hides, tallow, oakum and pitch, that it was deemed safe for her to return to England'. From St Helena, in blowing weather, en route for home, she was to keep near to HMS *Raisonable* (64), which led the convoy and was herself over forty years old, but it was noticeable how well *Inconstant* sailed, and she reached Spithead without trouble.[58]

The voyages back to England from both stations, often with ships heavily loaded with bulk materials, were arranged to take advantage of favourable seasonal winds and avoidance of tropical storms, though, as we shall see, that could go very wrong. Perhaps the luckiest homecoming was the convoy commanded by Vice-Admiral Peter Rainier on his return to England after his twelve years as commander-in-chief in the East Indies. He sailed in his flagship, HMS *Trident* (64) on 10 March 1805, having on board as a passenger Major-General Sir Arthur Wellesley, the future Duke of Wellington. The convoy called at St Helena on 20 June, where the rest of the China fleet joined. On 12 July the convoy set sail with forty-one ships, on a course well out into the Atlantic, west of the Azores, and did not head east for the Channel until it was at the latitude of the north coast of Spain.* Rainier's homecoming convoy missed the French and Spanish fleet returning from the West Indies by nearly two months. The real danger was posed by the

---

* On 16 August 1805 the convoy was at its most westerly position, longitude 34 degrees 05 minutes. It cleared the Azores on 28 August, latitude 41 degrees 02 minutes, longitude 33 degrees 13 minutes (TNA, ADM 51/1494). The French and Spanish fleet had crossed this track six weeks earlier (Knight, *Pursuit of Victory*, pp. 490–91).

powerful French raiding squadron commanded by Captain Zacharie Allemand, which left Rochefort on 17 July.[59] Rainier was always a lucky admiral. The exceedingly valuable convoy avoided discovery, reaching the Downs in safety on 9 September. The admiral struck his flag on the 18th.* According to the newspapers, the *Trident* carried some exotic cargo: a leopard and Indian livestock, while Rainier brought with him a fortune of half a million pounds.[60]

A more typical example of a homeward East Indies convoy is provided by HMS *Monmouth*, a thirty-year-old 64-gun ship, commanded by Captain Edward Durnford King, which left Madras in 1808 to pick up some returning East Indiamen and store ships. She had on board some invalids and a French diplomat prisoner of war. She left Point de Galle at the southern tip of Ceylon with twenty-one ships on 14 March, but in getting under way the HCS *Worcester* collided with HCS *Airly Castle*. The damage sustained meant that the *Worcester* had to be left behind. The convoy took the north-easterly monsoon towards the Cape of Good Hope, at which point the four transports left the convoy for the colony. The convoy reached St Helena after three months, on 12 June, where King found three more merchant ships to join the convoy, including a South Sea whaler. Here they stayed for a week watering. The *Monmouth*'s course took them well to the west in the Atlantic and they arrived at the Downs without incident on 14 August.[61] The convoy was competently handled and uneventful, not unlike Captain King's career, marked by longevity rather than distinction or excitement.†

From the West Indies, returning ships aimed to leave by the end of July to avoid the hurricane season, though convoys often did not get

---

* Immediately after landing, Wellesley went to London and paid his respects to the Foreign Secretary, Lord Castlereagh. In the anteroom, Wellesley met Lord Nelson, who was taking his leave before joining his fleet blockading Cadiz, before the Battle of Trafalgar. It was the only time that they met (Muir, *Wellington*, I, pp. 166–70; Knight, *Pursuit of Victory*, p. 497).

† King entered the navy as a midshipman in 1789, and was made lieutenant in 1795, therefore as captain he was young to command a ship of the line, even an old 64. He ended his career successively in the early 1840s as commander-in-chief, Brazils and the Cape, then c-in-c, the Cape alone and finally c-in-c, Nore. He died in 1862 (O'Byrne, *Naval Dictionary*).

away until after this deadline if the sugar crop and its processing was delayed. A strong northward current along the coast of Florida helped homegoing West Indies convoys. Robert Hay, a seaman aboard the ill-equipped *Edward* under a bad-tempered master in 1811, described the course. 'In sailing from Jamaica we do not, as many would suppose, steer a direct course. We first sail in a westerly direction till we draw near the Floridas, we then sail along the coast of America to the banks of Newfoundland, and from thence shape our course with almost always a fair wind for the south end (if for England) of Ireland.'[62] The convoys swept past Amelia Island where they picked up the ships loaded with American cotton. The prevailing south-westerlies in the North Atlantic and Western Approaches, together with the Gulf Stream and North Atlantic Drift moving in the same direction, made for swift homeward passages from the West Indies.* But there were still difficulties. The condition of some warships that had been out on station was poor, their hawsers being susceptible to rot.[63] Sometimes, owing to sickness or accident, there would be no one of sufficient seniority or experience to command a convoy and someone had to be sent out from England. Commander Edward Crofton escorted one convoy home commanding a ship in urgent need of repair, as he described in a letter to an Admiralty commissioner, then was ordered out to 'the West Indies in a Packet to bring home another in equally bad condition; and in both cases having done what I believe, unprecedented – brought home winter convoys safe.'[64]

In some years the hurricane season took its toll, if convoys left too late. One of the summer 1806 Jamaican convoys, escorted by the frigates HMS *Magicienne* (36) and HMS *La Franchise* (40) and the sloop HMS *Penguin* (16), lost 25 out of 102 ships. Nevertheless, the escorts received the public thanks of the West India merchants. Captain

---

* In the Western Approaches the convoy would split into two, one part heading up St George's Channel for Bristol, Liverpool, Glasgow and the Irish ports, the other up the Channel to London. In 1809, for instance, customs records show that 324 entered London, compared to 211 to the outports (Horsfall, 'West Indian Trade', p. 162).

Charles Dashwood of *La Franchise* replied in print: 'Although it is the duty of a Naval Officer to be peculiarly attentive to the Commerce of his Country, yet, when the endeavours of an humble individual is attended with success ... it cannot but be highly flattering ...'[65] The Committee of Lloyd's took a bleaker view. The Secretary, John Bennet, wrote to William Marsden concerning the loss of 6,000 tons of shipping, 'which is of the most serious consequence'. He pressed for three convoys to leave the islands a year, the last by 20 July.[66]

Strong south-westerly Atlantic winds were the cause of most complaints to the Admiralty from Lloyd's about West Indies convoy commodores in frigates, sailing too fast and out of sight of the merchant ships. The temptation for some naval officers to get home was too much. In 1808 Captain Sir Charles Brisbane, having led the expedition which captured the Dutch colony of Curacao, flew home in the frigate HMS *Arethusa*, signalling all the while for the convoy to keep up, 'several vessels in attempting to do so carried away their topmasts'. The masters of fifty-three merchantmen complained to Lloyd's that 'on no former occasion have they ever seen a convoying ship uniformly carrying so great a press of sail'.[67] Some of Brisbane's haste can be attributed to the fact that the *Arethusa* was transporting an enormous quantity of specie back to England.* He left the navy to become Governor of Dominica.

The problem of keeping convoys together in the long run across the Atlantic was always there. In May 1812 HMS *Dauntless* (24), not a fast frigate, left Jamaica with twenty-four ships and arrived in Britain, 'without a single ship of her convoy', as John Bennet wrote indignantly from Lloyd's to Croker, 'and that seven days after her arrival, only thirteen sail in all had arrived and ... nineteen sail of very valuable ships were missing...' Croker ordered the home waters commanders-in-chief to order out their cruisers to find and protect the stragglers.[68] Very slow merchant ships were also the problem. In the summer of 1811, the

---

* *Arethusa* carried 1,530,000 dollars on private account and 700,000 for the state (Knight, 'Achievement and Cost', p. 125; Aldous, 'Prize Money', p. 199).

Edward, seaman Robert Hay's unhappy, undermanned and leaky ship, was loaded with sugar, rum and coffee. Struggling to keep up by carrying more sail than was safe, her master was threatened with being left behind by one of the escorting warships. Only a vigorous protest secured a tow. After this, the *Edward* was towed whenever she fell behind. 'On one of these occasions,' Hay recounts, 'when it blew very fresh the ship that had us in tow was apprehensive of dragging us down and thought it prudent as she changed watches to let us go. We, also, afraid of being dragged under let go our hawser at the same time. Of course, away it went. A few days after, when we got within hail of the same ship, we requested her to drop the end of our hawser aboard, but behold instead of the hawser we got a knowledge of the events above named.'[69] Hay did not record the reaction of his choleric captain to the loss of his cable.

During the occasional prolonged periods of easterly winds in the Western Approaches, when the homecoming West India convoys were delayed, warships were sent out from Plymouth or Cork with food and water supplies to scour the seas for merchantmen who might be running perilously short of sustenance. It could happen in mid-ocean. In 1813, on the homeward run from the West Indies, only a month out, the brig *William* of Whitehaven ran out of provisions. The crew had been on short rations for all this time and had nothing to eat for three days, before victuals sent from the convoy commodore saved them from starvation.[70]

The most dangerous situation on the long-distance trade routes was the effect of severe storms on merchant ships with crews weakened by the loss of pressed men. Lack of manpower was less of a problem on the West Indies route, though the stresses of weather were similar in the western Atlantic and in the Indian Ocean. Even so, in 1805 at Port Royal, Jamaica, Captain Samuel Chambers of the HMS *Port Mahon* (18) boarded the

Anne looking for men and was resisted 'with muskets, pikes, blunderbusses and pistols' and the crew of the merchant ship attempted to break the naval boat to pieces.[71] That year was a particularly bad one for small warships; six foundered or sank, one was captured, while in 1806 as many as ten were lost and the subsequent three years were not much better.*

Lack of crew forced masters of merchant ships to use prisoners of war as crew members. In 1809 several of the crew of the *Lady Penryhn* were pressed in Grenada, though, according to the master, he 'accidentally met with some prisoners when on the point of sailing, he must have lost [missed] the convoy for want of hands'. Rear-Admiral Dacres, commander-in-chief, Jamaica, forwarded this account to the Admiralty, though his opinion was that masters took on prisoners of war to reduce the wage bill.[72] In the summer of 1809, a Jamaica convoy ran into the Tortola convoy, on different tacks, in mid-ocean, at night, described by Commander Benjamin Clement, HMS *Favourite* (18), as 'a perfect Hurricane ... At Daylight a most shocking s[cene] presented itself, nothing but dismasted Ships in every direction'.[73] Clement put himself under the command of the other convoy commodore, HMS *Captain* (74). The *Favourite* assisted in repairs, towed a damaged merchant ship for days and made it home, as the ships had the wind behind them. Clement was also able to deliver 800,000 dollars freight money.

East Indies casualties were also heavy. Between 1803 and 1815, thirty-five East Indiamen were lost, of which only seven (20 per cent) were captured by French frigates in the Indian Ocean.[†] The worst period was the two years of 1808 and 1809 when fourteen Indiamen were lost in the Indian Ocean, foundering during the sudden, short cyclones on the route back to the Cape.[‡] Four Indiamen were lost in British coastal waters

---

* See Appendix.
† All captures were in the Indian Ocean: *Cullands Grove* (1803), *Admiral Aplin*, *Princess Charlotte* (1804), *Warren Hastings*, *Fame* (1806), *Charlton, United Kingdom* (1809).
‡ Losses from a total of 508 sailings from 1800 to 1809 amounted to 5.9 per cent, and from 238 voyages between 1810 and 1814 to 3.8 per cent (Bowen, 'Shipping Losses', p. 326; Davey, *In Nelson's Wake*, p. 221).

in the winter.* Nine came to grief in the Indian Ocean.[74] In late 1808 in the Indian Ocean three foundered in a cyclone east of the Mascarene Islands, their crews weakened by naval impressment, when being convoyed home by HMS *Albion* (74), also severely damaged ('a perfect wreck'), as were others which just managed to reach the Cape.[75]

As the survivors repaired their battered ships at the Cape in preparation for the voyage home via St Helena, the commander-in-chief at the Cape, the recently-promoted Vice-Admiral Albemarle Bertie, had orders which he interpreted as instructions to join the expedition to Mauritius, with its promise of prize money.[76] However, his ships being short of men, he sent a lieutenant aboard HCS *Ann* who impressed eleven seamen. Impressment at the Cape was not customary. The short-handed captain of the *Ann* protested to Bertie that his ship was 'so much reduced as to be wholly unequal to carry on the duty of the ship or prepare her for sea'. When Bertie sent an officer to investigate, his launch was not, as custom demanded, offered a mooring rope. Tempers flared. The chief mate of the *Ann* explained coolly to the officer 'that he had not a man to spare for the purpose': his 'impertinence' was reported to the commander-in-chief, who demanded that the mate be punished. The company's agent at the Cape, John Pringle, refused, replying to Admiral Bertie:

> The State of the East India Fleet just arrived is such as requires no comment and with every exertion it is evident how unequal the crews are to work those ships home in safety. I therefore hope, Sir, that when you consider the state of these ships, their value and the importance of their safe arrival to the nation at large, that you will give directions that those who have already been entered may be returned and that no others be taken from them on any account whatever.[77]

---

* In 1805 HCS *Earl of Abergavenny* went ashore off Portland, in the winter of 1808–9, HCS *Walpole* was wrecked in the Thames Estuary on the way home, and HCS *Britannia* and HCS *Admiral Gardner* on outward voyages never got further than the Goodwin Sands (Bowen, 'Shipping Losses', pp. 355–6).

Bertie's bluff was called. Such a determined and dignified defence of the Company unnerved the commander-in-chief. He blustered to the agent: 'I shall not fail to represent to the Admiralty the marked hostility against rendering any assistance to HM Service and the insults offered to its officers'.* However, he returned the eleven seamen to the *Ann*. It did not often happen.

This convoy was followed by another in early 1809 when eighteen ships led by Admiral Pellew, after nearly five years as commander-in-chief, returned to England in HMS *Culloden* (74). Nine of them came from the Hoogli, escorted by a frigate, HMS *Terpsichore* (32). They had been crammed with saltpetre on the orders of the Master Attendant at Diamond Harbour, destined for the Ordnance, some of them with as much as 700 tons, so much so that four ships had to offload 50 tons of pig iron ballast each to make space in the hold. Because of the structure of the organisation, whereby officers, crew and ship were contracted to the Company, the person who was responsible for the navigation and safety of the ship did not have the final say over the stowage of his ship. The protests of each of the commanders were overruled by a shore-based official. It was no wonder that the Company was to lose its charter and monopoly in 1813.

As the pilots left them at the mouth of the river, it was noted that the bows of HCS *Calcutta* and HCS *Bengal* were low in the water, or 'trimmed by the head'.[78] Pellew joined the gathering ships from Penang at the Point de Galle and the eighteen-strong convoy left for London on 15 February 1809. His company commanders were dismayed when he ordered a course near to the Mascarenes. It was known that there were dangers of cyclones in this part of the ocean at this time of the year. Why Pellew decided to do this is unknown: perhaps his instincts as a frigate captain got the better of him and he was hoping to find a French prize near Mauritius. It was a decision that was to leave a blot on a distinguished

---

* As indeed he did, which is why the details of the row are to be found in the In-correspondence to the Secretary of the Board of Admiralty (Taylor, *Storm and Conquest*, pp. 101–2, quoting TNA, ADM 1/61, Pringle to Bertie, 28 January; Bertie to Pringle, 5 February 1809).

career. Near the Mascarenes the cyclone hit the convoy. Four of the Indiamen, *Calcutta, Bengal, Lady Jane Dundas* and *Jane Duchess of Gordon* disappeared without trace. The first two had cargoes valued at over £120,000.* Even a warship as powerful as the *Culloden* was hard pressed, and a vivid and terrifying account of that night at sea has been left to us by a seaman, Robert Hay. It was suggested to Pellew that the guns might be jettisoned to ease the ship. The admiral demurred: 'She will do very well, and what would become of the convoy if we meet the enemy?'[79]

In India, relations between navy and Company worsened under the next commander-in-chief, Rear-Admiral Drury, who was unrealistic, certainly undiplomatic and often out of his depth. Impressment of European seamen increased. When HCS *Asia* arrived at Madras in April 1809, seamen were impressed, then a further batch, tempers flared, shots were fired. Over thirty were impressed, a third of her crew. In sailing for Calcutta, she was unable to manoeuvre in a squall at the mouth of the Hoogli, and was lost on a sandbar on 1 June. Here was direct evidence that crew weakened by impressment directly led to ship-wreck. The sense of crisis was heightened as French raids on settlements in the Bay of Bengal became more effective, which led to the long-overdue decision to take Mauritius from the French in 1810. By the end of 1810, Reunion and Mauritius were in British hands, in spite of the disastrous attack on Grand Port, Mauritius in August of that year, when four British frigates were lost. Distant Java was taken from the Dutch in August 1811.[80]

From 1810 there were no East India casualties when ships were sailing in convoy.† The dangers of the English Channel were lessened by

---

* The Company carried its own insurance. The invoice value of the *Calcutta*'s cargo was £124,452 and *Bengal*'s £121,262, either of which would have paid for a 100-gun battleship (e.g. HMS *Nelson*, launched 1814, £123,469) or nearly ten Cruizer-class brig sloops, for example, HMS *Wasp*, launched in 1812, cost £5,837 to build and £7,216 to fit out (Bowen, 'Shipping Losses', p. 335; Winfield, *British Warships*, pp. 11, 301).

† Four ships were lost on the Indian coast and four were burnt in Bombay harbour or the river Hoogli, or wrecked while at anchor (Bowen, 'Shipping Losses', p. 336; Sutton, *Maritime Service*, p. 223).

not sailing in the depths of winter. Rather than January or February, three convoys left from the end of March until May, usually in smaller numbers, each consisting of between six and a dozen, totalling around thirty outward per year. Only in 1813–14, with the end of the monopoly, did numbers of outward convoyed merchant ships reach over eighty.[81]

A distinct lull of nearly three years in enemy threats to convoys followed, before the declaration of war by the United States. In the West Indies, the Spanish changed sides after the Madrid revolt of spring 1808 and their colonies were no longer hostile. Dutch, Danish and French naval bases in the Caribbean were captured, which eliminated the dangers from enemy warships or privateers. Martinique was captured in February 1809 and Guadeloupe a year later. Casualties of small warship more than halved. More and more shipowners applied to the government and were granted licences to sail without convoy in the Atlantic. This freedom abruptly ended when the Americans declared war in June 1812; United States warships and privateers were only too effective. From that date no licences were issued by the government.[82]

The balance shifted in Britain's favour after Napoleon's Moscow defeat in the autumn of 1812, when the Admiralty was able to make ships of the line available for Atlantic convoys. These large warships were easily identified and their tall masts provided seamen with a high platform for scanning the horizon. In January 1813 Charles Dashwood, by now commanding the 74-gun HMS *Crecy*, took 102 ships out to the West Indies. Convoy problems persisted. He reported to Lloyd's that the brig *William* of Whitehaven ran out of provisions after only a month at sea, during which time the crew were on short rations. By the time victuals from the flagship reached the *William*, they had had nothing to eat for three days.[83] Dashwood returned to Britain with 166 ships, with the approval of his merchant masters, who 'gave him a chronometer, for the very great attention he had paid them during the voyage'. In September 1814 Captain Lord Colville, commanding the cut-down 90-gun ship *Queen*, launched as early as 1769, brought back 370 ships, the last West Indian convoy of the war.[84]

The relationship between the navy and the merchant service on distant stations, far from those centres of authority, the Admiralty and the City of London, can at best be described as fragile. In the far corners of the British worldwide convoy system, the shortage of skilled seamen was at its most critical. The dangers of storms to merchant ships, accentuated by undermanning caused by impressment by the navy, would always outweigh the likelihood of their capture by the enemy.

NINE

THE BATTLE FOR THE BALTIC
Timber, Hemp and Wheat, 1807–1812

We were mostly employed convoying large bodies of merchant vessels through the Great Belt, an arduous service; the passage was so swarming with privateers and rowboats . . . At one time, with over 400 vessels, under the charge of the Hero, ourselves, two frigates and a bomb, we never saw the head of the convoy from the time of leaving Wingoe Sound. We had charge of the rear.

Midshipman John Harvey Boteler, HMS *Dictator* (64), June 1810[1]

Of 2,000 ships which entered the Baltic this year, not one was neutral: all were sent by the English; all were loaded in London, loaded on English account. They were, it is true, disguised under American, Spanish or Swedish flags; they had papers and dispatches of each country and perhaps false certificates of French consuls, certificates manufactured in London.

Napoleon to the Tsar of Russia, 2 December 1810[2]

The number of convoys and the ships within them sailing to and from the Baltic, mostly via the large anchorage outside Gothenburg, were by far the most numerous of any organised by Britain, doubling the next largest, those to and from the West Indies.* Moreover, this number was achieved without sailing in the three coldest months of the year, January, February and March, when ice prevents entry into the Baltic. The safest and largest convoys took place in midsummer. For instance, in July 1809, 6 convoys escorted 720 ships back to England. A huge expansion of trade in 1813, following Napoleon's Moscow defeat, resulted in vast convoys.† In April Commander Thomas Renwick, HMS *Mercurius* (18), who from 1808 until the end of the war did nothing else but convoy ships to and from the Baltic and Archangel, 'conducted in safety a fleet of between 400 and 500 sail through the Sound under a continued fire from Cronenburg Castle'.‡ In June 1813 Captain Samuel Butcher, HMS *Antelope* (50) took 332 to the Baltic, 209 back again and 142 to the Baltic again in October. On 29 October the tiny HMS *Cherokee* (10), Commander William Ramage, brought back 366 from Gothenburg to England. Ramage had been promoted from the lower deck and made commander in 1807 by St Vincent because of 'his superior merits and ability'.[3] The same could be said of many officers and seamen escorting convoys in the North Sea and Baltic.

Heavy concentrations of merchant ships tended to occur in the Sound or the Great Belt. In 1810 Count Bernadotte, on his way to take up the Swedish throne, crossed the Great Belt on 14 October 1810, with British permission. In the middle of the Belt, near the island of Sproe, two homeward convoys met six hundred bound for the Baltic. Bernadotte's Swedish yacht passed close to HMS *Victory* (100), flagship

---

* According to the Admiralty/Lloyd's log, 234 convoys took 9,237 ships into the Baltic between 1809 and 1813, averaging nearly 40 ships per convoy. The lowest total of ships was in 1811 (31 convoys taking 1,031 ships), the largest was 1813 (78 convoys, 3,702 ships). Homecoming convoys numbered 156, escorting 11,728, an average of 75 per convoy. The lowest number of convoys was in 1812 (22 convoys, 773 ships) and the highest was 1813, 35 convoys with 3,541 ships (TNA, ADM 7/64).

† Out of a total of 3,702 outward voyages in 1813, the peak months were June (946 ships) and August (1,790 ships). Voyages back to England totalled 3,541, peaking at 1,157 in September (TNA, ADM 7/64).

‡ Renwick claimed to have escorted 2,000 ships in all. 'Of these not one was at any time captured or lost' (O'Byrne, *Naval Dictionary*, p. 967).

of Vice-Admiral Sir James Saumarez, and six other ships of the line, protecting over a thousand merchantmen, flying a multitude of national flags. Saumarez's biographer claimed that Bernadotte thought that it was 'the most beautiful and most wonderful sight that he had ever beheld'.[4]

The strategic and financial importance of the Baltic led the government to position a considerable fleet in the Baltic under Saumarez. He reached Gothenburg to take up his command in April 1808. Before the end of the year his naval force had increased to eleven thousand men in eleven ships of the line and two sixty-fours, four frigates and ten sloops, as well as bomb vessels, a total of forty-four warships, which by 1809 had risen to sixty-two.[5] Most of them returned to England each year during the ice-bound winter, giving ships and men some respite. Saumarez's task was to block Napoleon's influence, bottle up the Russian fleet, maintain good relations with Sweden, resist the Danes and in doing so keep the trade flowing back and forth to Britain. When Napoleon forced Sweden to declare war on Britain, the commander-in-chief's common sense and diplomatic finesse maintained very good informal relations between two nations which were formally at war.[6] In Sweden, even today, Saumarez is highly regarded, having protected the country from both Russia and Napoleon.*

One of the functions of the Baltic convoys was to protect the transports and victuallers that supplied Saumarez's warships, a task which tested the organisation of the British navy to the full. The most difficult year was 1809, when naval and mercantile resources were tightly stretched across Europe, facing crises at Corunna in Spain early in the year and demand for unprecedented numbers of vessels to transport and supply the Walcheren expedition at the end of it. Demand for ships was

---

* Saumarez's great Swedish friend and confidant, Count von Rosen, wrote to him in 1813: 'you were the first cause that Russia had dare to make war against France: had you fired one shot when we declared war against England, all had been ended, and Europe would have been enslaved' (Voelcker, *Saumarez*, p. 3, quoting Suffolk Record Office, HA/93/6/1/2447, 22 August 1813).

heightened by the recovery of trade, so that hiring transports to supply the Baltic fleet was difficult. However, by 1810, the organisation of the Transport and Victualling Boards proved to be more than adequate, and, as we will see, that capability had far-reaching strategic results.[7] Saumarez and his fleet remained in the Baltic until 1812, when Napoleon's disastrous defeat in Russia led to the unravelling of the Continental System and the reduction of his influence, allowing British warships to be moved elsewhere, primarily to the North American station.*

Convoys to and from the Baltic were the most important to Britain for the means of fighting the war and they were the most complex.† Their routes lay through a war zone where effectively two wars were being fought, one by Britain against France and her allies Denmark, Sweden and Russia, while Sweden and Russia were fighting an intense land and sea war in the northern Baltic. The situation improved on the last day of 1810, when Russia again opened her ports to British ships. With her economy suffering, the Tsar realised that he could no longer afford to support Napoleon's Continental Blockade, though his change of sides met with a great deal of suspicion amongst British merchants and naval officers, doubtful about Russian intentions during 1811.[8]

In spite of these difficulties, trade flourished. Not only was the Baltic the only region that could supply the enormous quantities of naval stores required in British shipyards and by other expanding industries, year after year, but the timber, hemp and iron from that region were of the first quality.‡ Homegrown oak in England for shipbuilding was almost exhausted. The royal forests could only deliver four thousand

---

* See Chapter 10.
† In the recent words of a historian of the region, the Baltic in this war 'took on an importance second to none'. British government policy was 'grounded in the knowledge that exclusion from her source of shipbuilding materials would decimate her economy and her national security' (Davey, 'Securing the Sinews', p. 168).
‡ Very often iron was carried in the bilges as ballast as timber was a relatively light cargo and when only a ballast cargo, iron commanded only a low freight rate (Currie, *Henley's*, p. 18; Davis, *English Shipping*, pp. 223–4).

loads a year to the dockyards, just short of what was required for building a single second-rate ship of the line.[9] Nor should the importance of timber for purposes other than shipbuilding be forgotten: pine for housebuilding, and spruce for piling docks and canals and for pit props in quarries and mines.[10] Ports on the southern Baltic coast supplied wheat. During the Peace of Amiens, for instance, 72 per cent of wheat imported into Britain came from Prussia.

For the industrial materials there were almost no other effective sources than the Baltic: because substitutes from other parts of the world could not match the quality of the Northern Europe products or because far distant routes increased their price.* At the start of the war there were considerable shortages. In 1801, just before Lord St Vincent was appointed First Lord of the Admiralty, Britain imported 37,000 tons of hemp from Russia.[11] St Vincent's obsessive economies during the Peace of Amiens resulted in cancelled contracts. Reserves were whittled down in dockyard storehouses. In June 1804 the Navy Board reckoned that it had no more than three months of sailcloth and only half a year's worth of hemp and plank.[12] Dependence upon Russia as the sole supplier had worried the British government for many years. Shortages in 1800 and 1801, caused by Russian hostility, had resulted in a real sense of crisis within the British government, though the attempt to find alternative sources ended in failure.[13] The only possibilities, apart from a thin supply from India, was the Black Sea region, but this was also dominated by Russia; in any case, the supply route from there was too precarious in wartime.[14] The consumption of hemp for rope making was prodigious, for it rotted in the humidity of the tropics and needed regular renewal. The safety of a ship depended upon it daily, as in the account related by William Richardson, on board the merchantman *Regulus*, just back

---

* An exception was the import of timber from North America. Following the imposition of duties in 1806 upon Baltic softwoods, by which the government hoped to damage the Napoleonic economy, by 1811, 154,000 loads of squared timber came across the Atlantic, compared with 125,000 loads from Europe. Similar increases of imports of masts and deals from Canada took place in these years (Fayle, 'British Shipping', p. 84; Lower, *Great Britain's Woodyard*, p. 49).

from the West Indies in 1799, which anchored in heavy weather in the Downs. The first anchor cable failed. The ship was,

> broadside to the wind ... on her beam ends, and was driving fast towards the Goodwin Sands, before the sheet anchor was let go, but (thank God) that brought her up. Fortunately for us, the cable was a new one and not like our old worn-out cables we had brought from the West Indies. But when it brought the ship up I never saw such a strain on a rope before – it absolutely shrank to near half its size.[15]

It was no wonder that so much hemp was needed.

The average Baltic convoy was usually composed of many ships, mostly small, between 100 and 300 tons.* They needed to have a shallow draft as there was little water over the bar at some of the ports of loading in the Baltic itself. At Kronstadt the depth of the bar at the harbour entrance was only 8 foot, though most ships made fast to the mole outside. At Memel, the height of the bar was susceptible to currents and the depth varied between 11 and 14 foot, and merchant ships often had to anchor outside the bar to complete the loading of their cargoes from lighters.[16] Many ships sailed to the Baltic in ballast, with no cargoes at all, particularly in the fallow years, such as 1811, although there could be advantage in doing so as an empty hold reduced the likelihood of confiscation by hostile warships or privateers or Napoleon's officials in those states under his control.[17] During May of that year, for instance, 2 convoys sailed from Vinga Sand towards the Belt: HMS *Plantagenet* (74) escorted 100 ships, 79 of which were in ballast, while HMS

---

* A representative sample appears in a list sent to the Admiralty of ships wanting convoy to England, loading and ready at Karlskrona, sent by Captain Bathurst of the *Salsette*, 19 April 1809. Eight ships flew the flags of Sweden, Lubeck, Konigsberg and Russia, with cargoes of hemp, flax, wool, iron, deals and timber. Six of them were under 200 tons, their average was 160. Two were of 330 and 350 tons (TNA, ADM 1/1545).

Tremendous (74) protected 110, of which 67 were ballasted. In the two convoys, those that did have a cargo carried salt (24 ships), sugar and coffee (17), five had coal and three tobacco.* Single ships took chalk, manufactured goods, logwood and pickled herrings.[18] Merchant ships in ballast floated high in the water and were unwieldy and difficult to sail, and thus to convoy.

As well as protecting trade and resupplying the fleet of Admiral Saumarez, convoys also carried muskets and munitions to Prussia, Russia and Sweden, after the Tsar allowed trade and to bolster Russian defence against Napoleon. In 1811 a very risky scheme was put to the Foreign Secretary by Samuel Thornton, one-time MP for Hull and Governor of the Bank of England. Gunpowder and lead were to be taken to Russia, where the Tsar had turned against Napoleon, and hemp would be brought back in return. Lord Wellesley acted immediately.[19] HMS *Grasshopper* (18) escorted four merchant ships carrying 500 tons of gunpowder and 1,000 tons of lead for the Russians, with the expectation that 2,500 tons of hemp would be sent back as payment. When the convoy reached St Petersburg, permission to land the cargoes was refused. The munitions eventually reached Prussia.[20] *Grasshopper* never made it home, as she was caught on the Haak Sands in the great storm of Christmas 1811, and surrendered to the Dutch.

The next year, another small convoy loaded with fifty thousand stands of arms found it even more difficult to reach Russia, as recalled by Samuel Jefferson, by this time mate of the *Mary Ann*. She was one of three ships escorted by HMB *Gallant* (10). The convoy sailed far too late in the year, in November 1812, from the Nore into a strong north-easterly gale, reaching Gothenburg in late December, where Admiral Hope 'asked us if the Ministers were mad' to send the ships out at that season, and sent the convoy back to Portsmouth. The convoy was then sent to the Black Sea, but could not get past Constantinople and spent the next year sailing around the Mediterranean, then back to Spithead,

* The Swedish population depended upon British salt (Davey, 'Supplied by the Enemy', p. 2).

where orders caught up with them. Sent to the Baltic again, the ships failed to get through the Belt because of the weather, and finally made Karlskrona in Sweden.[21] Other convoys were more successful. Muskets, gunpowder, cartridges, pistols and flints munitions were sent in very large quantities. Prussia and Russia received over 100,000 muskets each, and those to Russia were of critical importance in the struggle of the Russians to re-arm after the battles of 1812. In 1813 over a hundred field pieces and 1,200 tons of ammunition followed.[22]

Although Baltic convoy routes were not the length of those in the oceans, they were a substantial distance, with difficult weather and hazardous pilotage. From the Humber, Gothenburg was a round trip of 800 miles and to and from Elsinore 1,000 miles. The trade from Liverpool and the west coast sailed 'northabout' the British Isles. It was not easy to get round the Butt of Lewis in northerly or easterly winds and fierce tides of the Pentland Firth were never easy to navigate, even with a fair wind.* The Archangel trade had to contend with difficult currents, fog and at latitudes that made compasses unreliable. Accounts by naval commanders of convoys from the North Cape at the end of the season make for dramatic and frightening reading, even two hundred years later.[23] But the trade continued to grow, with corn, tallow and hemp, 6,000 tons of which were anticipated in 1807.[24] In 1809, for instance, more than a hundred merchantmen loading at Archangel for ports in England and Lloyd's complained to the Admiralty in that year when Danish privateers were successful in that area and later when American privateers were becoming a danger.[25]

Not only were imports from the Baltic critical to industry and the war effort, it was also an important export market for British goods and grew at a faster rate than any other region of the world during these years. A variety of tropical re-exports found a ready market: sugar,

* One report from a merchant ship in 1793 runs: 'The Butt of Lewis ... with the wind from the NE we were for two days after before we could get round ... flowing very hard with a heavy sea and she was going with a fair wind' (GL, GG/245, Murray Gladstone to John Gladstone, 1 August 1793).

tobacco, coffee, cotton, hardwoods and currants from the Mediterranean. From Britain itself came manufactured goods, cloth, coal, salt and tallow candles.[26] War did not prevent the export of luxury or exotic goods to Russia. The cargo for Samuel Jefferson's first voyage as an apprentice to the Baltic in 1804 consisted of twenty-four horses, from Hull to St Petersburg, taking the owner of the horses and three grooms as passengers. Remarkably, the next year his ship repeated the voyage, this time delivering four kangaroos, a present from King George to the Emperor Alexander of Russia.[27]

Exports to most of Northern Europe went mostly through the Baltic as Napoleon's land conquests extended northwards. Unsurprisingly, the markets were volatile, subject to the varying effectiveness of Napoleon's anti-British trade measures, but the Baltic benefitted from the diversion of trade from elsewhere in Northern Europe.[28] In 1808, the year after the introduction of the Continental System, exports to the Baltic fell to half the value of the previous year. They recovered over the next few years, climbing again in 1809, but uncertainty over trading relations with Russia, as she was breaking with France, resulted in a spectacular fall in 1811 to a level just under a fifth of the previous year.[29] By 1814, when Napoleonic influence in the region had been eliminated, it had recovered to nearly £23 million, almost ten times the lowest point in 1811.* Admiralty organisation, the shipping industry, exporters and importers had to be flexible in dealing with the capricious combinations of war and trade.[30]

Nevertheless, war against Denmark did not start well for Britain after the attack on Copenhagen in the autumn of 1807. The year 1808 was, as Samuel Jefferson recalled, 'a black one for the Baltic trade, nearly every port being closed against us; only a few licensed ships under American colours got up through the Belts'.[31] As a result, multiple rises in prices followed on the London market. In 1808 and 1809 a ton of

---

* Exports to the Baltic: 1807 £9.4 million; 1808 £4.7m; 1809 £13.7m; 1810 £11.2m; 1811 £2.3m; 1812 £5.4m; 1813 not available; 1814 £22.9m; 1815 £19.8m (Mitchell & Deane, *Historical Statistics*, p. 311; Davey, 'Securing the Sinews', pp. 163–4).

St Petersburg clean hemp doubled in price, from 68/- to 118/- and flax from 80/- to 140/-. Steep rises were also recorded for Russian bar iron and tallow, while the price of Stockholm tar pushed up that of American tar. Fir from Memel nearly doubled, the price of pine from Quebec followed.[32] Large quantities of wheat had been imported into Britain from the southern shores of the Baltic, but none came to Britain in 1808.* However, alternative supplies could be obtained from the United States or Ireland. A large part of the determinant of the price of wheat was the success or failure of the domestic harvest in England. The import of wheat from 1810 onwards saw a large quantity coming from France under licence, and dependence upon the Baltic for wheat began to lessen.

Though the British had stripped Denmark of sixteen ships of the line and fifty-eight smaller warships after the expedition against Copenhagen in 1807, and had destroyed half-completed ships in the dockyard, the Danes rapidly built many brigs and gunboats which harassed the convoys. In all, 173 gunboats were built in Denmark and 100 in Norway; in the ensuing 7 years they were to lose 94 of them.[33] The entrance to the Baltic is an area which is susceptible to long periods of windless weather, giving these small vessels the crucial advantage of forward movement and manoeuvrability, being rowed when their larger antagonists were becalmed. Conversely, when the wind sprang up, the Danes were no match for the speed of British sailing warships. The smaller Danish gun vessels were armed with a single long 24-pound gun, firing from the bow, placed longitudinally so that the vessel could absorb the recoil and powered by oars (or sweeps) as much as by sail. In order to man the heavy sweeps, as many Danes as possible

---

* In 1800 and 1801, 665,955 and 528,032 quarters of wheat were imported from Prussia, with figures for the following years slowly decreasing. But in 1808 the figure was nil: Galpin, *Grain Supply*, Appendix 8, p. 246.

were packed into a small space. In late 1810 the Danes introduced an improved design of gunboat, more manoeuvrable and seaworthy, which enabled them to attack convoys in windy conditions, under cover of darkness, which brought them some immediate successes, but the British adapted new defensive tactics by using ships' boats.[34]

In October 1810 George Coggeshall, master of the schooner *Eliza*, described the scene at Gothenburg:

> Many merchant ships of different nations were daily arriving at this place of rendezvous to proceed up the Categat and Baltic. The merchant vessels had been collecting for several weeks, and as it was the last convoy into the Baltic for the season a great number of them of all descriptions had assembled: I believe at least 600 sail. The whole of this vast fleet were nominally neutral ships, sailing under the different flags of nearly all the petty states of Germany, and their cargo purported to be the bone fide property of their respective countries, which in point of fact, the most of them were English property, cloaked or covered by the flags of these different nations by simulated or counterfeit papers.[35]

Almost all merchant ships sailed under neutral flags, carrying two sets of papers, of which at least one set was forged. One set was to convince British intercepting warships that the ship had touched at a British port, had paid duties and obtained a licence for its journey and cargo. The other set would be to satisfy customs officers in southern Baltic ports under French control, or to convince Danish or French privateers that they had not called at a British port or carried British cargo.[36]

The likelihood of a merchant ship carrying two sets of papers was high. A Danish privateer owner instructed his captain in 1810:

> Should you chance to meet a vessel with French licence, endeavour to find an English licence on board, <u>which you cannot fail to do.</u> Her you must take as a prize ... These vessels are generally cleared from two

places, and are to be condemned as prizes even if they had a licence. The captains hide their papers under the hearths or about the body. As soon as you have detained a ship, you must treat the men with the greatest kindness and politeness; and endeavour to make them afraid of the punishment inflicted on anyone who does not declare the truth.[37]

The Danes issued letters of marque to some six hundred privateers from Denmark and three hundred from Norway between 1807 and 1813, enabling them to take British merchant ships. Up until the late summer of 1809 this was profitable, but by 1812 this was no longer the case, partly because of the effectiveness of British convoys but also because from 1810 Britain allowed Danish merchant ships to trade with Britain under licence.[38] Some Danish merchants took advantage of this arrangement, in spite of the trenchant punishments meted out by the Danish state to those who had any contact with the British. This included imprisonment and fines, and in one case in Flensburg the death sentence, though this was commuted.[39]

On the declaration of war with Denmark in 1807, British warships caused considerable havoc with the Danish merchant fleet and in all some 1,400 Danish-Norwegian ships were made prize.[40] Lieutenant Thomas Mansell, just thirty years old, from Guernsey and a protégé of Saumarez, commanded the 350-ton, ship-sloop HMS *Rose* (16).* Just how complex the prize situation with both Danes and Russians as adversaries is shown by a memorandum in Mansell's papers listing the questions to be asked of the masters of Russian merchant ships, so that they could prove that the cargo came from Britain. The Bill of Lading was to be produced and the licence under which they sailed, and proof

---

* Rear-Admiral Sir Thomas Mansell (1777–1858) was flag lieutenant of HMS *Victory* and was given command of the *Rose* 'for the time being' in September 1808. He claimed to have 'contrived to make prize of 170 vessels of various descriptions' in the Baltic and North American stations (GSA, AQ 365/02–13, order signed by Saumarez, 2 September 1808; O'Byrne, *Naval Dictionary*).

of the voyage should have been decided by charts of the North Sea or the coasts of England. Questions should be translated into German, Swedish and Danish in case there was no translator on board.[41]

Mansell and his crew did very well at the expense of the Danes. His correspondence and accounts with his agent list 28 Danish merchant ships taken in 1809, which grossed nearly £11,000, a calculation by his agent after the value of the prizes had been shared with other British warships. As much as £8,904 was available to his crew, with a complement of 121, for distribution at the end of that year. Russian merchant ships, fair prize up to 1811, were additional lucrative targets for Mansell and the *Rose*, so that his total prize money for 1810 was approaching £15,000.[42] In May 1812 he captured six Danish sloops laden with corn and provisions for North Bergen.[43] It was a time for rich pickings. One seaman aboard the *Victory* reported that 'our fleet Captures about 40 sail of prizes every week & sometimes More but Seldom less'. Even the pessimistic James Whitworth, seaman aboard HMS *Portia* (14), stood to gain from a valuable prize in 1812; characteristically in his letter to his wife he was doubtful if it would get through the courts, though, as he wrote to his wife, 'If she is condemned I shall get at least £100.'[44]

Saumarez facilitated the passage of convoys by taking and securing islands and bases on the approaches to the Sound and the Belt, and within the Baltic itself. His subordinate in the southern Baltic was Rear-Admiral Sir Richard Goodwin Keats, a cold, peevish but talented man who would personally supervise every detail of any operation for which he was responsible. One of his first tasks was to ensure a reliable and plentiful fresh water supply. This was essential, especially for the more numerous warship crews, for it was used constantly on board for steeping salt provisions before cooking to make them edible, as well as for cooking itself. The commanders of warships operating at any distance from a water supply carefully noted the tonnage remaining every day.* The lack of access to fresh water was one of the factors which led Keats to abandon Marstrand in December 1808 as the main base on the west coast of Sweden, choosing instead the Hawke Roads within Vinga Sand, fourteen miles east of Gothenburg.[45] The best protection for large ships was in the lee of the islet of Buskaer, sheltered from south-westerly or southerly winds. Here the crews of British ships planted vegetables. Smaller merchant ships anchored near Hano and Foto, and the best source of fresh water was on Hissing Island.† One captain described it as, 'A most dreary situation, but a very convenient anchorage for our fleet, being very secure, and plenty of water in the small islands, or rather rocks, the hollows of which, where there is any soil, the different ships have made into gardens and have raised plenty of vegetables for the use of officers.'[46] Although, as we shall see, the anchorage was vulnerable in extreme weather.

Gothenburg did well out of the war. When the British fleet entered the Baltic in 1808, 434 ships cleared the port. Four years later, that figure had quadrupled (1,617 ships).[47] It was a city of about 14,000, with a merchant class of 1,500, with an estimated English population of 200–300. One German visitor thought that, 'the city was virtually a piece of England set in Sweden ... English taste prevails from the breakfast table until late at night ... people drink Porter and Port, one is served Toddy not only before but also while having tea ... dressing habits are the same as those among the modern gentlemen on Pall Mall and in Westminster'.[48]

There were regularly vast gatherings of ships in Vinga Sand. A month before Bernadotte's crossing of the Belt, westerly winds had delayed two homeward convoys, when 19 warships and 1,100 merchant ships

---

* For instance, HMS *Forward*, a gun brig, with a complement of fifty crew, carried a maximum of 10 tons of water. Consumption was between a quarter and half a ton a day (TNA, ADM 51/2384, *Forward*'s log, June–July 1810). See also Davey, *Transformation*, pp. 128–9.
† Here there are still remains of wells, walls and buildings, known as the Englishman's Garden (my thanks to Henrik Karlssen for this local information).

were observed by Count Rosen, Saumarez's Swedish friend and ally. 'Since the Creation', he wrote, 'the outer roads of Gothenburg have probably not looked as now.'[49] On another occasion in mid-1812, a lack of escorts detained 250 vessels, and the Committee of Lloyd's wrote to Croker, Secretary of the Admiralty, complaining of the delay to the homeward voyages.[50]

Further down the Kattegat lay Anholt, a small sandy island, which was captured by the British in mid-1809, plentiful water being one of its advantages.[51] Its lighthouse not only marked some dangerous reefs, but also acted as a rendezvous for convoys heading towards the Baltic. Midshipman Boteler of HMS *Dictator* noted, 'Pure fresh water was to be had at any part, even within twenty yards of the sea, we only had to sink an empty flour cask in the sand and it would instantly be filled, and with this contrivance ships would complete their water.' The importance of Anholt was emphasised by a determined Danish attack in late March 1810 by 1,500 troops, transported by gun vessels, who landed one dark and foggy night. They were beaten back by a force of 150 marines. A large number of the Danes had to surrender, and lost forty men killed, while their retreating gunboats were pursued by a frigate and a sloop.[52]

There was no chance to establish a base in the Great Belt itself, where the larger warships were effectively floating bases for ships' boats in their defence of the convoys against attacks by Danish gunboats. An exception was the uninhabited island of Sproe, in the middle of the Belt, where the midshipmen were encouraged to exercise to work off some of their energy.* Nevertheless, these islands were fiercely contested by the Danes. In May 1809 HMS *Ardent* (64) landed about eighty men to collect water on the island of Romso in the Great Belt. They were surprised and captured by the Danes.[53]

---

* Boteler remembered Sproe as 'Of no great size, chiefly of fine turf, a pond or two, and myriads of frogs. Many of the ships had gardens on it: running the chance of reaping produce, for it was the anchoring place for most ships; we used to land there for leap-frog and other games' (Bonner-Smith, *Boteler Recollections*, pp. 12, 15).

It was important to have an equivalent rendezvous point within the Baltic itself for returning convoys, mirroring the function of Anholt for outward convoys. Saumarez's ships made a half-hearted attempt to capture a small island off the north-east of Bornholm called Christianso, but more because it was a base used by Danish privateers and the Baltic merchants were keen to have the islands taken. Saumarez, his attention taken up with more urgent matters, never gave its capture any priority and no serious attempt was made on it.[54] The main rendezvous for England-bound convoys became the island of Hano on the southern Swedish coast, south of Karlshamn. Between 1810 and 1812 a slaughter house was erected here, which enabled fresh beef to be supplied to British ships, while British seamen dug wells for water. The French did not know about this contravention of its treaty with Sweden.[55] George Coggeshall, at this time the master of the American schooner *Eliza*, came there in June 1811: 'between it [the island] and the mainland there is a good, safe anchorage, the entrance being open and easy of access'. He found twenty merchant ships anchored there and within eight days there were fifty, at which point he joined a convoy through the Great Belt.[56]

But these were dangerous waters in winter. Neither British naval captains nor merchant masters could relax, for in very bad weather there were no completely safe harbours or refuges. In the first week of October 1813, Samuel Jefferson in the 300-ton *Mary Ann* left Gothenburg for Riga in a small convoy, but a hard south-westerly gale forced the convoy commodore to anchor near Anholt. Cables soon parted and the convoy was forced back towards Vinga Sand. Jefferson was at main top, 'to look out for the rocks on the Swedish coast. It was a bitterly cold berth, with pelting and pitiless showers of sharp hailstones, but so anxious were we about the lee shore that we seemed not to feel the weather.' The ship found the Vinga Beacon and anchored, but unable to find a safe berth, Jefferson paints a vivid picture of a chaotic, crowded anchorage in a storm. The *Mary Ann* immediately began to drag her anchor, passing stern first close to the static ship of the line HMS *Warrior*, which had a loaded dismasted brig towing astern by a cable out of one of the quarter ports. A brig with her foremast and bowsprit gone, and riding by her only anchor, was obliged to cut her cable to prevent us driving on board of her. She had her top-gallant-yard on the stump of her foremast, and with this sail got before the wind, but where she went without anchors we never heard ... We continued driving towards a large ship that was riding by her only bower anchor ... but she held on, and our mizzen rigging caught the end of her bowsprit and carried it away, and at the next pitch away went her foremast and mainmast head, also our mizzen-mast, besides other damages. Our ship now brought up and we rode out the remainder of the hurricane.

This was the gale of 16 October 1813, when dozens of ships were lost or driven ashore and 'it was said that some 400 to 500 anchors were lost'.[57]

Geography concentrated the convoys so that guarding them from attack was very difficult. The Baltic sea can only be entered by two very narrow channels, the Sound and the Belt. The east passage, the Sound, had the advantage of being bordered by friendly Sweden, but narrow channels and shoals, from which the Danes removed the buoys and marks, made navigation very difficult. The Great Belt, on the other hand, was less well known and sixty miles long, with stronger currents. Whichever was chosen, the narrowness of both passages had the effect of acting as a bottleneck, a cause in itself of larger convoys. For these, if they experienced contrary winds, it could take as much as four days to get through the Belt.[58]

It was calm conditions rather than unknown hazards that were dangerous for convoys in these narrow waters. A period of calm in early June 1808 resulted in three losses. HMB *Tickler* (12) was attacked when cruising in the Great Belt and she surrendered after a four-hour battle, with her captain killed.* Four days later in the Sound off Saltholm the wind died on a homeward convoy of seventy-six ships, the rear protected by two bomb-vessels, HMS *Turbulent* and HMS *Thunder*, when they were attacked by twenty-five Danish gun vessels. They both lost steerage way. The *Turbulent*'s main topmast was shot away and she was overwhelmed by six in the evening. The captain of the *Thunder* tried firing shells and grapeshot at the Danes, but to little effect. He reported to the Admiralty: 'I had the mortification of seeing her fall, without a possibility of affording the smallest aid.' Then followed four hours' incessant gunfire in an attack on the *Thunder* until dark, when the Danish gun vessels withdrew. 'Many were the efforts of the enemy to close on all sides. Had we fallen, nothing could have saved the convoy . . . I believe the Enemy took 12 sail, 4 of which they burnt . . . Those now in the ship, who were in Lord Nelson's last action at Trafalgar say, this surpassed it for hard fighting.'[59]

Admiral Keats's role in evolving a method of ensuring safe passage of convoys into the Baltic was critical. The first difficulty was lack of knowledge of the waters; though this had been improved by ships which took part in the 1801 Copenhagen expedition, great gaps still remained. In early August 1807, a month before the attack on Copenhagen, Keats led ships of the line and sloops through the Belt to ensure that the main Danish army in Funen could not cross the Belt into Zealand to defend Copenhagen. Guided by the brig sloop HMS *Musquito* (16), with three gun brigs marking the banks and shoals, Keats reported to Admiral Gambier that he had navigated the Great Belt, 'with no delays than what unavoidably arose from calms, light or contrary winds and currents, which latter particularly affected and considerably retarded the ships-of-the-line, while its operations on smaller vessels was scarcely perceptible'.[60] It was from here that in the

---

* Lieutenant John Skinner was killed when his head was struck by grapeshot. His wife was on board according to Saumarez (Ipswich Record Office, James to Martha Saumarez, 17 June 1808), for which references I am indebted to Tim Voelker. The third capture was HMS *Seagull* (16) in the Skagerrak.

summer of 1808 Keats directed the remarkable removal and repatriation of over seven thousand Spanish troops commanded by the Marquis of Romana from Funen, via Gothenburg to Santander in northern Spain in a convoy of forty-one transports.[61]

Over the next four years, the British captains came to know the waters of the Great Belt well. Keats positioned his ships of the line at each end of the Belt and sloops and gunboats in the middle, creating a protective screen for convoys.* Both naval and merchant ships spent a great deal of time surveying these waters and, as the war progressed, the accuracy of the Hydrographic Office and commercial charts improved significantly and few problems of navigation were encountered after 1808.[62]

British tactics to fight the Danish gun vessels by guarding convoys with substantial ships' boats, also armed with a long gun, had some success. Aboard the *Dictator*, Midshipman Boteler recalled:

> We were supplied with two extra twenty-oared barges, which were stowed on skids outside the waist hammock nettings, just above the main deck guns. No sooner was the night set in, when there would be a tar-barrel on fire, or a rocket, or lights shewn at different parts of the convoy; then the exciting pipe was 'Away there, all boats' crews'. Barges and pinnaces and two cutters would be sent in various directions.[63]

Occasionally, the British would turn the tables, ambushing the Danes. One of the bomb vessels, HMS *Meteor*, had been converted from a merchant ship and was made to look as little like a warship as possible, 'a main top-gallant and royalmast, a fore-top gallant mast only and no mizen. The ropes were sixes and sevens, none kept taut, and her hull was painted with a sheer. Her own carronades were hidden, and

---

* 'The principal difficulty appeared to me to arise from currents, the set and velocity of which being frequently a few fathoms down very different from what it is on the surface, resists in large ships particularly the effect of the helm and sometimes, in what we think very commanding breezes, renders them quite unmanageable' (Ryan, 'Copenhagen Operation', p. 317, Keats to Gambier, 9 August 1807).

four quaker guns secured to the ship's sides, and she captured more privateers and row boats than all the squadron. They were taken in, all boarding her making sure she was a prize.'[64]

The shuttle system established by Keats lasted for the length of the war. Keats was not in the Baltic for long. His successor, Rear-Admiral Manley Dixon, followed Keats's principles with success. Two sixty-fours, HMS *Dictator* and HMS *Africa*, were attacked in the Sound in 1808, but thereafter few convoys went through the Sound and only the Great Belt was used. After this time, there were no British naval ships lost in the Belt.[65] Between mid-June and early November 1809, 2,210 merchant ships were escorted through the Belt without loss from enemy action. The next year between 30 May and 4 August, 1,815 passed through. The passage through the Sound was resumed regularly in 1813 after the defeat of Napoleon in Russia.[66]

The greatest single loss to British trade, however, occurred in 1810 more than 150 miles to the north, outside the Baltic, off the Naze of Norway. During the summer months, a convoy would leave Long Hope Sound in the Orkneys for Gothenburg on the first and fifteenth of the month, within the area for which the commander-in-chief, Leith, Vice-Admiral Sir Edmund Nagle, was responsible. Nagle had nowhere near enough warships for all the escort duties within his station and only two ships were available, with HMB *Forward* (10) separately sharing escort duties with the much larger, fifth-rate HMS *Hebe* (36). One warship took the outward convoy while the other brought back the homeward convoy, an arrangement which had been approved by the Admiralty.

The number of Danish naval brigs had increased in this area, and on the outward passage on 27 June the *Forward* lost a ship to two of them, in very light airs, 'inclined to calm'; the gun brig unsuccessfully 'swept after them', as the commanding officer, Lieutenant Richard Bankes entered in the log.[67] *Forward* and her outward-bound convoy reached Vinga Sand on 11 July and set out for the return to Long Hope with her new convoy on the thirteenth, by which time the wind had strengthened, squally with heavy rain. She issued convoy instructions to eleven ships only, before joining a larger convoy of two hundred ships escorted by the HMS *Solebay* (36), which was heading for the North Sea.[68] On 18 July the *Forward* parted from the *Solebay*, in light airs, and headed north, with a convoy of forty-seven ships. The next day the weather was 'moderate and hazy', twenty-five miles south-west of the Naze of Norway. On 19 July 1810 Captain Kreiger and his small squadron of five Danish/Norwegian naval brigs lay in wait, ready for a predatory raid. For many years, the Norwegians had been observing the low level of protection of homeward-bound convoys and it was surprising that it had not happened earlier.

At two in the afternoon, Lieutenant Bankes saw seven ships to the east, and 'immediately made the Signal to the Convoy for an enemy being in sight, and to haul on the Larboard tack and stand to the westward'. Outnumbered, *Forward* fled, though her attackers got within range. There was just enough breeze to allow the gun brig to escape, taking drastic measures to increase her speed: 'I cut away one of my anchors and blew away my stern boat in using the stern chasers.'[69] After an hour's chase, his pursuers turned back to the convoy.

While the light wind enabled the relatively fast *Forward* to escape, it was not enough to propel the forty-seven heavily laden merchant ships. Bankes complained to Vice-Admiral Nagle that his signals to scatter and sail to the west were ignored by every ship in the convoy.[70] But the conditions favoured the captors and there was almost no darkness in July to aid an escape. Every merchant ship in the convoy, Kreiger reported, flew a neutral flag. Only one of the forty-seven, a 'Papenburgher', was not condemned in the Admiralty court at Kristiansand. For the Norwegians, the convoy was the single most valuable capture of the entire war, contributing 25 per cent of their total prize money. Twenty-three of the ships were loaded with timber and iron, not so beneficial since Norway exported these products. Ten carried hemp and sailcloth, of considerable value, and three carried tallow and wax; but what was particularly prized by the blockaded and beleaguered Norwegians was the grain from north Germany, which was transported in ten ships.[71] The sailcloth was sent to the naval yard at Kristiansand, while the ships themselves sold well.* Only one other complete convoy had been taken during the war, by Villeneuve's fleet in the West Indies on 8 June 1805.[72]

The next year it was a different story. More warships were available for the defence of the Baltic convoys. Samuel Champion, Saumarez's secretary, reported to Lloyd's in July 1811 that the enemy was 'coming down the Belt on 1st and 5th June in great force but did not succeed in capturing a single vessel, the next day they mustered 17 large Gunboats and 10 heavy row Boats. Four of the gunboats were taken by the *Cressy*, *Dictator* and *Sheldrake* and nothing but a fog saved the rest. They suffered severely in killed & wounded, and we have besides 120 prisoners.'[73]

The most difficult decision that Admiral Saumarez had to make every year was the timing of the sailing of the last convoy to set out to cross the North Sea before the ice set in. The Board of Admiralty watched the situation very closely and issued firm guidelines to the commander-in-chief, but recognised that such a decision had to be taken locally because many variable factors had to be taken into account.† Annual differences included the extent and thickness of the ice, but the most finely balanced assessment was over the loading and readiness of merchant ships, which might have been delayed by contrary winds, or late deliveries at their port of departure. Shipowners had to weigh a delayed sailing against the expense of financing ships frozen in ice in the Baltic for the winter months. While Saumarez and the navy wanted the convoys off as early as possible

* The sudden influx of wealth caused problems for Norwegian naval officers (some of whom became wealthy) because they wished to see the cargoes sold gradually so that prices would hold up, but everything was sold in two days. The dispute was one cause of the resignation of Admiral Fisker later that summer (Tønneson, *Kaperfart og skipsfart*, p. 266).
† First and last convoys 1812: First, Nore to the Baltic 20 April; Gothenburg to Baltic 10 May. Last convoys, first favourable wind after: Gothenburg through Belts, 15 September; Hano south, 1 October; Convoy to Gothenburg 15 October or at least 1 November. Last convoy from Gothenburg to Britain, at discretion of the commander-in-chief (TNA, ADM 7/795).

to minimise risk, he had to judge how far to bow to commercial pressures and wait for delayed merchant ships.*

More ships and lives were lost at the beginning of winter through hostile weather than at any other time of the year. The winter of 1808/9 was especially harsh and December saw devastating losses. On 6 December 1808 HMS *Crescent* (36), sailing singly from Great Yarmouth with supplies of winter clothing for Saumarez's fleet and transporting seamen's families, was wrecked in thick weather on the north Danish coast. Two hundred and twenty people died, including six women and one child. On 23 December a convoy of twelve set out from Karlskrona for England, escorted by HMS *Salsette* (36), HMS *Fama* (38), HMS *Magnet* (16), a brig sloop, HMS *Salorman* (10), an ex-Danish prize cutter, and two Swedish warships. Every ship bar one was either forced ashore or cut to pieces by drift ice, driven by fresh easterly winds. Some merchant ships were taken by the Danes who walked over the ice to capture them. Only the *Salsette*, built of teak in Bombay, luckily survived, though she had no masts by the time she reached a safe port.[74] Less than three weeks later, HMB *Constant* (12), escorting a transport, was forced by ice from her anchorage in the Belt, sailing north, pumps going continuously, with the brig 'a mass of ice almost unmanageable', but managed to reach Harwich. The next month Keats's ship HMS *Superb* (74) had to cut her way 3 miles into the Hawke Roads (Hakefjorden) at Vinga Sand by means of ice saws, for the frost had, as he wrote to Saumarez at the end of January 1809, 'extended the solid ice, apparently as far as the eye could reach into the Kattegat . . . and thickened the ice to an extent from all accounts uninstanced at this season.'[75]

Fog could also be devastating, a particular problem in the late autumn of 1812. In October HMB *Sentinel* (12), escorting a large

---

* On occasion, no warships were available at the end of the season to provide an escort through the Belt. The *Oeconomy* and the *Alice* had to stay at Karlskrona during the winter of 1812–13, the only time that any of Henley's ships were forced to winter in the Baltic. This was a tiny percentage of the 157 Baltic voyages made by the firm's ship between 1784 and 1830 (Currie, *Henley's*, pp. 18, 21).

homeward convoy in the Baltic itself, ran into prolonged fog off the island of Rugen. A strong current took the ship and twenty-two of the convoy ashore on the island. Some were floated off, but eight merchant ships were set on fire and eight captured by the enemy. The dismasted *Sentinel*, fired on by enemy militia, was abandoned. Her crew was taken off by a merchant brig, setting fire to their ship as they went.[76] Six weeks later, HMS *Belette* (16), leading some Russian warships through the passage south-west of Anholt, immersed in thick fog and at night, hit a rock off the island of Laeso near Gothenburg.[77] By midnight, the ship had broken in two and most of the crew were clinging to the rigging, in intense cold. One by one they succumbed to exposure. Six survived, 116 perished. Between 1808 and 1813, seventeen small warships were lost in the Baltic, nine of them through winter weather and eight through capture by the Danes.*

Until the end of 1811, convoying from the Baltic had gone well, so much so that on 5 November the *Hull Packet* celebrated 'the exemplary conduct of the British commanders in the Baltic. The many and large fleets from that sea this year have been convoyed to the British shores almost without loss.'[78] As that complacent editorial was being published, the convoy that experienced the worst weather disaster in the entire war was gathering for the homeward passage. It was to be battered by a succession of gales, which took their toll on warships and their crews far more ruthlessly than it affected the escorted merchant ships. Saumarez tried to ensure that the merchants in the Russian ports knew that the last major convoy through the Belt back to Britain would leave Hano on 1 October, with a sweeping-up convoy on 15 October, 'which will positively be the very latest period . . . I am aware People may think the period fix'd upon is too early.' After that, he recommended that ships should winter in Riga in preference to the hazard of being detained in Sweden.[79] The concern over the Swedish political position was to affect the decisions that were to be made in the next month. Ten days of gales

* See Appendix.

followed by light winds ensured that it was not until 9 November that the end of the season convoy left Hano for England. It was led by HMS *St George* (98) under Captain Daniel Guion, the flagship of Rear-Admiral Robert Carthew Reynolds, with other ships of the line and several smaller warships, escorting a 120 merchant ships.

The first storm hit the convoy at the southern end of the Belt when it was anchored, waiting for a fair wind, not far from Nysted. Thirty merchantmen were lost or driven onshore and some returned to Hano. A large merchantman drove across the cable of the *St George*, which went ashore. 'While the foremast was falling,' wrote one crew member, 'a heavy sea lifted the ship up to the very heavens, from whence she was precipitated against a sand-bank (at two o'clock in the morning), with the most furious impetuosity, and with a dreadful crash, that appeared to shake all her timbers to pieces.' *St George* lost all her masts and her 7-ton rudder. With a 'Pakenham' (substitute) rudder and masts rigged from spare spars, with the wind behind her, escorted by the other warships, she managed to make it to Vinga Sand.

Here Saumarez conferred with his second-in-command, the sixty-six-year-old Rear-Admiral Reynolds, and Guion, his flag-captain. A fortnight passed with continual repairs on *St George*. The commander-in-chief's doubts increased over her seaworthiness, and he wanted her to remain at Vinga for the rest of the winter. But Saumarez allowed himself to be persuaded that she should return immediately. It was a risky decision made by tired men. The convoy set out for England on 17 December, with the patched-up *St George* under tow by HMS *Cressy* (74), under Captain Charles Pater, with HMS *Defence* (74), under Captain David Atkins, both ordered to stand by. HMS *Victory* with Admiral Saumarez, with eight ships of the line, led the convoy of a hundred merchant ships. *Victory* went on safely to England. On 23 December yet another gale, this time from the north-west, hit *St George*'s convoy. After a miserable two days trying to weather The Skaw, the three ships were swept down the Jutland coast. Towing large warships in these conditions was never going to be possible.

'Heavy and severe as the gale was, there was considerable light, as we had a moon,' Pater later reported to the Admiralty. As the *St George* made no signal, 'I considered I had his approbation to use every endeavour to clear the land.' Heading southwards, under only the mainsail, jib and storm staysail, 'the *Cressy* was pressed so hard that the lee gunwale was under water most of the night.' With the pumps manned continually, she finally cleared Horns Reef late on 24 December. By contrast, Captain Atkins in the *Defence* could not be persuaded to leave without a signal from the admiral giving him permission to do so.[80]

Defence stayed with the *St George*. The two ships were stranded on sand, and waves swept over them. The admiral and two captains and all the crews perished, although a handful of seamen reached the shore.* HMS *Hero* (74) too was lost. In heavy sleet and snow, with 120 merchant ships, hopelessly disorientated, she struck the Haake Sand off the Texel on 25 December. Five hundred drowned, eight seamen survived. Within twenty-four hours, the navy had lost two thousand officers and men.[81] Fewer casualties, by contrast, occurred among the merchant ships they were escorting, as the *Hull Packet* reported, since their masters knew the waters well, knowing the 'strong currents that set in the coasts of Jutland and Holland, by steering well off, they saved themselves from the destruction that befell the unfortunate *Hero*'.[82]

Captain Charles Dashwood, HMS *Pyramus* (38), was left behind, commanding a squadron of ten frigates and smaller vessels, as he remembered years later, 'to collect and bring home the remnant of Rear-Admiral Reynold's unfortunate convoy. On this occasion he took upon himself the responsibility of passing through the Malmo Channel instead of the Great Belt and thereby saved the whole from destruction.'[83]

---

* The Strandingsmuseum St George in Thorsminde commemorates this disaster through arte-facts excavated from the wrecks of the two warships. The *St George*'s 7-ton rudder lost off Nysted is also on display (Jepsen, *Last Voyage*).

William Henry Dillon, far away in Portsmouth, recalled, 'These losses made a lamentable impression on the whole nation ... All the Navy were called upon for a subscription to relieve the widows and relatives. At Portsmouth all the officers and seamen contributed two day's pay to their assistance.'[84] On 13 February 1812, John Wilson Croker sent out a printed letter to all captains on 'the later numerous and calamitous losses ... from extraordinary errors in the reckoning ... some by running indiscreetly in thick weather or by night for a Port, and others again from neglecting to keep the lead carefully going'. He reminded them of their responsibilities outlined in the Masters' General Printed Instructions and that, when a pilot was onboard, 'it does not relieve you from responsibility'.[85]

A month later, Charles Philip Yorke, the First Lord of the Admiralty, suffering continual attacks in Parliament, and under acute financial pressure from the Treasury, found this extra blow too much to bear and resigned.

Worried about costs, shipowners and masters did everything they could to get their loaded ships away before the ice set in, but every year dozens of merchant ships did not make the last convoys and had to winter in the Baltic. On the other hand, the seamen on these delayed ships welcomed the chance of between three and five months ashore, living in quickly built timber houses, working on the maintenance of their ships, where fuel, food and drink were inexpensive and camaraderie was plentiful. Samuel Jefferson when still an apprentice arrived at Kronstadt on 29 October 1804 and his ship was rapidly unloaded and then reloaded by 10 November. However, by the next day, 'we were all frozen fast for the winter, where we remained in the ice until the middle of the following May ... the Captain soon found us a house on shore, no fires being allowed on the ship.' Jefferson and his fellow apprentices enjoyed 'plenty of sleep and easy work, which pleased us much better than the cold winter wind at sea'. They spent the rest of the winter overhauling the ship's rigging in the house and Jefferson even had Russian lessons.[86]

George Coggeshall of the American schooner *Eliza* had a similarly sociable time during the winter of 1810/11 at Boldera, a few miles down the river Dwina from Riga. Houses were built there for wintering crews, 'and as there was no want of female society among the lower classes, balls and dances were very frequent'. The ship's rigging was overhauled and a new suit of sails made. As he was now in command, Coggeshall hired an apartment in Riga: 'as the river was frozen some two or three feet thick, there was an excellent road for sleighs on the ice to the ships at the Boldera, so that in a very short time we could visit our ships whenever it became necessary.'[87]

The next year, 1812, saw even more ships wintering, with the commander-in-chief and the Admiralty very cautious about sending home a late convoy after the 1811 disaster. The Admiralty also left a small squadron of ships and brig sloops at Marwyck, for there were 350 sail lying in Karlskrona, Hano and Marwyck frozen in. The *Hull Packet* lamented: 'The merchants and shipowners will ... suffer severely by this ... as many of the former are under heavy acceptances for cargoes which now cannot be brought to market for many months. The expense of keeping the crews in Sweden will be immense and even provisions must be sent out for this purpose.'[88] Two years later, Samuel Jefferson, by this time master of the *Mary Ann*, still convoying government munitions, found himself in Karlskrona during the severe winter of 1814/15. He recalled that he was very comfortable: 'We had in the harbour some fifty merchant vessels, five English men-of-war and one Russian sloop of war, indeed a town of all nations on the ice, and could visit each other quite comfortably without going at all into the city.'[89]

Jefferson was happy with this situation because on this voyage the government was paying. His general optimism over profitability in the Baltic is notable. For instance, 1815 was a good year. For the 7 months his ship, the *Mary Ann*, was contracted to government she earned 20/- per ton per month, but he made a late voyage to St Petersburg, taking cargo and passengers, arriving in late October, picked up tallow and hemp for London at 50/- and 80/- per ton per month respectively and made £1,300 on the voyage, clearing over £3,000 for the whole year, a high figure for a ship which was valued at £4,000.[90] An analysis of the wartime profits made by Henley's ships demonstrates an average profit for a reasonably large ship was between £1,000 and £2,000 a year.[91] Immediately after the peace, freight rates plummeted and, by 1816, Jefferson recorded, 'several hundreds of ships were out of employ.'

Of course, shipowners' costs went up steeply in wartime, including crew wages, provisions, port charges, dues, pilotage loading and delivery charges, but these were more than balanced by the increase in freight rates, in line with the increased risk and demand. They rose at the beginning and end of the Baltic season, so that shipowners made greater profits per ship at this time of any year.* Many of the shipowners in the Baltic trade insured their ships and cargoes, though not necessarily to the full cost, with insurance clubs at the north-east ports. The one at Shields would not cover any voyage to the Baltic that started after 15 October.[92] Insurance premiums for the Baltic, which stood at between 3 and 5 per cent of the value of the cargo and/or ship in the first years of the war, jumped to 20 or 30 per cent. In 1808 as much as 40 per cent was levied on cargoes in neutral vessels bound to Baltic ports occupied by the French.[93] The high point of these premiums occurred during 1810, though they started to decline in 1812.[94] In the event, the greatest loss incurred by Lloyd's was caused by the Prussians, who under pressure from Napoleon, seized ships in their ports along the southern shores of the Baltic in late 1810. It was discovered the following year that information that this was going to happen was already held in Lloyd's, sent by Samuel Champion, Saumarez's secretary,

* Typically, Baltic timber rates, per ton per month, rose to 30/- in March, fell to 27/- in July and August and rose to 31/- in November (Currie, *Henley's*, p. 21; Ville, *English Shipowning*, pp. 125–6).

to the Secretary of the Committee of Lloyd's, which caused a great furore within Lloyd's itself and led to a change of staff and systems.[95]

Economic warfare in the Baltic slowly fizzled out. Russia changed sides between 1811 and 1812 and Sweden, dependent on British trade and the need to import wheat, was muzzled by Saumarez's friendly, non-combative approach. The endgame for the war against Denmark was drawn out. The blockade of the Norwegian coast continued, although British raids against northern settlements had died out by 1809. Considerable hardship, which at some points reached starvation levels, was caused because the British prevented the import of wheat from the southern Baltic. The few sizeable Danish warships that survived the 1807 Copenhagen action were eliminated, notably in the bloody destruction of *Najaden* at Lyngor in early July 1812 by HMS *Dictator*, accompanied by sloops, though by the time of this attack the convoy battle had been won.[96] By January 1813 the Danish state was effectively bankrupt. It was not until January 1814 that peace was made at the Treaty of Kiel, complicated by Russia's insistence that Sweden should take over Norway. It was a sad end when the Norwegians hopelessly defended Frederikstad against the incoming Swedes with forty-seven sloops and yawls.[97] As with many great power conflicts, it was the adjacent smaller nations that suffered most.[98]

Britain had gained massively by subverting Napoleon's Continental System, keeping open the arteries of trade and forcing Russia away from France, in turn provoking the Emperor to invade. The decimation of the Grand Armee in the retreat from Moscow swung the strategic advantage in this long war, for the first time, towards Britain and the allies.[99] This would not have happened without a successful convoying system to and from the Baltic ports.

TEN

THE NORTH ATLANTIC
War on Two Fronts, 1812–1815

Each convoy therefore equalled in force the whole American navy;
the consequence of which was, that not a single merchant ship had
been taken which sailed under convoy, and that no convoy had been
at all disturbed, except by weather.

John Wilson Croker, Secretary to the Board of Admiralty,
speaking in Parliament during the annual debate on the
Convoy Act, 13 May 1814[1]

The United States declared war on Britain on 18 June 1812. Merchants in Boston and New York sent fast vessels to warn American ships before the British learnt of the news. While one ship from Boston was captured by a Danish privateer and taken into a Norwegian port, the *Champlin* from New York reached Gothenburg on 23 July. Forty American ships there, awaiting a British convoy, heard the news first and retreated up the river to the city, to moor under the Swedish fortifications. Efforts to alert those American ships at Hano were nullified by American masters believing that there would be no war once their government in Washington heard about the repeal of the Orders-in-Council, which the British government had announced on 16 June. Besides, most American ships were trading on English accounts. It was a confusing picture. Some American merchant ships made it home, some were captured and some were marooned in European ports for the rest of the war.[2]

The British first heard the news from incoming merchant ships on 29 July. Captain Clotworthy Upton in HMS *Sybille* (44) was cruising off the Old Head of Kinsale, under the orders of Vice-Admiral Edward Thornborough, commander-in-chief, Irish Station. Disobeying his orders, Upton immediately extended his cruise and headed towards Cape Clear to warn all merchant ships, ordering them into Cork Harbour. He wrote a tentative letter, defending his actions to his admiral: 'I am aware of the responsibility I am subjecting myself to, but I cannot serve the commercial interests of my country without some responsibility at times, I hope prolonging my cruise until 6th [August] may meet your approbation, and that by that time I may have prevented some of those vessels from falling into the hands of their new enemy. And I trust it will appear to you that had I waited until I coud [*sic*] have received express orders from you on this subject it might have been too late.'[3]

Events on land in Europe slowly shaped Britain's new trade protection war against the United States. On 24 June 1812 Napoleon had invaded Russia. On 19 October he began his retreat from Moscow and entered Paris on 18 December, having lost his army to the Russian winter, his global power fatally wounded. On 5 January 1813, in what was effectively a public announcement that Denmark was bankrupt, the Danish/Norwegian currency was converted and a new bank was established. The Danish naval threat to British convoys was almost eliminated, although peace was not signed until 14 January 1814.[4] Thus, during 1813 and 1814 Britain was able to move 15 per cent of its warships from the Baltic and other European theatres of war westward into the Atlantic to escort convoys and tighten her grip on the blockade of United States ports. This was critical if Britain was to succeed because her seamen numbers were declining steeply through the attrition of war, disease and desertion. The number of warships in the navy as a whole 'in Sea Pay' declined from 595 in 1809 to 515 in 1812 and by mid-1813 was down to 504. The newly built, 450-ton trade protection sloops had to be laid up in Ordinary as they were launched. The number of seamen fell by 20,000 between 1813 and 1814, from 147,000 to 126,000.[5] The army suffered a similar manpower decline in these two years.* The country was running out of men.

British North Atlantic convoys had to keep trade flowing, build up naval stores in Halifax to maintain warships, while troops had to be transported to defend British North America, and later take part in raids on United States soil.[†] Combined convoys to Halifax, St John's, Newfoundland and Quebec would leave the Solent or Cork, escorted by several warships, and when nearing the American coast, would then split up when ordered to do so by signal from the commodore, a designated warship taking each part of the convoy to their separate destinations. Westward, outgoing convoys from Spithead or Cork were smaller than those returning to Britain and because of the prevailing south-west winds would take a southerly course, often sailing more than a thousand miles further than the returning convoys which had the wind with them. Those sailing in the late spring or summer had kinder weather and an easier passage than those leaving in the autumn.

The conflict in the North Atlantic went through several phases during this short, 2 1/2-year war, in which 78 convoys escorted 2,661 transports and merchantmen from Britain to and from Halifax, St John's, Newfoundland and Quebec. There was also the much larger West Indies trade to protect, because the homeward-bound route passed close to the American eastern seaboard. From mid-1812 to the end of 1814, 149 convoys protected 6,233 ships engaged in this trade, figures that do not include the cross trades such as the route between the

* 'The British Army was able to continue to the end of the war without suffering a complete breakdown of its systems of manpower supply, but it was able to do so by the narrowest of margins and even eighteen months later, in the campaign of Waterloo, the legacies of 1813 and 1814 can be seen in the mixed quality and performance of some of the regiments sent to Flanders' (Bamford, 'Finding Manpower', p. 43; see also Knight, *Britain Against Napoleon*, chapter 15).
† Halifax experienced a boom at this time from the increase of the garrison and the navy, as well as the distribution of prize money (Gutridge, 'Hulbert', pp. 33–5; Knight, 'North Atlantic Convoys', pp. 47–8).

West Indies and British North America.[6] By the end of 1812, the commander-in-chief, Admiral Sir John Borlase Warren, was given the command of the combined naval stations of North America, Bermuda, Jamaica and the Leeward Islands. Although this might have looked, from London, to be a sensible way of controlling warships and convoys, the combined station was far too large a command, although Warren took advantage of moving to Bermuda during the winter and back to Halifax during the sticky Bermuda summer months.[7]

In the initial six months of the American war, British convoys to the West Indies and North America were very vulnerable to American warships and privateers because the number of available naval escorts were thin, as they were still engaged in the European war. Between July and December 1812, more than 200 American privateers and 'letters of marque' merchantmen captured approximately 350 British vessels, though a third of these were subsequently lost or recaptured, or were not taken into port to be condemned.[8] In all, 600 private armed ships from America and 40 from the British provinces of New Brunswick and Nova Scotia sought to capture mercantile prizes from each other. A few, powerful American 'long-range' letters of marque merchantmen took British prizes from as far away as the eastern North Atlantic, or from the Archangel trade, sending them into France or Norway to be condemned in prize courts sympathetic to the American cause.

Most prizes were, however, captured off the North American coast, although American success declined as the British blockade tightened, when it became difficult to get prizes back to the privateers' home ports. American privateers captured 190 prizes between 12 June and 26 September 1812, the Americans having managed to get most of them back to port; only 16 prizes were burnt or sunk. However, between 25 June and 29 October 1814, American privateers captured 170 British ships, but had to burn or sink 67 of them, or 39 per cent. A recent analysis is that 1,900 prizes, during the war as a whole, were taken by American privateers, 'with perhaps a third only getting as far as an admiralty court'.[9]

Local American commerce suffered too. The notorious, fast British *Liverpool Packet* (a privateer in spite of its name), from Liverpool, Nova Scotia, started operations in August 1812 against American trade, and before the war was out, had captured a hundred prizes, getting fifty of them to port. These were captured entirely within the waters around New England, for, in twelve cruises under four different captains, she never ventured beyond Cape Cod.[10] These were difficult, foggy waters, where local knowledge counted for a great deal and British warships, though superior, had to fight hard to defend their convoys. Captain William Henry Dillon, commanding the powerful frigate HMS *Horatio* (38), sailing in May 1814 from St John's, Newfoundland, to Halifax for repairs to his rigging and sails, took a convoy south. He nearly caught 'a Yankee privateer', as he called it in his journal. The 'chace' steered towards some rocks near the shore to try to shake her pursuer off. With every sail hoisted, trying to capture the privateer before darkness in the dusk of a May evening, Dillon was just about to give the order to fire the 'chace gun', when a squall caused the *Horatio*'s main topmast studding sail boom to give way. Dillon had to give up, but, as he reflected, 'She had not taken any of my convoy, and that, under my disappointment, was some satisfaction.'[11]

One consequence of the general warship shortage in the early stages of the war was that small warships had to be employed as convoy escorts on the long North Atlantic routes, operating above their design specification. In the first six months of the war, nine were lost, the worst in September 1812 when HMS *Magnet* (16) foundered escorting a convoy to Halifax, with a crew of 90; HMB *Plumper* (10) was wrecked in December near St John's, New Brunswick, when 42 were drowned. Altogether between 1812 and the end of 1814, 26 small warships were lost and approximately 600 officers and seamen perished, of whom over 400 were drowned in 5 ships that foundered.[12]

Hand in hand with the diminutive size of the escorts was the problem of the steady and less visible deterioration of crew quality. Evidence of this can be found among the Admiralty in-letters from the Cork station in a summary of the musters of HMS *Spy*, a modest storeship of 274 tons. In November 1810, having been fitted at Woolwich, her crew of thirty-six were all able seamen, except three. Two years later, on passage to Halifax, she was taken by a French privateer: impressment by more senior officers, and probably desertion, had halved her able seamen to sixteen; seven were ordinary seamen, and eleven landsmen and invalids.[13] When HMS *Leander* (60) arrived in Halifax in the spring of 1814, 'People naturally expected to see a picked crew of British seamen. Instead of which, they saw tall and short, old and young, and soon learnt that there were very few seamen in the ship.'* The weakness of the new Cruiser-class brig sloop HMS *Epervier* (16) became notorious. Returning north in April 1814 from the West Indies with specie, she was taken near the Bahamas by USS *Peacock*. Eight were killed and fifteen wounded. One observer declared that the *Epervier* had 'decidedly the worst crew of any ship on the station. They were principally invalids from the hospital.'[14] Two of her crew were reported to be seventy years old.[15]

Poor morale was a real problem on British warships on the North American and West Indies station, demonstrated by the heavy incidence of summary punishment, some of which angered the Admiralty Board. After a close inspection of quarterly punishment returns, logs and reports of courts martial, it tried to pressurise captains to eliminate severe flogging.[16] By the end of 1813, Warren received heavy criticism of some of the ships under his command, many of them involving small warships, with the Board citing some ugly incidents of over-heavy punishments. The only Admiralty praise went to the small schooner, the Spanish prize HMS *Paz* (12), 141 tons, with a crew of forty. She 'exhibits no case of offence or punishment [and] has met their Lordships' approbation'.[17] During the early part of 1813 she had captured two

---

* According to the combative historian William James, who published his *War of 1812* in 1817, *Leander* had a complement of 485, 44 of whom were boys (p. 66).

American privateers. Prizetaking was always an aid to morale and therefore discipline, but the different dynamics of a small warship and a firm but understanding captain could result in a happy ship.

Low morale led to desertion to the Americans. In the spring of 1813, the British agent for prisoners of war in America, Colonel Thomas Barclay, reckoned that two-fifths of British prisoners taken in Chesapeake raids had gone over to the Americans, assisted by irregular exchanges of prisoners.[18] The crews of eight British whaling ships, captured by USS *Essex* in 1813, entered into American service, enabling her captain, David Porter, to man three of the ships as privateers, as the petition from the Southern Whale Fishery to the Admiralty put it: '200 of the primest seamen taken from our nation and most of them fighting against us.'[19]

The American government was explicit on the desirability of destroying prizes, leaving the crew of the British ships to be ransomed, and unable to fight after accepting parole. On 16 March 1814, orders from the United States Secretary of the Navy, William Jones, to Master Commandant Charles G. Ridgely, USS *Erie*:

> It is evident that policy, interest and duty combine to dictate the destruction of all captures ... It is a great object with the enemy to capture and detain, in prison, our Seamen, and this can only be counteracted by capturing and bringing into Port ... an equal number; this is an object of great National Importance; the releasing at Sea, on Parole, though practised by all civilized Nations, is utterly disregarded by our enemy.[20]

The two governments had come to a cartel agreement on 12 May 1813, and some prisoner exchanges had taken place at American ports. One modern estimate is that 2,650 British naval seamen were captured and that between 6,000–7,000 Americans.[21] Many Americans were incarcerated in Dartmoor, a prison they shared with French prisoners. A modern estimate of the combined numbers of all nations in 1814 in British prisons, depots or hulks is conservatively put at 100,000.[22]

The drain of British seamen continued through captures by privateers in areas where convoys were thin. The quality of seamen on British warships deteriorated further. An American privateer prisoner kept on board HMS *Curlew* (18), based at Halifax, reported: 'We were kept very close while on board the Curlew because her crew were very weak, principally old men and boys.'[23] On the other side of the Atlantic, the route to Archangel for tar, hemp and tallow suffered repeated attacks. The American privateers *Scourge* and *Rattlesnake* took at least 22 merchantmen off the North Cape between 8 and 25 August 1813, capturing 212 men and boys, at a time of the year and at a latitude when there was no darkness in which to escape.[24] When she returned to New York in the autumn of 1813, the *Scourge* took 420 prisoners, which was more than the crew of a 38-gun frigate.[25]

In order to conduct this warfare at a great distance from the United States, American warships and privateers changed their tactics, destroying prizes, after taking aboard everything portable of value. This, however, left them with the crew of the prize to deal with. One solution was to ransom the crew, giving the ship back to the master for a price, to be redeemed by bills of exchange signed between the captor and the master of the prize. The crew had also to agree not to fight in the war until officially exchanged. However, the British government had recognised neither ransoming at sea nor the exchange of prisoners at sea for thirty years. British shipowners and insurers hid behind this law when presented with ransom documents, as in the case of the whaler *Eliza Swan* captured to the north of the Faroe Islands on 24 July 1813, with 146 tons of whale blubber on board. She was boarded by an American officer dressed in British uniform, but when her master, John Young, was escorted aboard the large frigate, he was met by her captain in American uniform, Commodore John Rodgers, and the ship turned out to be USS *President*. Rodgers had twenty-eight prisoners from prizes already taken and burnt. Rather than burden himself with more, Rodgers came to an agreement with Young, that instead of burning the ship and its full load of whale oil, the American commodore would ransom the cargo for £5,000, a sum for which Young signed bills of exchange. But Rodgers never received the money owed to him, in spite of continuing to press for it after the war was over.[26]

Britain was losing the war for seamen, and not just in the Atlantic: on 3 September 1813, Lord Melville, First Lord of the Admiralty, wrote a private letter to Admiral Lord Keith, commander-in-chief, Channel Fleet: 'the ships in commission are too frequently short of complement ... not less than six sail of the line and sixteen frigates, with a great number of sloops and smaller vessels, are at this moment ready to receive men, and are lying useless because men cannot be supplied to them.'[27] Commanders-in-chief across the world were in need of ships and men, so that Warren was not alone on the North American station with insufficient ships. He had been given an impossible job, nor had he the means to maintain those he had. He wrote to Croker in February 1813: 'There is not any Rope ... left in the Stores of the Royal Yard nor any to be had in the Island, the ships are in great want, and the stores at Halifax being likewise drained ...'[28]

Warren did not have much luck. In August 1813 a hurricane devastated shipping in St George's Harbour in Bermuda, where sixty merchantmen were anchored and were driven on shore and the recently developed dockyard was badly damaged.[29] On 12 November the same happened in Halifax, with far more damage to warships. HMS *San Domingo* (74), Warren's flagship, was driven on shore with half a dozen others, and all sustained damage: 'the following day never was witnessed in Halifax such a scene or destruction & devastation.'[30] The deficiency of naval stores on the station worsened the situation, matched by the shortage of strong and competent seamen.

One of the most flourishing trades in the North Atlantic during the Napoleonic Wars was to and from Newfoundland, which exported mainly dried cod, some barrelled salmon, codfish oil, seal products and timber to Britain. Convoys also took fish and oil to the West Indies and Southern Europe. The timber trade, stimulated by the anti-French duties on Baltic timber imposed by Britain in 1808, grew in leaps and bounds; by 1811 timber imports to Britain from British North America reached 175,000 loads.* Goods exported westwards from Britain included salt, bread, flour and casked meat provisions, as well as woollen goods and hardware. For much of the eighteenth century these trades had been dominated by English Channel ports, such as Poole, Dartmouth and Teignmouth, but the trade was steadily moving north. Liverpool was to become the most important centre, as the exploitation of the nearby Cheshire salt deposits, required for curing fish, gave it a trading advantage.[31] Between 1805 and 1815 exports from Newfoundland tripled and imports doubled. In 1815, 852 vessels entered St John's harbour. In spite of the outbreak of war in 1812, a considerable trade continued in foodstuffs with New England.[†]

A valuable witness to the Newfoundland convoys was a civilian, Thomas Bulley, a member of a well-established family fishing concern, based in Teignmouth, which ran a business in St John's, Newfoundland. Every year from 1809 to 1816, he took passage in a ship which left Torbay, or sometimes Liverpool, which was convoyed to St John's, Newfoundland. The observations in Bulley's notebooks are mixed with long passages of gloomy Nonconformist religious introspection, the pessimism induced by the long and uncertain westward voyages and the fact that he was newly married and was missing 'the partner of my

---

* Lower, *Great Britain's Woodyard*, p. 59. Of particular strategic value were large pine trees for great masts carried by specially adapted merchant ships, which were allotted single warships (or a very small group) as escort, usually from Halifax to England, though they were occasionally sent directly to the West Indies. Only a handful every year made the voyage, 35 between 1803 and 1810 (Gwyn, *Ashore and Afloat*, pp. 182–7).
† The ports of registry for those vessels entering St John's in 1807: Liverpool (60 vessels), Poole (58), Greenock (39), Dartmouth (37), Teignmouth (34), London (23), Bristol (12), with a handful each from Cork, Topsham, Waterford, Dublin and Leith. The value of exports from Newfoundland grew from £590,000 in 1805 to £1,247,503 in 1815, imports from £231,000 in 1805 to £659,280 in 1815 (Wardle, 'Newfoundland Trade', pp. 231–2, 243).

bosom', as he called his wife.* Thomas Bulley spent the second half of each summer in St John's hiring ships and supervising the loading of cargoes of dried, salted fish and oil destined for Britain or Southern Europe.[32]

Bulley's hitherto unpublished observations are of particular interest as he was neither a naval nor a merchant seaman, but a passenger in both naval and merchant ships. On 23 April 1812, he boarded HMS *Electra* (16), commanded by Commander William Gregory, off Torbay, which was escorting twenty-seven vessels for Newfoundland, New Brunswick, Nova Scotia and Quebec, 'my cot swinging in the Gun Room', as he recorded. On 5 May a seaman fell from the topmast head, and in spite of heaving to, and recovering the body, the seaman was dead. Bulley's depressed mood is noticeable. 'How wearisome is the time become, how anxious am I to be released from this floating Prison.' This was the prelude to impressments in mid-ocean. On 26 May the *Rodney* of Whitby, one of the convoy, was boarded, and two seamen taken, an incident which does not appear in the official log of the *Electra*, although the next day it records: 'Fired a shot at a brig in chase. Light breezes, several shot to bring to the chase. Shortened sail and boarded an American Brig from London to Massachusetts. Impressed from her some men.'[33] Bulley's diary entry recorded that a man was impressed, and, a 'negro for captain's cook'.[34] A sleight of hand by Captain Gregory had included in the official record all the impressed men as being from the American ship.

Bulley's entries describe the near misses and accidents unrecorded in the official log. On 19 May 1812 he described how HMS *Electra* was 'taken aback by a sudden squall from the NNE in great danger of going down by the Stern thro' Mercy she shortly fell round and we were

---

* The Bulley family was beginning to move its business to Liverpool and owned the *Steady*, though she was burnt by the American privateer *Prince de Neufchatel* in July 1814 (Kert, *Privateering*, p. 83 database). Bulley usually records little about the much shorter and more comfortable journey home, with strong westerly winds (Bulley Diaries, private collection). The company Bulley and Job continued trading in Liverpool until the twentieth century (Wardle, 'Newfoundland Trade', p. 248).

preserved'. A sudden and marked change of wind direction, which brings the wind to the wrong side of the sails and stops the ship, driving her astern, was the greatest danger to square-rigged ships. Only an alert crew instantly letting the sheets fly can retrieve the situation, although in the case of the *Electra* she appears to have fallen slowly round onto the opposite tack. Five warships of *Electra*'s size or smaller foundered in the North Atlantic in the American war, but as they disappeared without trace, we cannot know if this was their fate.

The rest of the 1812 voyage was relatively uneventful, dominated by the poor visibility and concerns over the ship's position due to the inaccuracies of dead reckoning over such a distance. There was much checking between ships, but a wide disparity of calculations, as Bulley noted on 1 June: 'Hitherto been disappointed, having spoke several vessels lately to have found their Longitudes to differ considerably from our own. The brig *Isabelle* 10 degrees to the westward, the Brig from Limerick 7 degrees, on the American Brig 5 degrees to the westward. Some others we spoke to were near to our own Long[itu]de and some to others to the Eastwards.' The next day he noted: 'Still confined on board this floating Prison.' But by 4 June they sounded at 70 fathoms on one of the Grand Banks, closing on their destination.

Bulley's next crossing was completely different, with very little wind when his convoy started out on 5 June 1813, during the most concentrated period of convoying for Britain during the American war.* This time he travelled in a merchant ship, the *Amy*, which joined the Newfoundland convoy in Torbay on 5 June. It was led by HMS *Majestic*, a 74-gun ship hastily cut down to 58 guns to make her

---

* From early May until the end of July 1813, 22 convoys were at sea, east and westbound, escorting 870 merchant ships and transports (TNA, ADM 7/64, 1813; see also Knight, 'North Atlantic Convoys', pp. 48–50).

more manoeuvrable, to try to combat the large American frigates.*
In extremely light easterly winds, the convoy rendezvoused near
Falmouth, but by 7 June was off the southern Irish coast, together with
130 ships, as several convoys converged, and none could weather Cape
Clear. The calm lasted a week. On 15 June, with a heavy sea swell, as
Bulley noted, 'Ships were in great danger of being thrown on board
each other in the event of which they must have sunk each other.'
Bulley's luggage had been left behind at Cork because of a misunder-
standing and he was more depressed than usual: 'And now we are
precisely steering by the same land we were leaving on this day week . . .
in all human probability we are likely to make a very long passage.' A
week later he wrote: 'I do confess that I have lost that relish I formerly
had for a mar[i]time life.'

One of the reliefs from the boredom of convoy life was visiting other
ships when the weather was quiet, though this was officially discour-
aged.† In the calm weather of June 1813, Bulley records multiple visits
of masters coming aboard the *Amy* for tea. On 7 June he went aboard
the *Penguin*, Captain Warren, to confirm that his luggage had indeed
been left at Cork. On 18 June: 'At 1 o'clock after Dinner lowered the
boat and with Captain Bloomfield went on board the Brig *Penguin* of
Teignmouth for some potatoes, from thence on board of the *Aurora*,
Captain Townsend, for a letter which he has for me from our dear
friends at Liverpool which afforded me delight.' Even with this clement
weather, danger could be at hand. On 25 June Bulley recorded another
near-fatal incident, when halfway across the Atlantic:

---

* HMS *Majestic* was accompanied by a large troop ship, HMS *Abundance* (16), a 16-gun ship
sloop, HMS *Pheasant* and two Cruizer-class brig sloops, HMS *Ringdove* (16) and HMS
Trincolo (16).
† 'In all convoys of merchantmen, there should be a general instruction to prohibit visiting.
Many dangers and inconveniencies attend it . . . Sometimes gales of wind arise, and the visitant
cannot regain his ship. Sometimes the visit and drinking are protracted till dark night. The
people are unnecessarily fatigued; there is a chance of ships falling on board such as have
brought to, to hoist their boats in; or of boats being run down, in crossing undiscovered to her
proper ship' (Blake, 'James Ramsay', p. 189).

This afternoon we were mercifully preserved from Fire and from being blown up, having upwards of 300 barrels of Gunpowder on board. The Cook while melting down some Grease suffered it to boil over into the Fire which burnt rapidly and ran to an amazing height. There was much danger of it communicating to the sails and rigging, but thro' mercy it was put under without much injury being done. Well may we constantly say, 'That in the midst of Life we are in Death'.

But by 27 June, Bulley's morale had improved: 'A Charming East Wind and pleasant weather, all the Fleet in Company. The Ships of War and the largest merchant vessels Towing the dull sailing Ships.' But by 30 June the fair weather had gone, it was blowing hard from the SSW. Only a few ships could be seen and they had lost sight of *Majestic*, though the convoy began to slowly close together the next day.

On 1 July the mood again turned sombre. 'As regards our Enemy we are now come into more immediate danger,' Bulley noted. 'One already captured and we have reason to believe that there are many more cruising in these Latitudes.' This was brought about by HMS *Majestic* chasing and capturing a 'brig privateer of 16 guns' on the previous day, recorded also in the log of another of the escorts, HMS *Ringdove*.[35] This was a time of high activity for the small escorts, mostly in thick fog, towing slow vessels, boarding strange ships or communicating with *Majestic*. *Ringdove* failed to stop the privateer *Snapdragon* from boarding several of the convoy to capture goods, though no ship was taken. On 13 July, *Pheasant* sounded 38 fathoms, shells and stones taken up from the bottom by the tallow at the bottom of the lead. Finally, on 22 July, she was warped through the Narrows into St John's Harbour, over six weeks from the start of the convoy. Bulley in the *Amy* had arrived on 17 July.

Unquestionably, the greatest and continuous concern reflected in both private and official logs for the North Atlantic convoys was the combination of fog and 'ice islands', which convoys met as they reached the Grand Banks off Newfoundland. Several times Bulley noted: 'The

Commodore firing Fog guns every hour and sometimes every half hour'.
Even Dillon's complacency was shaken when he later related an incident
on the Grand Banks. 'Thinking it unsafe to carry sail, I hove to and
struck soundings on the Bank in 38 fathoms ... the fog cleared a
little ... I made sail and, when going at the rate of seven knots, the ship
nearly ran upon a large island of ice. It was at least 400 feet in height and
aground on the Bank ... We just tacked in time to clear it. This was a
very narrow escape.'[36] Another naval officer recalled that he would take
the unusual step of sailing from a Newfoundland harbour at night,
because it was 'proven by experience to be safe and judicious on this
coast, from the general prevalence of fogs in the day-time, which are
remarked to be less dense and frequent on moon-light nights'.[37]

As 1813 drew to a close, disparate requests reached the Admiralty
from around the North Atlantic for increased trade protection. The
Southern Whale Fishery, the Cornish copper merchants and the House
of Assembly in the Bahamas all registered their dissatisfaction. Requests
by the latter to Warren for more warships to be on station had received
no reply.[38] By late 1813, Warren was a shadow of his former self,
worrying only over his share of prize money. His secretary and prize
agent, George Redmond Hulbert, wrote to his brother in November
1813 that he was glad that Warren was returning to England, because
the admiral was thinking about nothing except how much prize money
he was going to receive. Hulbert wrote of Warren: 'he is so miserably
stingy and parsimonious, nothing occupies his thoughts but remit-
tances, and it is an increasingly worrying conversation ten times a day.'[39]

The Board responded to this pressure and separate stations were
re-established in December 1813 when Warren was recalled, and
replaced by the more aggressive Vice-Admiral Sir Alexander Cochrane.[40]
One of the first things that Cochrane did was to bolster the British
blockade of the American coast. He now had twice as many warships,
and larger, than were on the North American station at the outbreak of
hostilities. By April 1814 a comprehensive and successful blockade
of the American coast was in place.[41] The changeover occurred as the

balance in favour of overwhelming British naval forces in the waters off the coast of the United States, was enabled by the end of the war in Europe. On 6 April 1814 Napoleon abdicated and the French threat at sea was no more. Britain continued to move warships to the North American coast.

In March 1814 a ship of the line and a large frigate, both far too fast and powerful for convoy escort duties, but strong enough to stand up to the American frigates if necessary, were being prepared to lead convoys to North America. Both left for Newfoundland within twenty-four hours of each other on 22/23 April.

Captain William Henry Dillon's appointment to HMS *Horatio* (44) had at last given him a warship which he felt was worthy of him. She was 154 feet long, measured over a thousand tons, and had a full crew complement of over three hundred.[42] Her orders were to complete her stores from Portsmouth dockyard and then proceed to Cork.* On 23 April she left with fifty-four merchantmen, assisted by HMS *Cyane* (22) and HMS *Dauntless* (18). Dillon was far more brazen and used impressment to improve his crew and as a means of disciplining his convoy. 'Whenever any particular ship was negligent in obeying signals,' he recalled, 'I ran alongside of her and sent an officer alongside to examine her crew. If she was well manned, one or two good seamen were taken away, and others from the *Horatio* sent to supply their places. By that arrangement the Masters could not complain, and I improved the complement of my Ship's Company.' He misjudged one master in April 1814, however, who, after such treatment, 'in a fit of passion, started to unreeve all his rigging, placing his ship in a position to prevent his making sail'. Dillon's threat to report the master to Lloyd's, as well as

---

* Dillon listed *Horatio*'s provisions in the log, including 20 tons of bread, 18 of flour, 4 tons of cheese and 4 of cocoa, 663 gallons of wine and 592 of rum. Her water capacity was 128 tons, consumed at 9 tons a week (TNA, ADM 51/2457).

the prospect of an 18-pound shot from the frigate, brought the incident to an end. 'Luckily he gave no further cause for my suspicion.'[43] But Dillon's official log records that when the ship was moored at Spithead, taking on provisions, a member of his boat crew deserted. Dillon soon made up his complement on the passage to Cork on 9 April when a random merchant ship was boarded, sailing from Passages to Cork, and a boy was pressed.[44]

The other over-powerful warship was HMS *Bellerophon* (74), commanded by Captain Edward Hawker, over 1,600 tons, with a crew of 550. She was taking out to St John's the commander-in-chief of the Newfoundland station, Vice-Admiral Sir Richard Goodwin Keats. He had served there in 1813, after a long period of sick leave and had come back to England during the winter, as was the custom. Though a fine organiser and planner, serving with distinction in the Baltic and at Cadiz, he suffered from anxiety and was quick to take offence. Keats had received his commission for Newfoundland on 10 February 1814, and before his departure met various committees of merchants, took three weeks leave, and conferred with the Secretary of State for the Colonial Department on 6 April. On 22 April *Bellerophon* left Spithead with seventy-two ships, was joined by HMS *Comet* with ten more, but experienced 'baffling winds'. Joined by another convoy, they proceeded down Channel accompanied by 157 ships.[45]

On 2 May *Bellerophon* anchored briefly in Torbay and picked up a group of passengers, among whom was Thomas Bulley.* For this voyage his 1814 diary reveals a changed man, for no time could be spent on morbid introspection when the continuously busy and exciting routine of a ship of the line was there to be observed, particularly when the admiral was the assiduous and obsessive Keats. Voluminous entries in his diary chronicle a passage of thirty-three days to St John's. The convoy, by now of seventy-seven ships, was off Start Point by eight p.m. that

---

* It is very likely that Bulley was given a passage by Edward Hawker, as they shared radical Nonconformist religious beliefs. According to *The Times*, Hawker was 'well known in low-church religious and philanthropic circles' (*ODNB*).

evening, blessed with light, easterly winds, but with a heavy swell. Two days later the swell caused the *Neptune*, a brig from London with a heavy cargo of 'shot and shell', to roll away her masts and the flagship supplied her with a replacement topmast.* Three other merchantmen lost their topmasts because of the swell, including the *Devonshire*; she had to be towed most of the way. Four days later Bulley was able to watch the 'general exercise of the great guns', while on 12 May a merchantman, the *Princess of Wales*, was run down and sunk, and eight men on a raft saved and put on board the flagship. That night he recorded that the *Bellerophon*'s gunners were refreshing the barrels of gunpowder: 'employed turning powder.' Every one of Keats's dinner guests was set down in the diary, and on 15 May Bulley himself was able to record: 'Dined with the admiral and Sir James Coburn [*sic*]'.†

The activities of the accompanying warships are fully recorded: the newly commissioned HMS *Medina* (22), HMS *Comet* fireship (18), HMS *Wolverine* Cruiser-class brig (16), HMS *Cormorant* storeship (16) and HMS *Pike* schooner (14). They chased and identified distant ships, repeated *Bellerophon*'s signals, towed slow merchantmen, sent their surgeons to assist sick merchant ship crew and escorted the constituent parts of the convoy to Halifax and Quebec, while the admiral proceeded to St John's. On 1 June Bulley had a final view of the great guns and small arms being exercised. With this panoply of naval power taking place in front of him, and with no responsibilities, no wonder Bulley's mood was transformed. His tone is confident, recording every detail of the ship's position as measured by the timekeeper, relishing its certainty. Nor was there any mention of American privateers.

By contrast, Keats's journal for the 1814 crossing, by the time that the convoy reached the fog and ice, is anxious and pessimistic. In spite of exceedingly full and complex instructions issued to the masters,

---

* A ship too densely loaded with a very heavy cargo could cause the masts to 'whip' and thus crack under the strain.
† Sir James Cockburn, older brother of Sir George Cockburn, was another passenger, taking up his post as Governor of Bermuda, 1814–16.

Keats had the usual difficulties in keeping the convoy together.* The entry in his journal for 11 May: 'those much spread and many far astern, paying no attention to signals; much delay & difficulty experienced in getting them to make sail'. The next day: 'many of which were very inattentive and disobedient to signals'. On 13 May the *Bellerophon* burnt blue lights. Out of character, on 16 May, he ordered the crew to fire muskets at ships in the convoy, which had crept ahead of *Bellerophon*. By 17 May, he notes, 'no less than 55 of the convoy separated.' By 20 May, the weather is a 'constant thick and wet fog'. *The Brothers* merchant ship lost her bowsprit, 'having lost it by running against an Ice Island in the night'. A final despondent entry: 'Am unable to account for the absence of the *Wasp* or *Plover*.'

Keats's anxious temperament did not suit the management of convoys and when ashore he continued to be irritable. He arrived at St John's on 4 June 1814 and within a week he wrote to Croker asking for more ships: 'American Privateers have been numerous and too successful.'[46] When Dillon arrived back in St John's in October in a storm-damaged HMS *Horatio*, having lost his convoy (the second of the year) when he had been ordered to the St Lawrence, Keats sent him straight out to sea again and threatened him with a court martial. There were stormy scenes. Although peace was eventually made with the prickly Dillon, Keats was clearly stressed and not coping. After his return to England in 1816, aged sixty, the admiral never took up an active command again.[47]

Large, well-escorted convoys in 1814 kept American warships and privateers at a distance and the sizeable warships that came with the

---

* One example from Keats's signal book demonstrates its complexity: 'Signals made to or from the Admiral requiring an Affirmative or Negative not to be considered as affirmatively replied to until the Admiral's Answering Flag, in Private Ships answering Pendant as the Case may be, shall after the acknowledgement of the Signal be hauled half down and rehoisted' (NMM, HAW/9, no. 3).

convoys across the Atlantic blockaded American ports. British superiority in North American waters had been foreseen by American naval officers before hostilities commenced. As early as June 1812, Commodore Rogers had written to the American Secretary of the Navy that 'the largest force they will soon be able to send to our Coast, will not prevent the few vessels we have from getting to sea, and annoying their Commerce to an extent not only to feel their effect seriously, but at the same time in a manner to astonish all Europe'.[48] While slow American merchant ships could not leave port, fast American warships and privateers could slip past the blockading British warships at night, or in bad weather, using their superior windward ability to keep out of trouble. George Coggeshall, who commanded the American privateer schooner *David Porter*, slipped out of Charleston in December 1813. He later wrote: 'Thus, while the whole coast of the United States was literally lined with English cruisers, on the broad ocean there were very few to be seen: a clear proof that the risk of capture between Newport and Charleston, was infinitely greater than in going to France.'[49]

Larger convoys led to delays in assembling and sailing. In May 1814 George Canning, MP for Liverpool, during the annual Parliamentary debate on the Convoy Act, represented the complaints of his West India merchant constituents over delay, citing four hundred ships currently waiting for a convoy, which 'was productive of great inconvenience in the market'. This was countered by John Wilson Croker, who was able to state that very highly defended convoys were now leaving Portsmouth and Cork every fortnight. Convoys were thus fewer but safer. Croker also defended the fact that licences to sail without convoy had been withdrawn because: 'The American merchant ships were almost universally converted into privateers. The seas swarmed with thousands of them. Vessels then running from Liverpool, and the other western ports, merely ran to fall into the jaws of the enemy.'[50]

It was at this time that British trade protection troubles in the north and eastern Atlantic really began, as the shortage of seamen and the consequent lack of escorts began to have an effect. Merchants and masters relaxed because the danger from French, Dutch, Danes and Norwegians had passed and they began to ignore convoys. Their ships became 'runners' or 'stragglers'. While Britain's transatlantic convoys were successful, and the blockade of the American east coast bottled up American trade and warships, damaging the American economy, it was a different story in northern waters, the Irish Sea and the Western Approaches. With the French beaten, civilian and commercial frustration levels at merchant ship destruction by American warships and privateers close to British coasts rose to new heights. In these areas, the lack of warships meant that the British navy was not defending trade, nor was it stemming the drain on its supply of seamen. Apart from the main routes from Britain to North America and back, the convoy system began to unravel.

American warships and privateers employed two methods to extend their cruising range. They used ports in sympathetic Norway and France for provisions and fresh water, at least until 1814 when those two countries withdrew from the war. Some privateers went further and operated out of France. One example was the *True Blooded Yankee*, built as a British gun brig, but captured by the French in 1811, owned by an American merchant living in Paris. The ship began its cruise from Brest with a mixed French and American crew in March 1813.* In just over a year, she turned a profit for her owner, capturing forty-three prizes in northern European waters before being taken, although half of her prizes were burned, recaptured or released.† In 1814, some powerful letters of marque ships traded with Canton and then took prizes in the Pacific.[51]

* Among the *True Blooded Yankee*'s crew was a former British sailor, John Wiltshire, who had spent three years as a prisoner of war in France and who pretended to be an American to get out of gaol. However, Wiltshire was recognised, when acting as a member of a prize crew of a British merchant ship, the *Margaret*, which was recaptured by the British. He was court martialled and hanged as a traitor (Kert, *Privateering*, p. 126).

† The urgency and detail of intelligence dispatches on American privateers sent to the Admiralty is striking. Captain Peter Rye, anchored in HMS *Ceylon* in the Hawke Roads at Gothenburg, sent Croker a detailed account of a prize crew from *True Blooded Yankee* captured in an open boat making its way from Jutland to Norway, with a summary of documents listing prize cargoes captured by the privateer (TNA, ADM 1/2422, 31 July 1813).

These American ships were formidable. In the Bay of Biscay, the schooner *Siro* of 225 tons, twelve long 9-pounder guns, was captured on 13 January 1814 by the new Cruizer-class HMS *Pelican* (16), Captain Thomas Mansell, and brought into Plymouth. She had been chased by several other British cruisers, 'but escaped by superior sailing, and was intended to cruise against our trade, after landing her cargo (cotton) at Bordeaux'.[52] Mansell received almost as much prize money for her than the total of his many Danish prizes.* Perhaps the most formidable was the 328-ton, schooner-brigantine *Prince de Neufchatel* (18), built in New York. Her windward sailing performance so impressed the officers of the three frigates who eventually captured her in December 1814 that after the war the Navy Board ordered a warship to be built on her lines, although in the event this was not done. In all she captured thirty-nine prizes, but only ten of them made it to port for condemnation. Many were recaptured, but between July and December 1814 she burnt or destroyed twelve merchant ships, contributing to the growing fury of British merchants. However, generally it was difficult for the privateers to make a profit at a distance. For instance, in 1814/15 the *Young Wasp* sailed 30,000 miles in the North and western Atlantic, took twelve prizes, but only five made it to port.[53]

Trade in the far north of the Atlantic was also at risk where convoy escorts were thin at the best of times. Long Hope Sound in the Orkneys, where 'northabout' convoys gathered, particularly those sailing between Liverpool and the Baltic, was particularly vulnerable. Operational responsibility lay with the commander-in-chief, Leith, well over two hundred miles to the south. If an American warship were to force an entrance and attacked a convoy which was gathering, it would be disastrous. A concerned Admiralty Board ordered the building of two Martello towers

* In the Mansell Papers: Account, Tor Point, 2 February 1814: 'Sold the schooner *Siro* with her Furniture, Ordnance, Stores and Provisions as she arrived from Sea with her Cargo, consisting of 254 Bales of Reed or Canes to Robert Feige & Son per of all Duties and Expenses (except those of Condemnation) to the Captors for the sum of £11,000'. Mansell and his crew netted £10,851/15/4d (GSA, AQ 365/10–25). HMS *Pelican* was a lucky ship. She had already taken USS *Argus* in Irish waters and was not sold out of the navy until 1865.

and a battery of eight guns on the island of Hoy in the Orkneys to protect the entrance to Long Hope Sound. It was an extremely expensive project and fortifications were not completed until after the war.[54]

Protecting the Greenland whaling trade was the most difficult. In an extravagant gesture, in June 1814 a ship of the line was sent up from Halifax to protect the trade. HMS *Victorious* (74), Captain John Talbot, had been blockading north-eastern American ports in 1813, based at Bermuda and Halifax. By June 1814 she was moored in the harbour at St John's, Newfoundland, and then sent, accompanied by Dillon in HMS *Horatio*, to the largely uncharted Davis Straits. The weather was very foggy, although the west coast of Greenland was sighted, but the ships found themselves amongst the ice. Dillon boarded a whaler and the master 'expressed himself completely astonished at beholding a line of battleship in such a high northern latitude . . . "You are surrounded by innumerable dangers". I explained to him that our reckoning was regulated by the lunar observations and our chronometers. He replied that the coast of Greenland was not properly laid down in the high latitudes, therefore all was uncertainty.'

The two warships sailed close to each other, but unable to see her, alerted by guns firing, Dillon came upon the *Victorious* ashore on a small island, 'lying over on her starboard side in a most awkward position . . . the streams of water, by pumping, coming out of the unfortunate ship caused a woeful impression.' The log entry for *Victorious* for 31 July runs: 'Ship making nine inches of water an hour'.[55] That evening, fortunately, *Victorious* floated off.[56] Canvas, well-lined with oakum, was put over *Victorious*'s damaged hull, secured by hawsers, and she limped back to Spithead. Neither the ship nor her captain went to sea again.* Many years later, her captain, by now Admiral Sir John Talbot, remembered that

---

* This was the third time in a year that HMS *Victorious* had been ashore. She was in Halifax harbour during the hurricane in November 1813, while in May 1814 she was 37 hours ashore on Fisher's Island, while blockading American warships in New London, 'and only got off with difficulty' (O'Byrne, *Naval Dictionary*). She was relatively new, commissioned in 1809. Had she been lost, especially with her triumphalist name, it would have been a grave embarrassment for the British government, even more so than the captures made by USS *Essex* suffered by the Southern Whale Fishery off the Galapagos in 1813 (Woodman, *Britannia's Realm*, pp. 320–44).

Victorious was making 44 inches of water an hour. *Horatio* also nearly ran ashore, Dillon describing her escape as 'quite miraculous'.

It was the loss of merchant ships in the western waters of the British Isles that prompted furious protests to the government from the merchants of Glasgow, Liverpool, Dublin and Bristol. By August 1814 insurance premiums for the Irish Sea, usually at 15/9d per cent, were now 5 guineas.[57] The level of anger over losses in home waters simmered throughout that summer. The *Caledonian Mercury* reported from a meeting in Glasgow on 7 September that an estimated eight hundred vessels had been lost from there in the last two years:

> it is equally distressing and mortifying that our ships cannot with safety traverse our own channels; that insurance cannot be effected but at an excessive premium; and that a horde of American cruizers should be allowed, unheeded, unresisted, unmolested, to take, burn and sink our own vessels, in our own inlets, and almost in sight of our own harbours.[58]

It was, however, the approaches to the Channel and the Western Approaches about which the Committee of Lloyd's was most worried. In June 1814, when Napoleon was imprisoned on Elba, Joseph Marryat, the Chairman of the Committee, travelled to France to speak with the French Foreign Minister, Prince de Bénevente, and Sir Charles Stuart, during his brief early spell as British minister in Paris. Marryat failed on the specific question of the restitution of prizes taken by American priva- teers currently in French ports, in particular by the *Prince de Neufchatel*, which had taken £14,000 worth of prizes. However, the French did agree not to support them any more, but this undertaking made no difference, for the rate of prizetaking of British merchant ships continued to rise.[59] During a four-week period in August and early September 1814, in the Channel, the Irish Sea and off Scotland, sixty-eight had been taken, at the rate of seventeen a week, or two and a half a day.[60]

Just how bad the situation was made clear to the Admiralty in a letter from Marryat to Croker on 19 September, which enclosed a detailed list of 172 merchant ship losses in home waters and the Western

Approaches. The analysis covered just under twenty weeks; losses were running at nine a week. The largest proportion, 94 or 55 per cent, were 'Running Ships', 38 or 22 per cent sailed in convoys, while the rest were coastal traffic. In fact, the situation was worse than the intelligence that Lloyd's had gathered. The *Prince de Neufchatel* was listed as having taken nine, but recent research makes it clear that she took eighteen in the same period.*

The problem was that merchant ships were now ignoring convoys, despite the withdrawal of Admiralty licences to sail without convoy. Insurance premiums on a British ship from Madeira was 70 guineas per cent and from the coast of Spain or Portugal 15, while the rate for neutral ships was only 5 per cent. The Committee of Lloyd's proposed desperate measures to the Admiralty, including passing new legislation to enforce coastal convoys and put forward a proposal for giving British consuls in foreign ports similar powers to commanders-in-chief, which was unlikely to have found favour. The underlying worry was the breakdown of the convoy system. As Marryat put it forcibly in his letter to Croker: 'The Public naturally look up to their Lordships for the protection of British commerce and the Committee for managing the affairs of Lloyd's . . . feel it their duty to state to them the extent of the disasters which their constituents have lately suffered, and are daily suffering . . . effective protection can only be given to British commerce, by a rigid adherence to the convoy system, the good effects of which for a long time past have been so well manifested.'[61] This was now a trade protection war which was not being won.

With tempers fraying in London, there were also ructions at sea, and weaknesses came to be displayed which would not have been apparent at the beginning of a war. Pressure from Lloyd's brought about the remarkable court martial of Captain Samuel Butcher, HMS *Antelope* (50), after a complaint of unreasonable delay by many of the masters in

---

* Lloyd's list of merchant ship captures, which appeared to be comprehensive, had far fewer instances of capture than took place (TNA, ADM 1/3994, Marryat to Croker, 19 September 1814, enclosure; Kert, *Privateering*, p. 154).

his Halifax and Bermuda convoy of 121 troopships and transports. The convoy set out from Portsmouth on 23 June 1814 and by 30 June was off the entrance of Cork Harbour, but on 5 July Butcher was still trying to get his convoy, by this time of 110 ships, round Cape Clear. He was accused of taking the convoy unnecessarily into Berehaven, when the wind was fair.* At this point, Butcher definitely broke the rules, by going to visit his wife, whom he had not seen for two years, at the family home three hours journey away in Killarney.

An already complicated convoy was also marked by sharp antagonism between Butcher and one of the captains of the escorts, Captain Lord George Stuart, commanding an exceptionally fast, lightly built of pitch pine HMS *Newcastle* (62), built at speed through the summer of 1813 to oppose the American 44-gun frigates. In a blow, she could achieve 13 knots close-hauled with reefed topsails.[62] While Butcher was the convoy commodore, having two year's seniority on Lord George, the latter's ship was 500 tons larger than Butcher's *Antelope*. The primary purpose of *Newcastle's* voyage to America was to strengthen the blockade against the big American frigates; she was a most unsuitable escort. It was a recipe for trouble, exacerbated by Stuart's aristocratic background.

Croker wrote to Butcher notifying him of the complaint and the fact that he could expect to be court martialled on his return to England. Within Butcher's seventeen-page answer to Croker was his defence that he could not get the convoy around Cape Clear, which is why he brought the convoy back to Berehaven.[63] Butcher then extended his defence by counter-charging Lord George with disobeying his orders, accusing him of chasing a prize rather than assisting with a disabled brig. The latter claimed to be surprised at this accusation, never having been told that he had displeased Captain Butcher.

---

* The charge against Captain Butcher read: 'For retarding the progress of a convoy of which he had charge, for not properly protecting the dull sailing ships of the said convoy, and for going on a party of pleasure, leaving the said ship and his duty of taking charge of the above mentioned convoy', 8 February 1815 (TNA, ADM 194/42, Courts Martial Register, no. 842).

Butcher's court martial did not take place until February 1815, at which point everyone knew the American war was over, and had no expectation that the war with France would flare up again after Napoleon escaped from Elba. After hearing the evidence, the court sat for five hours before it came to a verdict; Butcher was lucky, getting away with a reprimand. Lord George Stuart's court martial in November 1815 was held on a ship at Sheerness. Butcher protested that he needed more evidence, and he would prefer Portsmouth to Sheerness, but Barrow ordered him to attend 'without delay'.[64] Stuart was acquitted of all charges, with the comment that Butcher's 'public reprimand in orders was most harsh and unusual'.[65] This was the bickering of tired men, commanding fast and over-powerful ships entirely unsuitable for convoy duty.

The end of the American war was a stalemate. In the western Atlantic, the Americans had plenty of seamen, but few warships and no merchant ships which could get to sea because of the British blockade.* In the northern and eastern Atlantic, the British had plenty of warships available, but were very short of seamen. British historians have been dismissive of this war with 'Cousin Jonathan', as the Americans were called, yet the impact of the war against America was more damaging to trade than anything in the previous nine years against France, Spain (briefly), the Dutch or Denmark/Norway. There was a blindness to this at the time. An article in the *Naval Chronicle* of 1815 presented a satisfactory naval tally of American warships, privateers and merchantmen taken by the beginning of 1814, but made no reference to losses of British merchant ships, nor, of course, those lost to winter weather.[†]

Nor is it obvious which nation 'won', confused by the division of public opinion in both countries on the advisability of fighting the

---

* Large numbers of seamen, unemployed because of the British blockade, were restive in American port cities, so that in July 1813 Congress passed an act to create 'a Corps of Sea Fencibles . . . who may be employed for the defense of the ports and harbours of the United States'. It was not a success (Luecke, 'American Tars', p. 678).
† Return of 26 January 1814: ships of war taken by the Americans: 3x38, 6x16, 2x12, 2x10, 3x4, capturing 2,025 men and boys. American losses: 42 national ships and 228 private vessels of war: 2,300 guns, 11,268 men. Number of seamen captured and detained: 20,961. Number of American merchantmen taken: 1,407 (*Naval Chronicle*, vol. 33, January–June 1815).

war in the first place. The New England states, with close trading links to the Maritime Provinces to the north, had been very much against it. The *Salem Gazette*, for instance, commented on President Madison's declaration of war, 18 June 1812: 'The mass of people shudder at such an event, as unnecessary, ruinous, and criminal as suicide.'[66] One British historian, writing in the 1970s and known for his bon mots, judged that it 'was a conflict which began over nothing, proved nothing and settled nothing'.[67] But this lordly view ignores the fact that, in some quarters, it was a heartfelt, hard-fought war, with instances of vicious conflict between British warships and American privateers. For instance, sickening slaughter marked the action between the *Decatur* and HMS *Dominica* in August 1813, while in October 1814 the boat crews of HMS *Endymion* took terrible casualties, and inflicted them in return on the *Prince de Neufchatel*, in a night attack during a windless night off Nantucket.[68] George Coggeshall, the American merchant ship master, having endured British superiority and disdain for many years when sailing in a neutral ship in British convoys, commented later: 'If ever there was a just and holy war, it was ours against Great Britain in 1812.'[69]

Hostilities took some time to conclude. Seven weeks after the signing of the Treaty of Ghent and four days after its ratification by the US Congress, a successful but bloody defence of a British convoy took place in the mid-Atlantic, with none of the combatants aware that the war had ended. On 17 December 1814 the powerful 44-gun USS *Constitution* had finally broken out of the British blockade of Boston and seven weeks later was off Madeira, where on 20 February 1815 it met two much smaller British vessels, HMS *Cyane* (22) with a convoy from Cork to St John's, Newfoundland, and HMS *Levant* (22), with another convoy.[70] In the evening, with a light breeze, which favoured the sailing qualities of the American warship, a running battle took place, with the smaller British warships taking severe punishment in the rigging, with twelve killed and twenty-two wounded.[71] The action was one of a small handful of incidents where the escorting warships sacrificed themselves for trade. The convoys managed to get away into the night.

Then suddenly it was all over. The news of Waterloo came to the mid-Atlantic in late July 1815 to a homeward-bound convoy of fifty government transports from Quebec, full of troops who were expecting to be taken to the Continent to fight Napoleon again. It was led by a ship of the line and two frigates. In the opinion of Samuel Jefferson, commanding the *Mary Ann*, with 150 artillerymen on board: 'I never knew a fleet that sailed so well . . . One Sunday morning we fell in with an American merchantman from Liverpool, bound for Philadelphia.' The merchantman had a copy of a newspaper containing the text of the Duke of Wellington's despatch after the battle. The *Mary Ann* was given the job by the convoy commodore of transmitting this news to all ships of the convoy. Jefferson described the scene:

> All our hen coops were soon converted into writing desks, and about a dozen artillerymen were set to work writing copies of the despatch; these, when finished, were folded up, put into glass bottles, and corked up for distribution. It being a fine top-gallant breeze, we now set to work, hailing each ship as we approached, and sheering up alongside as near as practicable, a soldier with a powerful arm hove a bottle on board with all his might, which was generally smashed to pieces against the side of the longboat, when the despatch being picked up and handed to the commanding officer, he, the moment he saw what the contents would order his men to stand up in the rigging and on the booms and give three hearty cheers. Thus we continued going from ship to ship the whole day, but some of the ships astern would not find out until the following day what all the confusion was about, never for a moment anticipating a peace. It was glorious and unexpected news.[72]

The account epitomises the sailing navy convoy: cumbersome, difficult to control and communicate with, yet, at its best, disciplined and effective.

CONCLUSION

In answer to your Letter of yesterday's date, I am commanded by my Lords Commissioners of the Admiralty to acquaint you that Hostilities having ceased it has been determined <u>not to issue any more convoy instructions</u>.

John Wilson Croker, Secretary to the Board of Admiralty
to Samuel Thornton, Governor of the Russia Company,
18 March 1815[1]

John Wilson Croker's answer to this convoy enquiry followed the news of Napoleon's escape from Elba, which had reached London on 15 March 1815. The Admiralty Board took the view that convoys were unnecessary in this new emergency, although it was not in a strong position to organise anything. Following Napoleon's abdication in 1814, large parts of the British army, navy and ordnance had been disbanded or paid off, because back-bench MPs were appalled at the size of the National Debt and voted for immediate and radical economies. The visual shutter signalling system that criss-crossed southern England had been dismantled. The rapid operation to move troops and cavalry from British ports to Ostend was only successful because of the skill and experience of the masters of transports, gained over many years of war. By the end of May, 36,000 troops had reached Wellington, and more were being transported across the Channel well into June. His army of 68,000 British, Dutch, Belgian and German soldiers was assembled only days before the battle of Waterloo.[2]

It was not easy to bring to a halt the convoy routine that had been established over a dozen years. In August in the West Indies, the commander-in-chief, Rear-Admiral Sir Philip Durham, gathered a convoy of fifty-five transports at Barbados with five thousand troops on board to attack Guadeloupe.[3] The last one recorded in the Admiralty/Lloyd's log is dated 27 September 1815.* One of the last of the convoys that sailed unauthorised in mid-1815 was that of the homeward bound East Indies fleet. Captain Thomas Browne in HMS *Ulysses* (44) had been appointed commodore of the West African station in 1813, in which time he had destroyed two slave factories. However, he happened to be at St Helena when the news of Napoleon's escape arrived at the same time as the homeward East Indies fleet. Browne decided to convoy it back to Britain without there being another warship to cover his absence. By the time he arrived, as he later described it, 'tranquillity having been restored to Europe previous to arrival, the service he had rendered was not looked upon in so important a light as it might otherwise have been.' His decision was 'to the great prejudice of his professional interests', although the East India Company voted him the largest sum 'than had ever been given to any captain before him'.[4] Browne never served again.

Britain had signed the Treaty of Ghent with America at the end of 1814, which ended the worrying merchant ship losses of that year, a situation that could only have worsened had the war continued. After 1807 and the imposition of the Continental Blockade and the Orders-in-Council, the Admiralty Board had ensured that British warships had protected the hugely increased size and load of the convoys. Convoy commodores were instructed to allow any merchant ship flying neutral or even foreign flags, whose master asked for protection, to join their convoy, as long as the ship stayed for the whole voyage, ensuring that the ship sailed from and to a port friendly to Britain. Destination

---

* HMB *Rinaldo* (10), a Cherokee-class sloop, is recorded as escorting five ships from Havana to England (TNA, ADM 7/64).

rather than the nationality of the ship became the deciding factor, a subtle change of strategy, moving away from outright blockade to regulation of trade.[5] Protection of these larger convoys had to be achieved at a time when the number of seamen and therefore available ships were declining.* Such was the pressure by the time of hostilities against the United States that in order to maintain convoy discipline, masters of merchant ships who broke convoy were successfully prosecuted and imprisoned.

Trade protection had been achieved with many warships which were far too small for the task they were asked to perform. More warships, if smaller, with correspondingly small complements, could get to sea with fewer men.[6] One regular correspondent in 1815 in the *Naval Chronicle* had no doubt about the drawbacks of small British warships: 'in time of war, specially with America, they have been found completely ineffective, and I hope will be gradually laid aside . . . I have already expressed my strong conviction of the necessity of continuing to build larger ships of every class.'[7] Newly built, larger warships became available in 1813, but by that time not enough seamen were available to man them.

In addition, the corrosive effects of impressment on morale and effectiveness had not been countered; one man who might have found solutions, Henry Dundas, first Viscount Melville, had had to resign precipitately as First Lord of the Admiralty in May 1805. The years of service put in by the seamen aboard HMAS *Providence* (16), based at Grimsby, who were paid merchant seamen's wages and were loyal to Captain Peter Rye RN, allow a tantalising glimpse of what the navy could have been like without impressment. However, the country could not afford to support this system.

The British shipbuilding industry built constantly and intensively to keep high numbers of warships and merchantmen at sea. From 1803

* Improvements had been made. Seamen were better fed, scurvy was no longer a problem (though fever was), ships were cleaner and surgeons had greater skills. The attempt to analyse the causes of these shortages by Michael Lewis is skewed by his choice of the relatively quiet 1810 as his sample year (Lewis, *Social History*, pp. 419–21).

during the war, over five hundred warships (323,000 tons) were built, largely in private shipyards, while nearly six thousand merchant ships (703,000 tons) were launched.[8] The estimated number of British merchantmen captured by French privateers was 5,314 between 1803 and 1814, but this does not include those captured by Danes or the Americans. Calculating recaptures after prize taking makes precise judgements difficult. Moreover, winter weather caused more casualties than enemy action. What is incontrovertible is that in 1815 on the British Register there were over 24,862 merchant ships, 3,417 more than at the start of the war in 1803.[9] Many of them were owned overseas, but in the long sea conflict, shipowners of many nationalities saw the advantage of British registry, an indication of the reliability of British trade protection. International business confidence was the most important trading commodity of all.

For a dozen years after 1803, the British convoying effort between Britain and her enemies attracted few headlines, although arrivals of convoys and casualties were reported in detail in the newspapers in mercantile centres, such as Liverpool and Hull, and these details were copied by papers published elsewhere. At times in the year, particularly the winter, they would be anxiously scanned. With high freight rates and large profits to be made, shipowners could afford the high premiums and risked their ships with the winter weather. Military convoys could not wait for gentle weather or the passing of winter storms before sailing, and likewise the details of sailings and arrivals in the naval ports in the south of England were similarly covered. Yet the impact of hostile weather, which cost more lives and ships than enemy action, has been largely overlooked by historians. In all, between 1803 and 1815, the navy lost 409 warships – 61 per cent wrecked or foundered, 37 per cent due to enemy action. Of this total, 275 were sloops of 18 guns and below, including gun brigs and boats, cutters and luggers. Five thousand seamen were drowned or killed and approximately the same number taken prisoner.[10] These casualty figures were approaching double those sustained during the French Revolutionary War.

The threat posed by French privateers has overshadowed those from the Danes and Americans.* The greatest dangers to British trade came during the last five years of the war, which fortunately for Britain did not occur concurrently. With Britain losing seamen fast, this was at its most apparent to contemporaries. Late American success against trade in the Western Approaches and home waters in the last stages of the conflict led to the contemporary reputation of convoys ending on a low note. The consequence was the subsequent rejection of convoys as a part of Britain's war strategy during its century as the dominant sea power.[11]

The British slowly exploited Napoleon's maritime weakness. Naval trade protection, and the ability of British merchants to outwit or bribe customs officials responsible to France, enabled its trade to flourish throughout Europe. The Emperor's stock reaction to any country or part of Europe that did not conform with the proclamations of his Continental System, was to invade and absorb it into the French Empire. Between 1805 and 1812 eight countries or regions were annexed.† Eventually tensions within that greater empire led to its undoing, when it became apparent to the rest of Europe that French interests alone were clearly the raison d'être of the whole vast undertaking. It was a process that reached its climax when Napoleon invaded Russia in 1812. Yet had British convoys not been able to penetrate the Sound and the Great Belt to tempt the Russians to trade with British goods, the Emperor would not have needed to risk everything to bring Russia to heel.[12]

Without the safety afforded by convoys, the British could not have paid for the war. Without bullion from Mexico, without coffee and sugar from the tropics, imported and re-exported, or without the income from its manufactured exports to the East and West Indies, the country could not have manufactured gunpowder without saltpetre

---

* For instance, 'Actual (merchant ship) losses were never sufficient to cause the British real anxiety' (Rodger, *Command of the Ocean*, p. 559).

† Genoa was annexed 1805, Tuscany and central Italy 1808, Ragusa and the eastern Adriatic coast 1808; Holland, Bremen, Hamburg and Lubeck 1810; Catalonia 1812 (Marzagalli, 'Continental System', p. 94).

from Bengal or sulphur from Sicily, run its machinery or lit its streets without tallow or whale oil from Archangel and the Greenland Fisheries, or built and maintained its navy and merchant fleets without timber and hemp from the Baltic. It could not have fed its population in times of dearth without wheat from the plains of north Germany, while Wellington's army in the Peninsula would have been destitute without grain supplies from the middle states of the United States.[13]

But Britain was lucky. Its war effort narrowly outlasted the shortage of skilled seamen. Also, it did not suffer as it might have done from the generally poor performance of a generation of old, tired or inept flag officers. At any one time, between thirty-five and forty flag officers were on the active list, kept there, at least in part, by the prize money system of 'flag-eighths', the one time in a career when prize money could flow in quantity to a senior naval officer.[14] Prize money provided incentives for the navy, but it could also cause trouble, as in the case of the quarrel between admirals Bertie and Drury on the East Indies station, and similar friction on the West Indies station which led to the court martial of Vice-Admiral Charles Stirling.

Admiral William Young was an honourable exception to the rule of inept admirals. He wrote to Thomas Grenville shortly after the latter had been appointed First Lord of the Admiralty in September 1806. 'When one looks at the top of the very long list of Flag Officers, it is wonderful to see how very few there are, especially among the higher classes, that are fitted for situations of importance, some incapable through age, and others from other causes.'[15] Two flag officers took dangerous risks by returning to Britain in large warships that were palpably unfit for likely weather conditions. Thomas Troubridge's anger and resentment got the better of his judgement when he decided to return from India in the undocked, forty-six-year-old HMS *Blenheim* in January 1807. A frigate also sank with the *Blenheim*, bringing the number of drowned officers and seamen to a thousand. A more complex decision was made by Admiral Saumarez in December 1811, when persuaded by the sixty-six-year-old Rear-Admiral Robert Carthew

Reynolds to allow him to sail home in his flagship HMS *St George*. This great 98-gun ship had been severely damaged in a grounding a month before, had lost her masts and rudder. A midwinter, jury-rigged passage across the North Sea in the face of the prevailing winds was suicidal and caused the loss of two thousand men. The combined casualties of these two flag officer decisions amounted to three thousand officers and seamen drowned, enough to man twenty-four Cruizer-class brig sloops.

However, Britain also experienced some operational luck. Had the French admiral Linois pressed on in 1804 to take the fabulously valuable East Indies convoy at Pulo Aor, had squadrons of French warships broken out of Brest to devastate a convoy taking troops to Wellington in the Peninsula, had Danish warships repeated their success in capturing an entire Baltic homegoing convoy, or had Napoleon not lost his army in Russia in 1812, the results of these wars would have been very different. The world is, after all, as much defined by events that do not happen as by things that do. Convoys had always been put in place to prevent dramatic events from happening and because they were largely successful, they have attracted little notice. When the threat had passed, convoys were forgotten for a hundred years. At the outbreak of war in 1914, they were passed over as a primary method of trade protection. Only when merchant ship casualties had soared were convoys reintroduced, after much debate, in 1917.[16]

The peacetime unemployment of seamen was soon apparent after the excitement of Waterloo had passed. On 24 July 1815, two hundred seamen marched on the Admiralty protesting against foreign seamen manning British ships. According to the report in the *Naval Chronicle*, the merchants of Hull and other northern ports agreed to employ only British seamen, if available.[17] The great majority of the young naval officers who had convoyed British trade between 1803 and 1815 never served again, for the post-war years saw mass unemployment. By 1818 only

10 per cent of the available 5,797 active officers were serving, the unlucky ones existing on half pay.[18] By and large, it was a disappointed navy.

Some officers were recognised with honours. The two captains who defended the convoy in the Mediterranean, losing their ships in 1804, Richard Budd Vincent and Arthur Farquhar, were made Commanders of the Bath when the government instituted the order in June 1815.* Captain the Honourable John Talbot, from an aristocratic Irish family, who commanded HMS *Victorious*, which limped back safely after going ashore in Greenland, received a knighthood and was promoted to rear-admiral in 1819. Those who had made prize money flourished. Captain Samuel Butcher, after his narrowly decided exoneration in his court martial in 1815, lived his life out in Killarney in Ireland with a large family; he had done well out of Danish prizes. His pension was improved when it became his turn to become a retired rear-admiral in 1837, progressing to vice-admiral in 1847 before his death in 1849. Captain Thomas Mansell built a substantial house in St Peter Port in Guernsey and invested successfully in Guernsey shipping. Although he applied for active service posts unsuccessfully, he was remembered in the last tranche of knighthoods awarded by William IV before his death in 1837.[19] Sir Thomas Mansell was made a rear-admiral in 1849 and died, aged eighty-one, in 1858.

The two North Sea captains, too, became retired rear-admirals many years later: John Hancock in 1839 and Peter Rye in 1846. Hancock's prize money had led to prosperity, and he married an heiress in 1811 and had six children.[20] By contrast, Rye's retirement in Northamptonshire was marked by the need to raise loans and mortgages. His bad luck continued until the end. A note in his collection of loose drafts and letters records that his personal journals and logs were lost in 1840 at Bristol when they were being sent by rail.[21]

---

* Vincent was presented with a Lloyd's Patriotic Fund sword for his action, but left the sea because of ill-health, and was appointed to a staff post ashore at Malta for the rest of the war. Farquhar distinguished himself in amphibious operations off the Elbe and Weser in 1814 and was knighted in 1831 (Marshall, *Naval Biography*, IV, pp. 925–9, 935).

John Wilson Croker and John Barrow, fast friends, with children eventually intermarrying, continued to serve at the Admiralty for many years. Croker also put his endless energy into founding the Athenaeum Club in 1823, his monument today.[22] By now a 'High Tory', he resigned in 1830 from the Admiralty when it was clear that the Whigs were coming into office. Barrow continued as Second Secretary in office until his death in 1848, completing forty years' service, becoming famous for masterminding naval exploration. Towards the end of his career, he was responsible for the Admiralty sponsorship of the publication of William O'Byrne's 1,400-page *Naval Biographical Dictionary*, which contains the career details of 5,000 living naval officers, many of whom were serving before 1815. Barrow did not live to see it as it appeared a year after his death, but without its publication, the writing of large parts of this book would not have been possible.*

France and Britain each possessed a unique yet totally different military elite upon which each country ultimately depended. Both were highly trained and well funded. Napoleon's army was all-conquering, public and magnificent, feared in every capital in Europe, its every movement a political act. Within the Grand Armee, the Imperial Guard, all veterans, was pre-eminent, which Napoleon used very sparingly until 1812. By contrast, Britain's navy was dispersed around the world, each ship commanded and controlled by the skill and abilities of its commissioned, warrant and petty officers, and the able seamen among the ordinary seamen and landsmen. This naval elite was hidden from public view, their uniforms rough and practical; in the main they were young

---

* The level of detail is remarkable, with one exception, noted by O'Byrne in the preface: 'With regards to Courts-martial, I have, whenever I have found it possible to do so, avoided any reference to them; the advantage to be derived from reviving the details of inquiries of this nature appearing to me anything but obvious; and I hope, for the Credit of the service, there are few, if any, of its members who would desire to enhance their reputation by recalling the errors, often trivial, of their brother officers' (O'Byrne, *Naval Dictionary*, vii).

and tough, overcoming dangerous situations by teamwork imposed by years of repetitive discipline, motivated in the main by the promise of prize money. Further, these skills and experience were also to be found among the crews of merchant ships, many of whom had served in the navy, and vice versa. Controversy over the impressment of seamen, both at the time and in recent years, has rightly emphasised its inefficiency and its cruelty. Sheer muscle power was essential for working the naval guns, hauling anchors and heaving on sheets and halyards. But what ultimately counted was the strength of the young topmen, combined with the skill and experience of the commissioned and warrant officers and the older hands.

These two elite groups, though different in character, were broadly comparable in size. The numbers of the Imperial Guard varied considerably, and by 1812 had swelled to 56,000, but by Waterloo had fallen to around 25,000, about 20 per cent of the whole.* The number of seamen borne in both larger and small warships in 1812 totalled just under 145,000, of which 30 per cent of the complements were commissioned, warrant or petty officers.† To which should be added a significant proportion of able seamen, though these were in short supply in the later stages of the war.

The fortunes of these two bodies of fighting men ultimately decided the outcome of the war, but they had a common enemy. British ships and seamen took heavy casualties from extreme weather, in random and sometimes unknown numbers, with a high proportion of them suffering in small warships.[23] Some of the devastating weather came in the form of tropical storms, but most occurred in the northern hemisphere between October and March. This body of skilled seamen was,

---

* At Waterloo they formed just under 26,000 of the French army's total of 124,000 (Chandler, *Dictionary*, p. 205; Forrest, *Waterloo*, p. 29; Zamoyski, *1812*, pp. 143, 537–40, 584).
† Rodger, *Command of the Ocean*, p. 639; Rodger, *Wooden World*, pp. 348–51; James, *Naval History*, V, appendix 20. The purpose of this comparison is not to disparage the contribution of the British army from the beginning of the Peninsular War, nor of the armies of Russia, Prussia or Austria, but is intended to emphasise the distinctiveness of the two types of military expertise that were extant and effective for the whole of the Napoleonic Wars.

however, never completely annihilated, unlike the Grand Armee under Napoleon in Russia in 1812. The unexpected destruction of the French army on the retreat from Moscow was the single most important strategic event, on land or sea, in the last five years of the war. Thus, winter weather was the most significant arbiter of this long conflict.

EPILOGUE
The Second World War

Our business is to bring home the merchantmen. The sinking of the enemy is only a secondary consideration at this stage.

Commander C.D. Howard-Johnstone, Senior Naval Officer, B.12 Escort Group, summer 1941[1]

Many of the lessons learnt at such cost in the last war are being forgotten, just as precisely the same lessons were forgotten after 1918 and after the Napoleonic Wars.

Vice-Admiral Sir Peter Gretton, Convoy Escort Commander, 1963[2]

It is difficult to consider the British convoys of the wars against Napoleonic Europe and America without automatically comparing them to those of the mid-twentieth century against Hitler's Germany. The most powerful and widely read accounts of the Second World War at sea were fictionalised, written by those who had served in small warships. Both Herman Wouk's *The Caine Mutiny* (1951) and Nicholas Monsarrat's *The Cruel Sea* (also 1951) were made into films and recount the vicissitudes and feelings of those who manned these ships in the Pacific and Atlantic: but the driving force of the plot in both novels is the extreme weather and rough seas of the oceans. Yet the non-fictional accounts of the Second World War are even more compelling.

There are many parallels and contrasts between British convoys of the Napoleonic Wars and the Second World War. The technological race, which was central to the success of Britain and the allies during the later conflict, did not exist before 1815, while the ability to communicate in 'real time' made a real difference. The shortage of seamen was not such a problem, because of the resources of the Canadians, Australians, Indians and other Dominions, and the Americans in their own right. Perhaps the most marked difference is the outcome of the war, with the contrast of the strength of the British economy in 1815 as opposed to the financial exhaustion of 1945. The scale of mid-twentieth-century warfare was, of course, vast and any comparison of the sizes of merchant ships and their cargoes is scarcely valid. The capacity of a Second World War Liberty ship was 10,000 tons while that of a good-size West Indiaman before 1815 was perhaps 500 tons. Nevertheless, in terms of relative effort expended, there was an equivalence, for, roughly calculated, more British convoys and escorted ships sailed between 1803 and 1815 than between 1939 and 1945.[3]

Convoys around the British coasts in the Second World War were just as vital and as vulnerable as 130 years earlier, for roads and railways could not cope with demand. In 1940, London, for instance, needed 40,000 tons of coal a week. Coastal losses were heavy: 1,431 colliers and other small merchant ships totalling 3.7 million tons were sunk. This compares with ocean losses of 2,232 ships, measuring 11 million tons.[4] Worldwide convoy routes were similar, though there was, of course, no Pacific war and no Suez Canal in the earlier period.

A more obvious similarity between these two wars was the lack of enough small warships to serve as convoy escorts. In both wars, very small ships had to do the job of larger ships, operating in oceans for which they had not been designed. Constant improvisation was required to provide enough escort warships in the Second World War. The sturdy *Flower* class corvettes, based on a whaler design, could be built in as little as five months, in the same way (and at the same speed) as many sloops and brigs were constructed before 1815. The corvettes after 1939 'became the workhorses of an oceanic war for which they had not been intended'.[5] One Canadian seaman remembered:

> It was sheer unmitigated hell. She was a short fo'c'sle corvette and even getting hot food from the galley to fo'c'sle was a tremendous job. The mess decks were usually a shambles and the wear and tear on bodies and tempers was something I shall never forget. But we were young and tough and, in a sense, we gloried in our misery and made light of it all. What possible connection it had with defeating Hitler none of us bothered to ask. It was enough to find ourselves more or less afloat the next day and the hope of duff for pudding and a boiler clean when we reached port.[6]

Even with the advantage of twentieth-century communications, radar and navigation techniques, in the Second World War, according to Admiral Gretton, over a thousand ships were lost through collision, grounding and weather damage, as well as damaged ships being put out of action for long periods for repair. The chief reason was 'undue insistence on not burning navigation lights and on maintaining radio silence'. These accidents caused over 25 per cent of all ships lost, an analysis that recalls the fate of many sailing warships and merchantmen before 1815.[7] Overall, winter weather was less significant because of the greater efficiency of steam power, but an Atlantic south-westerly gale could still stop convoys in their tracks. Commander Denys Rayner, the captain of an old destroyer, described a west-going convoy of fifty ships in January 1944, during the worst period of Atlantic weather in the war. After five days, in mountainous seas and the loss of a 3-inch gun, torn out of its mountings and swept overboard, the convoy only made 40 miles in 24 hours. Rayner was forced to signal the commander-in-chief, Western Approaches: 'Convoy scattered by continuous gale. Have only eight merchant ships with me . . . No U-boat can operate in this weather. Request permission to return.' The answer soon came: 'Approved'.[8]

But there were good moments. Another destroyer captain wrote a lively passage describing the terrible food, similar discomfort and heart-stopping moments in 1942, but also indicating, though laced with irony, high moments in the life of a convoy: 'But comes the dawn and the sunlight and you see your convoy and you swell with pride and satisfaction . . . Now I'm doing a job worth doing . . . Life is good and sweet and strong. Then a dollop of spray hits you in the back of the neck to put you in your place and the Midshipman's sight turns out to be right and he shows you the mistake in yours and you realize you're just a worm after all.'[9]

Moments of calm and reflection like these are all but impossible to detect in the evidence available to us from the Royal Navy's fight against Napoleon. With the paucity of detailed personal accounts, we only have logs and official records of those who manned the wooden warships. By contrast, a very large number of Second World War convoy memoirs have been published, detailing the hardships and heroism of naval and merchant seamen. At their heart is the fascination of the unseen, lurking U-boats and the threat of sudden death. Their equivalents before 1815, enemy warships and privateers, do not pose the same immediacy or menace to a reader today.

There were, however, notable similarities. In both these world wars Britain had to import almost all its strategic war materials with which to fight the war. In the days of the sailing navy, the flow of naval stores from the Baltic was crucial in this respect, as well as saltpetre from India and sulphur from Sicily, while in the later conflict it was oil, steel and machinery that drove the war. By the mid-twentieth century, the North Atlantic was of central importance for the import of war materials, not so marked in the war against Napoleon, though it had been for a period when the supply of wheat from the middle states of the United States to Wellington's Peninsular armies was critical and in the later years, when supplies of timber from North America were transported to Britain in considerable quantities.

In the Mediterranean, with intense land fighting on its shores in both wars, Malta was crucial as the location for concentrating British convoys. Before 1815, it played its part as the base from which British troop expeditions sailed, and from which goods penetrated Napoleon's Continental System, while also serving as a base from which homeward Levant convoys ventured. By the twentieth century, it was essential for the protection of the route to the Suez Canal and supplies to the army in North Africa and, in order to retain the island, much was sacrificed in convoys to Malta, which according to the most detailed book on the subject, 'came within a whisker of surrender'.[10] The refusal of the British government to give up the island, which led to the failure of the Peace of Amiens in 1803, can be seen in retrospect as long-sighted stubbornness.

Both convoy generations had to solve the central conundrum of trade protection. How was naval instinct, trained and equipped for warfighting to destroy the enemy, to be fused with its duty to ensure the safety of merchant ships? By the First World War, prize money was not the complication that it once was, though it was not formally abolished until 1945.[11] The debate over which was the more important, the sinking of a U-boat or the safe arrival of a merchantman, was still intense when convoys were introduced again in 1917.[12]

There were remarkable individual connections in this respect between the convoy escort commanders of the two world wars. Though they were not alone in doing so, both Commander Peter Rye and Captain Peter Gretton, over 130 years apart, fired live ammunition at merchantmen which did not obey orders. Rye did not hesitate to fire two shots at a straying merchantman, for instance, the *Lord Carrington*, in the middle of the North Sea in September 1807 during a convoy to Copenhagen, 'for not obeying the signal . . . spoke her and ordered her to join the ships to leeward', as the log ran.[13] Similarly, although Gretton thought that the prohibition of lights during a convoy was overdone, 'when the convoy was being shadowed, or in a danger area, a light gave an aiming mark and was highly dangerous. I found that a few well aimed rounds of machine-gun bullets quickly doused the offender.'[14] These escort commanders stood no nonsense in their quest for the safety of their charges.

Individual officers and seamen had to cope with the stress and fatigue of convoying for months at sea. Wooden ships, naval or merchantmen, required continuous maintenance, much of it done while in port and mostly by the crews but a considerable part of the year was spent at sea. Stress and illness had to be managed, but such was the requirement to sail immediately with the next convoy that it was not easy to obtain Admiralty leave. Remarkably, however, officers who were Members of Parliament were given shore leave by the incumbent First Lord if their vote was required in the House of Commons. Captain Sir Charles Hamilton, for instance, was ordered ashore in April 1804 by Lord St Vincent, to come to the aid of Addington's government. He also came ashore in 1807 and 1810 for political reasons.[15]

In the days of patrons and political influence, there were far more anomalies and unfairness in the early nineteenth-century navy than in the twentieth century. Those who were influential enough and could afford to do so declined to serve for a time, altogether a wasteful and inequitable arrangement. As there were far more officers than there were ships to which to appoint them, the less privileged applied for shore jobs such as regulating officers in various ports, overseeing recruitment and impressment, or applied to command the local land-based Sea Fencibles. Lieutenants sought an appointment ashore to run coastal signal stations. Disabled officers tried for commands of prison or harbour hulks or hospital ships.[16] The mid-twentieth century navy was not so short of men, training many 'hostilities only' officers and seamen. The Royal Naval Volunteer Reserve played a vital role in escorting convoys and manning small craft.[17]

Convoy duty wore commanders out. Captains Richard Budd Vincent in 1807 and Peter Rye in 1812 were found staff jobs after long years of toil afloat. At the end of 1944, Commander Denys Rayner,

R.N.V.R., one of the longest-serving convoy escort commanders in the North Atlantic, recounts dispassionately in his memoirs how, after five years, having steamed tens of thousands of miles, been battered by North Atlantic storms, torpedoed and very nearly grounded, with one U-boat to his credit, he reached the end of his tether. He was relieved of his command in 36 hours. Admiral Sir Max Horton, commander-in-chief, Western Approaches, ensured that Rayner was given an important job ashore, using his convoy expertise, responsible to the commander-in-chief, Portsmouth. With his wry humour, Rayner described his new posting as 'Senior Officer of Escorts (Chairborne)'.[18]

While the Napoleonic seaman had to endure the morale-destroying scourge of impressment when reaching port, those who served in the Second World War when ashore found disruption of a different kind. One ordinary naval seaman noted the conditions during a particularly tough Atlantic convoy crossing in February 1941: 'The cold is unbearable, the blankets are frozen to the ironwork and frost is round the portholes . . . the oil in our messes is 2" deep in places.' Back on shore, he then had to pass through Portsmouth, where for the first time he saw the results of German bombing, which put his recent discomforts into some proportion: 'Amazed at the wreckage; stations, hospitals, shelters, shops, houses and acres of smoking ruins.'[19]

Without convoys effective enough to contain losses, neither war would have been won, given the potentially disastrous merchant ship losses when convoys either failed, or failed to materialise. In both wars, lone merchant ships and those which 'straggled' from convoys were always vulnerable to predators, be they privateers or U-boats. The hostile Norwegian coast in summer, with very long daylight hours, was always dangerous. This was the scene of the loss of HMB *Forward*'s convoy in 1810 and much further north, 130 years later, the destruction of two-thirds of convoy PQ17 in July 1942 when ordered to disperse and scatter. Twenty-four merchant ships were sunk and 153 merchant seamen died. No naval personnel died in their defence, which stirred up feeling between the service and civilian seamen. The Arctic convoys to Murmansk were slowly run down as other routes, through Iran and Vladivostok, were used to transport Lend-Lease materials to Russia.[20]

In the Second World War, Britain was in a weak position between 1941 and 1943. United States public opinion could have been turned had there been a dramatic convoy disaster, and the wholesale loss of troops at sea would have been the most difficult problem for President Roosevelt to weather. Dominion troops were moved in fast, well-escorted convoys, while thousands of American troops were transported to Europe by huge passenger liners travelling at 28 knots, too fast for any attacking U-boats. By May 1944 over 1.5 million American troops came across the Atlantic, 60 per cent in escorted convoys and 30 per cent in the large liners. The SS *Queen Elizabeth* and SS *Queen Mary* carried 425,000 between them. Allied luck held. There were no major casualties. The only 'monster' sunk was the 42,000-ton SS *Empress of Britain*, but on this voyage the ship was not packed with troops, passengers were evacuated and loss of life was light, as was the case when SS *Avoceta* was sunk north of the Azores in September 1941. In March 1943 the much smaller *Empress of Canada* was sunk on the way back to Australia with Italian prisoners of war, with the loss of nearly four hundred lives. The worst British maritime disaster was in September 1940 when SS *Lancastria* was evacuating 5,200 servicemen from northern France, with 2,000 casualties. News of the disaster was delayed by the British government for five weeks, fearful of the effect of the news on public morale.[21]

However, the greatest loss of allied merchant ships occurred after the Japanese attack on Pearl Harbour in early December 1941 when Germany and the United States found themselves at war. The failure of the American navy to organise convoys along the United States eastern seaboard enabled the U-boats to wreak havoc. Over a thousand merchant ships were sunk along the Atlantic coast in 1942. Of this number, 180 were sunk in the Caribbean, measuring nearly a million tons. By this time, the British had concluded that even weakly defended convoys were better than ships voyaging alone, but the Americans, beset by a sudden Pacific war, did not act on this advice. One historian described it as 'the greatest maritime massacre in US history'.[22]

The threats faced by Britain in the early nineteenth and mid-twentieth centuries, which the convoy system was designed to combat, were severe and potentially disastrous. In either conflict, had the war materials supply chain been broken, military reverses could have been catastrophic. Of greater fragility was the potential weakening of political will in the countries which despatched or received the convoys, which could have led to the reduction or abandonment of convoys altogether. Such political crisis points were never reached in either war, though there were some narrow shaves. Napoleon's Moscow defeat in 1812 enabled Britain to release large and small warships in 1813 from European waters to transfer them to protect troop and material convoys to North America. In the event, the British ran out of seamen and left great swathes of the eastern Atlantic and home waters undefended.

Storms, fog and ice, singly and in combination, tested and often overwhelmed the warships and seamen of the Royal Navy, and those ships carrying cargo whom they escorted. The threats posed by weather for wooden sailing ships, naval and merchant, were greater than those posed by the enemy. Yet the convoy chain was kept intact. Commander Denys Raynor, veteran of the Battle of the Atlantic, spoke for both wars when he wrote in 1955:

> I write only of ships and men, both of whom have character, and change from one generation to another . . . I do not write of the sea, which has no personality of its own and does not change. The sea is neither cruel nor kind. It is supremely indifferent . . . Any apparent virtues it may have, and all its vices, are seen only in relation to the spirit of man who pits himself, in ships of his own building, against its insensate power. To conclude otherwise is to diminish its majesty.[23]

APPENDIX: LOSSES OF SMALL WARSHIPS BY STATION, 1803–1815
(18 GUNS AND BELOW: SLOOPS, BRIGS, GUN BRIGS AND GUNBOATS)

Each entry includes: ship type, number of guns, tonnage, place of build (or prize, purchase or hire). Where known: duties of ship at time of loss, type of loss, place of loss, number of casualties.

HOME WATERS: CHANNEL INCLUDING IRISH SEA

1803

25 Dec: *Suffiisante* (brig sloop, 16 guns, 286 tons, French prize) cruising: **wrecked**, ashore at Cork, no casualties.

31 Dec: *Grappler* (gunboat, 12 guns, 170 tons, Northfleet) cruising: **wrecked**, Isles Chausey, burnt.

1804

20 Jan: *Fearless* (gunboat, 12 guns, 149 tons, Gravesend) convoying: **wrecked**, Plymouth Sound, no casualties.

20 Feb: *Cerbere* (gunboat, 10 guns, 138 tons, French. Prize) **wrecked**, Torbay, no casualties.

26 Aug: *Constitution* (cutter, 10 guns, 120 tons, hired) blockade duty: **sunk**, artillery off Boulogne, no casualties.

25 Sep: *Georgiana* (cutter, 12 guns, 129 tons, hired) blockade duty: **wrecked**, near Honfleur, burnt, no casualties.

13 Oct: *Firebrand* (fireship, 140 tons, prize) anchored in Downs, **wrecked**, 1 dead.

24 Oct: *Conflict* (gunboat, 12 guns, 180 tons, Deptford) blockade duty: **wrecked** off Ostend, captured, no casualties.

25 Nov: *Duke of Clarence* (cutter, 10 guns, 64 tons, hired) blockade duty: **wrecked**, Iles Chausey, no casualties.

20 Dec: *Tartarus* (bomb vessel, 8 guns, 344 tons, purchased) **wrecked**, anchored in Downs, 1 killed.

21 Dec: *Althorpe* (cutter, 14 guns, 163 tons, hired) **foundered**, Channel, no survivors.

24 Dec: *Julia* (schooner, 12 guns, 157 tons, hired) **wrecked**, entering Dartmouth, no casualties.

24 Dec: *Starling* (gunboat, 12 guns, 188 tons, Buckler's Hard) blockade duty: **wrecked**, captured near Gris Nez, no casualties.

24 Dec: *Mallard* (gunboat, 12 guns, 178 tons, Deptford) blockade duty: **wrecked**, near Calais, crew prisoners.

Dec: *Hawk* (ship sloop, 18 guns, 320 tons, French prize) **foundered**, Channel, no survivors.

1805

17 Jan: *Commerce* (brig, 6 guns, 117 tons, hired) cruising: **wrecked**, west coast of Ireland, 2 drowned.

Feb: *Bouncer* (gunboat, 12 guns, 177 tons, Newcastle) blockade duty: **wrecked**, near Dieppe, crew prisoners.

Feb: *Seagull* (brig sloop, 18 guns, 318 tons, Rotherhithe) **foundered**: Channel, no survivors.

Feb: *Mary* (cutter, 12 guns, 100 tons, hired) **foundered**, Channel, no survivors.

11 Jul: *Orestes* (ship sloop, 16 guns, 280 tons, purchased) blockade duty: **wrecked**, off Dunkirk, captured, no casualties.

16 Jul: *Plumper* (gunboat, 12 guns, 177 tons, Deptford) blockade duty: **captured**, Isles Chausey, crew prisoners.

16 Jul: *Teazer* (gunboat, 12 guns, 177 tons, Deptford) blockade duty: **captured** with *Plumper* (**recaptured** 25 Aug 1811).

19 Jul: *Ranger* (ship sloop, 16 guns, 367 tons, Limehouse) cruising: **captured** Channel Islands, crew prisoners.

10 Aug: *Pigmy* (cutter, 14 guns, 215 tons, French Prize) cruising: **wrecked**, off Jersey, no casualties.

11 Oct: *Squib* (fireship, not known, purchased) **wrecked**, near Deal, not known.

10 Nov: *Biter* (gunboat, 12 guns, 177 tons, Blackwall) blockade duty: **wrecked**, off Etaples, crew prisoners.

13 Nov: *Woodlark* (gunboat, 12 guns, 182 tons, Leith) transferring seamen: **wrecked,** off Calais, crew prisoners.

1806

31 Jan: *Venus* (cutter, 10 guns, 51 tons, hired) **captured** by French privateer.

16 Mar: *Ant* (cutter, 4 guns, 27 tons, hired) **captured** by French privateer.

Sep: *Flight* (cutter, 4 guns, 187 tons, purchased) **foundered** Channel, no survivors.

9 Dec: *United Brothers* (tender, 4 guns, 143 tons, hired) transferring seamen: **captured** off Lizard, 2 killed.

Dec: *Clinker* (gunboat, 12 guns, 178 tons, Northfleet) blockade duty: **foundered** off Le Havre, no survivors.

1807

18 Feb: *Inveterate* (gunboat, 12 guns, 182 tons, Bridport) blockade duty: **wrecked**, off Etaples, 4 drowned.

18 Feb: *Griper* (gunboat, 12 guns, 179 tons, King's Lynn) blockade duty: **wrecked**, off Etaples, no survivors.

18 Feb: *Magpie* (gunboat, 4 guns, 76 tons, Newcastle) blockade duty: **wrecked**, run ashore North Brittany, no casualties.

18 Feb: *Prospero* (bomb vessel, 8 guns, 400 tons, purchased) blockade duty: **foundered**, Dieppe, 6 survivors.

18 Feb: *Speedwell* (gunboat, 14 guns, 193 tons, purchased) blockade duty: **wrecked**, Dieppe, no survivors.

18 Feb: *Ignition* (fireship, 4 guns, 130 tons, purchased) blockade duty: **wrecked**, near Dieppe, 4 survivors.

30 May: *Jackal* (gunboat, 12 guns, 186 tons, Blackwall) cruising: **wrecked**, near Calais, crew prisoners.

1808

24 Jan: *Carrier* (cutter, 10 guns, 54 tons, purchased) **wrecked**, near Etaples, crew prisoners.

2 Feb: *Sussex Oak* (ketch, number of guns unknown, 124 tons, hired) not known: **captured** by French privateer.

20 Apr: *Widgeon* (schooner, 8 guns, 80 tons, Brixham) convoying: **wrecked**, Scottish east coast.

26 Oct: *Crane* (schooner, 4 guns, 80 tons, Gt Yarmouth) **wrecked**, anchored Plymouth Sound, no casualties.

31 Oct: *Cricket* (ketch, number of guns unknown, 97 tons, hired) not known, **captured** in Channel, crew prisoners.

26 Dec: *Bustler* (gunboat, 12 guns, 180 tons, Topsham) cruising: **stranded & captured** near Cap Gris Nez, no casualties.

1809

22 Jan: *Primrose* (brig sloop, 18 guns, 384 tons, Fowey) convoying: **wrecked** on the Manacles, 119 crew died.

7 Dec: *Harlequin* (ship sloop, 16 guns, 185 tons, hired) convoying: **wrecked** near Seaford, 2 drowned.

14 Dec: *Defender* (gunboat, 12 guns, 179 tons, Chester) **wrecked**, near Folkestone, no casualties.

1810

15 Feb: *Wild Boar* (brig sloop, 18 guns, 238 tons, Frindsbury) cruising: **wrecked**, Scillies, 12 drowned.

1 Jun: *Black Joke* (lugger, 4 guns, 109 tons, hired) cruising: **captured**, Channel, crew prisoners.

28 Oct: *Racer* (cutter, 12 guns, 203 tons, Sandgate) cruising: **wrecked**, off Calais, crew prisoners.

31 Dec: *Satellite* (brig sloop, 16 guns, 289 tons, Sandwich) **foundered**, Channel, no survivors.

1811

2 Mar: *Olympia* (cutter, 10 guns, 150 tons, Bermuda) blockade duty: **captured**, Channel, crew prisoners.

29 Jun: *Firm* (gunboat, 12 guns, 177 tons, Frindsbury) blockade duty: **wrecked**, near Cancale, set on fire, no casualties.

1812

3 May: *Skylark* (brig sloop, 16 guns, 283 tons, Newcastle) blockade duty: **wrecked and captured** near Cap Gris Nez, no casualties.

3 May: *Apelles* (brig sloop, 14 guns, 151 tons, Woolwich) blockade duty: captured near Cap Gris Nez, no casualties.

10 Sep: *Alphea* (schooner, 10 guns, 111 tons, Bermuda) cruising: **blew up** during action with French privateer off Start Point, no survivors.

1813

Oct: *Vautour* (brig sloop, 18 guns, 336 tons, French Prize) presumed **foundered**, Channel, no survivors.

1814

28 Feb: *Anacreon* (ship sloop, 16 guns, 423 tons, Plymouth) **foundered**, Channel, no survivors.

22 Mar: *Decoy* (cutter, 10 guns, 203 tons, Fishbourne, Isle of Wight) cruising: **wrecked** off Calais, no casualties.

WESTERN APPROACHES, CORK, BRITTANY, GIBRALTAR

1804

8 May: *Vincejo* (brig sloop, 16 guns, 277 tons, prize) blockade duty: **captured**, Quiberon, 2 killed, crew prisoners.

16 Dec: *Gertrude* (schooner, 16 guns, 148 tons, hired) blockade duty: **foundered**, collision off Ushant, no casualties.

1805

5 Aug: *Dove* (cutter, 4 guns, 103 tons, purchased) carrying despatches: **captured**, Bay of Biscay, crew prisoners.

1806

9 Dec: *Adder* (gunboat, 12 guns, 180 tons, Topsham) blockade duty: **wrecked**, Brittany, no casualties, crew prisoners.

1807

23 Jan: *Felix* (schooner, 14 guns, 158 tons, prize) cartel: **wrecked**, Santander, 3 survivors, 57 died.

12 Feb: *Atalante* (brig sloop, 16 guns, 310 tons, prize) blockade duty: **wrecked**, off Rochefort, no casualties.

13 Feb: *Woodcock* (schooner, 4 guns, 76 tons, Gt Yarmouth) **wrecked**, Azores, no casualties.

13 Feb: *Wagtail* (schooner, 4 guns, 76 tons, Gt Yarmouth) **wrecked**, Azores, 1 drowned.

16 Feb: *Jackdaw* (schooner, 4 guns, 76 tons, Newcastle) carrying despatches: **captured**, Portugal (recaptured 17 Feb).

5 Mar: *Pigmy* (gunboat, 12 guns, 217 tons, purchased) blockade duty: **wrecked**, Isle d'Oleron, crew prisoners.

Mar: *Cesar* (brig sloop, 16 guns, 320 tons, prize) blockade duty: **wrecked**, near Gironde, not known.

13 Aug: *Casandra* (cutter, 10 guns, 111 tons, Bermuda) carrying despatches: **foundered**, 12 drowned.

21 Nov: *Bolina* (brig, 6 guns, 181 tons, hired) cruising: **wrecked**, north Cornwall, no casualties.

1808

25 Mar: *Milbrook* (schooner, 12 guns, 148 tons, purchased) cruising: **wrecked**, Portuguese coast, no casualties.

18 May: *Rapid* (gunboat, 12 guns, 178 tons, Topsham) cruising: **sunk** by batteries, Sagres Bay, no casualties.

28 Jun: *Capelin* (schooner, 4 guns, 70 tons, Bermuda) blockade duty: **wrecked**, off Brest, no casualties.

1809

Feb: *Viper* (schooner, 8 guns, 81 tons, purchased) **foundered**, Cadiz to Gibraltar, no survivors.

25 Mar: *Caca Fuego* (gunboat, 2 guns, tonnage unknown, purchased) carrying despatches: **wrecked**, Gibraltar Bay, no casualties.

13 Apr: *Aeneas* (brig, number of guns unknown, 276 tons, hired) blockade duty: **wrecked**, Basque Roads, no casualties.

26 Nov: *Gibraltar* (gunboat, 3 guns, 43 tons, place of build unknown) carrying despatches: **foundered**, off San Pedro, Spain, no survivors.

1810

28 Oct: *Camperdown* (gunboat, 3 guns, 43 tons, place of build unknown) blockade duty: **wrecked**, off Cadiz, 15 drowned.

9 Nov: *Conflict* (gunboat, 12 guns, 182 tons, Topsham) **foundered**, off Corunna, no survivors.

25 Dec: *Monkey* (gunboat, 12 guns, 188 tons, Rochester) blockade duty: **wrecked**, off L'Orient, 2 drowned.

1811

23 Feb: *Shamrock* (schooner, 10 guns, 150 tons, Bermuda) cruising: **wrecked**, SW Spain, 2 drowned.

12 Mar: *Challenger* (brig sloop, 16 guns, 285 tons, Blackwall) blockade duty: captured off Brittany, 2 killed.

14 Jul: *Snapper* (schooner, 4 guns, 70 tons, Bermuda) cruising: captured off Les Sables d'Olonne, no casualties.

26 Dec: *Ephira* (brig sloop, 10 guns, 237 tons, Upnor, Medway) convoying: **wrecked**, Cadiz Bay, crew prisoners.

1812

19 Feb: *Gunboat 11* (gunboat, 3 guns, 43 tons) blockade duty: **wrecked**, Cadiz Bay, no casualties.

11 Jul: *Encounter* (gunboat, 12 guns, 185 tons, Northam) cruising: **wrecked**, Cadiz Bay, 1 killed, 14 wounded.

21 Sep: *Gunboat 10* (gunboat, 3 guns, 51 tons) carrying despatches: **wrecked**, off Cape Trafalgar, no casualties.

8 Dec: *Fearless* (mortar brig, 12 guns, 180 tons, Harwich) convoying: **wrecked**, Cadiz Bay, no casualties.

1813

25 Feb: *Linnet* (gunboat, 14 guns, 197 tons, purchased) cruising: **captured**, Channel, no casualties.

Aug: *Gunboat 23* (gunboat, 3 guns, 53 tons, place of build unknown) **wrecked**, River Ebro, Spain, no casualties.

1814

29 Jan: *Holly* (schooner, 10 guns, 172 tons, Bermuda) blockade duty: **wrecked**, San Sebastian, Spain, 4 drowned.

2 Apr: *Gleaner* (ketch, 10 guns, 154 tons, purchased) **wrecked**, St Jean de Luz, no casualties.

28 Jun: *Reindeer* (brig sloop, 18 guns, 385 tons, Rotherhithe) cruising: **captured, then sunk**, 25 killed, 42 wounded.

12 Jul: *Landrail* (schooner, 4 guns, 75 tons, Ringmore) carrying despatches: **captured**, off Ushant, 5 wounded.

27 Aug: *Avon* (brig sloop, 18 guns, 391 tons, Falmouth) convoying: **captured** off Portugal, **sank**, 10 killed, 32 wounded.

NORTH SEA INCLUDING SKAGERRAK

1803

5 Dec: *Avenger* (ship sloop, 14 guns, 264 tons, purchased) blockade duty: **wrecked**, River Elbe, no casualties.

1805

30 Nov: *Pigeon* (cutter, 4 guns, 85 tons, purchased) **wrecked**, off the Texel, captured, no casualties.

1806

Jan: *Manly* (gunboat, 12 guns, 178 tons, Sandwich) blockade duty: **captured**, Dutch coast, crew prisoners.

25 Mar: *Agnes* (lugger, 4 guns, 27 tons, hired) **foundered**, off Texel, no survivors.

1807

31 Mar: *Ferreter* (gunboat, 12 guns, 184 tons, Blackwall) blockade duty: **captured** off the River Ems, no casualties.

10 Sep: *Explosion* (bomb vessel, 12 guns, 323 tons, purchased) carrying despatches: **wrecked** off Heligoland, no casualties.

11 Nov: *Leveret* (brig sloop, 18 guns, 384 tons, Dover) **wrecked**, off Harwich, no casualties.

1808

11 Jan: *Lord Keith* (cutter, 10 guns, 72 tons, hired) blockade duty: **captured**, forced into Cuxhaven, crew prisoners.

13 Jan: *Sparkler* (gunboat, 12 guns, 178 tons, Brightlingsea) blockade duty: **wrecked**, Terschelling, 14 died.

19 Jun: *Seagull* (brig sloop, 16 guns, 285 tons, Dover) cruising: **captured** by Danish gunboats, 8 killed, 20 wounded.

4 Aug: *Delphinen* (brig sloop, 16 guns, 306 tons, prize) blockade duty: **wrecked**, Dutch coast, crew prisoners.

1809

5 Jan: *Pigeon* (schooner, 4 guns, 75 tons, Gt Yarmouth) cruising: **wrecked**, Margate Sands, 8 crew died.

20 Jan: *Claudia* (cutter, 10 guns, 111 tons, Bermuda) cruising: **wrecked** off Kristiansand, 14 died.

18 Jun: *Sealark* (schooner, 4 guns, 80 tons, Brixham) cruising: **foundered**, North Sea, 9 survivors.

5 Aug: *Lord Nelson* (cutter, 8 guns, 69 tons, hired) **wrecked** near Flushing, no casualties.

10 Aug: *Alaart* (brig sloop, 16 guns, 306 tons, prize) cruising: **captured** by Danish gunboats, off Norway, 1 killed.

1810

4 Apr: *Cuckoo* (schooner, 4 guns, 78 tons, Gt Yarmouth) blockade duty: **wrecked**, Dutch coast, 2 died, the rest prisoners.

4 May: *Fleche* (ship sloop, 16 guns, 279 tons, prize) blockade duty: **wrecked**, River Elbe, no casualties.

4 Jun: *Idas* (cutter, 10 guns, 102 tons, hired) blockade duty: **wrecked**, off Schoonereldt, no casualties.

4 Jun: *Porgey* (schooner, 4 guns, 78 tons, Bermuda) blockade duty: **wrecked**, off the Scheldt, no casualties.

1811

2 Sep: *Manly* (gunboat, 12 guns, 178 tons, Sandwich) blockade duty: **captured**, south Norway, 1 killed, 3 wounded.

24 Dec: *Fancy* (gunboat, 12 guns, 180 tons, Gt Yarmouth) convoying: **foundered** off Jutland, no survivors.

25 Dec: *Grasshopper* (brig sloop, 18 guns, 383 tons, Hythe) convoying: **wrecked**, off Texel, no casualties.

1812

8 Jul: *Exertion* (gunboat, 12 guns, 181 tons, Gt Yarmouth) **wrecked** in Elbe at Cuxhaven, no casualties.

18 Dec: *Alban* (cutter, 10 guns, 111 tons, Bermuda) **wrecked**, Aldeburgh, Suffolk, 2 survivors.

1813

7 Jan: *Ferret* (brig sloop, 18 guns, 387 tons, Dartmouth) **wrecked**, Northumbrian coast, no casualties.

Jul: *Gunboat 17* (3 guns, 53 tons, place of build unknown) **foundered** after collision at the Nore, 2 drowned.

1814

Jul: *Gunboat 8* (3 guns, 53 tons, place of build unknown) **wrecked** in Elbe, no casualties.

BALTIC INCLUDING THE KATTEGAT

1807

16 May: *Dauntless* (ship sloop, 18 guns, 426 tons, Hull) **captured** during the siege of Danzig.

1808

4 June: *Tickler* (gunboat, 12 guns, 178 tons, Brightlingsea) cruising: **captured** by Danish gunboats in the Great Belt.

9 Jun: *Turbulent* (gunboat, 12 guns, 181 tons, Dartmouth) convoying: **captured** in the Sound by Danish gun vessels.

2 Aug: *Tigress* (gunboat, 12 guns, 177 tons, Deptford) carrying despatches: **captured** by Danish gun vessels, 2 killed, 8 wounded.

5 Dec: *Proselyte* (bomb vessel, 4 guns, 404 tons, purchased) **wrecked**, Anholt, crushed by ice, no casualties.

23 Dec: *Fama* (brig sloop, 18 guns, 315 tons, prize) convoying: **wrecked**, Bornholm Island, 3 died.

23 Dec: *Salorman* (cutter, 10 guns, 121 tons, prize) convoying: **wrecked**, Ystad, no casualties.

1809

11 Jan: *Magnet* (brig sloop, 18 guns, 382 tons, Northam) convoying: **wrecked**, Malmo, destroyed by ice, no casualties

2 Sep: *Minx* (gunboat, 12 guns, 179 tons, Northfleet) acting as a light vessel off the Skaw: **captured**, 2 killed, 9 wounded.

1810

12 Sep: *Alban* (cutter, 12 guns, 111 tons, Bermuda) **captured** off Laeso by Danish gun vessels, 2 killed, 3 wounded.

1811

13 Feb: *Pandora* (brig sloop, 18 guns, 383 tons, Gt Yarmouth) cruising: **wrecked** off the Skaw, 27 died.

25 Apr: *Swan* (cutter, 10 guns, 119 tons, hired) cruising: **captured** by Danish gunboats, **foundered**, 2 killed, 1 wounded.

29 Jun: *Safeguard* (gunboat, 12 guns, 178 tons, Topsham) **captured** by Danish gunboats off Jutland.

1812

28 Feb: *Fly* (brig sloop, 16 guns, 286 tons, Bridport) convoying: **wrecked**, NE Kattegat, no casualties.

19 Aug: *Attack* (gunboat, 12 guns, 181 tons, Chapel) convoying: **captured** near Fornaes by Danish gun vessels, 2 killed.

6 Oct: *Nimble* (cutter, 10 guns, 145 tons, Cowes) **wrecked** off Marstrand, no casualties.

10 Oct: *Sentinel* (gunboat, 12 guns, 194 tons, purchased) convoying: **wrecked**, Rugen island, no casualties.

24 Nov: *Belette* (brig sloop, 18 guns, 384 tons, Dover) convoying: **wrecked** off Laeso, 116 died.

1813

1 Jan: *Sarpedon* (brig sloop, 10 guns, 241 tons, Eling) **wrecked**, Norwegian coast, no survivors.

NORTH ATLANTIC (INCLUDING AMERICAN WATERS)

1804

24 Mar: *Wolverine* (brig sloop, 12 guns, 286 tons, purchased) convoying: **sunk** in action off Newfoundland, 5 killed.

15 Jul: *Lily* (ship sloop, 14 guns, 200 tons, purchased) cruising: **captured** by French privateer off Georgia, 2 killed.

1805

Apr: *Papillon* (gunboat, 14 guns, 145 tons, French prize) convoying: **foundered**, Jamaica, no survivors.

30 Sep: *Flying Fish* (schooner, 4 guns, 70 tons, Bermuda) **taken** by French prisoners at Bermuda.

1806

Aug: *Martin* (ship sloop, 16 guns, 367 tons, Dartmouth) convoying: **foundered**, North Atlantic, no survivors.

30 Oct: *Zenobia* (schooner, 10 guns, 111 tons, Bermuda) **wrecked**, Norfolk, Virginia, no casualties, 18 out of 24 deserted.

1807

Feb: *Busy* (brig sloop, 18 guns, 337 tons, Harwich) convoying: **foundered** off Halifax, no survivors.

26 Oct: *Subtle* (schooner, 10 guns, 102 tons, prize) cruising: **wrecked**, off Bermuda, no casualties.

1808

Feb: *Tang* (schooner, 4 guns, 78 tons, Bermuda) **foundered**, new ship to England, disappeared.

1809

Mar: *Pelter* (gunboat, 12 guns, 177 tons, Deptford) convoying: **foundered**, Halifax to West Indies, no survivors.

Aug: *Foxhound* (brig sloop, 18 guns, 384 tons, Dover) **foundered**, Halifax to England, no survivors.

Dec: *Contest* (gunboat, 12 guns, 178 tons, Chester) **foundered**, America to England, no survivors.

1811

6 Mar: *Thistle* (schooner, 10 guns, 150 tons, Bermuda) carrying despatches: **wrecked**, near Sandy Hook, New York, no casualties.

1812

2 Aug: *Emulous* (brig sloop, 18 guns, 383 tons, Newcastle) cruising: **wrecked**, Nova Scotia, no casualties.

13 Aug: *Alert* (ship sloop, 16 guns, 393 tons, purchased) cruising: **captured**, off Azores, crew prisoners.

14 Aug: *Chubb* (schooner, 4 guns, 78 tons, Bermuda) **wrecked**, near Halifax, no survivors.

22 Aug: *Whiting* (schooner, 4 guns, 70 tons, Bermuda) **captured** off the Chesapeake, crew prisoners.

8 Sep: *Laura* (cutter, 12 guns, 111 tons, Bermuda) blockade duty: **captured** in the Delaware River, 15 killed & wounded.

Sep: *Magnet* (brig sloop, 16 guns, 286 tons, prize) convoying: **foundered**, England to Halifax, no survivors.

8 Oct: *Avenger* (ship sloop, 14 guns, 390 tons, purchased) cruising: **wrecked** entering St Johns harbour, Newfoundland, no casualties.

18 Oct: *Frolic* (brig sloop, 18 guns, 384 tons, Bridport) convoying: **captured** off Bermuda, 15 killed, 43 wounded, recaptured.

5 Dec: *Plumper* (gunboat, 12 guns, 177 tons, Halifax, NS) convoying: **wrecked** at St John's, New Brunswick, 42 drowned.

1813

4 Jul: *Eagle* (sloop, 1 gun, tonnage unknown, purchased) cruising: **captured** off Sandy Hook, crew prisoners.

Jul: *Herring* (schooner, 4 guns, 70 tons, Bermuda) **foundered** off Halifax, no survivors.

5 Aug: *Dominica* (schooner, 14 guns, 203 tons, prize) convoying: **captured** by an American privateer 19 killed, 41 wounded.

22 Aug: *Colibri* (brig sloop, 16 guns, 365 tons, prize) blockade duty: **wrecked** near Savannah, no casualties.

5 Sep: *Boxer* (brig sloop, 12 guns, 182 tons, Redbridge) cruising: **captured**, Portland, Maine, 4 killed, 17 wounded.

24 Sep: *Highflyer* (schooner, 8 guns, 144 tons, prize) cruising: **captured** off Nantucket, crew prisoners.

27 Sep: *Bold* (gunboat, 12 guns, 180 tons, Bursledon) convoying, **wrecked**, Prince Edward Island, no casualties.

5 Nov: *Tweed* (ship sloop, 18 guns, 431 tons, Littlehampton) convoying: **wrecked**, Newfoundland, 64 died.

10 Nov: *Atalante* (ship sloop, 18 guns, 399 tons, Bermuda) blockade duty: **wrecked** off Halifax, no casualties.

Dec: *Dart* (cutter, 10 guns, 127 tons, purchased) **foundered**, sailed from Halifax, no survivors.

1814

14 Feb: *Pictou* (brig sloop, 16 guns, 211 tons, prize) convoying: **captured**, Bermuda to Surinam, crew prisoners.

29 Apr: *Ballahou* (schooner, 4 guns, 70 tons, Bermuda) cruising: **captured** off South Carolina, crew prisoners.

29 Apr: *Epervier* (brig sloop, 18 guns, 388 tons, Rochester) convoying: **captured** in the Bahamas, 8 killed, 15 wounded.

Jul: *Peacock* (ship sloop, 18 guns, 434 tons, prize) **foundered** off North Carolina, no survivors.

Sep: *Crane* (brig sloop, 18 guns, 385 tons, Frindsbury) **foundered**, Bermuda to Canada, no survivors.

24 Nov: *Fantome* (brig sloop, 18 guns, 385 tons, prize) convoying: **wrecked** off Halifax, no casualties.

No date available: *Atalante* (schooner, 14 guns, 225 tons, prize) **reported captured** by Americans, no details known.

1815

17 Jan: *Sylph* (ship sloop, 18 guns, 399 tons, Bermuda) **wrecked**, Long Island, 6 survivors.

[South Atlantic 1815]

23 Mar: *Penguin* (brig sloop, 18 guns, 387 tons, King's Lynn) cruising: **captured**, Tristan de Cunha, 10 killed, 28 wounded.

WEST INDIES

1803

23 Jun: *Surinam* (ship sloop, 18 guns, 413 tons: ex-French prize) cruising: **arrested** in Curacao by the Dutch.

30 Jul: *Calypso* (ship sloop, 16 guns, 342 tons, Deptford) convoying: **foundered**, run down, no survivors.

1804

23 Jun: *Fort Diamond* (sloop, 20 guns (estimate), tonnage unknown, purchased) cruising: **ambushed** at anchor, St Lucia.

12 Jul: *Drake* (brig sloop, 14 guns, 212 tons, French prize) convoying: **wrecked** off Nevis, no casualties.

14 Jul: *Demerara* (schooner, 6 guns, 106 tons, purchased) cruising: captured off Demerara, 1 killed, 9 wounded.

6 Dec: *Morne Fortunee* (schooner, 6 guns, 106 tons, purchased) carrying despatches: **wrecked**, Bahamas, no casualties.

1805

26 Feb: *Redbridge* (schooner, 10 guns, 170 tons, French prize) **wrecked: sank** at anchor in Jamaica, no casualties.

8 Mar: *Fly* (ship sloop, 16 guns, 369 tons, Burlesdon) convoying: **wrecked**, Florida Straits, no casualties.

12 Mar: *Imogen* (ship sloop, 18 guns, 399 tons, French prize) convoying: **foundered**, leak in mid-ocean, no casualties.

12 May: *Cyane* (ship sloop, 18 guns, 428 tons, Frindsbury) cruising: **captured** near Martinique, **recaptured** 5 Oct.

30 Sep: *Seaforth* (gunboat, 14 guns, 215 tons, purchased) **foundered**, off Antigua, 2 crew survived.

3 Oct: *Barracouta* (schooner, 4 guns, 70 tons, Bermuda) cruising: **wrecked**, off Cuba, no casualties.

7 Nov: *Orquijo* (ship sloop, 18 guns, 384 tons, prize) cruising: **foundered**, off Jamaica, few survivors.

1806

23 Feb: *Unique* (schooner, 10 guns, 120 tons, purchased) cruising: **captured** by French privateer, then **foundered**.

21 May: *Dominica* (schooner, 6 guns, 85 tons, purchased) **mutiny** off Dominica, soon **recaptured**.

24 May: *Berbice* (schooner, 4 guns, 78 tons, purchased) **foundered** off Demerara, no casualties.

3 Jul: *Kingfish* (schooner, guns and tonnage unknown, purchased) carrying despatches: **captured** near St Kitts, no casualties.

31 Aug: *Prevost* (schooner, 10 guns, tonnage unknown, purchased) carrying despatches: **captured** near Martinique, 3 killed.

4 Sep: *Wolf* (ship sloop, 16 guns, 367 tons, Dartmouth) cruising: **wrecked**, Great Inagua, no casualties.

Sep: *Serpent* (ship sloop, 16 guns, 322 tons, Plymouth) **foundered**, no survivors.

28 Oct: *Tobago* (schooner, 10 guns, 120 tons, purchased) cruising: **captured** by French privateer, 1 killed.

4 Nov: *Redbridge* (schooner, 12 guns, 170 tons, purchased) **wrecked**, New Providence, Bahamas, no casualties.

17 Dec: *Netley* (gun brig, 16 guns, 133 tons, purchased) cruising: **captured** off Guadeloupe, 1 killed.

1807

18 Mar: *Pike* (schooner, 4 guns, 70 tons, Bermuda) carrying despatches: **captured** by French privateer, 1 killed, 4 wounded.

29 Mar: *St Lucia* (schooner, 14 guns, 183 tons, French prize) cruising: **captured** near Guadeloupe by a French privateer, 7 killed, 8 wounded.

Aug: *Bacchus* (cutter, 10 guns, 111 tons, Bermuda) **captured** by French ship, no details.

15 Sep: *Barbara* (schooner, 10 guns, 11 tons, Bermuda) cruising: **captured**, 4 killed, 6 wounded (**recaptured**: 17 Jul 1808).

Sep: *Elizabeth* (cutter, 12 guns, 110 tons, prize) **foundered**, no details, no survivors.

16 Oct: *Marie* (schooner, 10 guns, 130 tons, prize) **foundered**, Leeward Islands, no survivors.

16 Oct: *Pert* (brig sloop, 16 guns, 206 tons, French prize) cruising: **wrecked**, Island of Mucana, 10 drowned.

17 Nov: *Firefly* (schooner, 12 guns, 130 tons, French prize) **wrecked** off Curacao, no survivors.

1808

15 Feb: *Raposa* (gunboat, 10 guns, 173 tons, prize) cruising: **wrecked** near Cartelegena, no casualties.

22 Apr: *Bermuda* (ship sloop, 18 guns, 399 tons, Bermuda) cruising: **wrecked**, Grand Bahamas, no casualties.

10 Jul: *Netley* (gunboat, 14 guns, 173 tons, prize) **foundered**, off Barbados, 9 crew survived.

18 Aug: *Rook* (schooner, 4 guns, 80 tons, Ringmore) carrying despatches: **captured** off Hispaniola: 3 killed, 11 wounded.

29 Sep: *Maria* (gunboat, 14 guns, 172 tons, purchased) cruising: **captured** by a French corvette, 6 killed, 9 wounded.

3 Oct: *Carnation* (brig sloop, 18 guns, 383 tons, Bideford) cruising: **captured** off Martinique, 10 killed, 30 wounded.

23 Oct: *Volador* (brig sloop, 16 guns, 273 tons, prize) cruising: **wrecked**, off Curacao, 1 drowned.

15 Dec: *Flying Fish* (schooner, 12 guns, 151 tons, purchased) **wrecked**, near Jamaica, no casualties.

1809

9 Jan: *Morne Fortunee* (gunboat, 12 guns, 184 tons, prize) **foundered** off Martinique, 41 died.

3 Aug: *Lark* (ship sloop, 18 guns, 429 tons, Northfleet) **foundered** off San Domingo, 3 survivors.

Aug: *Dominica* (cutter, 14 guns, 153 tons, prize) **foundered** in a hurricane off Tortola, no survivors.

22 Sep: *Curieux* (brig sloop, 18 guns, 317 tons, prize) **wrecked** off Guadeloupe, no casualties.

24 Oct: *Glommen* (brig sloop, 16 guns, 303 tons, prize) **wrecked**, sank at anchor in Bridgetown harbour, no casualties.

12 Nov: *Haddock* (schooner, 4 guns, 75 tons, Bermuda) carrying despatches: **captured**, no casualties.

1810

7 Feb: *Achates* (brig sloop, 18 guns, 238 tons, Rotherhithe) **wrecked** near Guadeloupe, no casualties.

29 Dec: *Fleur de la Mer* (schooner, 8 guns, 117 tons, purchased) convoying: **foundered**, leak in mid-ocean, no casualties.

1811

7 Jul: *Guachapin* (brig sloop, 16 guns, 176 tons, prize) **wrecked** at anchor in Antigua by hurricane, no casualties.

21 Oct: *Grouper* (schooner, 4 guns, 70 tons, Bermuda) cruising: **wrecked**, off Guadeloupe, no casualties.

1812

30 Nov: *Subtle* (schooner, 12 guns, 139 tons, prize) **wrecked** off St Bartholomew, no survivors.

1813

21 Feb: *Rhodian* (brig sloop, 10 guns, 240 tons, Northam) **wrecked** off Jamaica, no casualties.

24 Feb: *Peacock* (brig sloop, 18 guns, 386 tons, Ipswich) **captured & sunk** off Demerara, 5 killed, 33 wounded.

20 May: *Algerine* (cutter, 10 guns, 197 tons, Upnor) convoying: **wrecked** in the Bahamas, no casualties.

26 Jun: *Persian* (brig sloop, 18 guns, 390 tons, Cowes) **wrecked**, Hispaniola, no casualties.

1814

Mar: *Rapide* (schooner, 10 guns, 90 tons, prize) **wrecked** on the Saintes, no survivors.

19 May: *Halcyon* (brig sloop, 18 guns, 384 tons, King's Lynn) **wrecked**, Jamaica, no casualties.

10 Oct: *Racer* (schooner, 12 guns, 250 tons, prize) cruising: **wrecked**, Florida Straits, no casualties.

31 Oct: *Elizabeth* (schooner, 12 guns, 141 tons, prize) **foundered**, pursuing American privateer, no survivors.

1815

26 Feb: *St Lawrence* (schooner, 16 guns, 240 tons, prize) carrying despatches: **captured** north of Cuba, 6 killed, 18 wounded.

7 Mar: *Cygnet* (brig sloop, 16 guns, 365 tons, Gt Yarmouth) convoying: **wrecked**, Surinam, no casualties.

MEDITERRANEAN

1803

4 Aug: *Redbridge* (schooner, 12 guns, 149 tons) carrying despatches: **captured** off Toulon.

1804

6 Jan: *Raven* (brig sloop, 18 guns, 390 tons, ex French prize) convoying: **wrecked**, Maretimo, off Sicily, no casualties.

1 Mar: *Weazle* (brig sloop, 12 guns, 214 tons, purchased) convoying: **wrecked**, Gibraltar, no casualties.

3 Apr: *Swift* (cutter, 8 guns, 77 tons, hired) carrying despatches: **captured** off Toulon, lieutenant killed.

1805

19 Jan: *Arthur* (cutter, 6 guns, 71 tons, hired) **captured**, no further details.

30 Jan: *Raven* (brig sloop, 18 guns, 383 tons, Blackwall) carrying despatches: **wrecked**, Spanish coast, 2 drowned.

4 Feb: *Acheron* (bomb vessel, 8 guns, 388 tons, purchased) convoying: **captured**, off North Africa, 3 killed, 8 wounded.

4 Feb: *Arrow* (ship sloop, 18 guns, 386 tons, Redbridge) convoying: **captured** with *Acheron*, then **sank**, 13 killed, 27 wounded.

1806

25 Oct: *Hannah* (gunboat, 12 guns, 59 tons, hired) convoying: **captured** off Gibraltar by a privateer, 8 killed, 11 wounded.

1807

4 Jan: *Nautilus* (ship sloop, 18 guns, 443 tons, Milford Haven) carrying despatches: **wrecked**, Aegean Sea, 59 died.

9 Mar: *Crafty* (schooner, 12 guns, 146 tons, French prize) carrying despatches: **captured** near Tetuan, 3 killed, 14 wounded.

Apr: *Moucheron* (brig sloop, 16 guns, 286 tons, prize) **foundered**, eastern Med, no survivors.

1808

31 Jan: *Delight* (brig sloop, 16 guns, 285 tons, Fremington) **wrecked**, off Sicily, captured, 2 killed.

23 Feb: *Hirondelle* (gunboat, 14 guns, 210 tons, prize) carrying despatches: **wrecked**, North African coast.

25 Mar: *Electra* (brig sloop, 16 guns, 282 tons, Ipswich) delivering/transferring specie: **wrecked**, Sicily, no casualties.

27 Jul: *Pickle* (schooner, 10 guns, 123 tons, purchased) carrying despatches: **wrecked**, then **captured**, Santa Maria, Spain, no casualties.

1811

26 May: *Alacrity* (brig sloop, 18 guns, 382 tons, Newcastle) cruising: **captured** off Corsica, 8 killed, 14 wounded.

1812

26 Jan: *Carlotta* (brig sloop, 14 guns, 204 tons, prize) **wrecked**, Cape Passaro, Sicily, casualties unknown.

Oct: *Gunboat 16* (gunboat, 3 guns, 51 tons), defending Cadiz: **wrecked**, near Malaga, no casualties.

1813

21 Nov: *Goshawk* (brig sloop, 16 guns, 285 tons, Blackwall) **wrecked** near Barcelona, no casualties.

EAST INDIES STATION, INCLUDING VOYAGES OUT AND BACK

1806

6 Jan: *Favourite* (ship sloop, 18 guns, 427 tons, Rotherhithe) cruising: **captured**, Cape Verde Islands, **recaptured** 1807.

12 Aug: *Belem* (schooner, 4 guns, 88 tons, prize) **captured** during capture of Buenos Aires.

1808

Aug: *Jaseur* (cutter, 12 guns, tonnage unknown, place of build unknown) **foundered**, Indian Ocean, no survivors.

28 Sep: *Seaflower* (gunboat, 16 guns, 203 tons, purchased) cruising: **captured**, Sumatra, crew prisoners.

1809

Mar: *Harrier* (brig sloop, 18 guns, 383 tons, Deptford) **foundered**, Indian Ocean, no survivors.

2 Nov: *Victor* (brig sloop, 16 guns, 425 tons, prize) cruising: **captured**, Bay of Bengal, 2 wounded.

1810

Nov: *Mandarin* (gunboat, 12 guns, 178 tons, prize) carrying despatches: **wrecked**, Singapore Straits, no casualties.

1811

Jun: *Staunch* (gunboat, 12 guns, 182 tons, Dartmouth) **foundered** off Madagascar, no survivors.

1813

27 Jan: *Daring* (gunboat, 12 guns, 177 tons, Ipswich) **captured** off the Iles de Los, West Africa, no casualties.

Small Warship Losses Summary

	Convoy	Blockade	Captured	Total
Channel	24	26	10	60
W. Approaches	11	20	7	38
North Sea	12	9	7	28
Baltic	10	0	9	19
North Atlantic	15	1	25	41
West Indies	40	0	20	60
Mediterranean	10	4	6	20
East Indies	4	0	5	9
TOTAL	126	60	89	275

APPENDIX

Seasonal Losses

	Convoy	Blockade	Captured	Total
Winter	84	39	41	164
Summer	42	21	48	111
TOTAL	126	60	89	275

Sources: David J. Hepper, *British Warship Losses in the Age of Sail, 1650–1859* (Rotherfield: Jean Boudriot Publications, 1994); Rif Winfield, *British Warships in the Age of Sail, 1793–1817: Design, Construction, Careers and Fates* (London: Chatham Publishing, 2005)

TIMELINE 1803–1815

1793

8 January   Vice-Admiral Peter Rainier appointed commander-in-chief, East Indies, until 10 March 1805

1795

3 March   Evan Nepean appointed First Secretary of the Admiralty, until 20 January 1804

1801

19 February   Admiral Lord St Vincent appointed First Lord of the Admiralty, until 15 May 1804

1802

27 March   Treaty of Amiens

1803

10 May   Vice-Admiral Sir William Cornwallis appointed commander-in-chief, Channel, until 22 February 1806

16 May	War declared by Britain against France; Admiral Lord Nelson appointed commander-in-chief, Mediterranean, until 21 October 1805
16 June	War declared by Britain against Holland
20 July	Admiral Lord Keith appointed commander-in-chief, North Sea, until 18 May 1807

1804

21 January	William Marsden appointed Secretary of the Admiralty, until 24 June 1807; Benjamin Tucker appointed Second Secretary, until 21 May 1804
14 February	French Admiral Linois' squadron withdraws at Pulo Aor, mistakenly believing that British warships were defending the East Indies homeward convoy
10 March	Rear-Admiral Sir Edward Pellew appointed commander-in-chief, East Indies, until 15 February 1809
2 April	HMS *Apollo* (36) wrecked on the Portuguese coast with 27 merchant ships in a convoy to the West Indies
10 May	Henry Addington's government falls, William Pitt forms government
15 May	Henry Dundas, Lord Melville, appointed First Lord of the Admiralty, until 2 May 1805
22 May	John Barrow appointed Second Secretary of the Admiralty, until 9 February 1806
14 August	John Bennet Jnr appointed Secretary of the Committee of Lloyd's, until February 1834
6 October	Spanish treasure ships attacked off Cadiz by British frigates
12 December	Spain declares war on Britain

1805

11 January	Britain declares war on Spain
2 February	HMS *Arrow* sunk and HMS *Acheron* burnt by French frigates in defence of a convoy off the North African coast
2 May	Charles Middleton, Lord Barham, appointed First Lord of the Admiralty, until 10 February 1806
23 August	Rear-Admiral Thomas Troubridge appointed joint commander-in-chief East Indies, until his return on 19 December 1806 and death on 1 February 1807
28 August	Captain Home Riggs Popham's expedition to the Cape of Good Hope sails from Cork
21 October	Battle of Trafalgar; Vice-Admiral Collingwood succeeds Lord Nelson as commander-in-chief Mediterranean, until 7 March 1810
2 December	Napoleon wins Battle of Austerlitz
10 December	General Lord Cathcart's force of 26,000 troops leaves for the Elbe, returns home having achieved nothing 15 February 1806
26 December	France gains Venice, Istria and Dalmatia from Austria by the Treaty of Pressburg

1806

23 January	William Pitt dies
10 February	Lord Grenville appointed Prime Minister, until 31 March 1807; Charles Grey, Lord Howick, appointed First Lord of the Admiralty, until 29 September 1806; Benjamin Tucker again appointed Second Secretary of the Admiralty, until 5 Apr 1807

14 February	Captain Home Riggs Popham convoys troops from the Cape of Good Hope to Montevideo, arriving 25 June
7 March	Admiral Lord St Vincent appointed commander-in-chief Channel, until 24 April 1807
5 April	Embargo on Prussian ships in, or which may enter, British ports
8 April	Order-in-Council promulgates a blockade of French ports between Brest and the River Elbe ('Fox's Blockade'), but allows neutral ships with cargoes not the property of Britain's enemies and not contraband (by British definition) to trade between the Seine and Ostend
14 May	War declared by Britain against Prussia
28 May	Prussian North Sea ports closed against British ships
29 September	Thomas Grenville appointed First Lord of the Admiralty, until 6 April 1807
21 November	Berlin decree. Napoleon declares the British Isles in blockade: all British property as lawful prize; all trade in British merchandise forbidden; any vessel from Britain or her colonies to be seized as enemy property

1807

7 January	Further British Order-in-Council prohibits any ship 'to trade between one port and another, both of which ports shall belong to or be in possession of France or her allies'
15 January	Admiral Sir John Duckworth's force sent to the Dardanelles, arriving there on 20 February
1 February	Foundering of HMS *Blenheim* (90) and HMS *Java* (32) in the Indian Ocean, drowning Admiral Troubridge and a thousand officers and seamen

3 February	General Sir Samuel Auchmuchty's forces capture Montevideo
3 March	Duckworth's squadron withdraws from the Dardanelles
17 March	British forces land in Egypt under Major-General Fraser Mackenzie but withdraw
31 March	Duke of Portland succeeds as Prime Minister, until his death on 30 October 1809
6 April	Lord Mulgrave appointed First Lord of the Admiralty, until 4 May 1810
9 April	John Barrow again appointed Second Secretary of the Admiralty, until 28 January 1845
25 April	Admiral Lord Gardner appointed commander-in-chief Channel, until 1 January 1809
24 June	William Wellesley Pole appointed Secretary of the Admiralty, until 12 October 1809
5 July	France and Russia sign the Treaty of Tilsit
10 July	Lieutenant-General Whitelock's attack on Buenos Aires fails disastrously
18 July	Admiral Lord Gambier, appointed commander-in-chief Baltic, until 28 October 1807
2 August	Ships under command of Captain Richard Goodwin Keats secure the Great Belt, isolating the Danish army on Zealand
2–5 September	British expedition under Gambier bombards Copenhagen and seizes the Danish fleet; 4 September: Vice-Admiral Thomas McNamara Russell leads force which captures Heligoland
11 November	Further British Orders-in-Council prohibit all trade with ports from which the British flag is excluded, unless the vessel in question first calls at a British port, pays duty on her cargo, and gains fresh clearances

17 November	Milan Decree. Napoleon declares as lawful prize any ship and cargo which sails to or from a British port or port occupied by the British, or which allows itself to be visited by a British naval officer, or which has paid any duty to the British government
29 November	British naval force commanded by Rear-Admiral Sir Sidney Smith evacuates the Portuguese Royal Family and fleet from Lisbon to Brazil
1 December	News of declaration of war on Britain by Russia reaches London
22 December	US Embargo Act. The United States interdicts all land and seaborne trade with foreign nations
26 December	British occupation of Madeira

1808

2 January	Vice-Admiral Sir James Saumarez appointed commander-in-chief Baltic, until 20 November 1812
17 April	Bayonne Decree orders the seizure of American ships in European ports
2 May	Spanish revolt against French occupation begins
10 May	Sir John Moore's army leaves Great Yarmouth for Sweden
21 May	British take Torshaven, Faroe Islands, destroying fortifications
15 July	Sir John Moore's army returns to the Downs
1 August	Wellesley's army lands at Montego Bay in Portugal
9 September	Convoy of 41 transports leaves Gothenburg with 9,000 Spanish troops under General Romana, arriving Santander, northern Spain, 9 October
23 December	HMS *Salsette* loses other escorts and a convoy of 12 merchant ships in the ice in the southern Baltic

1809

5 January	Anglo-Turkish war ends
11–19 January	Battle of Corunna, death of Sir John Moore and evacuation of British troops back to Britain
24 February	Martinique captured by British
1 March	US Non-Intercourse Act repeals the Embargo, reopens trade with all nations except France and Britain
14–17 March	Four East Indiamen lost in a severe storm homeward bound from Bengal
26 April	British Order-in-Council lifts the blockade from all European ports north and east of the river Ems
18 May	British capture Anholt to secure entry to the Baltic
28 July	Walcheren expedition sails from the Downs
15 August	British capture Flushing
August	Danish government limits its privateers to the waters around Heligoland, though in March 1810 full powers resumed for the waters around Denmark
17 September	Peace treaty of Fredrikshamn ends war between Russia and Sweden. Sweden gives up Finland, joins Continental System
12 October	John Wilson Croker appointed Secretary of Admiralty, until 29 November 1830
30 October	Duke of Portland dies, succeeded as Prime Minister by Spencer Perceval, until his assassination on 11 May 1812
23 December	Final British evacuation of Walcheren

1810

January	British capture Guadeloupe

23 March	Napoleon issues the Rambouillet Decree, ordering the seizure of those American ships in ports of France since 20 May 1809
1 May	United States repeals the Non-Intercourse Act of 1 March 1809
4 May	Charles Philip Yorke appointed First Lord of the Admiralty, until 25 March 1812
9 July	Capture of Reunion by British expedition
19 July	Loss of convoy off the Skaw of 47 fully loaded merchant ships escorted by HMB *Forward* (10) from Gothenburg to Long Hope Sound, Orkney
5 August	Trianon Decree imposes swingeing French duties on coffee, tea, sugar and other colonial imports .
September	Surrender of Dutch forces in Java
18 October	Fontainebleau Decree tightens the Continental System
17 November	Sweden declares war on Britain
3 December	Mauritius surrenders to British expedition
31 December	Alexander I opens Russian ports to neutral shipping

1811

2 March	US Congress renews commercial non-intercourse with Britain
18 September	Java surrenders to the British
24 December	Losses of HMS *St George* (98), HMS *Defence* (74) and HMS *Hero* (74) returning from the Baltic with convoys

1812

January	Napoleon occupies Swedish Pomerania
25 March	Robert Saunders Dundas, 2nd Viscount Melville, appointed First Lord of the Admiralty, until 2 May 1827

3 May	Britain joins Sweden and Russia in alliance
11 May	Spencer Perceval murdered, succeeded as Prime Minister by Lord Liverpool
June	British force of 10,000 troops convoyed to Alicante
16 June	Britain repeals the Orders-in-Council
18 June	USA declares war on Britain
24 June	Napoleon invades Russia
19 August	USS *Constitution* captures the British frigate HMS *Guerriere* (44)
15 September	Napoleon enters Moscow
13 October	British government authorises general reprisals against United States
19 October	Napoleon begins his retreat from Moscow
22 December	HMS *Sentinel* (12) loses convoy of 22 merchant ships on the island of Rugen in the Baltic
25 October	USS *United States* captures HMS *Macedonian* (38)
29 December	USS *Constitution* captures HMS *Java* (44) off Brazil

1813

March	Prussia and Russia declared war
1 June	HMS *Shannon* (38) defeats USS *Chesapeake* off Boston
August	Austria re-enters the war
8 September	San Sebastian surrenders to Wellington
16 October	Great storm causes widespread destruction in the anchorages outside Gothenburg
12 November	Brief hurricane at Halifax, Nova Scotia, causes extensive damage to warships and merchantmen at anchor

1814

14 January	Treaty of Kiel. Denmark makes peace with Britain and Russia

4 April	Abdication of Napoleon
30 May	First Treaty of Paris
19 September	Lloyd's reports loss of 172 ships in the summer months in the Western Approaches to the Admiralty
24 December	Treaty of Ghent signed between Britain and USA

1815

8 January	British army defeated in the Battle of New Orleans
15 January	HMS *Endymion* (46) captures USS *President*
16 February	Ratification of the Treaty of Ghent by the US Congress
20 February	USS *Constitution* severely damages and captures HMS *Cyane* (22) and HMS *Levant* (22), defending convoys in the Atlantic
26 February	Napoleon leaves Elba with 600 troops
March	War renewed against Napoleon
18 June	Battle of Waterloo
20 November	Second Treaty of Paris

Sources: Crosby, *America, Russia, Hemp and Napoleon*; Davey, *In Nelson's Wake*; Hill, *Prizes of War*; Knight, *Britain Against Napoleon*; Rodger, *Command of the Ocean*; Roscoe, *Prize Cases*; Sainty, *Admiralty Officials*

GLOSSARY

able seaman experienced seaman, with a higher rate and pay than an ordinary seaman or landsman

bare poles to run before a strong wind without sail, used by faster warships to slow progress when escorting a convoy

barilla A Mediterranean alkaline plant which when burnt produces soda ash, used in the manufacture of soap and glass

betel nut the nut of a palm chewed as a narcotic in the Far East. A dangerous cargo, liable to heating

bomb vessel vessel built or converted to carry two heavy mortars amidships (usually one 13-inch and one 11-inch) to throw explosive shells at a high trajectory during shore bombardments; often used to escort convoys

bottomry bond entered into to enable a master to get credit in a foreign port, pledging the ship as security for repayments

braced by yards braced as far as possible fore and aft on the mast, in order to slow progress

brig sloop a warship or merchantman with two masts and a square rig; more economical to man than three-masted ships, and more manoeuvrable, but more vulnerable if they lost a mast. Large brig sloops (18 guns, 300 tons) were commanded by a 'master

	and commander', the smaller ones, usually called gunbrigs (12, 10 or 4 guns) by a lieutenant
broach	caused by the head of a ship flying up into the wind, by carrying too much sail aft, resulting in the vessel lying dangerously parallel to the wind and the waves
carronade	short, light, low velocity cannon, very effective at close quarters, but which could not reach distant targets
chase (noun)	the ship being pursued
chasse-mare	fast lugger from the north French coast, a rig favoured by French privateers
Cherokee class	smallest class of naval sloop, 90 foot, 237 tons, 10 carronades, with a complement of 75 crew; designed by the Surveyor Henry Peake, the first launched in 1807/8. 34 were built during the war, and five were wartime losses, all wrecked. Many more were built in the dockyards after 1815, when they became known, unfairly, as coffin brigs
c-in-c	an admiral commanding a naval station as commander-in-chief
cochineal	a scarlet dye stuff made of the bodies of insects found in Mexico, of great value
colours	the national flag of a ship
commander	naval rank between post-captain and lieutenant
condemned (as a prize)	a vessel or cargo judged as lawful prize by a vice-admiralty court
country ship	a merchant ship owned in an Indian port, though often officered by Europeans, which traded between India, the East Indies and China, but not with Britain
course made good	direction and measured distance between two points, not reflecting the actual course travelled, inevitably much longer because of the need to tack against the wind

crank	when a ship is liable to lean over or even capsize being built too deep or narrow, or has too little ballast to carry full sail
Cruizer class	highly effective naval sloop, 100 foot, 16-gun, 382 tons, with a complement of 121 crew. Designed by Sir William Rule in 1797; 105 were built between 1802 and 1813, of which 18 were wartime losses; 7 were captured, 9 wrecked and 2 foundered in the Atlantic
culm	cargo of coal dust transported for the Ordnance Board
cut-down ship (razee)	a warship, originally with two gundecks, with the upper guns removed to improve sea keeping qualities, e.g. a cut-down 64 would mount 44 guns and be rated as a frigate
cutter	small warship, rigged fore and aft
Downs, the	anchorage off Deal on the Kent coast, sheltered from south-west winds
drive, driving	the course of a ship, moving stern first, resulting from the anchor ceasing to hold
extra ship	a merchant ship allowed to trade with India, but taken on only for one year
fireship	a ship filled with explosives sent to sail into an anchored enemy fleet, as in the battle of the Aix Roads in 1809. Some were built as specialised vessels, but more were purchased and were thus a variety of sizes from 50 to around 100 tons; often as big as 400 tons, fireships were used as convoy escorts
Flag eighth	the share of prize money due to the c-in-c of the station on which the prize was taken
fleet	often used to describe a convoy
foundering	a ship sinking at sea, as opposed to being wrecked when going aground

freight money   a percentage payment to commanding officers of warships for carrying gold or silver bullion, by the owners of the money

frigate   fifth- or sixth-rate warship, between 24 and 44 guns, with a crew of between 200 and 300

fustic   yellow dye brought from the West Indies, boiled and processed from wood

galiot, galliot   a small, fast galley, with one mast and sixteen to twenty oars; also a Dutch or Flemish cargo vessel

gruff goods   bulk goods in the East India trade, applying especially to saltpetre

gunboat   built for anti-invasion duties, with long guns firing forward and a broadside of carronades, single-masted, usually brig rigged; also conversions of hoys or barges, purchased Dutch vessels for anti-invasion duties

gun brig   development of the single-masted sailing gunboats of 1794. In practice, very little different from a gunboat

Haak Sands   very dangerous sandbanks off the Dutch coast outside the Texel estuary

Hawke Roads   British name for Hakefjorden, part of Vinga Sand (see below) outside Gothenburg

HCS   Honourable (East India) Company Ship

HMAB   His Majesty's (hired) Armed Brig

HMAC   His Majesty's (hired) Armed Cutter

HMAS   His Majesty's (hired) Armed Ship

HMB   His Majesty's (commissioned) Brig

HMC   His Majesty's (commissioned) Cutter

HMS   His Majesty's (commissioned) Ship or Sloop

head money   prize money for an enemy warship or privateer captured, burnt or driven on shore, based on the number of enemy crew at the start of the action

indigo	a plant-based dye in blue powder form of considerable value, produced in India and Spanish America
landsman	an unskilled seaman on a warship
Leith smack	see smack
letter of marque	(1) a document issued by the government which enabled a privately owned ship to capture enemy merchant ships legally. (2) A merchant ship, usually large, well-armed and well-manned, which sailed with a letter of marque document. Having delivered its cargo, the ship would then turn to privateering, a method used very effectively by the Americans after 1812
Lloyd's	marine insurance organisation in London
logwood	the heart wood of an American tree used for dyeing cloth, so called because it was imported as a log and processed in Britain
lugger	general term for a small coasting vessel, which might have two or three masts, but more specifically with four-cornered, fore and aft loose-footed sails. Between 1810 and 1814 some French luggers, as well as Guernsey privateers, were as large as 300 tons
Malouin	ship, privateer or individual from St Malo
Mascarene islands	the collective name for a group of islands in the Indian Ocean, the largest of which is Mauritius
master	aboard merchant ships, the person in command responsible for the ship's conduct, and the safety of the ship. On warships, a warrant officer in charge of the ship's navigation under the captain
mate	second in command of a merchant ship
missed stays	failure of a ship, when beating against the wind, to turn into the wind and sail away on the other tack
mulct	a monetary fine

nankeens	cotton of brownish yellow colour from the city of Nanking, China
neaped	a ship ashore or in dock at high spring tides, unable to float at neap tides, until the spring tides two weeks later
Nore	anchorage in the Thames Estuary
northabout	a course round the north of Scotland
opium	a sedative and intoxicant from India, though also transported through the Mediterranean, manufactured from poppy seed
ordinary seaman	rated below able seaman, may be competent to go aloft, but not yet able
pitch	boiled tar and coarse resin used when hot with oakum for caulking a ship
pooped	breaking of a heavy sea over the stern of a ship, especially if scudding before the wind in a gale; extremely dangerous, especially if deeply laden
private signal	a numbered flag signal, used by warships and merchant ships to identify themselves
privateer	a privately owned ship, carrying a letter of marque, fitted out and heavily manned, to prey on enemy merchant shipping
prize agent	an agent, usually based in London, engaged to look after the prize affairs of officers or a ship's crew
protest	a formal, written notification by a merchant ship master to attest that damage was not caused through the fault of the ship's crew
quintal	a 100-pound weight, often used to measure fish
roads	sheltered anchorage outside a port, such as at Leith, Yarmouth or Madras
saltpetre	the main agent in gunpowder, formed by mixing nitric acid with potash, imported in quantity from Bengal where it was produced by mixing water with

	human waste, from which evaporation produced crystals of potassium nitrate
salvage	money claimed from the recapture of a ship or cargo from the enemy or from a sinking
saving the premium	a practice whereby a ship's master would send a letter to his insurers in London by another ship making an earlier passage, itemising his cargo; it might happen that the original ship reached port safely before the letter was delivered, in which case he would cancel his insurance, saving his premium
scammony	medicine made from gum resin obtained from roots of a plant grown in Syria and Asia Minor, used as a strong purgative
schooner	ships built from 1804 in Bermuda, 75–8 tons, with four 12-pounder carronades, with a crew of 20, nicknamed 'Tom Tit' cruisers; their small size ensured a high casualty rate
scud, scudding	to run before a gale propelled only by a forward sail to keep the vessel ahead of the sea, to avoid the danger of being pooped
ship of the line	a warship of 100 guns (1st rate), 90 or 80 guns (2nd rate) or 74 guns (3rd rate)
ship sloop (or 'ship rigged')	a three-masted sloop
slops	seaman's clothing
smack	usually a cutter, fore and aft rigged vessel, used for cargo or for carrying passengers. The largest were the Leith smacks, which could be as much as 200 tons
Soundings	relatively shallow area between the Atlantic and the Channel
Spithead	anchorage within the Solent outside Portsmouth harbour

springs
(or spring tides)
the highest and lowest tides, occurring bi-monthly with the moon's phases, occurring alternately with neap tides, which have the least tidal range

stations
designated sea areas, with warships under the orders of the c-in-c of the station, appointed by the Admiralty Board, who was responsible for convoys within the station

strike the
colours
lower the national flag, to signal surrender in battle, or to end the commission of the commanding officer

sulphur
a highly inflammable crystalline solid, used in gunpowder to increase the rate of combustion, imported from Sicily

sweeps
very long oars, used by small warships to propel themselves in windless conditions

tacking
turning a ship into the wind, in order to steer onto the other tack

Tagus
the river on which Lisbon is situated, important for assembling convoys

tallow
processed animal fat, imported in quantity from the Baltic, Archangel and the East Indies, primarily used for making candles and soap, but also aboard ship for greasing and weatherproofing rope and blocks

ticket men
trusted seamen sent from a warship to take the place of pressed men. The ticket was issued to protect the holder from being pressed into yet another warship

tierce
a provisions cask. A beef tierce contained 280 pounds, while a pork tierce 260 pounds

tonnage
a measurement of the volume of a ship, calculated by multiplying the length of the keel by the extreme breadth, multiplying the product by the half breadth, then dividing by 94

train oil	cod oil, important cargo from northern latitudes, especially from Newfoundland and Archangel, used as a lubricant and for oil lamps; sold by the tun of 252 gallons
vice-admiralty courts	courts in major seaports that adjudged prize money cases
Vinga Sand	sheltered anchorage and assembly area for convoys, 14 miles from Gothenburg, named by the British as Wingo or Wingoe Sound
wearing	turning the ship with the wind blowing from behind the ship, the opposite to tacking; the modern equivalent is gybing
weatherly, to weather	a ship that goes well to windward, hence 'to weather' is to steer safely past a hazard when sailing against the wind
windward	towards the direction from which the wind is blowing

NOTES

PROLOGUE

1. TNA, ADM 52/3591, *Apollo's* log, 27 Mar 1804.
2. NMM, MRK/105/11/48, 12 Jul 1804, 'List of Ships lost, drove on Shore, Sep 1803–1 Jun 1804'.
3. Rodger, *Command of the Ocean*, pp. 382–3; 'Weather', p. 187.
4. Dunn & Higgit, *Ships, Clocks & Stars*, p. 192.
5. *Naval Chronicle*, XXVII, 1812, pp. 121–2; Woodman, *A Low Set of Blackguards*, II, pp. 327–33.
6. TNA, ADM 1/627, 12 Dec 1814, King to Vice-Admiral Herbert Sawyer.

INTRODUCTION

1. Syrett, 'British Trade Convoys', p. 172, quoting James Allan Park, *A System of Law of Marine Insurance* (London, 7th edn, 1817), p. 498.
2. Knight, 'Achievement and Cost', pp. 121–2.
3. Rodger, *Command of the Ocean*, pp. 500–501; Brunsman, *Evil Necessity*; Pfaff & Hechter, *Genesis of Rebellion*; Rogers, *Press Gang*; 'British Impressment', pp. 52–73; Davey, *In Nelson's Wake*, pp. 22–3.
4. Caputo, 'Alien Seamen', pp. 685–707; 'Transnational History', pp. 13–32.
5. Sutton, *Maritime Service*, pp. 177–82, 196–7.
6. TNA, ADM 36/15311.
7. Knight, *Pursuit of Victory*, p. 521.
8. Hepper, *Warship Losses*, p. 213.
9. Jepsen, *Last Voyage*, p. 165.
10. Jefferson, *Merchant Marine*, pp. 26–41.

1 CONVOYING BEFORE 1803

1. Merriman, *Queen Anne's Navy*, p. 346.
2. Knight, 'Defensive Strategy', pp. 88–9.
3. Unger, 'Channelling Violence', pp. 36–7; Rodger, *Safeguard of the Sea*, pp. 106–7, 157; Blakemore & Murphy, *British Civil Wars at Sea*, p. 176.
4. Capp, *Cromwell's Navy*, pp. 102–3.
5. Hornstein, *Restoration Navy*, p. 260.
6. Rodger, *Command of the Ocean*, pp. 78, 153–4, 158–9, 176–7; Davis, *English Shipping*, p. 328.
7. Bromley, *Corsairs and Navies*, pp. 215–16.
8. Davis, *English Shipping*, p. 327n.
9. Richmond, *Instrument of Policy*, pp. 237–46.

10. Wright & Fayle, *Lloyd's*, p. 43; Bromley, *Corsairs and Navies*, p. 64.
11. Rodger, *Command of the Ocean*, p. 153; Pearsall, 'Trade Protection', pp. 117–18.
12. Wright & Fayle, *Lloyd's*, p. 43; Rodger, *Command of the Ocean*, p. 153.
13. Rodger, *Command of the Ocean*, pp. 159–60.
14. Pearsall, 'Archangel Trade', p. 65.
15. e.g. Harding, *Amphibious Warfare*, p. 200; Gradish, *Manning*, pp. 203–12.
16. Pearsall, 'Trade Protection', pp. 120, 123.
17. Merriman, *Queen Anne's Navy*, pp. 334, 339; 'The Cruisers and Convoy Act'.
18. Hattendorf, *Spanish Succession*, pp. 170–71, 308–17; Bromley, *Corsairs and Navies*, p. 61.
19. Waters, 'Notes on the Convoy System', pp. 16–20.
20. Richmond, *War of 1739–48*, I, pp. 183–94; Pares, *War and Trade*, p. 304; Hill, *Prizes of War*, p. 61.
21. Baugh, *Global Seven Years War*, p. 303; Gradish, *Manning*, pp. 209–11.
22. Crowhurst, 'Seven Years War', p. 173.
23. I am indebted to Professor Daniel Baugh for the sight of an unpublished paper on this subject which allows me to assert this with confidence.
24. Baugh, *Global Seven Years War*, pp. 318–19; 'British Navy Superiority', pp. 235–6; McLeod, *Naval Captains*, pp. 24–35, 39–41.
25. Syrett, *Shipping and Military Power*, pp. 23–4, 75–7; Baugh, *Global Seven Years War*, pp. 319–21.
26. Crowhurst, 'Seven Years War', p. 173; Steele, *English Atlantic*, pp. 23–50.
27. Davis, *English Shipping*, pp. 318–19.
28. Corbett, *Seven Years War*, I, pp. 361–2.
29. Mackesy, *War for America*, p. 173.
30. Syrett, *Shipping and the American War*, pp. 154–60; Sutcliffe, *Expeditionary Warfare*, pp. 40–43.
31. *Dublin Evening Post*, 2 Dec 1780: Baugh, 'British Navy Superiority', p. 247.
32. Syrett, *European Waters*, pp. 134–7; *Norfolk Chronicle*, 16 Sep 1780.
33. Mackesy, *War for America*, p. 357; Rodger, *Command of the Ocean*, p. 347; Syrett, *European Waters*, pp. 136–7; Rutter, *Red Ensign*, p. 80.
34. *Reading Mercury*, 28 Aug 1780.
35. Wright & Fayle, *Lloyd's*, p. 155.
36. Petrie, 'Eliza Swan', pp. 103–4; Wright & Fayle, *Lloyd's*, pp. 153–4.
37. Fayle, 'British Shipping', p. 73; Crowhurst, *Defence of British Trade*, pp. 70–71; Wright & Fayle, *Lloyd's*, p. 185.
38. Marzagalli, 'Sea Power and Neutrality', p. 101, quoting Pierrick Pourchasse, 'La Guerre de la faim: l'approvisionnement de la République, le blocus britannique, et bonnes affaires des neutres au course des guerres révolutionnaires (1793–1795)', HdR thesis, Université de Bretagne Sud, 2010.
39. Knight, *Pursuit of Victory*, p. 142.
40. *London Gazette*, 24 Oct 1796.
41. *Hull Advertiser and Exchange Gazetteer*, 29 Oct 1796.
42. Crowhurst, *French War on Trade*, pp. 46–78, 199, 203–4; Foynes, *East Anglia*, pp. 59–66.
43. Knight, *Britain Against Napoleon*, p. 111.
44. Mahan, *French Revolutionary War*, II, p. 205.
45. Geo. III c.66; 38 Geo. III c.76 (Ehrman, *Younger Pitt*, II, pp. 502–3); Crowhurst, *Defence of British Trade*, p. 71.
46. Sutcliffe, *Expeditionary Warfare*, pp. 73–5.

2 THE ADMIRALTY AND TRADE PROTECTION, 1803–1815

1. TNA, ADM 7/71. The *Sybella*, bound for Gibraltar from London, was granted licence no. 22, 125, 2 Nov 1811.
2. TNA, ADM 2/1107/434–5, quoted in McCranie, 'War of 1812', p. 1089.

3. Davis, *British Overseas Trade*, pp. 32–3.
4. Rodger, *Command of the Ocean*, p. 636.
5. Dancy, 'Naval Administration', p. 61; Starkey, 'Market for Seafarers', p. 29.
6. Aldous, 'Prize Money', pp. 107, 183–92.
7. Knight, *Britain Against Napoleon*, chaps 12 & 13.
8. Marzagalli, 'Neutrality Issues in the Mediterranean', pp. 112–13.
9. TNA, ADM 1/3993, Admiralty Office to the Committee of Lloyd's, 14 Mar 1809.
10. Dowling, 'Convoy System', pp. 343–4.
11. TNA, ADM 7/72, 1814 and 1815, licence 26, 295 on 21 Jun 1814 to number 27, 423 on 31 Dec 1814.
12. TNA, ADM 1/3993, 'Admiralty Office statement on a letter transmitted from the Committee at Lloyd's on the 8th March 1809'.
13. Wright & Fayle, *Lloyd's*, p. 179.
14. Lloyd, *Keith Papers*, III, p. 191, Marsden to Keith, 1 Mar 1804.
15. e.g. Kert, *Privateering*, p. 62.
16. Crosby, *America, Russia, Hemp and Napoleon*, pp. 258–9.
17. Hill, *Prizes of War*, p. 98.
18. Thorne, *House of Commons*, I, p. 278.
19. Ibid., pp. 4, 320–21, 325–6.
20. e.g., TNA, ADM 1/3993, John Bennett, Lloyd's, to Barrow, 13 Apr 1808; to Croker, 30 Jun 1812.
21. TNA, ADM 1/3992, Bennett and White to Marsden, 27 Jul 1804.
22. Avery, 'Naval Protection', pp. 249–50.
23. Davey, *In Nelson's Wake*, p. 179.
24. Knight, *Britain Against Napoleon*, pp. 399–400.
25. Jane Knight, 'Eastern Mediterranean', p. 198, quoting NMM, Croker Collection, CRK/6/163, Sir John Hippersley to Nelson, 27 Jul 1801; BL, Add. Mss 34953, Nelson to Francis Wherry, 7 Oct 1803.
26. Collingwood, *Private Correspondence*, p. 169, to J.E. Blackett, 11 Jan 1806, *Queen*, off Malaga.
27. Dowling, 'Convoy System', p. 322.
28. Dowling, 'Convoy System', pp. 330, 323, quoting 'Lloyd's Proceedings', 30 Oct, 24 Nov, 8 Dec 1806, 23 May 1808.
29. TNA, ADM 1/3898, Doctors' Commons, Gostling to Wellesley Pole, 24 July, 8 Aug 1807.
30. Bourguignon, *Scott*, pp. 172–242.
31. Aldous, 'Prize Money', p. 77.
32. Roscoe, *Reports of Prize Cases*, p. 492.
33. Thorne, *House of Commons*, III.
34. Davey, *In Nelson's Wake*, p. 205.
35. Hamilton, *Modern Admiralty*, p. 9, quoting NMM, Middleton Papers, MID/6/10, nd, but 1805–6.
36. Knight, *Britain Against Napoleon*, pp. 137–40.
37. Mead, 'Telegraphs', pp. 200–203.
38. e.g. NMM, MRK/101/5/48, Rear Admiral Rowley to Markham, 18 May [1806].
39. Knight, *Britain Against Napoleon*, pp. 300–303.
40. TNA, ADM 7/589, Barrow to lieutenants of signal stations, copied to Port Admirals, 6 Nov 1807.
41. Lloyd, *Keith Papers*, III, p. 191, Keith to Admiralty Secretary, 12 Mar 1804.
42. Davey, *In Nelson's Wake*, p. 138.
43. TNA, ADM 1/557, 16 Nov 1807.
44. Knight, *Britain Against Napoleon*, pp. 313–30.
45. Gutridge, 'Prize Agency', pp. 50–52; Knight, *Britain Against Napoleon*, pp. 348–9.
46. Pool, *Croker Papers*, pp. 14–15.
47. Jennings, *Croker Papers*, I, 20; Knight, *Britain Against Napoleon*, pp. 336–44.
48. Pool, *Croker Papers*, p. 38, letter to Lord Exmouth, 23 Oct 1816.

49. Thorne, *House of Commons*, III, p. 538; Hamilton, *Byam Martin*, III, 'Reminiscences', p. 330.
50. Hamilton, 'Croker and Patronage', pp. 53–4, 57, 66.
51. Muir, *Wellington*, p. 550, quoting Hartley Library, Southampton University, Wellington Papers 1/378.
52. Jennings, *Croker Papers*, I, p. 55.
53. Wright & Fayle, *Lloyd's*, pp. 254–9; Avery, 'Naval Protection', pp. 237–8.
54. Dowling, 'Convoy System', p. 321, quoting T. Edwards, *Reports of Cases argued and determined in the High Court of Admiralty 1808–1812* (London, 1815) p. 81.
55. Knight, *Britain Against Napoleon*, pp. 397–8.
56. TNA, ADM 1/1430, Admiral Murray to Croker, 10 Jul 1811.
57. TNA, ADM 1/624, 8 Aug, 9 Nov 1812; 1/626, 25 Mar, 23 Apr 1813.
58. TNA, ADM 1/625, Thornborough to Croker, 16 Jun 1813, also 27 Jul 1813.
59. TNA, ADM 1/4369, 'Convoys', 1812, 1813.
60. TNA, ADM 1/3994, Marryat to Croker, 19 Sep 1814.
61. Dowling, 'Convoy System', p. 322, quoting TNA, ADM 1/3902, 8 Feb, 26 Apr 1814; 1/3903, 30 May 1815.
62. Kingston, 'America, 1720–1820', pp. 206–7.
63. TNA, ADM 1/3994, Bennett to Croker, 17 Jul 1813.
64. Davis, *British Overseas Trade*, pp. 27, 31.
65. Knight, 'Achievement and Cost', p. 126.
66. Galpin, *Grain Supply*, p. 122; Solar, 'Shipping between Europe and Asia', pp. 625–61; Vale & Edwards, *Trotter*, pp. 114–21.
67. GL, GG/108, Kirkman Finlay to John Gladstone, 11 Oct 1812.
68. TNA, ADM 7/64.
69. GL, GG/92, Canning to Gladstone, 8 Feb, 10 Apr, 17, 18 May 1814; Jennings, *Croker Papers*, I, p. 55.

3 WARSHIPS AND MERCHANTMEN

1. Coggeshall, *Thirty-Six Voyages*, p. 127.
2. TNA, ADM 1/1664, 23 Apr 1813.
3. Rodger, *Command of the Ocean*, pp. 476–80; Davey, *In Nelson's Wake*, pp. 36–8; Morriss, *Royal Dockyards*, pp. 120–26, 198–9; Thorne, *House of Commons*, IV, pp. 143–4.
4. James, *Naval History*, III and IV, Appendices 10–14.
5. Winfield, *British Warships*, pp. 369–71, 391–3.
6. Bonner-Smith, *St Vincent*, II, p. 322, St Vincent to Nelson, 24 Sep 1803.
7. HL, STG 158 (13) 14 Oct 1806; also Davey, *In Nelson's Wake*, p. 234.
8. Davey, *In Nelson's Wake*, p. 234.
9. Gardiner, *Frigates*, p. 183.
10. Jefferson, *Merchant Marine*, p. 18; see also *Hull Packet*, 31 Mar 1812; Bonner-Smith, *Boteler Recollections*, p. 52.
11. Hughes, *Private Correspondence*, p. 309, 15 Dec 1809.
12. Quoted in Rodger, *Command of the Ocean*, p. 523.
13. TNA, ADM 1/1950, Hancock to Barrow, 1 Dec 1814.
14. Bulley Diaries, 6, 9, 10 May 1814.
15. Winfield, *British Warships*, p. 291.
16. Markham, *Correspondence*, p. 175, 1 May 1804.
17. NMM, MRK/101/3/205, 6 Apr 1806.
18. Winfield, *British Warships*, pp. 257, 306–8, 310–13.
19. Winfield, *British Warships*, p. 310.
20. Winfield, *British Warships*, p. 305.
21. 'Commander', *The State of the Navy*, pp. 39–41.
22. NMM, MRK/101/11/64, Thompson to Markham, 26 Aug 1806.

23. Hall Gower, *Dangers Attendant on Convoys*, pp. 12–13.
24. NMM, MRK/101/10/40, Erasmus Gower to Markham, 25 Jan [1807].
25. Lewis, *Dillon Narrative*, II, p. 78. Dillon's account was written many years later, and contains much self-justification, and occasionally bombast, but his achievements were remarkable.
26. Lewis, *Dillon Narrative*, II, p. 102.
27. Brunsman, *Evil Necessity*, p. 163; Rodger, *Command of the Ocean*, pp. 504–5; Hattendorf et al., British *Naval Documents*, p. 549, J. Powell to his mother, 12 Jun 1805.
28. Hay, *Landsman Hay*, p. 49.
29. Larpent, *Private Journal*, p. 2.
30. Rubinstein, *Durham Papers*, p. 273, 18 Jul 1812.
31. Hepper, *Warship Losses*, p. 125; James, *Naval History*, IV, pp. 331–3.
32. Watt & Hawkins, *Letters of Seamen*, pp. 328, 332, 334, 338–40, 7 May–27 Sep 1812.
33. *Naval Chronicle*, XXVIII, 1812, pp. 504–5.
34. Lohnes, 'Halifax', p. 325; Gwyn, *Frigates and Foremasts*, p. 138.
35. Beck, 'Patronage and Insanity', pp. 5–9.
36. Wilson, *British Naval Officers*, p. 56.
37. *Naval Chronicle*, XIX, 1808, p. 289; Wilson, *British Naval Officers*, p. 151; Rodger, *Command of the Ocean*, p. 522; Benjamin, 'Golden Harvest', p. 18.
38. Winfield, *British Warships*, examples from pp. 283, 344, 353, 360. See the comprehensive table for the mid-eighteenth century, from which there had been little change, in Rodger, *Wooden World*, Appendix 1, especially p. 351.
39. Parkinson, *Trade*, p. 212.
40. MacInnes, 'Slave Trade', p. 259, quoting the *Memoirs of Captain Hugh Crow of Liverpool*, pp. 89–90.
41. NMM, HNL/99/39:91, HNL/101/8; Currie, *Henley's*, p. 40; Davis, *English Shipping*, pp. 58–61, 380.
42. Dowling, 'Convoy System', p. 287, fn.1, quoting TNA, ADM 1/325, no. 24, 29 Mar 1804.
43. TNA, ADM 1/694, Otway to Croker, 19 Nov 1811.
44. TNA, ADM 1/261, Commander Lewis Shepheard to Admiral Rowley, 18 Oct 1810, with memorandum by John Finlaison on previous recent grants; ADM 2/940.
45. *Naval Chronicle*, XXVIII, 1812, pp. 112–13.
46. e.g. GL, GG/102, Edgar Corrie to John Gladstone, 13 May 1787.
47. GL, GG/345, John Gladstone to Messrs Maclean & Sampson, 18 Oct 1785.
48. TNA, ADM 7/795, Lieutenant John Reynolds to Lloyds, 29 Jul 1811.
49. TNA, ADM 1/557, 3 Apr 1807.
50. TNA, ADM 1/626, Aug 1814.
51. Dowling, 'West Indies Convoys', p. 326.
52. Dann, *Nagle*, pp. 282–4.
53. Willis, 'Topmen', pp. 161–3.
54. Dowling, 'West Indies Convoys', p. 315, quoting TNA, ADM 1/4481, no. 112, Memorial, 18 Oct 1806.
55. Jefferson, *Merchant Marine*, pp. 3–4.
56. Jefferson, *Merchant Marine*, pp. 16–18, 22, 24–5.
57. ADM 51/4075, HMAS *Prince William*'s log, 16 Jun 1805.
58. NMM, LBK/66, 24 Oct 1809.
59. Hay, *Landsman Hay*, pp. 200, 202.
60. NMM, HNL 99/20; 56/2, 17 Sep 1810, quoted in Barney, 'North Sea and Baltic, pp. 435–7.
61. Dowling, 'Convoy System', p. 295, quoting TNA, DM 1/3901, Gostling to Croker, 30 Sep 1813, enclosure Dashwood to Gostling, 9 Sep 1813.
62. Bulley Diaries, 18 Dec 1812.
63. Woodman, *A Low Set of Blackguards*, II, pp. 580–85.
64. Rodger, *Command of the Ocean*, pp. 546–7.

65. Parkinson, *War in the Eastern Seas*, p. 222.
66. Knight, *Britain Against Napoleon*, p. 311.
67. TNA, ADM 7/263, 21 Jan 1813.
68. Knight, *Britain Against Napoleon*, p. 433, 3 Sep 1813.
69. Knight, 'North Atlantic Convoys', pp. 52-4.

4 COASTAL WATERS AND THE WESTERN APPROACHES, 1803-1814

1. Craig, 'St Vincent Letters', p. 479.
2. Marcus, *Age of Nelson*, pp. 362-3.
3. *Royal Cornwall Gazette*, 4 Feb 1804; *Exeter Flying Post*, 1 Nov 1804.
4. Marzagalli, 'A Vital Link', p. 206.
5. Crowhurst, 'French Privateering Expeditions', p. 164.
6. Woodman, *A Low Set of Blackguards*, II, pp. 609-12, 643-5; Grocott, *Shipwrecks*, pp. 194-5, 273-4.
7. Bulley, *Country Ships*, p. 237; Grocott, *Shipwrecks*, pp. 304-5.
8. NMM, LBK/66, Longstaff to Mellish and Captain William Day, 22, 24, 26, 29 Mar, 22 Apr 1812.
9. TNA, ADM 1/3993, Bennet to Croker, 17 Apr 1812.
10. *Hampshire Telegraph*, 11 Feb 1805; Grocott, *Shipwrecks*, pp. 194-5.
11. TNA, ADM 1/557, Russell to Marsden, 18 Feb 1807. The *Snipe* was a hired 30-ton lugger, not the gun brig of the same name.
12. Grocott, *Shipwrecks*, pp. 230-32, quoting *The Times*, 21 Feb, 24 Mar 1807.
13. TNA, ADM 1/557, Lieutenant Dennis to Vice-Admiral Russell, 13 Nov 1807.
14. *Hampshire Telegraph*, 28 Mar 1814.
15. *Hull Packet*, 3 Feb, 8 Dec 1807.
16. Jefferson, *Merchant Marine*, p. 15.
17. Knight, *Britain Against Napoleon*, pp. 164-5, 370-71.
18. NMM, MRK/101/8/27, Colpoys to Captain John Markham, 24 Sep 1803.
19. TNA, ADM 1/3992, John Bennet to William Marsden, 13 Oct 1804.
20. TNA, ADM 1/3993, John Bennet to William Wellesly Pole, 5 Nov 1807.
21. Crowhurst, *French War on Trade*, p. 54.
22. Knight, *Britain Against Napoleon*, pp. 299-302.
23. Foynes, *East Anglia*, pp. 134-41.
24. Crowhurst, *French War on Trade*, pp. 101-4, 199-200; Harrison, 'Privateers on the East Coast', pp. 301-6.
25. Marcus, *Age of Nelson*, p. 364, quoting the *Naval Chronicle*, XXV, 1811, p. 291; XXVII, 1812, p. 102.
26. NMM, ADM B/230, enclosure, Charles Ellis to Navy Board, 8 Feb 1809.
27. Grocott, *Shipwrecks*, pp. 285-6, quoting the *Naval Chronicle*, XXIII, 1810, pp. 111-12.
28. TNA, ADM 1/1940, Captain William Hill to Croker, 7 Dec 1809.
29. Crowhurst, *French War on Trade*, pp. 60-62; James, *Naval History*, III, p. 191.
30. NMM, HNL/99/40:6-33, 27 Jan, 2, 17 Feb, 13, 19 Mar 1809.
31. NMM, HNL/99/40, 15, 16 Jan 1810; 99/41, 20 Feb 1812, 27 Feb 1813, 2 Nov 1814, 4 Jan 1815.
32. TNA, ADM 1/3993, 14 Mar 1809, 'Admiralty Office Statement on a letter transmitted from the Committee of Lloyd's on the 8th March 1809'.
33. Davey, *In Nelson's Wake*, p. 249; Crowhurst, *French War on Trade*, p. 47.
34. Wright & Fayle, *Lloyd's*, pp. 252-60.
35. *Hull Packet*, 22 Jan 1811.
36. *General Evening Post*, 24 Jan 1811, quoted in Marcus, *Age of Nelson*, p. 369; see also Mahan, *French Revolutionary War*, II, pp. 208-9.
37. TNA, ADM 1/1430, Rear-Admiral Alan Hyde, Lord Gardner to Croker, 9 Mar 1811.

38. Knight, *Britain Against Napoleon*, p. 397.
39. TNA, ADM 1/3993, 24 May 1812; *Hull Packet*, 2, 9 Jun 1812; James, *Naval History*, V, pp. 320–23.
40. TNA, ADM 1/625, Julian to Vice-Admiral Thornborough, 11 Apr 1813.
41. Kaplan, *Rothschild*, p. 80; Muir, *Wellington*, I, pp. 568–70.
42. TNA, ADM 51/2263, log of HMS *Desiree*, 22 Jan–6 Feb 1814.
43. Knight, *Britain Against Napoleon*, p. 413.
44. TNA, ADM 51/2338, log of HMS *Earnest*, 4–18 Jan 1814.
45. Kaplan, *Rothschild*, pp. 87–8.
46. TNA, ADM 7/64, 24 Feb 1814.
47. TNA, ADM 51/2195, log of HMS *Comus*.
48. TNA, ADM 51/2914, log of HMS *Thais*.
49. Knight, *Britain Against Napoleon*, p. 413.
50. Kaplan, *Rothschild*, pp. 88–9, 95–6.

5 NORTH SEA CONVOYS, 1804–1812

1. Bonner-Smith, *Boteler Recollections*, p26. No evidence of this incident exists in the captain's log (TNA, ADM 51/2293) and no master's log exists. However, this mishap would hardly be emphasised in the official record and Boteler's description is too detailed and circumstantial to be dismissed.
2. Marshall, *Naval Biography*, IX, Supplement, pt 1, p. 6.
3. NMM, KEI/L/165, Lord Keith in account with John Jackson, 30 Sep 1806–2 Sep 1807.
4. Thorne, *House of Commons*, IV, p. 298.
5. TNA, ADM 1/2407, 'R', 25 Mar 1804.
6. TNA, ADM 1/2408, 'State and Condition', Rye in the Humber, 27 Sep 1805.
7. TNA, ADM 1/1427, Rye to Vice-Admiral Billy Douglas, 11 Jun 1810.
8. TNA, ADM 1/2407, Rye to Marsden, 17 May 1804.
9. TNA, ADM 51/4032, Log of the *Providence*; TNA, ADM 1/2407, Rye to William Marsden, 17 May 1804.
10. TNA, ADM 41/59, Muster book of the *Providence*.
11. NMM, MRK/101/2/52, Admiral Vashon to Admiral John Markham, 9 Jan 1807.
12. *Naval Chronicle*, XII, 1804, pp. 454–8; Foynes, *East Anglia*, pp. 135–6.
13. NMM, KEI/30, Journal of the *Cruizer*, Jan–Jun 1805.
14. TNA, ADM 36/15006, 17047, 17048, *Cruizer*'s muster books, 1803–7.
15. NMM, KEI/30, *Cruizer*'s Journal, 14 Jan, 10, 22 Feb, 9 Mar, 29 Jun 1805.
16. TNA, ADM 1/1937, Hancock to William Marsden, 10 Apr 1806.
17. Marshall, *Naval Biography*, IX, p. 21.
18. Marcus, *Age of Nelson*, pp. 318, 370, 410.
19. Redford, *Manchester Merchants*, p. 34, 174–6.
20. Redford, *Manchester Merchants*, pp. 32–3.
21. Jackson, *Hull*, pp. 60–64.
22. Schulte-Beerbuhl, 'Trading Networks', pp. 140, 143.
23. NMM, MRK/101/5/49, B.S. Rowley to Markham, 20 May [1806].
24. Rüger, *Heligoland*, p. 1.
25. Laughton, 'Seizure of Helgoland', Russell to Admiralty, 6 Sep 1807.
26. Marcus, *Age of Nelson*, p. 320; Adams & Woodman, *Light Upon the Waters*, p. 144.
27. TNA, FO 36/2, 11 Oct 1809, enclosure of 18 Sep 1809.
28. Coggeshall, *Thirty-Six Voyages*, p. 102.
29. Rüger, *Heligoland*, p. 23; TNA, CO/118/1, John Hall to Canning, 16 Jul 1808.
30. TNA, CO 118/9, Thomas Morgan Certifying Officer, 'Total of goods exported from this Island to the Continent', 1 Jan 1813–1 Jan 1814, 18 Jan 1814.
31. Quoted by Rüger, *Heligoland*, p. 25.
32. Schulte-Beerbuhl, 'Crossing the Channel', pp. 46–8.

33. Rüger, *Heligoland*, pp. 29–30; Glenthøj & Ottosen, *Denmark and Norway*, p. 114.
34. TNA, CO/118/1, Hamilton, Governor of Heligoland to Castlereagh, Jan 1808.
35. e.g. TNA, FO 36/2, Canning to Chatham, 7 Jul; Ordnance Office to Foreign Office, 18 Jul 1809.
36. TNA, ADM 7/64, 1808–13.
37. TNA, ADM 51/4032, *Providence*'s log, 7–16 Aug 1808.
38. TNA, ADM 51/4079, 11 Jan 1807, 12 Nov, 8 Dec 1809.
39. NRO, Rye/X/7243/157, nd. In the muster book Westcott was marked DD ('Discharged Dead') on 11 Apr 1807 (TNA, ADM 41/59, 11 April 1807).
40. TNA, ADM 1/4079, Log, 17 Jan, 5 Sep 1810.
41. TNA, ADM 41/59, Muster book of the *Providence*.
42. TNA, ADM 1/2408, Return to the Admiralty, 27 Sep 1805.
43. NRO, RYE/X/7243/122, Rye to Hartwell (draft), 8 Apr 1809.
44. TNA, ADM 1/2409, 13 Dec 1806.
45. TNA, ADM 51/4079, 30 Sep 1807.
46. TNA, ADM 51/4079, 6 Nov 1807.
47. TNA, ADM 1/2409, 26 Aug, 30 Dec 1806, 2 Jan 1807.
48. Jackson, *Grimsby and the Haven Company*.
49. TNA, ADM 51/4079, Log, 20 Nov–20 Dec 1811.
50. TNA, ADM 1/2407, Rye to Admiralty, 12 Nov 1804.
51. TNA, ADM 51/4032, *Providence*'s Log, 15 Sep–13 Nov 1804.
52. e.g. TNA, ADM 1/2411, Rye to Marsden, 14 Feb 1807.
53. TNA, ADM 51/4032, Log of the *Providence*, 16–21 Dec 1804; TNA, ADM 1/2407, Captain's Letters 'R', 16, 21 Dec 1804.
54. e.g. the rescue of the *Joseph and Mary*, TNA, ADM 1/2413, Rye to Pole, 24 Dec 1809.
55. TNA, ADM 51/4032, 28–9 February 1806; NRO, Rye/X/7243, March 1806 (draft).
56. Sutcliffe, *Expeditionary Warfare*, pp. 171–7.
57. NRO, Rye/X/7243/104, Rye to Mossin, Gluckstadt, 6 Apr 1806.
58. TNA, ADM 1/2409, Rye to Marsden, 2, 28 March, 14 Apr 1806.
59. NRO, Rye/X/7243/104 (draft) nd; 7243/105, Marsden to Rye, 18 Apr 1806.
60. TNA, ADM 51/4032, 11 Apr 1805, 30 Sep 1806; O'Byrne, *Naval Dictionary*, 'Peter Rye'.
61. TNA, ADM 1/2407, Captain Peter Rye to Isaac Wolley, 21 Dec 1804.
62. TNA, ADM 1/2408, Rye to Marsden, 2 Mar 1805.
63. NRO, Rye/X/7243/115, Marsden to Rye; also a commission also signed by Marsden appointing Rye to the Hermes, 21 Oct 1806.
64. TNA, ADM 1/2409, Rye to Marsden, 3 Dec 1806, enclosure of Thomas Bell.
65. TNA, ADM 1/2412, 19 Apr 1808; see also TNA, ADM 1/2408, for his application for leave because of health to Marsden, 2 Mar 1805.
66. Davey, *In Nelson's Wake*, p. 138.
67. NRO, Rye/X/7243/128, Douglas to Rye, 12 Jun 1807.
68. NRO, Rye/X/7243, Vice-Admiral Billy Douglas to Rye, 12 Jun 1807.
69. NRO, Rye/X/7243/136, G. Eggerton et al., 8 Oct; 7243/137, Francis Clifton et al. to Rye, 9 Oct 1807.
70. TNA, ADM 51/4079, 15 Sep 1808; NRO, X/Rye/7243/188, Douglas to Rye, 24 Sep 1808.
71. NRO, Rye/X/7243/199, Douglas to Rye,7 May; 7243/198, 31 Aug 1810.
72. TNA, ADM 1/1937, Hancock to Marsden, 17 Jun 1807; Marshall, *Naval Biography*, p. 22.
73. TNA, ADM 1/1937, Hancock to Pole, 23 Sep, 19 Oct 1808.
74. TNA, ADM 1/1937, Hancock to Pole, 27 Apr 1809.
75. James, *Naval History*, IV, p. 212.
76. TNA, ADM 1/1942, Hancock to Barrow, 14, 19 Aug, 16 Oct, 9, 11 Nov 1810.
77. Wold, *Privateering and Diplomacy*, pp. 216–26.
78. TNA, ADM 51/2604, *Nymphen*'s log, Jul–Aug 1812, 20–29 May 1813.
79. Marshall, *Naval Biography*, IX, p. 28, 24 Nov 1813.
80. e.g. TNA, ADM 2/993, 9 Feb, 11 Mar, 5 Apr, 8 Aug 1811.

81. NRO, Rye/X/7243/201, Jona Brown to Rye, 1 Jan 1811.
82. TNA, ADM 51/4079, *Providence's* log, 13 Jan 1811.
83. TNA, ADM 1/1430, 16 Jan 1811.
84. TNA, ADM 1/1430, Gardner to Croker, 11 May 1811.
85. TNA, ADM 51/4079, *Providence's* log, 19 Jan to 4 May 1811; TNA, ADM 7/64.
86. TNA, ADM 1/1430, Murray to Croker, 3 Jun 1811.
87. TNA, ADM 1/2416, 23, 28 May, 2, 8, 15, 27, 28 Jun, 11 Jul 1811; see also TNA, ADM, 1/2413, 1809.
88. TNA, ADM 51/4079, *Providence's* log, 21 Sep 1812.

6 ESCORTING THE TROOPS, 1803–1816

1. *Kentish Gazette*, 20 Nov 1807. It also reported that 54 transports were missing.
2. Liddell Hart, *Letters of Private Wheeler*, p. 47.
3. Duffy, *Soldiers, Sugar and Seapower*, pp. 199–216.
4. Knight, *Britain Against Napoleon*, pp. 188, 198–201.
5. Davey, *In Nelson's Wake*, passim, but especially pp. 113–21, 139–47, 298–301.
6. Sutcliffe, *Expeditionary Warfare*, Appendix 3, p. 252.
7. Sutcliffe, *Expeditionary Warfare*, pp. 1–122.
8. Hall, *Strategy*, p. 43.
9. Clammer, 'Soldiers' Wives', p. 56.
10. Sutcliffe, *Expeditionary Warfare*, chapter 6.
11. Duffy, *Soldiers, Sugar and Seapower*, pp. 168–70, 186–7, 214–15; Sutcliffe, *Expeditionary Warfare*, pp. 164–7.
12. Bunbury, *Narratives*, p. 93.
13. Sutcliffe, *Expeditionary Warfare*, p. 165.
14. Wellington, *Supplementary Despatches*, I, pp. 19–24. Wellesley's orders of 1797 were copied by troops being transported on board EIC ships (Parkinson, *Trade*, pp. 383–4).
15. Davey, *In Nelson's Wake*, pp. 190, 192, 199–200; Taylor, *Sons of the Waves*, pp. 357–9.
16. TNA, ADM 51/1693, *Mermaid's* log; Crumplin, *Guthrie's War*, p. 12.
17. Knight, *Britain Against Napoleon*, pp. 184–6.
18. Knight & Wilcox, *Sustaining the Fleet*, pp. 23–9.
19. O'Keefe, 'Old Halberdier', p. 19.
20. Sutcliffe, 'Bringing Forward', pp. 171–2; *Expeditionary Warfare*, p. 212.
21. Howard, *Walcheren*, p. 229.
22. Davey, *In Nelson's Wake*, p. 187.
23. *Bury and Norwich Post*, 15 Jan 1806.
24. TNA, ADM 51/1524, *Regulus's* log, 23–4 Dec 1805; Grocott, *Shipwrecks*, pp. 205–7.
25. TNA, ADM 51/1686, *Inflexible's* log, 4–28 Oct 1807.
26. *Lloyd's List*, 16 Nov 1807; Grocott, *Shipwrecks*, pp. 244–6; Glover, *Copenhagen*, pp. 268–9.
27. Ompteda, *King's German Legion*, p. 213.
28. *York Herald, Norfolk Chronicle*, 28 Nov 1807.
29. *Hampshire Chronicle*, 11 Jan; *Star* (London), 28 Jan 1808.
30. Sutcliffe, *Expeditionary Warfare*, pp. 54–80.
31. NMM, HNL/13/20, 15, 18, 30 March 1811.
32. Currie, *Henley's*, p. 33; also her full cataloguing notes in the NMM Caird Library.
33. NMM, HNL/56/7, July 1809–Mar 1810.
34. Grocott, *Shipwrecks*, p. 244, quoting *The Times*, 1 Jan 1808.
35. O'Keefe, 'Old Halberdier', p.20.
36. Ibid., pp. 18–26.
37. NMM, YOR/2, Berkeley to Yorke, 29 Sep 1810.
38. TNA, ADM 7/64.
39. See Hall, 'Royal Navy and the Peninsular War', pp. 404–5; *Wellington's Navy*, p. 112, which gives the out and back unconsolidated figures as 404 convoys, totalling 13,427 voyages, quoted in Knight, *Britain Against Napoleon*, pp. 425–6.

40 Knight & Wilcox, *Sustaining the Fleet*, p. 54–6; Currie, *Henley's*, p. 12.
41. Muir, *Defeat of Napoleon*, pp. 35–6.
42. Hall, 'Royal Navy and Peninsular War', p. 406.
43. See Davey, 'Repatriation', passim.
44. Knight, *Britain Against Napoleon*, chapter 7.
45. HL, STG 136 (21), Captain James Bowen to the Transport Board, 28 Jan 1809; Oman, *Peninsular War*, I, p. 595–6, 646–7.
46. Knight, *Britain Against Napoleon*, p. 204.
47. Hall, 'Royal Navy and Peninsular War', p. 410.
48. TNA, ADM 12/37; Oman, *Peninsular War*, II, pp. 640–42.
49. Knight & Wilcox, *Sustaining the Fleet*, p. 53.
50. Sutcliffe, 'Bordeaux to Ostend', p. 1.
51. Burnham, 'Filling the Ranks', p. 201.
52. Cohen, 'Brothers in War', pp. 15, 18.
53. Fernyhough, *Military Memoirs*, pp. 164–7.
54. Hall, 'Royal Navy and Peninsular War', p. 410; see also Sutcliffe, *Expeditionary Warfare*, pp. 221–2.
55. Davies, *Wellington's Wars*, quoting *Wellington's Supplementary Dispatches*, VIII, pp. 223–6, 3 Sep 1813; *Wellington's Dispatches*, XI, pp. 238–41, 1 Nov 1813.
56. Clammer, 'Soldiers' Wives', p. 61.
57. Grocott, *Shipwrecks*, pp. 310–12.
58. TNA, ADM 51/2382, *Franchise*'s log, 1811.
59. Robinson, *Bloody Eleventh*, pp. 332–3.
60. Kruk, 'Queen', p. 7, quoting John Bechervaise, *Thirty Six Years of a Seafaring Life by an Old Quarter Master* (1839).
61. Kruk, 'Queen', p. 8.
62. Grocott, *Shipwrecks*, p. 367.
63. Sutcliffe, 'Bordeaux to Ostend', p. 4.
64. Grocott, *Shipwrecks*, pp. 369, 371, 381–5.
65. *Morning Post*, 8 Nov 1814.
66. Mahan, *War of 1812*, II, p. 236; Kert, *Privateering*, p. 125.
67. Wilson, 'Napoleon's Escape', pp. 265–91.
68. Muir, *Defeat of Napoleon*, pp. 353–4.
69. Sutcliffe, 'Bordeaux to Ostend', p. 13, quoting Ian Fletcher, *'A Desperate Business': Wellington, the British Army and the Waterloo Campaign* (Staplehurst: The History Press, 2001), p. 12.
70. Sutcliffe, 'Bordeaux to Ostend', p. 13.
71. Mercer, *Journal*, pp. 6, 8; see also Knight, *Britain Against Napoleon*, pp. 456–7.
72. Glover, *Corunna to Waterloo*, pp. 247–52.
73. Muir, *Defeat of Napoleon*, p. 377.

7 THE MEDITERRANEAN, 1803–1814

1. Collingwood, *Private Correspondence*, II, p. 320; Hughes, *Private Correspondence*, Collingwood to his sister, 12 Feb 1809, pp. 267–8.
2. Anderson, *Levant*, pp. 430–48.
3. Krajeski, *Cotton*, p. 144, quoting Bonaparte, *Unpublished Correspondence*, III, pp. 656–7, Napoleon to Clarke, 19 Jul 1810.
4. Anderson, *Levant*, p. 476.
5. Hattendorf, 'Mediterranean', pp. 212–17.
6. Krajeski, *Cotton*, p. 153.
7. Crowhurst, *French War on Trade*, pp. 164–70, 213–14.
8. Galani, *British Shipping*, pp. 69–70, 224.
9. Roberts, *Napoleon*, p. 323; Esdaile, *Napoleon's Wars*, pp. 140–49.

10. Knight, *Britain Against Napoleon*, pp. 198–9, 218, 241; Davey, 'European Islands', p. 49.
11. Coad, *Support for the Fleet*, p. 240.
12. Macdonald, 'Gibraltar', pp. 63–4.
13. TNA, ADM 1/3993, Bennet to Marsden, 26 Jun 1805.
14. Mackesy, *Mediterranean*, pp. 274–5.
15. MacDougall, 'Malta Dockyard', p. 209.
16. Galani, *British Shipping*, pp. 74–5, 194.
17. Jane Knight, 'Eastern Mediterranean', p. 198; Thorne, *House of Commons*, I, pp. 321–3.
18. Nicolas, *Nelson Dispatches*, VI, p. 193, 6 Sep 1804.
19. Anderson, *Levant*, pp. 462–81.
20. Rodger, *Command of the Ocean*, p. 554.
21. Wellcome 3667, Nelson's in-letters from captains, Sep–Dec 1803.
22. Mackesy, *Mediterranean*, pp. 398–9, 403.
23. Davey, *In Nelson's Wake*, p. 141; Hughes, *Private Correspondence*, p. 214, to Purvis, 16 Jul 1807; p. 242, 15 Apr 1808.
24. Panzac, *The Barbary Corsairs*, pp. 144, 147, 161–2.
25. Jane Knight, 'Eastern Mediterranean', p. 200, quoting NMM, CRK/1, Ball to Nelson, 15 Dec 1803.
26. Krajeski, *Cotton*, p. 146.
27. Wellcome 3681, 'List of ships under convoy of HMS *Tribune*', Oct–Nov 1804.
28. Mackesy, *Mediterranean*, p. 115.
29. Galani, *British Shipping*, p. 149.
30. Jane Knight, 'Eastern Mediterranean', p. 211, fn. 26; Wellcome 3681, 9 Apr 1804.
31. Vale & Edwards, *Trotter*, pp. 120–21.
32. Knight, *Pursuit of Victory*, p. 467.
33. Wellcome 3681, letter conveyed by HMS *Seahorse*, 24 Sep 1803.
34. Cole, *Arming the Navy*, p. 72; Knight, *Britain Against Napoleon*, pp. 44–5.
35. Knight, *Pursuit of Victory*, pp. 464–5, 583–5.
36. Flayhart, *Counterpoint to Trafalgar*, pp. 84–120.
37. Jane Knight, 'Eastern Mediterranean', p. 198.
38. Jane Knight, 'Eastern Mediterranean', p. 210, quoting Nicolas, *Nelson Dispatches*, VI, to Marsden, 23 Jul 1805, p. 486.
39. Jane Knight 'Eastern Mediterranean', p. 210, quoting Nicolas, *Nelson Dispatches*, to Benjamin Hallowell, 20 Mar 1804.
40. Morriss, *Bentham*, p. 99.
41. Jane Knight, 'Eastern Mediterranean', p. 212, fn. 54; p. 214, fn. 104; Wellcome 3667, 3 Jun 1804.
42. James, *Naval History*, IV, pp. 13–17.
43. *London Gazette*, 27 Mar 1805, quoting letter of 26 Feb 1805; also Woodman, *Britannia's Realm*, pp. 182–3.
44. *London Gazette*, 18 Mar 1805; see also Henderson, *Frigates, Sloops and Brigs*, pp. 304–11.
45. *Aberdeen Press and Journal*, 3 Apr 1805.
46. Mackesy, *Mediterranean*, p. 117.
47. Laughton, *Barham Papers*, III, p. 116, 'Memorandum for King and Cabinet', 11 Jan 1806.
48. Anderson, *Levant*, p. 444.
49. Hughes, *Private Correspondence*, Collingwood to Purvis, *Ocean*, Malta, 7 Feb 1809.
50. Knight & Wilcox, *Sustaining the Fleet*, pp. 221–2; Mackesy, *Mediterranean*, Appendix II, p. 339.
51. Galani, *British Shipping*, pp. 40, 224.
52. Galani, *British Shipping*, pp. 6, 78, 82, quoting Crouzet, *L'economie Britannique*, pp. 305–7.
53. Galani, *British Shipping*, p. 67.
54. Marzagalli, 'French Wars', pp. 117–18.
55. NMM, LBK/66, 4 Aug 1808, 31 Jan 1809.
56. NMM, LBK/66, 24 Oct 1809.

57. NMM, LBK/66, 18 Dec 1817.
58. Davey, *In Nelson's Wake*, p. 149.
59. Hill, *Prizes of War*, pp. 98–9.
60. Crowhurst, *French War on Trade*, pp. 202–3.
61. Mackesy, *Mediterranean*, pp. 115–16.
62. Mackesy, *Mediterranean*, p. 398.
63. Davey, *In Nelson's Wake*, pp. 232–4.
64. Hall, *Wellington's Navy*, pp. 146–7.
65. Esdaile, *Peninsular War*, pp. 370–74, 400–401; Davey, *In Nelson's Wake*, p. 294.
66. Galani, *British Shipping*, p. 209.
67. TNA, ADM 1/664, In-letters 'C' to Admiralty Secretary, 1813.
68. TNA, ADM 7/64, 13 Jul 1813.
69. Krajeski, *Cotton*, p. 144, quoting TNA, ADM 7/41, 21 May 1810.
70. McCranie, 'War of 1812', p. 1076.
71. Anderson, *Levant*, pp. 479–81.
72. Jefferson, *Merchant Marine*, pp. 29–30.

8 THE EAST AND WEST INDIES, 1803–1814

1. TNA, ADM 1/3993.
2. Dann, *Nagle*, pp. 269–70.
3. TNA, ADM 51/1627, log of HMS *Canada*, 28 Jan–2 Feb 1806; 51/1625, log of HMS *Caesar*, 1806.
4. Davey, *In Nelson's Wake*, pp. 110–11, 117, 124–5.
5. Childers, *Mariner of England*, pp. 220, 222–3.
6. TNA, ADM 7/64.
7. Bonner-Smith, *St Vincent*, II, 16 Sep 1803, p. 334.
8. TNA, ADM 1/3993, John Bennet to W.W. Pole, 5 Nov 1807.
9. TNA, ADM 1/3993, 1 Jan 1810.
10. TNA, ADM 7/64.
11. Davis, *British Overseas Trade*, pp. 31, 36, 46.
12. Ward, *Naval Power in the East*, pp. 427–32.
13. Horsfall, 'West Indian Trade', p. 173.
14. Edwards, *Cotton Trade*, pp. 69, 243; Petley, *Slaveholders in Jamaica*, p. 16.
15. Horsfall, 'West Indian Trade', p. 176.
16. Dickson, *Cork*, chapter 10.
17. Knight & Wilcox, *Sustaining the Fleet*, pp. 32, 168.
18. NMM, HNL/101/8:6, Customs Declaration, 9 Nov 1811.
19. Bowen, 'Trading with the Enemy', p. 40.
20. TNA, ADM 7/64, 17 Sep 1808.
21. Hylton, *Paget Brothers*, 1 Sep 1808, p. 87.
22. TNA, ADM 51/2777, *Revenge*'s log, 5, 29 Sep, 10 Oct, 18 Nov 1808.
23. Hylton, *Paget Brothers*, 1, 13 Oct 1808, pp. 91, 92.
24. Parkinson, *Trade*, pp. 310–14.
25. Taylor, *Storm and Conquest*, p. 214, quoting TNA, ADM 1/180, Drury to William Wellesley Pole, 8 May 1809.
26. Day, 'Securing an Ocean', p. 63.
27. Captain Tremenhere, HEICS Asia, quoted in Parkinson, *War in the Eastern Seas*, p. 342.
28. Southam, *Jane Austen and the Navy*, p. 98.
29. Aldous, 'Prize Money', pp. 201–3.
30. Davey, *In Nelson's Wake*, p. 132.
31. Marcus, *Age of Nelson*, pp. 419–20.
32. Edwards, *Cotton Trade*, p. 99.
33. Mui & Mui, *Management of Monopoly*, pp. 92–4.

34. Bowen, *Business of Empire*, p. 234.
35. Parkinson, *Trade*, p. 84.
36. Coggeshall, *Thirty-Six Voyages*, p. 163.
37. Horsfall, 'West Indian Trade', pp. 163, 168, 181.
38. Knight, *Britain Against Napoleon*, pp. 406–7.
39. TNA, ADM 2/1384, Board of Admiralty (Secret) to Hotham, 22 Aug 1804, 8.
40. Marichal, *Bankruptcy of Empire*, pp. 210, 235.
41. TNA, ADM 51/1660, *Resistance*'s log, 21 Nov 1806–16 Mar 1807.
42. Knight, *Britain Against Napoleon*, pp. 406–7.
43. TNA, ADM 1/261, Rowley to Croker, 21 Nov 1810; Gwyn, *Ashore and Afloat*, p. 205.
44. Hall, *Wellington's Navy*, pp. 134–5.
45. TNA, ADM 1/262, Matthew Lawrence Murphy to Vice-Admiral Rowley, 3 Dec 1810 (copy).
46. Marichal, *Bankruptcy of Empire*, p. 234; Hall, *Wellington's Navy*, p. 136.
47. Woodman, *A Low Set of Blackguards*, II, p. 708.
48. Barton, 'Duelling', p. 303.
49. Knight, *Britain Against Napoleon*, p. 215.
50. Crimmin, 'Troubridge', p. 319.
51. Taylor, *Commander*, p. 204.
52. Malcolmson, *Order and Disorder*, pp. 150–52; Davey, *In Nelson's Wake*, pp. 130–31; Morrow, *British Flag Officers*, pp. 67–8.
53. Woodman, *A Low Set of Blackguards*, II, pp. 654, 647.
54. Day, 'Securing an Ocean', p. 60.
55. TNA, ADM 51/1866, log of HMS *Culloden*, 13–28 Jan 1809; Woodman, *A Low Set of Blackguards*, II, p. 657.
56. Taylor, *Storm and Conquest*, p. 166.
57. TNA, ADM 1/2705, Ward to W.W. Pole, 13 Apr 1809.
58. Parkinson, *Samuel Waters*, p. 101.
59. Rodger, *Command of the Ocean*, pp. 542–3.
60. Woodman, *A Low Set of Blackguards*, II, p. 599; *Royal Cornwall Gazette*, 24 Aug; *Morning Post*, 9 Sep; *British Press*, 14 Sep 1805.
61. TNA, ADM 1/2023, Captain's Letters 'K', 1809, 14 Aug 1808; ADM 7/64.
62. Hay, *Landsman Hay*, p. 204.
63. e.g. Childers, *Mariner of England*, pp. 162–3.
64. NMM, MRK/102/1/165, Edward Crofton to Rear-Admiral John Markham, 26 Nov 1806.
65. *Morning Chronicle*, 27 Nov 1806.
66. TNA, ADM 1/3993, 31 Dec 1806.
67. Knight, 'Achievement and Cost', p. 125.
68. TNA, ADM 1/3993, 25 May 1812.
69. Hay, *Landsman Hay*, pp. 194, 205–6.
70. Captain Charles Dashwood to Lloyd's, 14 Aug 1813, West India Convoy Register (Admiralty Library) Red 5/54, f.63, quoted in Dowling, 'West Indies Convoys', p. 312.
71. Dowling, 'Convoy System', p. 316, quoting TNA, ADM 1/255, Chambers to Dacres, encl. 16 Apr 1805.
72. Dowling, 'Convoy System', pp. 314–15, quoting ADM 1/4833, deposition of Thomas Burghes (enclosure), 23 Dec 1809; ADM 1/256.
73. TNA, ADM 1/1654, Clement to the Secretary of the Admiralty, 18 Sep 1809; Knight, 'Achievement and Cost', pp. 132–3.
74. Taylor, *Storm and Conquest*, p. xv.
75. Woodman, *A Low Set of Blackguards*, II, pp. 648–52; Taylor, *Storm and Conquest*, pp. 76–7.
76. Davey, *In Nelson's Wake*, p. 220.
77. Taylor, *Storm and Conquest*, p. 102, quoting TNA, ADM 1/61, Pringle to Bertie, 28 Jan 1809; Woodman, *A Low Set of Blackguards*, II, pp. 652–3.
78. Taylor, *Storm and Conquest*, p. 120; Woodman, *A Low Set of Blackguards*, II, p. 654.
79. Hay, *Landsman Hay*, p. 166.

80. Davey, *In Nelson's Wake*, p. 134.
81. TNA, ADM 7/64, 1810–14; Bowen, 'Shipping Losses', p. 324.
82. Dowling, 'Convoy System', p. 343; Knight, 'Achievement and Cost', p. 125, quoting TNA, ADM 1/3994, William Driscoll to the Committee of Lloyd's, 1 Oct 1814.
83. Dowling, 'Convoy System', p. 312, quoting Admiralty Library, Convoy Register 5/54, f. 63.
84. O'Byrne *Naval Dictionary*.

9 THE BATTLE FOR THE BALTIC, 1807–1812

1. Bonner-Smith, *Boteler Recollections*, p. 10.
2. Crosby, *America, Russia, Hemp and Napoleon*, p. 183, quoting *Correspondance de Napoleon*, XXI, p. 298.
3. Brenton, *Life of St Vincent*, II, p. 341, quoting St Vincent to Thomas Grenville, 25 Mar 1807; TNA, ADM 7/64, 1808–14.
4. Marcus, *Age of Nelson*, p. 394.
5. Davey, *Transformation*, p. 127.
6. Voelcker, *Saumarez*, chapter 5; Davey, *In Nelson's Wake*, pp. 242–3.
7. Davey, *Transformation*, pp. 99–100, 193–6 and passim; Sutcliffe, *Expeditionary Warfare*, p. 130; Knight, *Britain Against Napoleon*, p. 210.
8. Davey, *In Nelson's Wake*, p. 250; 'Securing the Sinews', p. 168; Anderson, *Baltic*, pp. 339–49; TNA, ADM 7/795, Samuel Champion, Saumarez's Secretary to Admiralty, 20 May 1811.
9. Morriss, *Royal Dockyards*, pp. 79–81.
10. Astrom, 'Timber Imports', pp. 17–18.
11. Davey, 'Securing the Sinews', p. 173.
12. Rodger, *Command of the Ocean*, p. 478.
13. Davey, 'British Hemp Crisis', pp. 668–9.
14. Davey, 'Securing the Sinews', pp. 174, 180 and generally 171–8.
15. Childers, *Mariner of England*, pp. 162–3.
16. Currie, *Henley's*, pp. 20–21.
17. Crosby, *America, Russia, Hemp and Napoleon*, p. 212.
18. TNA, ADM 7/795, Admiralty correspondence with Lloyd's, 7, 20 May 1811.
19. Thorne, *House of Commons*, V, pp. 375–8.
20. Sherwig, *Guineas and Gunpowder*, pp. 273–4.
21. Jefferson, *Merchant Marine*, pp. 26–35.
22. Knight, *Britain Against Napoleon*, p. 375; Lieven, *Russia Against Napoleon*, pp. 30–31; Sherwig, *Guineas and Gunpowder*, p. 287.
23. e.g. TNA, ADM 7/801, Captain John Ross, *Acteon*, at Lerwick, to Rear-Admiral George Hope, 22 Oct 1814.
24. Davey, 'Securing the Sinews', p. 175.
25. Marcus, *Age of Nelson*, p. 370.
26. *Hull Packet*, 14 Jul 1807.
27. Jefferson, *Merchant Marine*, pp. 4, 11.
28. Knight, *Britain Against Napoleon*, p. 392; Ryan, 'Defence of British Trade', p. 445.
29. TNA, ADM 7/795, Samuel Champion, secretary to Saumarez, to John Bennett of Lloyd's, 20 May, 2 Jun 1811.
30. Davey, 'Securing the Sinews', pp. 163–4.
31. Jefferson, *Merchant Marine*, p. 18.
32. Tooke, *High and Low Prices*, pp. 15–57; Davey, *Transformation*, pp. 22–4; 'Securing the Sinews', pp. 168–72.
33. Davey, *In Nelson's Wake*, p. 243; Anderson, *Baltic*, p. 370.
34. Ryan, 'Defence of British Trade', pp. 446, 456.
35. Coggeshall, *Thirty-six Voyages*, pp. 119–20.
36. Voelcker, *Saumarez*, p. 95.
37. Ryan, *Saumarez Papers*, Jun 1810, p. 127.

38. Witt, 'Smuggling and Blockade-Running', pp. 156–7; Glenthøj & Ottosen, *Denmark and Norway*, pp. 106–10.
39. Witt, 'Smuggling and Blockade-Running', pp. 162, 164.
40. Glenthøj & Ottosen, *Denmark and Norway*, p. 101.
41. GSA, AQ 365/10–34, nd.
42. GSA, AQ 365, 10–1, 'List of Prizes, 1809'; 10–10, nd; 10–13, Nov 1809; 10–19, 21 Mar 1810; Jonas Browne & Co., Hull to Mansell, 10–21, 8 Dec 1810; 10–22, 14 Jan 1812; 10–23, Henry Abbott to Mansell, Jan 1812; 10–27, Frederick Mansell in account with Henry Abbott, Dec 1814, lists another eighteen prizes; 10–24, 26 Jun 1813.
43. *Hull Packet*, 12 May 1812.
44. Watt & Hawkins, *Letters of Seamen*, p. 312, John Whick to his father, 4 Jun 1811; p. 318, Whitworth to his wife, 2 Feb 1812.
45. Voelcker, *Saumarez*, p. 77.
46. Rodger, *Command of the Ocean*, pp. 560–61, quoting Captain David Milne, *Impetueux*, 4 Sep 1811, HMC *Milne Home*, p. 146.
47. Marzagalli, 'Continental System', p. 92.
48. Aberg, 'Communities in Western Sweden', pp. 178, 187–9.
49. Voelcker, *Saumarez*, p. 117; Marcus, *Age of Nelson*, p. 327.
50. TNA, ADM 1/3993, Bennet to Croker, 30 Jun 1812.
51. Marcus, *Age of Nelson*, p. 326; Voelcker, 'Battle of Lyngor', p. 90.
52. James, *Naval History*, V, pp. 222–6; Voelcker, *Saumarez*, p. 102; Davey, *Transformation*, pp. 130–31.
53. Anderson, *Baltic*, p. 338.
54. Voelcker, *Saumarez*, chapter 6.
55. Davey, 'Supplied by the Enemy', pp. 279–82; *Transformation*, p. 179; Voelcker, *Saumarez*, pp. 109–13.
56. Coggeshall, *Thirty-Six Voyages*, p. 139.
57. Jefferson, *Merchant Marine*, p. 33.
58. Ryan, 'Defence of British Trade', pp. 455–6.
59. Marcus, *Age of Nelson*, p. 373, quoting TNA, ADM 1/6, 9 Jun 1808.
60. Ryan, 'Copenhagen Operation', p. 316, 9 Aug 1807.
61. Davey, 'Repatriation', pp. 689–707; *In Nelson's Wake*, pp. 188–9.
62. Davey, 'Charting of the Baltic', pp. 94–7.
63. Bonner-Smith, *Boteler Recollections*, p. 10.
64. Bonner-Smith, *Boteler Recollections*, p. 20.
65. Woodman, *Victory of Seapower*, pp. 129–35; Marcus, *Age of Nelson*, pp. 373–4.
66. Ryan, 'Defence of British Trade', p. 457; Glover, *Copenhagen*, Appendix 35.
67. TNA, ADM 51/2384, *Forward*'s log; ADM 1/693, Nagle to Admiralty, 31 Jul 1810.
68. TNA, ADM 7/64.
69. TNA, ADM 1/693, Leith to Admiralty, 27 Jul 1810; Ryan, *Saumarez Papers*, pp. 141–2.
70. TNA, ADM 1/693, Leith to Admiralty, 31 Jul 1810.
71. Tønnesson, *Kaperfart og skipsfart*, pp. 265–6.
72. James, *Naval History*, III, p. 351.
73. TNA, ADM 7/795, Samuel Champion to John Bennet, 12 Jul 1811.
74. Ryan, *Saumarez Papers*, pp. 59–61.
75. Voelcker, *Saumarez*, p. 78, quoting Suffolk Record Office, HA/93/6/1/487, 31 Jan 1809.
76. Grocott, *Shipwrecks*, quoting *The Times*, 3 Nov 1812; *Hull Packet*, 10 Nov 1812.
77. *Hull Packet*, 22 Dec 1812.
78. *Hull Packet*, 5 Nov 1811.
79. TNA, ADM 7/795, Champion to Bennet, 14 Sep 1811.
80. Jepsen, *Last Voyage*, pp. 142–4, 147, 151–3.
81. Voelcker, *Saumarez*, pp. 174–5; James, *Naval History*, V, pp. 231–2.
82. *Hull Packet*, 28 Jan 1812.
83. O'Byrne, *Naval Dictionary*.

84. Lewis, *Dillon Narrative*, p. 192.
85. NRO, Rye/X/7243/208.
86. Jefferson, *Merchant Marine*, pp. 7-8.
87. Coggeshall, *Thirty-Six Voyages*, pp. 132-3.
88. *Hull Packet*, 15, 29 Dec 1812.
89. Jefferson, *Merchant Marine*, pp. 39, 26-38.
90. Jefferson, *Merchant Marine*, pp. 52-3; see also Ville, *English Shipowning*, p. 124.
91. Ville, *English Shipowning*, appendices, pp. 174-81.
92. Currie, *Henley's*, p. 21; Ville, *English Shipowning*, pp. 128-33.
93. Fayle, 'Marine Insurance', p. 43.
94. Wright & Fayle, *Lloyd's*, p. 190; Ryan, 'Defence of British Trade', p. 461; Marcus, *Age of Nelson*, pp. 318-19.
95. Wright & Fayle, *Lloyd's*, pp. 263-7.
96. Voelcker, 'Battle of Lyngor', p. 90; Robson, 'Lyngor', p. 423
97. Anderson, *Baltic*, p. 349.
98. Witt, 'Smuggling and Blockade Running', pp. 164, 166.
99. Davey, *Transformation*, pp. 187-96; *In Nelson's Wake*, pp. 250-51.

10 THE NORTH ATLANTIC, 1812-1815

1. Hansard, vol. 27, col. 869.
2. Crosby, *America, Russia, Hemp and Napoleon*, pp. 247-60.
3. TNA, ADM 1/624, 29 July 1812.
4. Glenthøj & Ottosen, *Denmark and Norway*, p. 120.
5. McCranie, 'War of 1812', pp. 1068-9, 1093-4; Kert, *Privateering*, pp. 37, 88; Rodger, *Command of the Ocean*, p. 639. See chapter 2.
6. Knight, 'North Atlantic Convoys', p. 48, figures from TNA, ADM 7/64.
7. Gutridge, 'Hulbert', p. 33.
8. Kert, *Privateering*, p. 23.
9. Kert, *Privateering*, pp. 35-6, 146.
10. Kert, *Privateering*, p. 116.
11. Lewis, *Dillon Narrative*, II, p. 298.
12. Knight, 'North Atlantic Convoys', p. 51; Appendix.
13. TNA, ADM 1/623, nd.
14. *Naval Chronicle*, XXXIII, 1815, p. 296.
15. James, *War of 1812*, p. 173.
16. Malcolmson, *Order and Disorder*, pp. 198-202.
17. Quoted in Malcolmson, *Order and Disorder*, p. 199.
18. Crimmin, 'Exchange of Prisoners', p. 150.
19. Crimmin, 'Exchange of Prisoners', p. 147, quoting TNA, ADM 1/5129, Petition of Adventurers in the Southern Whale Fishery to Admiralty, 4 Nov 1813.
20. Crawford, *Naval War of 1812*, III, pp. 28-9.
21. Crimmin, 'Exchange of Prisoners', p. 148.
22. Knight, *Britain Against Napoleon*, pp. 445-6.
23. Crimmin, 'Exchange of Prisoners', p. 153, quoting Benjamin Waterhouse, *Journal of a Young Man from Massachusetts* (Boston, MA: Rowe & Hooper, 1816), p. 15.
24. Crimmin, 'Exchange of Prisoners', p. 152, quoting TNA, ADM 1/5129, Petition of masters of merchant ships, 17 Sep 1813.
25. Mahan, *War of 1812*, II, p. 223.
26. Petrie, *'Eliza Swan'*, pp. 102-8; also Kert, *Privateering*, p. 33.
27. Knight, *Britain Against Napoleon*, p. 433.
28. Lohnes, 'Halifax', p. 324, 22 Feb 1813.
29. Wilkinson, *Bermuda*, I, pp. 318-20.
30. Lohnes, 'Halifax', pp. 326, 332.

31. Wardle, 'Newfoundland Trade', p. 248; Knight, *Britain Against Napoleon*, p. 164.
32. Wardle, 'Newfoundland Trade', pp. 247–8.
33. TNA, ADM 51/2342, 27 May 1812.
34. Bulley Diaries, 27 May 1812.
35. TNA, ADM 51/2766, Log of the *Ringdove*, 30 Jun 1813.
36. Lewis, *Dillon Narrative*, II, p. 295.
37. Wardle, 'Newfoundland Trade', p. 231.
38. Crimmin, 'Exchange of Prisoners', pp. 145–6, quoting TNA, ADM 1/5129, Petitions, 11 Sep, 4 Nov 1813; CO 23/61, Report from the House of Assembly, 9 Dec 1813.
39. Gutridge, 'Hulbert', p. 38, quoting Portsmouth City Records Office, 626A/1/1/3–21, 11 Nov 1813.
40. Arthur, *War of 1812*, p. 104.
41. Arthur, *War of 1812*, pp. 110, 222–6; Lohnes, 'Halifax', p. 327.
42. TNA, ADM 51/2457, *Horatio*'s log; ADM 37/5322, *Horatio*'s muster book, 1814.
43. Lewis, *Dillon Narrative*, II, pp. 293–4, April 1814.
44. TNA, ADM 51/2457, *Horatio*'s log, 1 Apr 1814.
45. TNA, ADM 50/75, Keats's Journal, pp. 247–59; NMM, HAW/9, Keats's Order Book, 19 Apr 1814.
46. TNA, ADM 1/478, 11 Jun 1814.
47. Lewis, *Dillon Narrative*, II, pp. 314–15.
48. Dudley, *Naval War of 1812*, vol. 1, p. 120, to Jones, 3 Jun 1812.
49. Coggeshall, *Thirty-Six Voyages*, pp. 164–5; Kert, *Privateering*, pp.111–43
50. *Hansard*, 27, cols 867–71, 13 May 1814.
51. Kert, *Privateering*, pp. 26–9.
52. Marshall, *Naval Biography*, VIII, p. 469.
53. Kert, *Privateering*, pp. 27, 154
54. Saunders, *Fortress Britain*, pp. 151–2.
55. TNA, ADM 51/2936, log of *Victorious*, 1813–14.
56. Lewis, *Dillon Narrative*, II, p. 301, Jun 1814.
57. *Saunder's Newsletter*, Dublin, 25 Aug 1814.
58. *Caledonian Mercury*, 10 Sep 1814; also *Bristol Mirror*, 17 Sep 1814.
59. London Metropolitan Archives, Guildhall Library: Lloyd's of London, minutes of General Meetings, CLC/B/148/MS 31570/001, 21 Sep 1814. I am grateful to Dr Evan Wilson for a transcript of this reference.
60. I am particularly grateful to Dr Faye Kert who sent me part of her invaluable database of prizes taken in this way, to prove this and other points; also TNA, ADM 1/3994, Marryat to Croker, 19 Sep 1814 (enclosure).
61. TNA, ADM 1/3994, Marryat to Croker, 19 Sep 1814 (and enclosure).
62. Gardiner, *Frigates*, p. 147.
63. TNA, ADM 1/1558, Butcher to Croker, 22 Nov 1814.
64. TNA, ADM 1/1561, Butcher to Barrow, 6 Sep 1815.
65. *London Courier and Evening Gazette*, 23 Nov 1815.
66. *Salem Gazette*, 19 Jun 1812, quoted in Kert, *Privateering*, p. 1.
67. Parkinson, *Britannia Rules*, p. 170.
68. Knight, 'North Atlantic Convoys', p. 51; McCranie, 'Obstinate and Audacious', pp. 25–6.
69. Coggeshall, *Thirty-Six Voyages*, p. 154.
70. TNA, ADM 7/64, 7 Nov 1814.
71. James, *Naval History*, VI, pp. 248–51.
72. Jefferson, *Merchant Marine*, p. 50.

CONCLUSION

1. TNA, ADM 7/801, 18 Mar 1815.
2. Knight, *Britain Against Napoleon*, pp. 456–7.

3. Rubinstein, *Durham Papers*, p. 468, quoting TNA, ADM 1/336, Durham to Croker, 15 Aug 1815.
4. Marshall, *Naval Biography*, IV, p. 709.
5. Rodger, *Command of the Ocean*, p. 559.
6. Knight, *Britain Against Napoleon*, p. 433.
7. *Naval Chronicle*, XXXIII, 1815, pp. 227–8.
8. Knight, *Britain Against Napoleon*, p. 363; Sutcliffe, *Expeditionary Warfare*, Appendix 2.
9. Sutcliffe, *Expeditionary Warfare*, Appendix 1.
10. Hepper, *Warship Losses*, p. 213; see also Appendix.
11. Knight, 'North Atlantic Convoys', pp. 54–8.
12. Davey, *In Nelson's Wake*, pp. 242–53.
13. Knight & Wilcox, *Sustaining the Fleet*, pp. 54–5.
14. Wilson, *British Naval Officers*, p. 152.
15. HL, ST/169 (43), 29 Nov 1806.
16. Knight, 'North Atlantic Convoys', pp. 54–8.
17. *Naval Chronicle*, XXXIV, 1815, p. 80.
18. Lewis, *Navy in Transition*, p. 69.
19. GSA, AQ 0365/03–09, 4 Mar 1831; 03–13, 14, 18 Mar, 8 Apr 1836; 03–19, 9 Oct 1849.
20. Marshall, *Naval Biography*, Supplement, part 1, pp. 4–31.
21. NRO, Rye/X/7244/191, 7244/255, list of debts, 1 Oct 1831; 7245/29, assignments to creditors, 13 Jun 1822; 7245/32, will, 4 Sep 1848; 7246/112, will, 25 Jul 1819.
22. Wheeler, *Athenaeum*, pp. 11–15.
23. Hepper, *Warship Losses*, p. 213; Lewis, *Social History*, pp. 361–412.

EPILOGUE: THE SECOND WORLD WAR

1. Rayner, *Escort*, p. 88.
2. Gretton, *Escort Commander*, Introduction, p. 2.
3. Comparison between TNA, ADM 7/64, and Murfett, *Naval Warfare, 1919–1945*, Appendix I, 'Allied Convoy Statistics', pp. 530–33. Figures for the earlier period are definitely an underestimate; Rutter, *Red Ensign*, p. 153.
4. Hewitt, *Coastal Convoys*, p. 1.
5. Mawdsley, *War for the Seas*, p. 313; Brown, 'Atlantic Escorts', pp. 455–6; Lyon, 'Order of Battle', pp. 267–8.
6. Brown, 'Atlantic Escorts', p. 47, quoting J.B. Lamb, *Corvette Navy: True Stories from Canada's Atlantic War* (London: Futura Publications, 1979); see also, Rayner, *Escort*, pp. 68–9.
7. Gretton, *Escort Commander*, pp. 190, 187–9.
8. Rayner, *Escort*, pp. 164–7.
9. Prysor, *Citizen Sailors*, pp. 170–71.
10. Woodman, *Malta Convoys*, p. xix.
11. Aldous, 'Prize Money', pp. 4–5.
12. Baugh, 'Richmond', p. 18.
13. TNA, ADM 51/4079, 10 Sep 1807.
14. Gretton, *Escort Commander*, p. 190.
15. Thorne, *House of Commons*, IV, pp. 132–3; HL, ST/103, 23 Mar 1807.
16. Rodger, *Command of the Ocean*, pp. 501–2.
17. Prysor, *Citizen Sailors*, pp. 112–14.
18. Rayner, *Escort*, pp. 223–4.
19. Prysor, *Citizen Sailors*, pp. 159–60.
20. Woodman, *Arctic Convoys*, pp. 254–6.
21. Prysor, *Citizen Sailors*, p. 168; Mawdsley, *War for the Seas*, p. 53.
22. Mawdsley, *War for the Seas*, pp. 255–8, quoting, p. 255, Gannon, *Drumbeat*, p. 240.
23. Rayner, *Escort*, Preface, p. 10.

BIBLIOGRAPHY

This book owes much to the work of an almost-forgotten generation of historians who wrote in the years following the Second World War. They had lived through and served in a global maritime conflict during which the continuity of trade to and from Britain and the movement of armies by sea were of everyday concern. Some of these distinguished academics applied their wartime experience to the parallel events of the Napoleonic period. C. Northcote Parkinson wrote on the East Indies, as well as editing a still-valuable book of essays on wartime trade in *The Trade Winds*, while Piers Mackesy analysed the war in the Mediterranean and A.N. Ryan the Baltic. Gerald Graham dedicated his *Empire of the North Atlantic* to the officers and ship's company of HMS *Harvester*, who were lost through enemy action on convoy duty in the North Atlantic in 1943.

However, as Britain's place in the world rapidly diminished, this flourishing field in the history of the sailing navy tailed off. Historians turned to other questions: how did a small island off Europe manage to create and defend a worldwide empire in the days before steam, coal and oil? How was British naval and mercantile power able to remain so effective for so long? Questions of financial resources, political control, shipbuilding capacity and the influence and impact of individual naval officers were analysed.[*] Economic historians explored the growth of industrialisation, though they often overlooked the maritime world and the effects of War.[†] Only John Bromley studied the economic war at sea in depth, largely during the early eighteenth century in European waters. He was as much at home in French archives as those in Britain, and he thus concentrated upon French privateering.[‡] Patrick Crowhurst, his student, contributed in 1977 a short but important book on British trade defence between 1689 and 1815. Some twenty years later he published *The French War on Trade: Privateering 1793–1815*, written in the main from archives in France, examining trade protection from the French ports of Dunkirk, St Malo, Nantes, Bordeaux and Bayonne, as well as Marseilles.

On the British side of the Channel, convoys have received very little consideration. It is unsurprising that the small warships and officers who commanded them during the Napoleonic Wars have been neglected, given the difficulty of penetrating the extensive naval records in the National Archives. This was made easier when compilations began to appear in 1993, starting with David Lyon's *The Sailing Navy List* on which he had been working for much of his career at the National Maritime Museum. The next year saw the publication of both David Hepper's *British Warship Losses in the Age of Sail, 1650–1859* and David Syrett and Richard Dinardo's *The Commissioned Sea Officers of the Royal Navy, 1660–1815*. Terence Grocott's *Shipwrecks of*

---

[*] e.g. Ehrman, *Navy in the War of William III* (1953); Baugh, *Naval Administration in the Age of Walpole* (1965); Kennedy, *The Rise and Fall of British Naval Mastery* (1976).

[†] Rodger, 'War as an Economic Activity', pp. 1–18.

[‡] Bromley's essays and papers were collected after his death in *Corsairs and Navies* (1987). He had been taught in turn by Richard Pares at Oxford, whose *War and Trade in the West Indies, 1739–1763* (1936) contains a fine, intricate analysis of English and French convoys and their parallel difficulties in the two mid-eighteenth-century wars (pp. 303–25).

the Revolutionary and Napoleonic Eras (1997) used newspapers as sources, and can now be amplified by using the digital British Newspaper Archive. The *Oxford Dictionary of National Biography* (2004) has, of course, been in constant use, but Rif Winfield's comprehensive *British Warships in the Age of Sail, 1793–1817* (2005) was the most consulted. So profuse are individual references to these works that I have not reproduced them in the text.

The final chapters of N.A.M. Rodger's all-encompassing *Command of the Ocean* (2004) started the process of gently levering the post-Amiens naval and mercantile history of Britain out of obscurity, followed by a number of specialist studies on the Baltic by Tim Voelcker (2008) and James Davey (2012). The bicentenary of the Anglo-American War of 1812 produced a flurry of good books, including a study of the blockade of the United States by Brian Arthur (2011) and a long article by Kevin McCranie (2012) on the movement of British warships to the North Atlantic after the defeat of Napoleon. In 2015 a comprehensive history of the whole naval conflict was provided by James Davey's *In Nelson's Wake: The Navy and the Napoleonic Wars* (2015). This was the first operational history since the volume in Laird Clowes's seven-volume history of the navy, published in 1900, which itself was based almost entirely on William James's work of the 1820s. Davey's book, of central importance when writing on the convoy system, has, perforce, only one chapter on economic warfare.

Evidence for merchant shipping is comparatively thin, when compared to the navy, which makes the work of Sarah Palmer, Simon Ville and Ann Currie of particular value. Richard Woodman's five-volume history of the merchant navy published the volume on the Napoleonic Wars in 2009, to which he added a comprehensive history of the shipping of the East India Company in 2017. Robert Sutcliffe's analysis of the Transport Board (2016) and its performance up to 1815 tells us as much about merchant shipping as it does about the complexities of Whitehall administration.

A most welcome addition to accessible scholarship has been the work of Continental scholars, such as Katherine Aaslestad and Silvia Marzagalli, published in English in the War, Culture and Society, 1750–1850 series, as well as Rasmus Glenthøj and Morten Ottosen (2014) on Denmark and Norway and the volume edited by Aaslestad and Johan Joor (2015) on the impact of the Continental System and the war at sea in several European countries. These books emphasise the degree to which smaller, neutral countries were dragged into the conflict and how badly they suffered.

PRIMARY SOURCES

National Archives (TNA) Kew, London

Admiralty Secretariat: In-letters

ADM 1/261–2 c-in-c Jamaica 1810; 1/327 c-in-c Leeward Islands 1806; 1/478, c-in-c Newfoundland 1813–15; 1/557–8 'B' 1814; 1/572 c-in-c North Sea 1807, 1813; 1/623–9 c-in-c Cork 1812–1815; 1/690–695 c-in-c Leith; 1/1426–1431 c-in-c Yarmouth ADM 1/1545–7 1807–12

Captain's In-letters: 'A' 1/4369 1814–16; 'B' 1809; 1/1558, 1561, 1815; 1/1591 'B' 1815; 1/1652–5 'C' 1809; 1/1664–5 'C' 1813; 1/1773 'D' 1813; 1/1770 'E' 1809; 1/1804 'F' 1805; 1/1937 'H'; 1/1940, 1809; 1/1950, 'H' 1814; 1/2023 'K' 1809; 1/2080–1; 'L' 1811–12; 1/2407–22, 'R' 1804–13; 1/2632, 1804–1; 1/2705 'W' 1809

ADM 1/3898 Doctors' Commons to Secretary of the Admiralty 1807

ADM 1/3992–4 In-letters from the Committee of Lloyd's 1809–14

Admiralty Secretariat: Out-letters

ADM 2/940 to c-in-c Jamaica; 2/993–5 to Flag Officers Thames, Downs, Yarmouth, Leith, Cork 1811–13; ADM 2/1101–14, to c-in-cs re convoy, 1807–14; 2/1384 Letters pertaining to convoy, correspondence with merchants, Transport Board etc. Secret Convoys, 1801–6

BIBLIOGRAPHY

Miscellaneous Admiralty Records

ADM 7/41–43 papers of Admiral Sir Charles Cotton, as c-in-c Channel; 7/64 Summary List of Convoys sent to Lloyd's 1808–14; 7/68 Orders to convoys 1808

7/69 Register of applications for licences 1811–12; 7/71 Register of licences to sail without convoy 1811–14; 7/72 Register of licences to sail without convoy 1814–15; 7/263–6 Admiralty Board Journal: orders and correspondence with commanders-in-chief, 1813–14

7/586–8 Signals and Signal Books: convoys 1800–45

7/793–5 Convoys to and from the Baltic, correspondence with Lloyd's, 1810–11; 7/801, Admiralty correspondence, miscellaneous, Baltic, 1814; 7/805 Register of licences to sail without convoy 1812–15

7/975 Popham's Telegraphic signals 1805–9

Lists and Digests

ADM 12/37 Lists and Digests of convoy requests, 1809; ADM 13/103–4 Courts Martial Indexes and Registers 1803–56

Muster Books

ADM 36/15006, 36/17047, 36/17048 *Cruizer*, 1803–7; 37/5322 *Horatio*, 1814; 41/59, 41/85 *Providence*, 1804–14; 36/15311 *York* 1803

Hired Ships

ADM 49/36 Papers relating to hired ships 1803–8; 49/96 Papers relating to hired ships 1804–12; 49/99 Volume of imprests 1804–18

Keats Papers

ADM 50/75, Keats's Journal, 1812; 50/143–5 Letter and Order books, 1808-9; ADM 50/151 Letter and Order books 1815–16

Captains' Log Books

ADM 51/2111 *Aggressor*, 1813–15; 51/2124 *Antelope*, 1813–14; 51/1970 *Alaart*, 1809; 51/2016 *Bulwark*, 1810; 51/1625 *Caesar*, 1806; 51/1627 *Canada* 1805–7; 51/1668 *Canopus* 1806–7; 51/4050 *Charles*, 1807–12, 1813–14; 51/2035 *Cherokee*, 1813; 51/1973 *Childers*, 1808–9; 51/2042; 51/2195 *Comus*, 1809–14; 51/2253 *Cracker*, 1810–11; 51/1866 *Culloden*, 1808–9; 51/2041-2 *Dauntless*, 1812-13; 51/2263 *Desiree*, 1814–15; 51/2253 *Cracker* 1808-12; 51/2293 *Dictator* 1809–16; 51/2257 *Diligence*, 1809; 51/2338 *Earnest*, 1810–15; 51/2342 *Electra*, 1812; 51/2384 *Forward*, 1810; 51/2382 *Franchise*, 1811; 51/2433 *Garland*, 1813; 51/2007, 51/2425 *Gluckstadt*, 1808–11; 51/2529 *Goshawk*, 1810; 51/2439 *Griffon* 1809–18; 51/2457 *Horatio*, 1814; 51/2478 *Implacable*, 1810–11; 51/1686 *Inflexible*, 1807; 51/2511 *Jalouse*, 1811–13; 51/2485 *Jasper*, 1812; 51/2543 *Majestic* 1813–15; 51/1693 *Mermaid*, 1807; 51/1941 *Nereide* 1806–8; 51/1933 *Owen Glendower*, 1809; 51/2646 *Pheasant*, 1813; 51/4075 *Prince William*, 1804–6; 51/4032 *Providence*, 1804–12; 51/1524 *Regulus*, 1805–6; 51/1660 *Resistance*, 1806–7; 51/2777 *Revenge*, 1808–10; 51/1971, 2766 *Ringdove*, 1808–9, 1813; 51/2052 *Talbot*, 1811; 51/2914 *Thais*, 1812–15; 51/1494 *Trident* 1805; 51/2936 *Victorious*, 1813–14; 51/2966 *Warrior* 1807–8; 51/2968–9 *Wolverine*, 1811–14; 51/2980 *Wrangler*, 1809

Masters' Logs

ADM 52/3591 *Carysfort*, 1804; 52/3738 *Culloden* 1808–9

Victualling Board

ADM 109/104 In-letters concerning army victualling 1800–3

Courts Martial Registers

ADM 194/42, 1812–55

Foreign Office Papers

FO 36/2 Heligoland

Colonial Office Papers

CO 118/1–9 Correspondence relating to Heligoland 1808–14

National Maritime Museum (NMM), Greenwich, London

ADM/B/230 Navy Board Out-letters, 1808
HAW/9 Hawker Papers, Order book of Vice-Admiral Keats, *Bellerophon*, 1813–15
HNL/99/39–41 Michael Henley & Son Papers
KEI/28/79–85 Keith Papers, Letters received, 1804–7; KEI/30 *Cruizer* journal, 1805;
    KEI/L/165 Keith's Account with his agent, John Jackson
LBK/66 Letter book of Thomas Longstaff master of the *Ellice* transport, 1806–17
MRK/101/2 Markham Papers, correspondence with naval officers
NEP/7 Nepean Papers
YOR/2 Correspondence with Charles Philip Yorke, 1810–12

Gladstone's Library (GL) Hawarden, Flintshire

Glynne Gladstone Archive, papers of Sir John Gladstone

Guernsey State Archives (GSA) St Peter Port, Guernsey

Thomas Mansell Collection

Huntington Library (HL) San Marino, California

Stowe Grenville Collection, papers of Thomas Grenville ST/103, 158, officers' appointments

Northamptonshire Record Office (NRO) Northampton

Culworth Papers: Rye/X/7243–4, Peter Rye papers 1795–1845

Private Collection

Diaries of Thomas Bulley, fish merchant of Teignmouth Devon, 1809–16

Wellcome Library (Wellcome) London

Western Mss 3667, 3681, Nelson documents, 1803–5

Contemporary Publications

Pamphlets and Books

[Anon] 'Commander', *The State of the Navy of Great Britain in the Year 1831*

Brenton, Edward Pelham, *Life and Correspondence of John Earl St Vincent*, 2 vols (London: Henry Colburn, 1838)

Childers, Spencer, *A Mariner of England: An account of the career of William Richardson from cabin boy in the merchant service to warrant officer in the Royal Navy (1780 to 1819) as told by himself* (London, 1908; repr. Greenwich: Conway Maritime Press, 1970)

Coggeshall, George, *Thirty-six Voyages to Various Parts of the World* (New York, 1858, repr. London: MacDonald and Jane's, 1974)

Fernyhough, Thomas, *Military Memoirs of Four Brothers* (1829; repr. Staplehurst: Spellmount, 2002)

Hall Gower, Richard, *A Treatise on the Theory and Practice of Seamanship* (London: Wilkie and Robinson et al., 1808)

—, *Remarks relative to the Dangers Attendant on Convoys* (pamphlet, 1811)

Jefferson, Samuel, *Life in the Merchant Marine one hundred years ago* (Blackheath: privately printed, 1905)

Marsden, William, *A Brief Memoir of the Life of William Marsden, Written by Himself, with Notes from his Correspondence* (London: Privately published, 1838)

Marshall, John, *Royal Naval Biography*, 9 vols (London: Longman, 1827)

O'Byrne, William R., *A Naval Biographical Dictionary* (London: John Murray, 1849)

Parliamentary Papers

HCP, 1808, no. 81, *Minutes of Evidence on considering Petitions of Merchants and Manufacturers Select Committee on Marine Insurance*, 1810–11

HCP, 1821, no. 283, *Commission of Enquiry into the Departments of Customs and Excise, 7th–10th Reports*

Ralfe, J., *The Naval Biography of Great Britain*, 4 vols (London: Whitmore & Fenn, 1828)

Tooke, Thomas, *Thoughts and Details on the High and Low Prices of the last Thirty Years* (London, 1823)

Newspapers and Periodicals

Cobbett's Annual Register
Cobbett's Parliamentary Debates
Hull Packet
Lloyd's List
Naval Chronicle vols 10–36
The Times

Printed Primary Sources

Blake, Richard, ed., 'James Ramsay's *Essay* of 1780 on the Duty and Qualification of a Sea Officer', in Brian Vale, ed., *The Naval Miscellany*, vol. VIII (London: Navy Records Society, vol. 164, 2017, pp. 129–204)

Bonner-Smith, David, ed., *The Letters of Earl St Vincent, 1801–1804*, vol. 1 (London: Navy Records Society, vol. 55, 1921)

—, ed., *Recollections of my Sea Life from 1808 to 1830 by Captain John Harvey Boteler* (Navy Records Society, vol. 82, 1942)

Cohen, Clive, 'Brothers in War: George (1788–1847) and John (1790–1875) Luard: Paths to Waterloo', in Andrew Cormack, ed., *A Peninsular and Waterloo Anthology* (London: Society for Army Historical Research, Special Publications, no. 17, 2015), pp. 9–92

Collingwood, G. L. Newnham, ed., *A Selection from the Public and Private Correspondence of Vice-Admiral Lord Collingwood* (London: James Ridgeway, 5th edn, 1837)

Craig, Hardin, 'Letters of Lord St Vincent to Thomas Grenville, 1806–7', in Christopher Lloyd, ed., *The Naval Miscellany*, IV (London: Navy Records Society, 92, 1952), pp. 470–93

Crawford, Michael J., ed., *The Naval War of 1812: A Documentary History*, III, 1814–15 (Washington DC: Naval Historical Center, 2002)

Dudley, William S., *The Naval War of 1812: A Documentary History*, II (Washington DC: Naval Historical Center, 1992)

Gurwood, J., ed., *The Dispatches of Field-Marshall the Duke of Wellington*, 13 vols (London: John Murray, 1852)

Hamilton, Sir Richard Vesey, ed., *Journal and Letters of Admiral of the Fleet Sir Thomas Byam Martin*, vol. 3 (London: Navy Records Society, 24, 1902)

Hattendorf, John B., et al., eds, *British Naval Documents, 1204–1960* (London: Navy Records Society, vol. 131, 1993)

Hay, M.D., ed., *Landsman Hay: The Memoirs of Robert Hay, 1789–1847* (London: Rupert Hart-Davis, 1953)

Hughes, Edward, *The Private Correspondence of Admiral Lord Collingwood* (London: Navy Records Society, vol. 98, 1957)

Jennings, Louis J., ed., *The Croker Papers: The Correspondence and Diaries of the Rt. Honourable John Wilson Croker*, 3 vols (London: John Murray, 1885)

Larpent, Francis Seymour, *The Private Journal of Judge-Advocate Larpent* (Staplehurst: Spellmount Library, 2000)

Laughton, Sir John Knox, 'Extracts from the Journals of Thomas Addison, of the East India Company's Service, 1801–1830'; 'The Seizure of Helgoland', in Laughton, ed., *The Naval Miscellany* 1 (London: Navy Records Society, 20, 1902), pp. 335–74, 377–86

—, *Letters and Papers of Charles, Lord Barham, 1758–1813*, III (London: Navy Records Society, 29, 1911)

Lewis, Michael A., ed., *A Narrative of my Professional Adventures (1790–1839) by Sir William Henry Dillon*, vol. II (London: Navy Records Society, 97, 1956)

Liddell Hart, B.H., ed., *The Letters of Private Wheeler, 1809–1828* (London, Michael Joseph, 1951)

Lloyd, Christopher, ed., *The Keith Papers*, vols 2 & 3 (London: Navy Records Society, 90, 1950, vol. 96, 1955)

Markham, Sir Clements, ed., *The Correspondence of Admiral John Markham during the years 1801–4 and 1806–7* (London: Navy Records Society, 28, 1904)

Mercer, General Cavalie, *Journal of the Waterloo Campaign* (London: Peter Davies, 1927)

Merriman, R.D., *Queen Anne's Navy: Documents concerning the administration of the Navy of Queen Anne* (London: Navy Records Society, 103, 1961)

Mundy, Godfrey B., ed., *The Life and Correspondence of the late Admiral Lord Rodney*, 2 vols (London: John Murray, 1830; repr. 1972)

Nicolas, Nicholas Harris, ed., *The Dispatches and Letters of Vice-Admiral Lord Viscount Nelson*, 7 vols (London: Henry Colburn, 1846; repr. 1998)

Pool, Bernard, ed., *The Croker Papers, 1808–1857* (1887; repr. London: Batsford, 1967)

Rubinstein, Hilary L., ed., *The Durham Papers: Selections from the Papers of Admiral Sir Philip Charles Henderson Calderwood Durham (1763–1845)* (London: Navy Records Society, vol. 166, 2019)

Ryan, A.N., ed., *The Saumarez Papers: Selections from the Baltic Correspondence of Vice-Admiral Sir James Saumarez 1808–1812* (London: Navy Records Society, vol. 110, 1968)

Watt, Helen, and Anne Hawkins, eds, *Letters of Seamen in the Wars with France, 1793–1815* (Woodbridge: Boydell Press, 2016)

Wellesley, 2nd Duke of Wellington, ed., *Supplementary Despatches and Memoranda of Field-Marshall Arthur, Duke of Wellington, 1797–1818*, 14 vols (London: John Murray, 1858)

SECONDARY SOURCES

Aaslestad, Katherine B., and Johan Joor, eds, *Revisiting Napoleon's Continental System: Local, Regional and European Experiences* (Basingstoke: Palgrave Macmillan, 2015)

Aberg, Martin, 'Migration, civic culture and politics: British middle-class communities in Western Sweden, 1730–1900', in Patrick Salmon and Tony Barrow, eds, *Britain and the Baltic* (Sunderland: University of Sunderland Press, 2003), pp. 169–94

Adams, Andrew, and Richard Woodman, *Light Upon the Waters: The History of Trinity House, 1514–2014* (London: Corporation of Trinity House, 2013)

Agnarrdottir, Anna, 'The Challenge of War on Maritime Trade in the North Atlantic: The case of British Trade to Iceland during the Napoleonic Wars', in Olaf Uwe Janzen, ed., *Merchant Organization and Maritime Trade in the North Atlantic* (St John's Newfoundland: IMEHA, 1998), pp. 221–58

Aldous, Grahame, 'The Law Relating to the Distribution of Prize Money in the Royal Navy and its Relationship to the Use of Naval Power in War' (PhD, King's College, London, 2020)

Anderson, R.C., *Naval Wars in the Baltic during the Sailing Ship Epoch* (London: C. Gilbert-Wood, 1910)

—, *Naval Wars in the Levant, 1559–1853* (Liverpool: Liverpool University Press, 1953)

Andress, David, *The Savage Storm: Britain on the Brink in the Age of Napoleon* (London: Little, Brown, 2012)

Arthur, Brian, *How Britain Won the War of 1812: The Royal Navy's Blockades of the United States, 1812–1815* (Woodbridge: Boydell Press, 2011)

Astrom, Sven-Erik, 'English Timber Imports from Northern Europe in the Eighteenth Century', *Scandinavian Economic History Review*, 1970, 18, pp. 12–32

Avery, R.W., 'The Naval Protection of Britain's Maritime Trade, 1793–1802' (University of Oxford D. Phil thesis, 1983)

Bamford, Andrew, '"Injurious for the Service Generally": Finding Manpower for Northern Europe, 1813 & 1814', *Journal of the Society of Army Historical Research*, 90, 2012, pp. 25–43

Barney, John, 'North Sea and Baltic convoys, 1793–1814, as experienced by merchant masters employed by Michael Henley and Son', *Mariner's Mirror*, 95, 2009, pp. 429–40

Barton, Mark, 'Duelling in the Royal Navy', *Mariner's Mirror*, 100, 2014, pp. 282–306

Baugh, Daniel A., *Naval Administration in the Age of Walpole* (Princeton: Princeton University Press, 1965)

—, 'Admiral Sir Herbert Richmond and the Objects of Sea Power', in James Goldrick and John B. Hattendorf, eds, *Mahan is not Enough: The Proceedings of a Conference on the Works of Sir Julian Corbett and Admiral Sir Herbert Richmond* (Newport, Rhode Island: Naval War College Press, 1993), pp. 13–49

—, 'Maritime Strength and Atlantic Commerce: the uses of a "grand maritime empire"', in Lawrence Stone, ed., *An Imperial State at War: Britain from 1689 to 1815* (London and New York: Routledge, 1994), pp. 185–223

—, 'Naval Power: what gave the British navy superiority?', in Leandro de la Escosura, ed., *Exceptionalism and Industrialism: Britain and its European Rivals, 1688–1815* (Cambridge: Cambridge University Press, 2004), pp. 235–57

—, *The Global Seven Years War, 1754–1763: Britain and France in a Great Power Contest* (London: Longman, 2011)

Beck, Catherine, 'Patronage and insanity: tolerance, reputation and mental disorder in the British Navy, 1740–1820, *Historical Research*, 94, 2021, pp. 73–95

Bell, David A., *The First Total War: Napoleon's Europe and the Birth of Modern Warfare* (London, Bloomsbury, 2007)

Benjamin, Daniel K., 'Golden Harvest: The British Naval Prize System, 1793–1815' (unpublished paper, 2009), pp. 1–49

—, and Anca Tifrea, 'Learning by Dying: Combat Performance in the Age of Sail', *Journal of Economic History*, 7, 2007, pp. 968–1000

—, and Christopher Thornberg, 'Organization and incentives in the age of sail', *Explorations in Economic History*, 44, 2007, pp. 317–41

Bibbings, Martin, '"An Awkward Engine": Captain Philip Broke's troublesome relationship with the carronade', *Mariner's Mirror*, 102, 2016, pp. 303–24

Blakemore, Richard J., and Elaine Murphy, *The British Civil Wars at Sea, 1638–1653* (Woodbridge: Boydell Press, 2018)

Bourguignon, Henry J., *Sir William Scott, Lord Stowell, Judge of the High Court of Admiralty, 1798–1828* (Cambridge: Cambridge University Press, 1987)

BIBLIOGRAPHY

Bowen, H.V., *The Business of Empire: The East India Company and Imperial Britain, 1756–1833* (Cambridge: Cambridge University Press, 2006)

—, 'Trading with the enemy: British private trade and the supply of arms to India ca 1750–1820', in Richard Harding and Sergio Solbes Ferri, eds, *The Contractor State and its Implications, 1659–1815* (Las Palmas de Gran Canaria: Universidad de las Palmas de Gran Canaria, 2012), pp. 35–56

—, 'The Shipping Losses of the British East India Company, 1750–1813', *International Journal of Maritime History,* 32, 2020, pp. 323–36

Brightfield, Myron F., *John Wilson Croker* (Berkeley, CA: University of California Press, 1940)

Bromley, J.S., *Corsairs and Navies, 1660–1760* (London: Hambledon Press, 1987)

Brown, D.K., 'Atlantic Escorts, 1939–1945', in Stephen Howarth and Derek Laws, eds, *The Battle of the Atlantic, 1939–1945: The 50th Anniversary International Naval Conference* (London: Greenhill Books, 1994)

Brunsman, Denver, *The Evil Necessity: British Naval Impressment in the Eighteenth-Century Atlantic World* (Charlottesville, VA: University of Virginia Press, 2013)

Bulley, Anne, *The Bombay Country Ships, 1790–1833* (Richmond: Curzon, 2000)

Bunbury, Henry, *Narratives of Some Passages in the Great War with France from 1799 to 1810* (London: Richard Bentley, 1854)

Burnham, Robert, 'Filling the Ranks: How Wellington kept his Units up to strength', in Rory Muir et al., eds, *Inside Wellington's Peninsular Army, 1808–1814* (Barnsley: Pen & Sword, 2006), pp. 201–25

—, and Ron McGuigan, *The British Army against Napoleon, 1805–1815* (Barnsley: Frontline Books, 2010)

Capp, Bernard, *Cromwell's Navy: the Fleet and the English Revolution, 1648–1660* (Oxford: Clarendon Press, 1989)

Caputo, Sara, 'Towards a Transnational History of the Eighteenth-Century British Navy', *Annales Historiques de la Révolution français,* 397, 2019, pp. 13–32

—, 'Alien Seamen in the British Navy, British Law, and the British State, ca. 1792–c1815', *Historical Journal,* 2019, pp. 685–707

Chandler, David, *Dictionary of the Napoleonic Wars* (New York: Simon & Schuster, 1993)

Clammer, David, 'Women All at Sea: Soldiers' Wives aboard Naval Transports during the Napoleonic War, *The Trafalgar Chronicle,* New Series 3, 2018, pp. 55–66

Clark, G.N., *The Dutch Alliance and the War against French Trade, 1688–1697* (Manchester: Manchester University Press, 1923)

Coad, Jonathan, *Support for the Fleet: Architecture and Engineering of the Royal Navy's Bases, 1700–1914* (London: English Heritage, 2013)

Coggeshall, George, *History of the American Privateers and Letters of Marque during our War with England in the years 1812, '13 and '14* (New York: published by the author, 1856)

Cole, Gareth, *Arming the Royal Navy, 1793–1815* (London: Pickering & Chatto, 2012)

Colville, John, *The Portrait of a General* (Salisbury: Michael Russell, 1980)

Consolvo, Charles, 'The Prospects and Promotion of British Naval Officers, 1793–1815', *Mariner's Mirror,* 91, 2005, pp. 137–59

Coote, J.O., *The Shell Pilot to the English Channel,* 2 vols (London: Faber and Faber, 1990)

Corbett, Julian S., *England in the Seven Years War: A Study in Combined Strategy,* 2 vols (London: Longmans, Green, 1907)

—, *Some Principles of Naval Strategy* (London: Longmans, Green, 1911)

—, 'Napoleon and the British Navy after Trafalgar', *Quarterly Review,* 1922, pp. 238–55

Cordingly, David, *Billy Ruffian: The Bellerophon and the Downfall of Napoleon: The biography of a ship of the line, 1782–1836* (London: Bloomsbury, 2003)

Cotton, Sir Evan, *East Indiamen: The East India Company's Maritime Service* (London: Batchworth Press, 1949)

Crimmin, Patricia, 'The Impact of the Exchange of Prisoners on the Defence of Shipping in the Americas, 1812–14', in Clark G. Reynolds, ed., *Global Crossroads: The American Seas* (Missoula, MT: Pictorial History Publications, 1998), pp. 145–54

—, 'Sir Thomas Troubridge', in Richard Harding and Peter Lefevre, eds, *British Admirals of the Napoleonic Wars: The Contemporaries of Nelson* (London: Chatham Publishing, 2005), pp. 295–321

Crosby, Alfred W., *America, Russia, Hemp and Napoleon: American Trade with Russia and the Baltic, 1783–1812* (Columbia, OH: State University Press, 1965)

Crouzet, François, 'The British Economy at the time of Trafalgar: Strength and Weaknesses', in David Cannadine, ed., *Trafalgar in History: A Battle and its Afterlife* (Basingstoke: Palgrave Macmillan, 2006), pp. 7–17

Crowhurst, Patrick, 'The Admiralty and the Convoy System in the Seven Years War', *Mariner's Mirror*, 57, 1971, pp. 163–73

—, *The Defence of British Trade, 1689–1815* (Folkestone: Dawson, 1977)

—, *The French War on Trade: Privateering, 1793–1815* (Aldershot: Scolar Press, 1989)

—, 'Experience, Skill and Luck: French Privateering Expeditions, 1792–1815', in David J. Starkey et al., eds, *Pirates and Privateers: New Perspectives on the War on Trade in the Eighteenth and Nineteenth Centuries* (Exeter: University of Exeter Press, 1997), pp. 155–170

Crumplin, Michael, *Guthrie's War: A surgeon of the Peninsular War and Waterloo* (Barnsley: Pen & Sword, 2010)

Currie, Ann, *Henley's of Wapping: A London Shipowning Family, 1770–1830* (London: National Maritime Museum, 1988)

D'Andrea, Diletta, 'Great Britain and the Mediterranean Islands in the Napoleonic Wars – the Insular Strategy of Gould Francis Leckie', *Journal of Mediterranean Studies*, 16, 2006, pp. 79–90

Dancy, J. Ross., *The Myth of the Press Gang: Volunteers, Impressment and the Naval Manpower Problem in the Eighteenth Century* (Woodbridge: Boydell Press, 2015)

—, 'British Naval Administration and the Lower Deck Manpower Problem in the Eighteenth Century', in N.A.M. Rodger et al., eds, *Strategy and the Sea: Essays in Honour of John B. Hattendorf* (Woodbridge: Boydell Press, 2016), pp. 49–63

—, 'Sources and Methods in the British Impressment debate', *International Journal of Maritime History*, 30, 2018, pp. 733–46

Dann, John C., *The Nagle Journal: A diary of the life of Jacob Nagle, sailor, from the year 1778 to 1841* (New York: Weidenfeld & Nicolson, 1988)

Davey, James, 'The Repatriation of Spanish Soldiers from Denmark: The British Government, Logistics and Maritime Strategy', *Journal of Military History*, vol. 74, 2010, pp. 689–707

—, 'Securing the Sinews of Sea-power: British Intervention in the Baltic, 1780–1815', *International History Review*, vol. 33, 2011, pp. 161–84

—, 'The Advancement of Nautical Knowledge: The Hydrographical Office, the Royal Navy and the Charting of the Baltic Sea, 1795–1815', *Journal of Maritime Research*, vol. 13, 2011, pp. 81–103

—, 'Supplied by the Enemy: The Royal Navy and the British Consular Service in the Baltic, 1808–1812', *Historical Research*, vol. 85, 2012, pp. 265–83

—, *The Transformation of British Naval Strategy: Seapower and Supply in Northern Europe, 1808–1812* (Woodbridge: Boydell, 2012)

—, *In Nelson's Wake: The Navy and the Napoleonic Wars* (New Haven and London: Yale University Press, 2015)

—, 'Atlantic Empire, European War and the Naval Expeditions to South America, 1806–7', in John McAleer and Christer Petley, *The Royal Navy and the British Atlantic World, ca 1750–1820* (London: Palgrave Macmillan, 2016), pp. 147–72

—, 'Serving the State: Empire, Expertise and the British Hemp Crisis of 1800–01', *Journal of Imperial and Commonwealth History*, 46, 2018, pp. 651–75

—, 'Britain's European Island Empire, 1793–1815', in Douglas Hamilton and John McAleer, *Islands and the British Empire in the Age of Sail: Oxford History of the British Empire* (Oxford: Oxford University Press, 2021), pp. 35–54

Davies, Huw J., *Wellington's Wars: The Making of a Military Genius* (London and New Haven: Yale University Press, 2012)

Davies, J.D., *Gentlemen and Tarpaulins: The Officers and Men of the Restoration Navy* (Oxford: Clarendon Press, 1991)

Davis, Ralph, *The Rise of the English Shipping Industry in the 17th and 18th Centuries* (1962; repr. Newton Abbott: David and Charles, 1972)

—, *The Industrial Revolution and British Overseas Trade* (Leicester: Leicester University Press, 1979)

Day, John, 'Securing an Ocean for an Empire: British Naval Bases and the Eastern Seas, 1784–1824', *Transactions of the Naval Dockyards Society*, 13, 2020, pp. 54–66

Dickson, David, *Old World Colony: Cork and South Munster, 1630–1830* (Cork: Cork University Press, 2005)

Dowling, C., 'The Convoy System and the West Indian trade, 1803–1815' (University of Oxford D. Phil. thesis, 1965)

Duffy, Michael, *Soldiers, Sugar and Seapower: The British Expeditions to the West Indies and the War against Revolutionary France* (Oxford: Clarendon Press, 1987)

—, 'World-wide War, 1793–1815', in P.J. Marshall, ed., *The Eighteenth Century: The Oxford History of the British Empire* (Oxford: Oxford University Press, 1998), pp. 184–207

—, 'Festering the Spanish Ulcer: The Royal Navy and the Peninsular War, 1806–1814', in Bruce A. Ellerman and S.C.M. Paine, eds, *Naval Power and Expeditionary Warfare: Peripheral Campaigns and New Theatres of Naval Warfare* (London, 2010), pp.15–28

Dull, Jonathan R., *The Age of the Ship of the Line: The British & French Navies, 1650–1815* (Barnsley: Seaforth, 2000)

Dunn, Richard, and Rebekah Higgit, *Ships, Clocks & Stars: The Quest for Longitude* (Glasgow: Collins, 2014)

Dunne, William M.P., and Frederick C. Leiner, 'An "Appearance of Menace": The Royal Navy's Incursion in New York Bay, September 1807', *Log of Mystic Seaport*, 44, 1993, pp. 86–92

Dziennik, Matthew P., 'The Fiscal-Military State and Labour in the British Atlantic World', in Aaron Graham and Patrick Walsh, eds, *The British Fiscal-Military States, 1660–c.1783* (London and New York: Routledge, 2016), pp. 159–177

Edwards, Michael M., *The Growth of the British Cotton Trade, 1780–1815* (New York: Augustus M. Kelly, 1967)

Ehrman, John, *The Navy in the War of William III, 1689–1697: Its State and Direction* (Cambridge: Cambridge University Press, 1953)

—, *The Younger Pitt:* vol. 1, *The Years of Acclaim;* vol. 2, *The Reluctant Transition;* vol. 3, *The Consuming Struggle* (London: Constable, 1969, 1983, 1996)

Ellerman, Bruce, and S. Paine, eds, *Naval Blockades and Seapower: Strategy and Counter-Strategies, 1805–2005* (London and New York: Routledge, 2006)

—, *Commerce Raiding: Historical Case Studies, 1755–2009* (U.S. Naval War College Proceedings, 2009)

Esdaile, Charles, *The Peninsular War* (London: Allen Lane, 2002)

—, *Napoleon's Wars: An International History 1803–1815* (London: Penguin, 2008)

Fayle, C. Ernest, 'Shipowning and Marine Insurance' and 'The Employment of British Shipping', in C. Northcote Parkinson, ed., *The Trade Winds: A study of British Overseas Trade during the French Wars, 1793–1815* (London: Allen & Unwin, 1948), pp. 25–48, 72–86

Feldbaek, Ole, 'Denmark-Norway 1720–1807: Neutral Principle and Practice', in Rolf Hobson and Tom Kristiansen, eds, *Navies in Northern Waters, 1721–2000* (London: Frank Cass, 2004)

Flayhart, William Henry, *Counterpoint to Trafalgar: The Anglo-Russian Invasion of Naples, 1805–1806* (Columbia: University of South Carolina, 1992)

Fletcher, Ian, *The Waters of Oblivion: The British Invasion of the Rio de la Plata 1806–7* (Stroud: Spellmount, 2006)

Forrest, Alan, *Great Battles: Waterloo* (Oxford: Oxford University Press, 2015)

Fox, Frank, 'Hired Men-of-War, 1664–67', parts I & II, *Mariner's Mirror*, vol. 84, 1998, pp. 13–15, 152–72

Foynes, Julian, *East Anglia Against the Tricolor, 1789–1815: An English Region Against Revolutionary and Napoleonic France* (Cromer: Poppyland Publishing, 2016)

Galani, Katerina, *British Shipping in the Mediterranean during the Napoleonic Wars: The Untold Story of a Successful Adaptation* (Leiden: Brill, 2017)

Galpin, W. Freeman, *The Grain Supply of England during the Napoleonic Period* (1925; repr. New York: Octagon Books, 1977)

Gannon, Michael, *Operation Drumbeat: The Dramatic, True Story of Germany's First U-boat Attacks along the American Coast in World War II* (New York: Harper & Row, 1990)

Gardiner, Robert, *Frigates of the Napoleonic War* (London: Chatham Publishing, 2000)

Gillett, Edward, *A History of Grimsby* (Oxford: Oxford University Press, 1970

—, *A History of Hull* (Hull: Hull University Press, 1980

Glenthøj, Rasmus, and Morten Nordhagen Ottosen, *Experiences of War and Nationality in Denmark and Norway, 1807–1815* (Basingstoke: Palgrave Macmillan, 2014)

Glete, Jan, *Navies and Nations: Warships, Navies and State Building in Europe and America, 1500–1860*, 2 vols (Stockholm: Almqvist and Wiksell International, 1993)

—, *Warfare at Sea, 1500–1650: Maritime Conflicts and the Transformation of Europe* (London: Routledge, 2000)

Glover, Gareth, *From Corunna to Waterloo: The letters and journals of Two Napoleonic Hussars, 1801–1816* (London: Greenhill Books, 2007)

—, *The Two Battles of Copenhagen, 1801 and 1807: Britain and Denmark in the Napoleonic Wars* (Barnsley: Pen & Sword, 2018)

Gordon, Iain, *Admiral of the Blue: The Life and Times of Admiral John Child Purvis, 1747–1825* (Barnsley: Pen & Sword, 2005)

Gough, Barry M., 'Specie Conveyance from the West Coast of Mexico, c.1820–1870: An Aspect of Pax Britannia', *Mariner's Mirror*, 69, 1983, pp. 419–33

Gradish, Stephen, *The Manning of the British Navy during the Seven Years War* (London: Royal Historical Society, 1980)

Graham, Gerald, *Empire of the North Atlantic: The Maritime Struggle for North America* (Toronto and Oxford: University of Toronto Press, Oxford University Press, 1950 and 1958)

Gray, Ernest A., *The Trumpet of Glory: The military career of John Shipp, the first veterinary surgeon to join the British army* (London: Robert Hale, 1985)

Gretton, Vice-Admiral Sir Peter, *Convoy Escort Commander* (London: Cassell, 1964)

Grocott, Terence, *Shipwrecks of the Revolutionary and Napoleonic Eras* (London: Chatham Publishing, 1997)

Gutridge, Tony, 'Aspects of Naval Prize Agency, 1793–1815', *Mariner's Mirror*, 80, 1994, pp. 45–53

—, 'George Redmond Hulbert: Prize Agent at Halifax, Nova Scotia, 1812–14', *Mariner's Mirror*, 87, 2001, pp. 30–42

Gwyn, Julian, *Frigates and Foremasts: The North American Squadron in Nova Scotia Waters, 1745–1815* (Vancouver: University of British Columbia Press, 2003)

—, *Ashore and Afloat: The British Navy and Halifax Naval Yard before 1820* (Ottawa: University of Ottawa Press, 2004)

Hall, Christopher D., *British Strategy in the Napoleonic War, 1803–15* (Manchester: Manchester University Press, 1992)

—, 'The Royal Navy and the Peninsular War', *Mariner's Mirror*, 79, 1993, pp. 403–18

—, *Wellington's Navy: Sea Power and the Peninsular War, 1807–1814* (London: Chatham Publishing, 2004)

Hamilton, C.I., 'John Wilson Croker: Patronage and Clientage at the Admiralty, 1809–1857', *Historical Journal*, 43, 2000, pp. 49–77

—, *The Making of the Modern Admiralty: British Naval Policy-making, 1805–1927* (Cambridge: Cambridge University Press, 2011)

Hancock, David, *Citizens of the World* (Cambridge: Cambridge University Press, 1995)

Harding, Richard, *Amphibious Warfare in the Eighteenth Century: The British Expeditions to the West Indies, 1740–1742* (London: Royal Historical Society, 1991)

—, *Seapower and Naval Warfare, 1650–1830* (London: UCL Press, 1999)

—, 'Expeditionary Armies and Naval Power: The North German Campaign of 1805–6', *Trafalgar Chronicle*, 15, 2005, p. 63–74

—, *The Emergence of Britain's Global Naval Supremacy: The War of 1739–1748* (Woodbridge: Boydell Press, 2010)

Harland, John, *Seamanship in the Age of Sail* (London: Conway Maritime Press, 1984)

Hattendorf, John B., *England in the War of Spanish Succession: A study in the English View and Conduct of Grand Strategy, 1701–1713* (New York and London: Garland Publishing, 1987)

—, 'Seapower as control: British defensive naval strategy in the Mediterranean, 1793–1815', French conference proceedings in *Français et Anglaise en Meditérranée, 1789–1830* (Vincennes: Service Historique de la Marine, 1991), pp. 203–20

—, 'The Royal Navy and Economic Warfare against the United States during the War of 1812', in David Morgan-Owen and Louis Halewood, eds, *Economic Warfare and the Sea: Grand Strategies for Maritime Powers, 1650–1945* (Liverpool: Liverpool University Press, 2020), pp. 137–56

Henderson, James, *The Frigates: An Account of the Lesser Warships of the Wars from 1793 to 1815* (London, 1970) and *Sloops and Brigs: An Account of the Smallest Vessels of the Royal Navy during the Great Wars 1793 to 1815* (London, 1972) (Two books combined, published in Barnsley: Pen & Sword, 2005)

Hepper, David J., *British Warship Losses in the Age of Sail, 1650–1859* (Rotherfield: Jean Boudriot Publications, 1994)

Hewitt, Nick, *Coastal Convoys, 1939–1945: The Indestructible Highway* (Barnsley: Pen & Sword Maritime, 2008)

Higgins, David, *Springboard to Victory: Great Yarmouth and the Royal Navy's Dominance in the North Sea and Baltic during the French Wars* (King's Lynn: Phoenix Publications, 2020)

Hill, Richard, *The Prizes of War: The Naval Prize System in the Napoleonic Wars, 1793–1815* (Stroud: Sutton Publishing, 1998)

Hilton, Boyd, *A Mad, Bad & Dangerous People? England, 1783–1846* (Oxford: Oxford University Press, 2006)

Hornstein, Sari R., *The Restoration Navy and English Foreign Trade, 1674–1688* (Aldershot: Scolar Press, 1991)

Horsfall, Lucy Frances, 'The West Indian Trade', in C. Northcote Parkinson, ed., *The Trade Winds: A Study in British Overseas Trade during the French Wars, 1793–1815* (London: Allen & Unwin, 1948), pp. 157–93

Howard, Martin R., *Walcheren, 1809: The Scandalous Destruction of the British Army* (Barnsley: Pen & Sword, 2012)

Hughes, Edward, *The Private Correspondence of Admiral Lord Collingwood* (London: Navy Records Society, 98, 1957)

Hylton, Lord, *The Paget Brothers, 1780–1840* (London: John Murray, 1918)

Jackson, Gordon, *Grimsby and the Haven Company, 1796–1846* (Grimsby Public Libraries, 1971)

—, *Hull in the Eighteenth Century* (Oxford: Oxford University Press, 1972)

Jaffer, Aaron, *Lascars and Indian Ocean Seafaring, 1780–1860: Shipboard Life, Unrest and Mutiny* (Woodbridge: Boydell Press, 2015)

James, William, *The Naval History of Great Britain*, 6 vols (London: Baldwin, Cradock and Joy, 1822–3; Richard Bentley & Son, 1878 edn)

—, *Naval Occurrences of the War of 1812* (London, 1817; repr. Conway Maritime Press, 2004)

Jennings, Louis J., *The Correspondence and Diaries of the late Right Honourable John Wilson Croker*, 3 vols (London: John Murray, 1885)

Jepsen, Palle Uhd, *The Last Voyage* (Ulfborg, Denmark: Holstebro Municipality, 2019)

Kaplan, Herbert H., *Nathan Mayer Rothschild and the Creation of a Dynasty: The Critical Years, 1806–1816* (Stanford, CA: Stanford University Press, 2006)

Kennedy, P.M., *The Rise and Fall of British Naval Mastery* (London: Allen Lane, 1976)

Kert, Faye M., *Privateering: Patriots and Profits in the War of 1812* (Baltimore: Johns Hopkins University Press, 2015)

Kingston, Christopher, 'America 1720–1820', in A.B. Leonard, *Marine Insurance: Origins and Institutions, 1300–1850* (Basingstoke: Palgrave Macmillan, 2016), pp. 205–26

Knight, Jane, 'Nelson and the Eastern Mediterranean, 1803–5', *Mariner's Mirror*, 91, 2005, pp. 195–215

Knight, Roger, *The Pursuit of Victory: The Life and Achievement of Horatio Nelson* (London: Allen Lane, 2005)

—, 'The Fleets at Trafalgar: The Margin of Superiority', in David Cannadine, ed., *Trafalgar in History: A Battle and its Afterlife* (Basingstoke: Palgrave Macmillan, 2006), pp. 61–77

—, *Britain Against Napoleon: The Organization of Victory, 1793–1815* (London: Allen Lane, 2013)

—, 'British Defensive Strategy at Sea in the War against Napoleon', in N.A.M. Rodger et al, eds, *Strategy and the Sea, Essays in honour of John B. Hattendorf* (Woodbridge: Boydell Press, 2016), pp. 88–97

—, 'The Achievement and Cost of the British Convoy System, 1803–1815', in David Morgan-Owen and Louis Halewood, eds, *Economic Warfare and the Sea* (Liverpool: Liverpool University Press, 2020), pp. 121–36

—, 'British North Atlantic Convoys, 1812–1814, and the Subsequent Rejection of the Convoy System', in Paul Kennedy and Evan Wilson, eds, *Navies in Multipolar Worlds: From the Age of Sail to the Present* (Abingdon and New York: Routledge, 2021), pp. 47–61

—, and Wilcox, Martin, *Sustaining the Fleet: War, the British Navy and the Contractor State* (Woodbridge: Boydell & Brewer, 2010)

Krajeski, Paul C., *In the Shadow of Nelson: The Naval Leadership of Admiral Sir Charles Cotton, 1753–1812* (London and Westport, CT: Greenwood Press, 2000)

Kruk, Sue, 'In Search of the *Queen* transport', *Troze* (online journal of the National Maritime Museum, Cornwall), 4, 2013, pp. 1–17

Lahari, Shompa, 'Contested Relations: The East India Company and Lascars in London', in H.V. Bowen, Margarette Lincoln and Nigel Rigby, eds, *The Worlds of the East India Company* (Woodbridge: Boydell Press, 2002), pp. 169–81

Lambert, Andrew, *The Challenge: America, Britain and the War of 1812* (London: Faber and Faber, 2012)

Leonard, A.B., 'Underwriting Marine Warfare: Insurance and Conflict in the Eighteenth Century', *International Journal of Maritime History*, XXV, 2013, pp. 173–85

—, ed., *Marine Insurance: Origins and Institutions, 1300–1850* (Basingstoke: Palgrave Macmillan, 2016)

Lewis, Michael, ed., *A Narrative of my Professional Adventures (1790–1839) by Sir William Henry Dillon K.C.H., Vice-Admiral of the Red*, vol. II, 1802–1839 (London: Navy Records Society, vol. 97, 1956)

—, *A Social History of the Navy, 1793–1815* (London: George Allen & Unwin, 1960)

—, *The Navy in Transition, 1814–1864: A Social History* (London: Hodder and Stoughton, 1965)

Lieven, Dominic, *Russia against Napoleon: The Battle for Europe, 1807 to 1814* (London: Penguin, 2009)

Lohnes, Barry J., 'British Naval Problems at Halifax during the War of 1812', *Mariner's Mirror*, 59, 1973, pp. 317–33

Lower, Arthur R.M., *Great Britain's Woodyard: British America and the Timber Trade, 1763–1867* (Montreal and London: McGill-Queen's University Press, 1973)

Luecke, Mirelle, 'American Tars: Impressment, citizenship and labour in early Republican New York City', *International Journal of Maritime History*, 30, 2018, pp. 663–80

Lyon, David, *The Sailing Navy List: All the Ships of the Royal Navy: Built, Purchased, Captured, 1688–1860* (London: Conway Maritime Press, 1993)

—, 'The British Order of Battle', in Stephen Howarth and Derek Law, eds, *The Battle of the Atlantic 1939–1945: The 50th Anniversary International Naval Conference* (London: Greenhill Books, 1994), pp. 266–75

—, and Rif Winfield, *The Sail & Steam Navy List: All the Ships of the Royal Navy, 1815–1889* (London: Chatham Publishing, 2004)

McAleer, John, 'The Route to the East's Atlantic Islands and Britain's Maritime Empire', in Douglas Hamilton and John McAleer, eds, *Islands and the British Empire in the Age of Sail: Oxford History of the British Empire* (Oxford: Oxford University Press, 2021)

McCarthy, Matthew, *Privateering, Piracy and British Policy in Spanish America, 1810–1830* (Woodbridge: Boydell Press, 2013)

McCranie, Kevin D., *Admiral Lord Keith and the Naval War against Napoleon* (Gainesville, FL: University Press of Florida, 2006)

—, 'The War of 1812 in the Ongoing Napoleonic Wars: The Response of Britain's Royal Navy', *Journal of Military History*, 76, October 2012, pp. 1067–94

—, 'Obstinate and Audacious' (*Prince de Neufchatel*), *Naval History*, 2014, pp. 22–7

Macdonald, Janet, 'The Victualling yard at Gibraltar and its role in feeding the Royal Navy in the Mediterranean during the Revolutionary and Napoleonic Wars', *Transactions of the Naval Dockyard Society*, 2, 2006, pp. 55–66

MacDougall, Philip, 'Malta Dockyard, 1800–1815: The Formative Years', *Mariner's Mirror*, 76, 1990, pp. 205–13

MacInnes, C.M., 'The Slave Trade', in C. Northcote Parkinson, ed., *The Trade Winds: A study of British Overseas Trade during the French Wars, 1793–1815* (London: Allen and Unwin, 1948), pp. 251–77

Mackesy, Piers, *The War in the Mediterranean, 1803–1810* (London: Longmans, 1957)

—, *The War for America, 1775–1783* (Cambridge, MA: Harvard University Press, 1965)

McLeod, A.B., *British Naval Captains of the Seven Years' War: The view from the Quarterdeck* (Woodbridge: Boydell Press, 2012)

Magra, Christopher, *Poseidon's Curse: British Naval Impressment and Atlantic Origins of the American Revolution* (Cambridge: Cambridge University Press, 2016)

Mahan, Alfred Thayer, *The Influence of Sea Power upon the French Revolution and Empire, 1793–1812*, 2 vols (London: Sampson, Low, Marston, 1893)

—, *Sea Power in its relations to the War of 1812*, 2 vols (Boston: Sampson, Low, Marston, 1905)

Malcolmson, Thomas, *Order and Disorder in the British Navy, 1793–1815: Control, Resistance, Flogging and Hanging* (Woodbridge: Boydell Press, 2016)

Marcus, G.J., *A Naval History of England: The Age of Nelson*, vol. II (Sheffield: Applebaum, 1971)

Marder, Arthur J., *From the Dardanelles to Oran: Studies of the Royal Navy in War and Peace, 1915–1940* (London: Oxford University Press, 1974)

Marichal, Carlos, *Bankruptcy of Empire: Mexican Silver and the Wars between Spain, Britain and France, 1760–1810* (Cambridge: Cambridge University Press, 2007)

Marshall, P.J., *The Eighteenth Century: The Oxford History of the British Empire*, II (Oxford: Oxford University Press, 1998)

Marzagalli, Silvia, 'A Vital Link in Wartime: The Organization of a Trade and Shipping Network between the United States and Bordeaux, 1793–1815', in Olaf Uwe Janzen, ed., *Merchant Organization and Maritime Trade in the North Atlantic, 1660–1815* (St John's Newfoundland: IMEHA, 1998), pp. 199–219

—, 'Napoleon's Continental Blockade: An Effective Substitute to Naval Weakness?', in Bruce A. Elleman and S.C.M. Paine, eds, *Naval Blockades and Seapower: Strategies and Counter-Strategies, 1805–2005* (London and New York: Routledge, 2006), pp. 25–34

—, 'The Continental System: A view from the Sea', in Katherine B. Aaslestad and Johan Joor, eds, *Revisiting Napoleon's Continental System: Local, Regional and European Experiences* (Basingstoke: Palgrave Macmillan, 2015), pp. 83–97

—, ' "However illegal, extraordinary or almost incredible such conduct might be": American and neutrality issues in the Mediterranean during the French Wars', *International Journal of Maritime History*, 28, 2016, pp. 118–32

—, 'Sea Power and Neutrality: The American Experience in Europe during the French Wars, 1793–1812', in David Morgan-Owen and Louis Halewood, eds, *Economic Warfare and the Sea: Grand Strategies for Maritime Powers* (Liverpool: Liverpool University Press, 2020), pp. 101–20

—, and Leos Muller, ' "In apparent disagreement with all law of nations in the world": Negotiating neutrality for shipping and trade during the French Revolutionary and Napoleonic Wars', *International Journal of Maritime History*, 28, 2016, pp. 108–17

Mawdsley, Evan, *The War for the Seas: A Maritime History of World War II* (New Haven and London: Yale University Press, 2019)

Mead, Hilary, 'Admiralty Telegraphs and Semaphores', *Mariner's Mirror*, 1938, 24, pp. 200–203

Mitchell, B.R., and Phyllis Deane, *Abstract of British Historical Statistics* (Cambridge: Cambridge University Press, 1962)

Morriss, Roger, *The Royal Dockyards during the Revolutionary and Napoleonic Wars* (Leicester: Leicester University Press, 1983)

—, *The Foundations of British Maritime Ascendancy* (Cambridge: Cambridge University Press, 2011)

—, *Science, Utility and British Naval Technology, 1793–1815: Samuel Bentham and the Royal Dockyards* (London, Routledge, 2020)

Morrow, John, *British Flag Officers in the French Wars, 1793–1815: Admirals' Lives* (London: Bloomsbury Academic, 2018)

Mui, Hoh-cheung, and Lorna H. Mui, *The Management of Monopoly: A Study of the East India Company's Conduct of its Tea Trade, 1784–1833* (Vancouver: University of British Columbia Press, 1984)

Muir, Rory, *Britain and the Defeat of Napoleon, 1807–1815* (New Haven and London: Yale University Press, 1996)

—, *Wellington: The Path to Victory, 1769–1814* (New Haven and London: Yale University Press, 2013)

Murfett, Malcolm, *Naval Warfare, 1919–1945: An operational history of the volatile war at sea* (London and New York: Routledge, 2009)

O'Brien, Patrick Karl, and Xavier Duran, 'Total Factor Productivity for the Royal Navy from Victory at Texel (1653) to Triumph at Trafalgar', in Richard W. Unger, ed., *Shipping and Economic Growth, 1350–1850* (Leiden: Brill, 2011), pp. 279–307

O'Keefe, Eamonn, 'The Old Halberdier: From the Pyrenees to Plattsburgh with a Welshman of the 39th Foot', *Journal of the Society of Army Historical Research*, 95, 2017, pp. 17–33

Olson, Mancur, *The Economics of Wartime Shortage: A History of British Food Supplies in the Napoleonic War and in World Wars I and II* (Durham, NC: Duke University Press, 1963)

Oman, Sir Charles, *A History of the Peninsular War*, 7 vols. (Oxford: Clarendon Press, 1902-30)

Ompteda, Baron L., *In the King's German Legion: Memoirs of Baron Ompteda, Colonel in the King's German Legion during the Napoleonic Wars* (London: Grevel & Co, 1894)

Page, Anthony, *Britain and the Seventy Years War, 1744–1815: Enlightenment, Revolution and Empire* (Basingstoke: Palgrave Macmillan, 2015)

Panzac, Daniel, *The Barbary Corsairs: The End of a Legend, 1800–1820* (Leiden: Brill, 2005)

Pares, Richard, *War and Trade in the West Indies, 1739–1763* (Oxford: Oxford University Press, 1936; London: Frank Cass, 1963)

Parkinson, Northcote C., *Trade in the Eastern Seas, 1793–1813* (Cambridge: Cambridge University Press, 1937)

—, 'The East India Trade', in Parkinson, ed., *The Trade Winds: A Study of British Overseas Trade during the French Wars 1793–1815* (London: George Allen and Unwin, 1948), pp. 141–56

—, *Samuel Waters, Lieutenant R.N.* (Liverpool: Liverpool University Press, 1949)

—, *War in the Eastern Seas, 1793–1815* (London: George Allen and Unwin, 1954)

—, *Britannia Rules: The Classic Age of Naval History* (London: Weidenfeld and Nicholson, 1977; repr. 1987)

Pearsall, Alan, 'The Royal Navy and Trade Protection, 1688–1714', *Renaissance and Modern Studies*, XXX, 1986, pp. 109–23

—, 'The Royal Navy and the Protection of Trade in the Eighteenth Century', *Guerres et Paix, 1660–1815* (Vincennes: Service Historique de la Marine, 1987), pp. 149–62

—, 'British Convoys in the North Sea, 1780–82', in Walter Minchinton, ed., *Britain in the Northern Seas* (Pontefract: Lofthouse, 1988), pp. 1–12

—, 'The Royal Navy and the Archangel Trade, 1702–14', in Poul Holm, Olaf Janzen and Jon Thor, eds, *Northern Seas Year Book 1996*, pp. 63–71

Petley, Christer, *Slaveholders in Jamaica: Colonial Society and Culture during the Era of Abolition* (London: Pickering and Chatto, 2009)

Petrie, Donald A., 'The Ransoming of *Eliza Swan*', *American Neptune*, 53, 1993, pp. 98–108

Pfaff, Steven, and Michael Hechter, *The Genesis of Rebellion: Governance, Grievance and Mutiny in the Age of Sail* (Cambridge: Cambridge University Press, 2020)

Philips, C.H., *The East India Company, 1784–1834* (Manchester: Manchester University Press, 1961)

Pietsch, Roland, 'Hearts of oak and jolly tars? Heroism and insanity in the Georgian navy', *Journal for Maritime Research*, 15, 2013, pp. 69–82

Prysor, Glyn, *Citizen Sailors: The Royal Navy in the Second World War* (London: Penguin, 2011)

Raash, A., 'American Trade in the Baltic, 1783–1807', *Scandinavian Economic History Review*, 13, 1965, pp. 31–64

Rayner, D.A., *Escort* (London: William Kimber, 1955)

Redford, A., *Manchester Merchants and Foreign Trade, 1794–1858* (Manchester: Manchester University Press, 1934)

Richardson, David, 'The British Empire and the Atlantic Slave Trade, 1660–1807', in P.J. Marshall, ed., *The Oxford History of the British Empire: The Eighteenth Century*, vol. II (Oxford: Oxford University Press, 1998), pp. 440–64

Richmond, H.W., *The Navy in the War of 1739–48* (Cambridge: Cambridge University Press, 1920)

—, *The Navy in India, 1763–1783* (London: Ernest Benn, 1931; repr. 1993)

—, *Imperial Defence and Capture at Sea in War* (London: Hutchinson, 1932)

—, *The Navy as an Instrument of Policy, 1558–1727* (Cambridge: Cambridge University Press, 1953)

Roberts, Andrew, *Napoleon the Great* (London: Allen Lane, 2014)

Robinson, R.E.R., *The Bloody Eleventh: History of the Devonshire Regiment*, vol. 1 (Exeter: Devonshire and Dorset Regiment, 1988)

Robson, Martin, *Britain, Portugal and South America in the Napoleonic Wars: Alliances and Diplomacy in Economic Maritime Conflict* (London and New York: I.B. Tauris, 2011)

—, 'The Destruction of the Danish Frigate *Najaden* at the Battle of Lyngor, 1812', *Mariner's Mirror*, 104, 2018, pp. 423–8

Rodger, N.A.M., *The Wooden World: An Anatomy of the Georgian Navy* (London: Collins, 1986)

—, *The Safeguard of the Sea: A Naval History of Great Britain* (London: HarperCollins, 1997)

—, 'Seapower and Empire, 1688–1793', in P.J. Marshall, ed., *The Eighteenth Century: The Oxford History of the British Empire* (Oxford: Oxford University Press, 1998), pp. 169–83

—, 'Weather, geography and naval power in the Age of Sail' (originally published in the *Journal of Strategic* Studies, 1999), reprinted in Rodger, *Essays in Naval History, from Medieval to Modern*, XII (Farnham: Ashgate 2009), pp. 178–200

—, 'Commissioned officers' careers in the Royal Navy, 1690–1815' (originally published in the *Journal for Maritime Research*, 2001), reprinted in Rodger, *Essays in Naval History, from Medieval to Modern*, XV (Farnham, Surrey: Ashgate, 2009), pp. 1–41

—, *The Command of the Ocean: A Naval History of Britain, 1649–1815* (London: Allen Lane, 2004)

—, 'The Significance of Trafalgar: Sea Power and Land Power in the Anglo-French Wars', in David Cannadine, ed., *Trafalgar in History: A Battle and its Afterlife* (Basingstoke: Palgrave Macmillan, 2006), pp.78–89

—, 'War as an Economic Activity in the "Long Eighteenth Century"', *International Journal of Maritime History*, 22, 2010, pp. 1–18

Rogers, Nicholas, *The Press Gang: Naval Impressment and its opponents in Georgian Britain* (London: Continuum UK, 2007)

—, 'British Impressment and its discontents', *International Journal of Maritime History*, 30, 2018, pp. 52–73

Roscoe, E.S., *Reports of Prize Cases determined in the High Court of Admiralty from 1745 to 1859* (London: Stevens and Sons, 1905)

Rose, J. Holland, 'British West Indies Commerce as a Factor in the Napoleonic War', *Historical Journal*, 3, 1929, pp. 34–46

Rüger, Jan, *Heligoland: Britain, Germany and the Struggle for the North Sea* (Oxford: Oxford University Press, 2017)

Rutter, Owen, *Red Ensign: A History of Convoy* (London: Robert Hale, 1942)

Ryan, A.N., 'The Defence of British Trade with the Baltic, 1808–1812', *English Historical Review*, 74, 1959, pp. 443–66

—, 'Documents relating to the Copenhagen operation, 1807', in N.A.M. Rodger, ed., *The Naval Miscellany*, V (London: Navy Records Society, vol. 125, 1984), pp. 297–329

Sanderson, M.W.B., 'English Naval Strategy and Maritime Trade in the Caribbean, 1793–1802' (London PhD, 1969)

Saunders, Andrew, *Fortress Britain: Artillery Fortifications in the British Isles and Ireland* (Liphook: Beaufort Publishing, 1989)

—, 'Upnor Castle and Gunpowder Supply to the Navy, 1801–4', *Mariner's Mirror*, 91, 2005, pp. 160–74

Schulte-Beerbuhl, Margrit, 'Crossing the Channel: Nathan Meyer Rothschild and his trade with the continent during the early years of the blockades (1803–1808)', *Rothschild Archive Review*, 2008, pp. 41–8

—, 'Trading Networks across the Blockades: Nathan Meyer Rothschild and his Commodity Trade during the Early Years of the Blockades (1803–1808)', in Katherine B. Aaslestad and Johan Joor, eds, *Revisiting Napoleon's Continental System: Local, Regional and European Experiences* (Basingstoke: Palgrave Macmillan, 2015), pp. 135–52

Sherwig, John M., *Guineas and Gunpowder: British Foreign Aid in the Wars with France, 1793–1815* (Cambridge, MA: Harvard University Press, 1969)

Smyth, W.H., *The Mediterranean: A Memoir Physical, Historical and Nautical* (London: John W. Parker and Son, 1854)

Solar, Peter, 'Opening to the East: Shipping between Europe and Asia, 1770–1830', *Journal of Economic History*, 73, 2013, pp. 625–61

—, 'Late eighteenth-century merchant ships in war and peace', *International Journal of Maritime History*, 28, 2016, pp. 36–73

Southam, Brian, *Jane Austen and the Navy* (London and New York: Hambledon and London, 2000)

Starkey, David J., *British Privateering Enterprise in the Eighteenth Century* (Exeter: University of Exeter Press, 1990)

—, 'War and the Market for Seafarers, 1736–1792', in Lewis R. Fischer and Helge W. Nordvik, eds, *Shipping and Trade, 1750–1950: Essays in International Maritime Economic History* (Pontefract: Lofthouse, 1990), pp. 25–42

—, 'A Restless Spirit: British Privateering Enterprise, 1739–45', in Starkey, E.S. van Eyck van Hesling and J.A. de Moor, *Pirates and Privateers: New Perspectives on the War on Trade in the Eighteenth and Nineteenth Centuries* (Exeter: Exeter University Press, 1997), pp. 126–40

Steele, Ian K., *The English Atlantic, 1675–1740: An exploration of communication and community* (New York and London: Oxford University Press, 1986)

Sutcliffe, Robert K., 'Bringing Forward Merchant Shipping for Government Service: The Indispensable Role of the Transport Service, 1793 to 1815' (PhD thesis, University of Greenwich, 2013)

—, *British Expeditionary Warfare and the Defeat of Napoleon, 1793–1815* (Woodbridge: Boydell Press, 2016)

—, 'From Bordeaux to Ostend: The Transport Service in 1814 and 1815 (unpubl. paper, 2015)

Sutton, Jean, *The East India Company's Maritime Service, 1746–1834* (Woodbridge: Boydell Press, 2010)

Syrett, David, 'The Organization of British Trade Convoys during the American War, 1775–1783', *Mariner's Mirror*, 62, 1976, pp. 169–81

—, *Shipping and the American War, 1775–83: A study of British Transport Organization* (London: Athlone Press, 1970)

—, *The Royal Navy in European Waters during the American Revolutionary War* (Columbia, SC: University of South Carolina Press, 1998)

—, *Shipping and Military Power in the Seven Years War: The Sails of Victory* (Exeter: University of Exeter Press, 2008)

—, and Richard Dinardo, *The Commissioned Sea Officers of the Royal Navy, 1660–1815* (London: Navy Records Society, 1994)

Taylor, Stephen, *Storm and Conquest: The Clash of Empires in the Eastern Seas, 1809* (New York and London: Norton, 2007)

—, *Commander: The Life and Exploits of Britain's Greatest Frigate Captain* (London: Faber and Faber, 2012)

—, *Sons of the Waves: The Common Seaman in the Heroic Age of Sail* (New Haven and London: Yale University Press, 2020)

Thorne, R.G., *The House of Commons, 1790–1820*, 5 vols (London: History of Parliament Trust, Secker & Warburg, 1986)

Tønnesson, J.N., *Kaperfart og skipsfart* [Privateering and Seaborne Trade] *1807–1814* (Oslo: J.W. Cappelens Forlag, 1955)

Unger, Richard W., 'Warships, Cargo Ships and Adam Smith: Trade and Government in the Eighteenth Century', *Mariner's Mirror*, 92, 2006, pp. 41–59

—, 'Channelling violence at sea: States, international trade and the transformation of naval forces from the high Middle Ages to the age of steam', *International Journal of Maritime History*, 31, 2019, 202–21

Vale, Brian and Griffith Edwards, *Physician to the Fleet: The Life and Times of Thomas Trotter, 1760–1832* (Woodbridge: Boydell Press, 2011)

Ville, Simon P., *English Shipowning during the Industrial Revolution: Michael Henley and Son, English Shipowners, 1770-1830* (Manchester: Manchester University press, 1987)

Villiers, Patrick, *La France sur Mer: De Louis XIII à Napoléon 1er* (Paris: Fayard/Pluriel, 2015)

Vine, P.A.L., *London's Lost Route to the Sea* (Dawlish: David & Charles, 1965)

Voelcker, Tim, *Admiral Saumarez versus Napoleon: The Baltic 1807–1812* (Woodbridge: Boydell Press, 2008)

—, 'The Battle of Lyngor, 1812', *Mariner's Mirror*, 105, 2019, pp. 88–91

Ward, J.R., 'The British West Indies in the Age of Abolition, 1748–1815', in P.J. Marshall, ed., *The Oxford History of the British Empire: The Eighteenth Century*, vol. II (Oxford: Oxford University Press, 1998), pp. 415–39

Ward, Peter, *British Naval Power in the East, 1794–1805: The Command of Admiral Peter Rainier* (Woodbridge: Boydell Press, 2013)

Wardle, A.C., 'The Newfoundland Trade', in C. Northcote Parkinson, ed. *The Trade Winds: A Study of British Overseas Trade during the French Wars* (London: George Allen & Unwin, 1948)

Wareham, Tom, *The Star Captains: Frigate Command in the Napoleonic Wars* (London: Chatham Publishing, 2001)

Waters, D.W., 'Notes on the Convoy System of Naval Warfare: Thirteenth to Twentieth Centuries', Part 1, 'Convoy in the Sail Era, 1204–1874' (Typescript, Historical Section, Admiralty, December 1957), pp. 1–55

Watt, Helen, and Anne Hawkins, eds, *Letters of Seamen in the Wars with France, 1793–1815* (Woodbridge: Boydell Press, 2016)

Webb, Paul, 'The Frigate Situation of the Royal Navy, 1793–1815', *Mariner's Mirror*, 82, 1996, pp. 28–40

West, Jenny, *Gunpowder, Government and War in the Mid-Eighteenth Century* (Woodbridge: Boydell Press, 1993)

Wheeler, Michael, *The Athenaeum: More than Just Another London Club* (New Haven and London: Yale University Press, 2020)

Wilcox, Martin, ' "These peaceable times are the devil": Royal Navy officers in the post-war slump, 1815–1825', *International Journal of Maritime History*, 26, 2014, pp. 471–88

Wilkinson, H.C., *Bermuda from Sail to Steam: A History of the Island from 1784 to 1901*, 2 vols (Oxford: Oxford University Press, 1973)

Williams, E. Cameron, 'The Four "Iron Laws" of Naval Protection of Merchant Shipping', *Naval War College Review*, XXXIX, 3, 1986, pp. 35–42

Willis, Sam, *Fighting at Sea in the Eighteenth Century: The Art of Sailing Warfare* (Woodbridge: Boydell Press, 2008)

—, 'The Capability of Sailing Warships, Part 1: Windward Performance', *Northern Mariner*, 2003, XIII, pp. 29–39

—, 'The High Life: Topmen in the Eighteenth-Century Navy', *Mariner's Mirror*, 90, 2004, pp. 152–66

Wills, Mary, *Envoys of Abolition: British Naval Officers and the Campaign against the Slave Trade in West Africa* (Liverpool: Liverpool University Press, 2013)

Wilson, Evan, *A Social History of British Naval Officers, 1775–1815* (Woodbridge: Boydell Press, 2017)

—, 'The Naval Defence of Ireland during the French Revolutionary and Napoleonic Wars, *Historical Research*, 92, 2019, pp. 568–84

—, 'The Limits of Naval Power: Britain after 1815', in Paul Kennedy and Evan Wilson, eds, *Navies in Multipolar Worlds from the Age of Sail to the Present* (London and New York: Routledge, 2021), pp. 62–81

—, 'The Monster from Elba: Napoleon's escape reconsidered', *Mariner's Mirror*, 107, 2021, pp. 265–81

Winfield, Rif, *British Warships in the Age of Sail, 1793–1817: Design, Construction, Careers and Fates* (London: Chatham Publishing, 2005)

Witt, James M., 'Smuggling and Blockade Running from 1807 to 1814', in Katherine B. Aaslestad and Johan Joor, eds, *Revisiting Napoleon's Continental System: Local, Regional and European Experiences* (Basingstoke: Palgrave Macmillan, 2015), pp. 153–69

Wold, Atle, *Privateering and Diplomacy, 1793–1807* (Basingstoke: Palgrave Macmillan, 2020)

Woodman, Richard, *The Victory of Seapower: Winning the Napoleonic War 1806–1814* (London: Chatham Publishing, 1998)

—, *The Sea Warriors: Fighting Captains and Frigate Warfare in the Age of Nelson* (London: Constable, 2001)

—, *Arctic Convoys, 1941–1945* (London: John Murray, 1994)

—, *Malta Convoys, 1940–1943* (London: John Murray, 2000)

—, *A History of the British Merchant Navy*: vol. I, *Neptune's Trident: Spices and Slaves, 1500–1807*; vol. II, *Britannia's Realm: in support of the State, 1763–1815*; vol. III, *Masters under God, Makers of Empire, 1816–1884* (Stroud: The History Press, 2008, 2009)

—, *A Low Set of Blackguards: The East India Company and the Maritime Service*, vol. 2, *Triumph and Decline* (Harwich: privately published, 2017)

Wright, Charles, and C. Ernest Fayle, *A History of Lloyd's from the Founding of Lloyd's Coffee House to the Present Day* (London: Macmillan, 1928)

Wyndham, Mrs Hugh ed., Correspondence of Sarah Spencer, Lady Lyttleton, 1787–1870 (London: John Murray, 1912)

Zamoyski, Adam, *1812: Napoleon's Fatal March on Moscow* (London: Harper Perennial, 2004)

INDEX

Abercromby-Christian expedition (1795–6)
        135
Aberdeen 173
Adam, Captain Charles, later Admiral Sir
        Charles (1780–1853) 195–6
Admiralty, Board of 13, 15–16, 18, 21, 24,
        26, 28–30, 33–5, 40–1, 43, 46–9,
        52, 54, 56–7, 59, 66, 70–3, 78–9, 82,
        86, 90–1, 93, 96–7, 104, 107–8,
        111, 113, 118, 120, 122, 124, 127,
        133, 139–40, 166, 174, 177, 179,
        182, 190, 196, 198–9, 201–2,
        205–6, 208, 210, 212–13, 221–2,
        231, 233, 235, 239, 241, 249, 250,
        258, 265, 267, 268, 273–4, 289
Admiralty, First Lord of 18, 37, 54, 78–9, 148,
        154–5, 174, 218, 240, 252, 275, 278
Admiralty, Secretary of Board 9, 42–3, 50,
        85, 94, 96, 105–6, 121, 124, 127–8,
        130, 165, 170, 184, 228
Admiralty, Second Secretary 9, 57, 96
Admiralty, High Court of 28, 31, 35–6,
        48–9, 248
Admiralty licences 32, 36, 268
Admiralty Office 9, 38–9, 62, 249, 274, 279,
        281
Adriatic Sea 165–7, 170, 177–8
Aegean Sea 166
Aire and Calder Navigation 112
Aix Roads, battle of 135n
Aleppo, Syria 168
Alexandria 162, 166–8, 174
Allemand, French Vice-Admiral Zacherie
        Jacques Theodore, Comte (1762–
        1826) 163, 204
Allen, Captain John, later Admiral
        (1774–1833) 154
America (United States) 9, 26–7, 136, 167,
        179, 205, 218, 247, 250, 269, 270,
        274–5, 284

American warships and merchantmen
        USS *Argus* 265n
            Constitution 271
            Erie 250
            Peacock 249
            President 251
        privateers *Decatur* 271
            Prince de Neufchatel (18) 254n, 265,
                268, 271
            Rattlesnake 251
            Saucy Jack 158
            Scourge 251
            Snapdragon 257
            True Blooded Yankee 264
            Young Wasp 265
        merchantmen *Alexandria* 70
            Champlin 244
            Eliza 53, 224, 229, 241
            Siro 265
Amelia Island, Georgia 193, 205
Amiens, Peace of (1802–3) 105
Amsterdam 48, 195
Anholt, island of 228, 229, 237
Anstruther, Lieutenant Philip 93–4
Archangel 13, 111, 125, 146n, 215, 221, 247,
        251, 278
armed ships 55, 107–8, 124
army regiments, 5th Foot 151n; 7th Foot
        141n; 8th Foot 141n; 11th Foot
        154; 28th Foot 138n; 29th Foot
        139; 30th Foot 156; 51st Foot 135,
        138n; 57th Foot 165; Queen's Own
        German Regiment 144
Athens 166
Atherfield Rocks, Isle of Wight 89
Atkins, Captain David (d. 1811) 238
Atlantic Ocean 1, 5, 17, 21, 27, 29, 47, 58,
        60, 65, 81, 85, 98, 146, 159, 179,
        180, 184, 186, 188n, 192, 194, 199,
        203–7, 212, 218, 245–8, 251–2,

255, 256, 258, 263–5, 270–2,
286–7, 290–2
Austen, Captain Francis, later Admiral of the
Fleet (1774–1865) 56–7, 191
Azores 189–203

Baird, General Sir David (1757–1829) 142,
150
Ball, Rear-Admiral Sir Alexander (1757–
1809) 166
ballast, ships in 29, 57–8, 87, 187, 210, 217n,
219–20
Ballingcollig, Cork, Ireland 169
Baltic 9, 18, 50, 54–5, 61, 68, 70, 74, 103,
108, 111, 118, 125–6, 131–2, 135,
146, 162, 168, 175, 179, 214–43,
245, 252, 265, 278–9, 287
Bankes, Lieutenant Richard 233
Bantry Bay 158
Barbary States 163, 167
Barham see Middleton
Barclay, Colonel Thomas, British agent for
POW in America 250
Barrow, John (later Sir John), Second
Secretary of the Admiralty
(1764–1848) 37n, 38n, 40, 43–6,
57, 97, 131, 270, 281
Bathurst, Captain Walter (d. 1827) 219n
Bathurst, Henry, Earl (1762–1809) 44, 99,
152n
Baugh, Lieutenant Thomas 128n
Bayonne, French port 83, 99, 101
Beachy Head, Sussex coast 91n, 93–4, 160
Bechervaise, John, merchant ship master 156
Benevente, Prince de, French Foreign
Minister 367
Bengal 8, 83, 86, 193, 211, 278
Benghazi 167
Bennet, John, Secretary of the Committee of
Lloyd's 49, 85, 90–1, 185, 206
Bentham, Samuel (1757–1831) 171
Berehaven, Ireland 27, 158, 269
Berkeley, Admiral Sir George Cranfield, later
Baron Berkeley (1753–1818) 148
Berlin Decrees 18, 112
Bermuda 59, 61, 136n, 159, 247, 252, 261n,
266, 269
Bernadotte, Count 215–16
Bertie, Captain, later Admiral Sir Albemarle
(1755–1824) 82, 183, 198, 209–10,
278
Biscay, Bay of 4, 54, 149, 152, 265
Black Sea 163, 147, 179, 218, 220
Blackrock, Dublin 144

Blanckeman, Jean, French privateer captain
109
Blankenburg, Flanders 109
blockade 4, 8, 11, 15–16, 29, 36, 64, 80,
82–3, 86n, 104–5, 110–11, 120,
128, 135, 164, 169, 178, 234, 243,
245, 247, 258, 263–4, 269–71, 275
Bolton, Captain Sir William (1777–1830)
35–6
Bombay 184n, 198, 201, 211n, 236
Bordeaux 27–8, 83, 101, 265
Bornholm, island of, Baltic 229
Boston 244, 271
Botany Bay, Australia 3, 64, 146n, 151n, 232
Boteler, Cdr John Harvey (b. 1790) 228
Brazil 192–3
Brest 12, 15, 27n, 61, 135, 182, 264, 279
Bridlington, Yorkshire 89
brimstone see sulphur
British North America 246, 253, 259, 264,
288, 292
British warships and merchantmen
HMAS Ceylon 132, 264n
Charles (14) 108, 125n
Harlequin (18) 93
Prince William (14) 75, 108, 125,
130–1
Providence (14) 104–9, 113, 116–26,
131–2, 275
HMB Aggressor (10) 108n
Cheerly (10) 191
Cherokee (10) 215
Constant (12) 236
Cracker (10) 46, 129
Earnest (10) 100–2
Forward (10) 233, 290
Gallant (10) 220
Growler (12) 64
Helicon (10) 57
Hirondelle 170
Plumper (10) 248
Renard (10) 170
Rinaldo (10) 274n
Sentinel (12) 236–7
Teazer (10) 98
Tickler (10) 230
HMS Abundance (troopship) 256n
Acheron (bomb) 172
Achille (74) 51
Africa (64) 233
Alarm (32) 18
Albion (74) 209
Alexander (hospital ship) 146
Alexandria (36) 70

Amelia (44) 56
Anson (44) 170
Antelope (50) 147, 215, 268–9
Apollo (36) 1–4
Ardent (64) 228
Arethusa (38) 206
Arrow (28) 167n
Bacchante (20) 202
Belette (16) 237
Bellerophon (74) 58, 260–2
Bittern (18) 170
Blenheim (90) 200–2, 278
Brazen (18) 71
Britannia (100) 79
Buffalo (storeship) 18
Bulwark (74) 64, 197
Caesar (80) 182
Cambridge (80) 128
Cameleon (10) 170
Canada (74) 182
Canopus (84) 56
Captain (74) 208
Carnation (18) 64
Carysfort (32) 3
Censeur (74) 21
Chichester (storeship) 93
Childers (14) 61–3
Christian VII (80) 127
Clio (16) 128n
Comet (18, fireship) 260
Comus (22) 101
Cormorant (16) 261
Courageux (74) 82, 91
Coventry (48) 14
Crecy (74) 212
Crescent (36) 72, 236
Cressy (74) 235
Cruizer (16) 104–5, 108, 110, 130
Culloden (74) 202, 210–11
Cumberland (74) 52
Curlew (18) 251
Dauntless (18) 239
Dauntless (24) 206
Defence (74) 238
Desiree (36) 99
Dictator (64) 103, 228, 243
Dominica (14) 140, 271
Electra (16) 254
Elizabeth (70) 14
Endymion (46) 187, 271
Epervier (16) 249
Espiegle (14) 56
Fama (36) 236
Favourite (18) 208

Fisgard (38) 36, 128
Fortitude (74) 21
Gluckstadt (18) 95
Grasshopper (18) 220
Griffon (16) 65
Harrier (18) 200
Hebe (36) 233
Horatio (38) 248, 259, 262, 266
Implacable (74) 197
Inconstant (32) 203
Inflexible (64) 18, 143
Java (32) 200–1
La Franchise or *Franchise* (40) 154, 205–6
Lavinia (44) 127
Leander (60) 249
Leonidas (38) 4, 151n
Levant (22) 271
Leviathan (74) 178
Liffey (50) 57, 129
Magicienne (36) 181, 205
Magnet (16) 236, 248
Majestic (74) 41, 255, 256n, 257
Medina (22) 58, 261
Melpomone (42) 156
Mercurius (18) 215
Mermaid (22) 139–40
Meteor (bomb) 232
Monarch (74) 128, 148
Monmouth (64) 204
Montagu (74) 182
Musquito (16) 231
Newcastle (62) 269
Northumberland (74) 98
Nymphen (42) 128
Paz (12) 249
Pelican (16) 265
Pelorus (16) 84
Penguin (16) 205
Pheasant (16) 256n, 257
Pike (14) 58, 261
Plantagenet (74) 219
Plover (18) 262
Pomone (44) 53, 87
Porpoise (16) 132
Port Mahon (18) 207
Portia (14) 64, 226
President (44) 192
Queen (90) 212
Raisonable (64) 203
Ramillies (74) 18–19
Ranger (16) 82
Recruit (18) 65
Regulus (50) 143

INDEX

Resistance (38) 195–61
Resolution (74) 127
Revenge (74) 138n, 188–9
Revolutionaire (40) 195
Ringdove (16) 256n, 257
Rose (16) 225
Salorman (10) 236
Salsette (36) 236
Scorpion (16) 120
Seagull (16) 94, 231
Seahorse (38) 101, 158n
Serapis (storeship) 84
Sheldrake (14) 235
Snipe (10) 86
Solebay (36) 234
Sophie (18) 165n
Southampton (32) 18
Spider (14) 170
Spy (storeship) 249
St Albans (64) 191
St George (98) 9, 183, 238–9, 279
St Vincent (100) 79
Sultan (74) 158
Superb (74) 236
Sybille (44) 245
Terpsichore (32) 210
Thais (bomb) 101
Thames (32) 120
Thetis (32) 18
Thetis (38) 46
Thisbe (28) 36–7
Thunder (bomb) 231
Tremendous (74) 220
Trident (64) 178, 203–4
Trincolo (16) 256n
Turbulent (bomb) 231
Undaunted (44) 192
Unicorn (38) 146
Unite (38) 177
Vautour (16) 63
Ventura (10) 170
Vesuvius (bomb) 76
Victorious (74) 266, 280
Victory (100) 215, 225n, 226, 238
Wasp (16) 211n
Weymouth (46) 86
Wolverine (16) 173n, 261
York (64) 8
Zealous (74) 99
British East India Ships
  HCS *Admiral Aplin* 208n
    Admiral Gardner 83, 209n
    Airly Castle 204
    Ann 209–10

Asia 211
Bengal 210–11
Britannia 83, 209n
Brunswick 83n
Calcutta 210
Charlton 208n
Cullands Grove 208n
Earl of Abergavenny 86, 209n
Fame 208n
Jane Duchess of Gordon 211
Lady Jane Dundas 211
Lord Nelson 94
Neptune 181
Perseverance 201
Princess Charlotte 208n
Retreat 191
Royal Admiral 8
United Kingdom 208n
Walpole 209
Warren Hastings 208n
Worcester 204
British hired government transports
  Amphititre 140
  Antiope 144
  Ariadne 142
  Augustus Caesar 143–4
  Aurora 143
  Baring 158
  Charlotte 157
  Crisis 140
  Dispatch 150–1
  Dominica 140
  Ellice 75, 84–5, 175–7
  Endeavour 144
  Helder 143
  Harry Morris 145
  Golden Fleece 158
  Hawke 146
  Jenny 142
  Lady Juliana 146
  Mary 159–60
  Norfolk 68
  Ocean 113
  Penelope 157
  Perseverance 151
  Queen 156–7
  Salisbury 134
  Sceptre 140
  Smallbridge 151
  Sovereign 157
  William 147–8
  Zephyr 139
British Merchant ships
  Anatolia 75

Anne 208
Arethusa 36
Ark, of Bristol 3
Atlas 114
Brilliant 73
Catharine of London 71
Charlotta 49
Coquette 48
Cumberland 98
Cynthia 45
Devonshire 261
Dolphin 179
Eagle packet 144
Edward 75, 205, 207
Eliza Swan 31, 251
Elizabeth 83
Fame 76
Findon 93
Intrepid 179
Isabelle 255
Kingsmill 51–2
Lord Carrington 288
Mary slave ship 68
Mary 123
Mary Ann 138n, 179, 229, 241, 272
Minerva 148
Neptune 261
Norfolk 76
Oeconomy 48–9, 69, 187, 236n
Penguin 256
Prince of Wales packet 144
Princess of Wales packet 144
Rambler 173
Regard 86
Robert and Mary 123
Rochdale 144
Rodney of Whitby 254
Supply 122
Sussex Oak 93
Triton 120–1
Venus 89
Wight 36–7
privateer
   Liverpool Packet 248
Second World War steam ships
   SS *Avoceta* 291
     Empress of Britain 291
     Empress of Canada 291
     Lancastria 291
     Queen Elizabeth 291
     Queen Mary 291
Brisbane, Captain Sir Charles, later
   rear-admiral (d.1829) 206
Bristol 3, 33, 186, 205n, 253n, 267

Brittany 83
Brown, Thomas, naval harbour master 114
Browne, Captain Thomas, later vice-admiral
   (d. 1851) 274
Bulley, Thomas, fish merchant 253–7, 260n,
   261
bullion 30, 168, 176, 191, 194, 196–7
Bunbury, Lt-General Sir Henry (1778–
   1860) 138
Butcher, Captain Samuel, later vice-admiral
   (d.1849) 215, 268–70, 280
Byam Martin, Captain Thomas, later
   Admiral of the Fleet Sir Thomas
   (1773–1854) 43
Byron, George Gordon, 6th Baron Byron
   (1786–1824) 44

Cadiz, siege of 153, 163–5, 178, 196–7
Cadiz, Spain 21, 27n, 60n, 136, 146, 149,
   154–5, 167n
Cagliari, Sardinia 179
Calder, Admiral Sir Robert (1745–1818) 84
Campbell, Captain Patrick, later Vice-
   Admiral (1773–1841) 177–9
Campbell, Thomas, RN master 131
canals 112, 218
Canning, George, politician (1770–1827)
   51, 263
Canton 86, 193, 264
Cape Breton Island 157
Cape Clear, southern Ireland 81, 94, 98, 45,
   269
Cape of Good Hope 3, 199, 204
Cape St Vincent 4, 13, 21
cargoes
   bale goods 89
   barley 167
   barrelled salmon 253
   bullion 30, 168, 176, 191, 194, 196–7,
     277
   candles 106, 146, 186–7, 222
   chalk 220
   cheese 259n
   chemicals 112
   coal 89–90, 101, 115, 187, 220, 222, 285
   cochineal 146, 197
   codfish oil 253
   coffee 5, 50, 70, 111, 115, 167–8, 185–6,
     192, 194, 207, 220, 277
   copper boilers 186
   cordage 111
   cotton 70, 86, 89, 115, 167–8, 184n,
     185–6, 193–4, 205, 222, 265
   dye wood 89

figs 168
fustic 187
geneva gin 111
glass 168, 186
grain 30, 89, 166, 235, 278
haberdashery 186
hemp 5, 55, 111, 165, 168, 217–18, 219n,
    220–1, 223, 234, 242, 251, 278
herrings 89, 220
indigo 111, 193, 197
iron 9–90, 111, 148, 167, 186, 210, 217,
    219n, 223, 234
lead 112, 167, 203, 220
lemon juice 168
logwood 73, 115, 220
mahogany 48, 49n, 69, 187
munitions 10, 187, 220–1, 241
muskets 187, 220–1
nankeens 193
oats 89, 167
olive oil 167–8
pepper 193
potatoes 89, 187, 236
raisins 111, 115, 147, 168
saddlery 186
sailcloth 218, 234
saltpetre 169, 193, 210, 277, 287
seal products 253
silk 168, 193
sugar 5, 49, 70, 75, 111, 115, 167–8,
    185–6, 192–4, 207, 220–1, 277
sulphur 167–9, 287
tallow 111, 146, 203, 221–3, 234, 242,
    251, 278
tea 185, 193
textiles 112
timber 54, 56, 76, 87, 90, 98, 111, 165–6,
    217–18, 219n, 234, 242n, 253
tobacco 111, 146, 220, 222
wheat 21, 71–2, 89, 111, 167–8, 196, 218,
    223, 243
wine 18, 146, 168, 176, 187–8
wool 146, 219n, 253
Carr, Andrew, merchant master 76
Carron Company, Scotland 90
Carthagena, Spain 35
Carthew, Captain James, later Admiral
    (1770–1855) 72
Castlereagh, Lord (1769–1822) 101, 114n,
    204n
Cattewater, inner harbour at Plymouth 84
Chambers, Captain Samuel (d. 1843) 207
Champion, Samuel, admiral's secretary 235,
    242

Channel 11, 16, 18–19, 22–3, 32, 55, 58, 62,
    65, 81–7, 91–7, 135, 144, 150, 154,
    160, 179, 182, 185, 203, 205n, 211,
    253, 260, 267, 273
Channel Fleet 17, 19, 21, 40, 59, 252
Chios, Greece 166
Chivers, William, merchant ship master 36
Christianso, island of, Baltic 229
chronometers 3–4, 212, 266
City of London 26, 33, 197, 213
Clancarty, Earl of (diplomat) 100
Clarence, Duke of, later William IV
    (1765–1837) 101
Clark, William, Shields shipowner 106,
    108n, 118
coastal trades 28, 72n, 88, 90, 111
Cochrane, Vice-Admiral Sir Alexander
    (1758–1832) 258
Cockburn, Captain George, later Admiral
    (1772–1853) 197, 261n
Coggeshall, George, American merchant
    master 53, 113, 137n, 224, 229, 241,
    263, 271
colliers 46, 55, 92–3, 108, 285
Collingwood, Vice-Admiral Cuthbert, Lord
    (1750–1810) 19n, 35, 57, 162–3,
    165, 174, 177–8
Colpoys, Admiral Sir John (1742–1821) 90
Colville, Captain Lord John, later admiral
    (d. 1849) 212
commanders-in-chief
    Cape of Good Hope 199
    Cork 46, 249
    East Indies 199, 203, 278
    Leith 41, 62, 70, 107, 124, 128n, 233,
        265
    Mediterranean 34, 162–3
    North America 247, 259
    North Sea 40–1, 59
    South America 193
    West Indies 274
Congreve, General Sir William (1743–
    1814) 169
Constantinople 165, 174, 220
Convoy Act (1798) 22; (1803) 28, 35, 48,
    88, 263
Copenhagen 28, 231
    expedition to (1807) 120, 126–7, 135,
        141, 143, 222–3, 243, 288
copper sheathing 107, 118, 202
Cordoba, Don Luis de, Spanish admiral 19
Cork Harbour 1, 14, 18, 27, 36, 46, 47n, 83,
    85, 87, 90, 94, 130–2, 136, 144, 150,
    151n, 159–60, 169, 184, 186, 207,

245–6, 253n, 256, 259–60, 263, 269, 271

Cornwall 90, 186

Cotton, Admiral Sir Charles (1753–1812) 150, 152n, 163, 167, 179

Courcy, Rear Admiral Michael de (d. 1824) 193

courts martial 64, 139n, 173, 249

Cowes, Isle of Wight 141

Craig, Lt-Gen Sir James (1748–1812) 170

Crofton, Commander Edward 205

Croker, John Wilson, Secretary of the Admiralty (1780–1857) 38n, 41–7, 48n, 50–1, 94, 97, 129, 131, 133, 170n, 179, 185, 195n, 206, 228, 240, 252, 262–3, 264n, 267–9, 273, 281

Cromwell, Oliver 11

Cronenburg Castle 215

cross trades 47, 163, 175, 246

Cruizer class of brig sloop 59, 67, 331

Dacres, Rear-Admiral James Richard (1749–1810) 83, 208

Dalby, Augustus, master RN 1

Dalmatian coast 162

Danish warship *Najaden* 243

Dardanelles 162, 174

Dartmoor 152

Dartmouth, Devon 253

Dashwood, Captain Charles, later Rear-Admiral (1765–1847) 206, 212, 239

Davidson, Meyer 100

Deal, Kent 39, 87, 134, 158n, 159, 191

Denmark 26, 113, 121, 150, 167n, 217, 222–3, 225, 243, 245, 270

Deptford 146

Dillon, Captain William Henry, later rear-admiral Sir William (1779–1857) 62–3, 240, 248, 258–60, 262, 266–7

Dixon, Captain John (d.1804) 1

dockyards 54, 79, 87, 90, 106–7, 132, 165–6, 171, 196, 200–2, 218, 223, 252, 259

Dogger Bank, North Sea 20

Domett, Rear-Admiral William, later Admiral (1752–1828) 64n

Douglas, Rear-Admiral Billy 118n, 125–7, 130–1

Downs, The, the anchorage off the Kent coast 27, 38–9, 41, 46, 86–7, 91n, 92–3, 101, 124, 130–1, 140, 142–3, 159, 179, 202, 204, 219

Drury, Vice-Admiral William O'Brien (d. 1811) 190, 198, 211, 278

Dublin 46, 136, 144, 253n, 267

Dundas, Henry, first Lord Melville, First Lord of the Admiralty 54, 78, 275

Dungeness 74, 91, 160

Dunkirk 11, 84, 91, 109, 111

Durham, Admiral Sir Philip (1763–1845) 274

East India Company 33, 50, 204, 274, 279

East Indies 51, 136n, 184, 187–8, 191, 201, 208

Elgin Marbles 170

Elsinore, Denmark 72, 75, 108–9, 118, 120, 123, 125, 221

Emden, German port 112

Etaples 83

Evans, John, Commander (d.1816) 65–6

exports 26, 112, 167, 175, 185–6, 221–2, 253, 277

Falmouth, Cornwall 27, 90–1, 95, 140, 147, 149, 154–6, 182, 184, 192, 256

Farquhar, Captain Arthur, later rear-admiral (d.1843) 99, 172–3, 280

Fernyhough, Richard, Royal Marines officer 152–3

Fisher, Peter, merchant master 114

fisheries 47, 278

Flamborough Head, Yorkshire 103, 118

Fleeming, Captain Charles, later Admiral (1774–1840) 197

Flower class corvettes 285

Folkestone, Kent 98, 160

Foto, Sweden 227

Foulerton, Thomas, Lieutenant 191–2

foundering 8, 15n, 17n, 23n, 54, 121, 208

French national warships and privateers warships *Andromache* (44) 98
    Arianne (44) 98
    L'Hortense (40) 172
    L'Incorruptible (38) 172
    Marmalouck (16) 98
    Palinure (16) 64
   privateers *Bellone* 94
    Contre-Amiral Magnon 109
    La Valeur 95
    Vengeur 110

France, National Convention 21

Frankfurt 115

freight money 70, 120, 191–2, 198, 200, 208

French Revolutionary War (1793–1801) 23–4, 34, 50, 59n, 104, 136, 138, 160n, 199, 276
fresh water 165, 226–8, 264
Funen, Danish island 231–2

Gamage, Lieutenant Richard (executed 1812) 65
Ganteaume, Honoré, French Admiral (1756–1833) 163
Gardner, Rear-Admiral Alan Hyde, Baron (1772–1815) 131
Garonne, River 83, 101
Geary, Admiral Sir Francis (1709–1796) 19
General Evening Post 97
George III 42
Ghent, Treaty of (1814) 271, 274
Gibraltar 18–19, 57, 71, 85, 113, 136n, 147–9, 151, 164–6, 168, 172–4, 176, 179
Gill, Lieutenant 71
Gladstone, John, MP and merchant, later Sir John (1764–1851) 50–1
Glasgow 47, 73, 126, 194, 205n, 267
Globe Insurance 45
Gluckstadt 121–2
Goodwin Sands 83, 144, 209n, 219
Gordon, Alexander, merchant master 71
Gothenburg, Sweden 71, 125–6, 129, 132, 142, 215–16, 220–1, 227–9, 232–3, 235n, 244
Gower, Richard Hall 46n
Grand Banks, Newfoundland 4, 257
Great Belt, passage through Denmark 61, 70n, 215, 228, 230, 232, 239, 277
Great Yarmouth, Norfolk 27, 38, 65, 87, 90, 92, 104n, 109–10, 116, 120, 124, 127, 129–31, 236
Greenland 128, 266, 278
Greenock, Scotland 73, 253n
Gregory, Commander William (d. 1844) 254
Grenville, Thomas, First Lord of the Admiralty (1755–1846) 37, 56, 278
Gretton, Vice-Admiral Sir Peter (1912–1992) 288
Griffiths, Major Edwin, 15th Light Dragoons 159
Grimsby 107, 109n, 117, 120–5, 131–2, 140–1
Guadeloupe 142n, 196, 212
Guernsey 225, 280
gun brigs 58, 60, 80n, 231, 276

gun vessels 60, 223, 232
gunpowder 90, 169, 220, 257, 277

Haak Sands, off the Texel 71, 143, 157, 220, 239
Halifax, Nova Scotia 27, 65, 139, 157, 196, 246–9, 251–2, 253n, 261, 266, 269
Hamburg 30, 112, 115, 122n, 167n, 277n
Hamilton, Captain Sir Charles, later Admiral (1767–1849) 289
Hamond, Captain Graham, later Admiral of the Fleet (1779–1862) 170
Hampshire Telegraph 144n
Hancock, Captain John, later rear-admiral (d. 1839) 57, 97, 104–5, 109–11, 127–9
Hano, Sweden 27, 226, 229, 233n, 237–8, 244
Hartwell, Captain Sir Francis (1757–1831) 118, 132n
Harvey, Captain John 182
Harwich, Essex 30, 87, 100, 104n, 110, 125, 130, 132, 140, 143, 159, 236
Hawke Roads, off Gothenburg (Hakefjorden) 227, 236, 264n
Hawker, Captain Edward (1782–1860) 260
Hay, Captain (HEIC) 191
Hay, Robert, seaman 75, 205, 207, 211
Heligoland 5, 103, 108n, 113–15, 120, 125–6, 135, 141, 194
Helvoetsluis 100–2
hemp 5, 55, 111, 165, 168, 217–20, 223, 234, 242, 251, 278
Henley, Michael, ship owner of Wapping 48, 68, 76, 95–6, 145–6, 187, 236n, 242
Herries, John Charles (1778–1855) 102
Holland 26, 30, 101, 112, 157, 160n, 239, 277n
Hollinworth, Mitchell, 3rd Confidential clerk, Admiralty Office 39
Hoogli River, Bengal 199, 210–11
Hope, Captain William Johnstone, later Admiral (1766–1831) 132n, 220
Horns Reef, off Danish coast 239
Horton, Admiral Sir Max (1883–1951) 290
Hotham, Captain, later Vice-Admiral Sir Henry (1771–1833) 98, 195
Howard-Johnstone, Commander C.D., Second World War escort group commander 284
Hoxton 66
Hoy, island of, Orkneys 266
Hulbert, George Redmond, admiral's secretary 258

Hull 74, 112, 118, 121, 124, 126, 128, 130–1, 140, 141n, 220, 222, 276, 279

Hull Packet newspaper 8, 97, 120n, 237, 239, 241

Humber, River 5, 27, 76, 103–4, 107–8, 111–12, 115–16, 119, 120n, 124–7, 130–1, 140, 221

Husum, Denmark 30, 112

ice, navigational hazard 5–6, 100, 103, 236, 240–1, 257, 261–2, 266

Imperial Guard 281–2

imports, to Britain 26, 30, 112, 169n, 178, 185, 218n, 253

impressment 7, 24, 34, 38, 54n, 72–4, 83, 98, 189–90, 201, 209, 211, 213, 249, 254, 259, 275, 282, 289–90

Ionian islands 36, 168, 175

Iran 291

Irish Sea 46, 55, 136, 144, 264, 267

Istria 162

Jamaica 18, 27, 56, 73, 75, 82, 85n, 91, 136n, 158, 181, 184n, 185, 195n, 196–8, 200–2, 205–8, 247

Jefferson, Samuel, merchant master 56, 74–5, 89, 138n, 179, 220, 222, 229, 240–2, 272

Jekyll, Joseph, MP (1754–1837) 105

Jenkinson, Robert Banks, Earl Liverpool, Prime Minister (1770–1828) 101, 152n

Jervis, John, Admiral Lord St Vincent (1735–1823) 1, 37, 53–5, 78, 81, 105, 184, 199–200, 215, 218, 289

Jones, Private John Morris, 39th Foot 147–8

Jones, Sir Hartford (diplomat) 87–8

Jones, William, American Secretary of the Navy 250

Julian, Commander John (1778–1828) 98

Kattegat (also 'Categat') 228, 236

Keats, Captain Richard Goodwin, later Admiral Sir Richard (1756–1834) 58, 150, 226, 231–3, 236, 260–2

Keith, Admiral George Keith Elphinstone, Lord Keith (1746–1823) 30, 40–1, 59, 105, 110n, 124, 252

King, Captain Edward Durnford, later Admiral Sir Edward (d. 1862) 204

King, Captain William (d. 1836) 4

King's German Legion 141n, 144, 151

Knightsbridge 74

Kristiansand, Norway 234–5

Kronstadt 219, 240

Laeso, island of, Sweden 237

Lascar seamen 83

Laugharn, Rear Admiral John (d. 1819) 178

Layman, Lieutenant William (d.1826) 60n

Leith, Scotland 27, 89, 109, 120, 141, 167, 186, 194, 253n

Lerwick, Shetland Islands 71, 129

letters of marque 32, 36, 225, 247, 264

Levant Company 165–6

Lewis, Butt of 221

licences, to sail without convoy 29, 32, 35, 46, 51, 212, 263, 268

licences, to trade with the enemy 30–1, 49, 119, 177

Limerick, Ireland 255

Linois, contre-amiral Durand de 77, 279

Lisbon 2–3, 27n, 44, 57, 62, 136, 145–6, 148–9, 151–4, 156, 165, 175n

Liverpool 32–3, 50–1, 68, 81, 85, 115, 131, 136, 141n, 144, 192, 205n, 221, 248, 253–4, 256, 263, 265, 267, 276

Liverpool, Lord *see* Jenkinson

Lloyd's 19, 23–4, 28–30, 33–5, 45, 47–9, 72, 78, 85, 91, 96, 98, 110, 114n, 115, 143n, 152n, 165, 175n, 184–5, 206, 212, 221, 228, 235, 242–3, 259, 267–8, 274

Lloyd's Patriotic Fund 34, 280n

London 11, 13–16, 23, 26, 32–3, 46, 48, 66, 69, 78, 83–4, 88n, 89–90, 96–7, 112, 115, 120, 125, 130, 137, 146, 154, 165–6, 168, 175–7, 185, 193–7, 201, 205n, 210, 213–14, 222, 242, 253n, 254, 262, 285

London Assurance 45, 48

Long Hope Sound, Orkneys 27, 109, 233, 265–7

Longstaff, Thomas, merchant ship master 84, 175–7

Louisiana Purchase 194

Luard, Cornet John, 4 Dragoons 152

Lyngor, battle of 123, 242

Lynn, Norfolk 126

Madagascar 200

Madeira 3, 5, 16, 18–19, 142n, 182, 184, 188, 268, 271

Madison, James, American President (1751–1836) 271

Majorca 167

Malmo, Sweden 239
Malta 75, 115n, 136n, 147–8, 162–70, 174–9, 280n, 288
Manacles, rocks off Cornwall 151
Manchester 112, 115, 193
Mansell, Captain, later rear-admiral Sir Thomas (1777–1858) 225, 265, 280
Mansell, Commander William 165n
Mansfield see Murray
marine insurance 16, 33, 45, 48, 97
Markham, Rear-Admiral John (1761–1827) 55n, 59, 61
Marryat, Joseph, Chairman of the Committee of Lloyd's (1757–1834) 33, 45, 48, 267–8
Marsden, William, Secretary of the Admiralty (1754–1836) 38n, 42, 105–6, 118, 122, 124, 206
Marshalsea Prison 48
Marstrand, Sweden 227
Martinique 64, 196, 212
Mediterranean 12, 27, 29, 44, 50, 84, 87, 127, 135, 148–9, 151, 152n, 154, 162–80, 220, 222, 280, 288
Mellish, William, government beef contractor 84, 175–6
Memel, Baltic port 146, 219, 223
Messina, Sicily 164–5, 169n, 174–6
Middleton, Charles, Lord Barham (1726–1813) 37–8, 174, 177
Minorca 165, 167, 176
mistral 180
Mitford, Captain Henry (d.1804) 8
Mondego, Cape, Portuguese coast 2
Moniteur, French newspaper 143
Monsarrat, Nicholas, author 285
Montagu, Admiral Sir George (d. 1829) 91
Montagu, John, 4th Earl of Sandwich (1718–1792) 17
Montego Bay, Portugal 150
Moore, Lt-General Sir John (1761–1809) 142, 150
Morris, Commander Henry, later Rear-Admiral (d. 1851) 56
Moscow 157n, 212, 215, 243, 245, 283
Motherbank, anchorage near Spithead 86
Mott, Lieutenant Andrew, later Commander 75, 108n, 125, 127, 131
Moutray, Captain John 18–19
Mulgrave see Phipps
Murmansk, north Russia 291
Murray, William, 1st Earl Mansfield (1705–1793) 6

Nagle, Jacob, seaman 73, 181
Nagle, Vice-Admiral Sir Edmund 233–4
Nantes, northern French port 83, 98
Naples 135, 163, 170, 177
Napoleon 97, 101, 135, 158, 164, 175, 194, 214, 216, 219, 245, 259, 270
Naval Chronicle 2, 4, 71, 270, 275
Naval Discipline Act 55
naval stores 111, 217, 246, 252, 287
Navy Board 8, 37n, 43, 54–5, 57, 59, 79, 90, 93, 108, 118, 122n, 139, 218
Naze of Norway 10, 233
Needles Channel 87, 91n, 145, 190
Nelson, Vice-Admiral Horatio, Viscount (1758–1805) 19, 34, 166, 168–70, 204
Nepean, Sir Evan, Secretary of the Admiralty (1752–1822) 38n
neutral flags 224
New Brunswick, Canada 247–8, 254
New York 244, 251, 265
Newburyport, Massachusetts 28
Newfoundland 45, 58, 61–2, 76, 155n, 157, 167, 173n, 205, 246, 248, 252–5, 257–60, 265, 271
Newland, John, merchant ship master 48
Newry, Northern Ireland 89
Nore, The 90, 92, 106, 111, 114–15, 120, 132, 13, 204n, 220, 235n
North America 18, 46, 152, 157, 167, 217, 218n, 225n, 246–7, 253, 259, 264, 288, 292
North Cape, Arctic 221, 250
North German states 26
North Sea 5, 20, 22, 30, 46, 54–5, 64, 68, 71–2, 92, 100, 103–33, 138, 179, 194, 215, 226, 235, 279–80, 288
Norway 26, 45, 223–4, 234, 243, 247, 264n, 270
Nova Scotia 27, 65, 136n, 139, 196, 247–8, 254
Nysted, Denmark 238, 239n, 281n

O'Byrne, William, naval author 280
Odessa, Black Sea port 167
Oporto, Portugal 149
Ordnance Board 166, 168–9, 194n, 209, 265n, 273
Orkneys 27, 109, 233, 266
Ostend 11, 110, 141, 159–60, 273
Otway, Captain Robert, later Admiral Sir Robert (1772–1846) 182
Otway, William Albany Vice-Admiral (b.1756) 70

Ouvrard, Gabriel-Julien, French banker (1770–1846) 194

Parkhurst Barracks, Isle of Wight 141
Parliament 13, 20, 32–3, 45, 48n, 50, 95, 139, 192, 240, 289
Paros, Greek island 166
Passages, northern Spain 99, 101, 149, 153, 156, 260
Pater, Captain Charles, later Rear-Admiral (d.1818) 238–9
patronage 66
Pellew, Admiral Edward, later Viscount Exmouth (1757–1833) 94, 128, 163, 177, 179, 199–202, 210–11
Peninsular War 160, 197, 282n
Penlee Point, Devon 84
Perceval, Spencer, Prime Minister (1762–1812) 42
Phipps, Henry, Earl Mulgrave, First Lord of the Admiralty (1755–1831) 37
Pitt, William, British Prime Minister 37, 54, 61
Plymouth 13, 27, 38–9, 82, 84, 90, 92–3, 95, 98, 101, 138, 140, 146, 152, 154, 189, 202, 207, 265
Pogen, island in the Elbe 121–2
Point de Galle, Sri Lanka 204, 210
Pole see Wellesley-Pole
Poole, Dorset 253n
Portland Bill 91n, 94
Portsmouth 38–9, 49, 76, 84, 87, 88n, 90–2, 99, 131, 144, 146, 156, 184, 188, 192, 201, 220, 240, 269–70, 290
PQ17 convoy 10n, 290
press gangs see impressment
Pressburg, Treaty of 162
Price, William, East India merchant 25
Pringle, John, HCS agent at the Cape 209
privateers 4n, 6, 9, 12, 15, 18, 22, 25, 29, 31, 40, 54, 59–60, 62, 86, 88, 90–1, 93, 96–7, 104–5, 119, 126, 128n, 137, 212, 219, 232, 287, 290
privateers, American 17–18, 20, 46–7, 77, 80, 101, 137, 158, 212, 221, 247–8, 250–1, 262–5, 267, 270–1, 276
privateers, Danish 214, 221, 247–8, 250–1, 262–5, 267, 270–1, 276
privateers, British 15, 32, 276
privateers, French 46, 81, 87–8, 91–2, 94, 97–8, 111, 129, 163, 166, 168, 170, 177–8, 224, 276
Privy Council 28n, 30, 32
Prize Acts 31

prize money 32n, 42, 46, 57, 66, 69–70, 105, 120, 173, 199, 209, 226, 234, 246n, 258, 265, 278, 280–1, 288
protections (from impressment) 54n, 98, 201
Prussia 26, 121, 218, 220–1, 223n, 282n
Prussian merchant ship Iphigenia 123
Purvis, Rear-Admiral John Child (1746–1825) 57, 174

Quebec 56–7, 129, 146n, 157, 223, 246, 254, 261, 272
Quiberon Bay 16

Rainier, Peter, Admiral (1741–1808) 199, 203–4
Ramage, Commander William (d.1828) 215
Ramsgate, Kent 46, 146, 156n, 159
ransoming prizes 20, 95, 137, 177, 251
Rayner, Commander Denys, RNVR (1908–1967) 286, 289–90
regulating officers 289
Renwick, Commander Thomas 215
Reynolds, Rear-Admiral Robert Carthew (d.1811) 238, 279
Rhine, River 100, 115
Richery, French contre amiral 21
Ridgely, Master Commandant, USN 250
Riga 146n, 229, 237, 241
Rochefort 15, 27n, 127, 135, 204
Rodgers, Commodore John, USN 251–2
Rodney, George Brydges, Admiral Sir George, 1st Baron (1718–1792) 20
Romana, Marquis de, Spanish general 232
Romso, island of, Great Belt 228
Rose, George, Treasurer of the Navy (1744–1818) 42
Rosen, Count, Swedish government official 216, 227
Rostock, Baltic port 146
Rothschild, Nathan Meyer (1777–1836) 100–2, 115
Rowley, Commander Joshua Ricketts, later Vice-Admiral Sir Josiah (d. 1857) 84
Rowley, Admiral Bartholomew (d. 1811) 195n, 198n, 200
Royal Exchange, insurance corporation
Royal Navy warships see British warships and merchantmen
Rule, Sir William, Surveyor of the Navy 59
Russell, Admiral Edward, 1st Earl Orford (1653–1727) 13
Russell, Thomas Macnamara, Vice-Admiral (ca. 1740–1824) 41, 86, 113

Russia 10, 26, 31, 50, 99, 162–4, 216–22,
    233, 243, 245, 277, 282–3, 291
Rye, Captain Peter, later rear-admiral
    (d.1851) 103–9, 112–18, 120–6,
    129–33
Ryswick, Peace of (1697) 13

Salonika 168
San Domingo 56, 69
San Sebastian, northern Spain 137n, 153
Sandwich see Montagu
Santander, northern Spain 149–50, 153, 232
Saumarez, Admiral James, Baron (1757–
    1836) 216–17, 220, 225–6, 229,
    235–8, 278
Sawyer, Sir Herbert, Vice-Admiral
    (fl. 1788–1820) 46
Scilly, Isles of 1, 83–4, 152, 160, 184
Scott, Sir William, 1st Baron Stowell, Judge
    of the High Court of Admiralty
    (1745–1836) 36
scurvy 19, 50, 168, 197
Select Commission on Marine Insurance
    (1811) 33
Seville 163, 178
Sheerness 39, 41, 103, 106, 120n, 124, 132,
    270
Shetland islands 71
Shields, North 106–8, 124, 126, 242
shipbuilding 27, 55, 59n, 111, 217–18, 275
Sicily 148, 163, 166, 168–70, 174, 278, 287
signal stations, coastal 40, 46, 91, 289
slave ship 68, 192
Sluys see Helveoetsluis
smugglers, English 40, 119, 126
Smyrna 10n, 12, 16, 34, 166, 171
Snipe, Dr John, naval surgeon 168
Soundings, The 16, 81, 94
Southern Whale Fishery 250, 258, 266n
Spain 15n, 17n, 26, 27n, 101, 138n, 149,
    153, 157, 163, 177, 179, 195–6, 216,
    232, 270
Spanish ships
    Span merch San Justo 196
    Span San Juan Baptista 49
Spartivento, Cape, Sardinia 176
specie see bullion
Spencer, Lieutenant-General Sir Brent
    (1760–1828) 149
Spithead 12, 22, 82–3, 91, 93, 140, 144, 146,
    149, 153, 183, 190–2, 196, 202–3,
    220, 246, 260, 266
Sproe, island in the Great Belt 215, 228
St Eustatius 19

St Helena 25, 184, 191, 203–4, 209, 274
St John's, Newfoundland 27, 266
St Lawrence river, Canada 157, 262
St Malo 80, 91n, 94–5
St Margaret's Bay, Kent 87
St Petersburg 138n, 220, 222–3, 242
St Vincent see Jervis
St Vincent, Cape 4, 13, 21
Staniforth, John, MP for Hull (d.1830)
    130
Start Point, Devon 182–3
Stirling, Charles, Vice-Admiral 200–1
Stockholm 76
Strachan, Admiral Sir Richard (1760–1828)
    182–3
Stuart, Sir Charles, British diplomat
    (1779–1845) 267
Stuart, Captain Lord George (d. 1841)
    269–70
Stuart, General Sir John (1759–1815) 175
Stuart, Captain Lord William (d. 1814)
    127
Suez Canal 285, 288
Sunderland 107
Sweden 27, 216–17, 219–21, 227, 229–30,
    237, 241, 243
Sydney, Nova Scotia 65

Tagus, river, Portugal 152–3
Talbot, Captain John, later Admiral
    (d. 1851) 266, 280
Tarragona, Spain 163, 177–8
Tate, James, merchant seaman 95–6
Teignmouth, Devon 253, 256
telegraph, shutter 39–40
Templar, Lieutenant Richard 100–1
Texel 8, 41, 124, 128, 143, 157
Thames, River 27, 74–5, 83, 88–9, 92, 108,
    157
Thompson, Commander Henry 64n
Thompson, Vice-Admiral Sir Thomas
    Boulden (1766–1828) 61
Thornborough, Admiral Sir Edward
    (1754–1834) 46–7, 85, 151, 245
Thornton, Samuel, MP (1754–1838) 220
Tinos, Greece 166
Tonningen, Denmark 30, 112–13, 120
Torbay 27, 84, 253–5, 260
Torres Vedras, lines of 153
Townsend, Captain, merchant master 256
Trafalgar, battle of 8, 37, 111, 162, 231
Transport Board 18, 55, 71, 113, 140, 145,
    157n, 176
Trefusis Point, Falmouth, Cornwall 156

Trieste 164–5, 167n, 177
Trinity House 113
Tripoli 166–7
Troubridge, Admiral Sir Thomas (1758–1807) 189, 198–202
Tunis 166–7
Turkey 162–3

United States *see* America
Upton, Captain Clotworthy 245
Ushant 15

Vashon, Rear-Admiral James (1742–1827) 62, 107
Venice 162, 165, 167n, 178–9
Vera Cruz, Mexico 195–7
Victualling Board 83, 140, 175, 187
Vigo 95, 150
Villiers, George, Paymaster of Marines (1759–1827) 42–3
Vincent, Captain Richard Budd (d.1831) 171, 280, 289
Vinga Sand, anchorage near Gothenburg 219, 227, 229, 233, 236, 238

Walcheren 44, 61, 135, 142, 160n, 216
Ward, Lieutenant William 202
Warren, Admiral Sir John Borlase (1753–1852) 247, 249, 252, 258
Warren, Captain, merchant master 256
Washington 244–5
Waterford, Ireland 253n
Waterloo, battle of (1815) 141, 160, 246n, 272–3, 279, 282
Watson, Lieutenant John, later commander 108n
Wayth, Francis, merchant ship master, 45

Wellesley-Pole, William, Secretary of the Admiralty (1763–1845) 42, 130
Wellington, Duke of 41, 44, 99–100, 151–4, 203, 273, 279
Wells, Rear-Admiral John, later Admiral Sir John (d.1841) 41
West Indian merchants 33
West Indies 1, 10n, 16, 17–18, 20, 27, 48, 56, 71, 81–2, 85, 90, 135–6, 139, 160n, 168, 171, 181–207, 212, 215, 219, 235, 246–7, 249, 253n, 277–8
Western Approaches 16, 23, 32, 82–3, 88, 90, 94–5, 98, 176, 182, 185, 205, 207, 264, 267, 277, 286, 290
Western Squadron 15–18
Wheeler, Private William, 51st Regiment of Foot 134, 138n
Whitworth, James, seaman 64–5, 227
Wight, Isle of 89, 140–1, 160
Willaumez, contre-amiral 182
Wingo Sund near Gothenburg, *see* Vinga Sand
Wolley, Captain Isaac 200
Wordsworth, John, HEIC captain (d. 1804) 86
Wouk, Herman, author 284

Yarmouth, Norfolk *see* Great Yarmouth
Yorke, Admiral Sir Joseph (1768–1831) 43, 127
Yorke, Charles Philip, First Lord of the Admiralty (1764–1834) 38, 148, 240
Young, Admiral Sir William (1751–1821) 65, 86n, 128–9, 278

Zante, Ionian islands 166–7, 169